The Hidden Power™ of Photoshop® Elements 4

The Hidden Power™ of Photoshop® Elements 4

RICHARD LYNCH

WILEY PUBLISHING, INC.

Acquisitions and Developmental Editor: PETE GAUGHAN
Technical Editors: MARK CLARKSON, WALT DIETRICH
Production Editor: DARIA MEOLI
Copy Editor: LINDA RECKTENWALD
Production Manager: TIM TATE
Vice President and Executive Group Publisher: RICHARD SWADLEY
Vice President and Executive Publisher: JOSEPH B. WIKERT
Vice President and Publisher: DAN BRODNITZ
Media Development Specialist: ANGIE DENNY
Book Designer: CARYL GORSKA
Compositor: CHRIS GILLESPIE, HAPPENSTANCE TYPE-O-RAMA
Proofreader: NANCY RIDDIOUGH
Indexer: NANCY GUENTHER
Cover Designer: RYAN SNEED

Dear Reader,

Thank you for choosing *The Hidden Power of Photoshop Elements 4*. This book is part of a family of premium-quality Sybex graphics books, all written by outstanding authors who combine practical experience with a gift for teaching.

Sybex was founded in 1976. Thirty years later, we're still committed to producing consistently exceptional books. With each of our graphics titles we're working hard to set a new standard for the industry. From the paper we print on to the writers and photographers we work with, our goal is to bring you the best graphics books available.

I hope you see all that reflected in these pages. I'd be very interested to hear your comments and get your feedback on how we're doing. To let us know what you think about this or any other Sybex book, please send me an e-mail at sybex_publisher@wiley.com. Please also visit us at www.sybex.com to learn more about the rest of our growing graphics line.

Best regards,

Dan Brodnitz
Vice President and Publisher
Sybex, an Imprint of Wiley

Acknowledgments

Many people who have helped with this book will likely never suspect that they did so, and, quite honestly, I don't know them well enough to name them. The list ranges from rustic tour guides, to people I've met in passing at camera stores and eBay auctions, to people who participate in image editing forums on the Internet, to those who post book reviews and mentions, to people at work who might ask the most innocent questions about images and cameras. Any time I am forced to consider results and what people are trying to achieve in their images, it helps me look back to where I was years ago when trying to learn image editing. A grand thanks to all the readers who purchased previous versions of the *Hidden Power* book and Hidden Power toolsets, those who have downloaded the free tools or purchased tools, and those who visit the website (www .hiddenelements.com). Your visits and activity confirm for me and assure the publisher that there really is a market of advanced Elements users.

The list of people I can name who help day-to-day remains much the same. My wife, Lisa, and children, Julia and Isabel, provide pointed critique, patience in allowing the work to go on, and dexterity in avoiding collisions with the by-product debris that accumulates in piles during the project, and they show enough interest in the result (whether faked or real) to help make the writing seem less isolated.

Thanks to companions in "the business": Al Ward (www.actionfx.com), Greg Georges (www.reallyusefulpage.com), Fred Showker (www.graphic-design.com), Doug Nelson (www .retouchpro.com), and Barbara Brundage. Thanks to those at the beginning (Stephanie Wall, Mitch Waite, and Beth Millett), those in the middle (Bonnie Bills), and the present Sybex/Wiley crew (Pete Gaughan, Walt Dietrich, Mark Clarkson, Daria Meoli, Linda Recktenwald, and Dan Brodnitz). Contracts be damned, Jeff (Schultz).

A round of applause for the chroma key backdrop: Sam, Murphy, Mom, Stephen L., Todd Jensen, Kevin H., Robert Blake, Larry Woiwode, Alan R. Weeks, Tony Zenos, Luke DeLalio, Rabelaise, Beckett, and various Nardecchias and Hongs. A blurry one out there to Vincent T. L.

About the Author

After graduating from college with an MFA in writing and separate careers as a chef, a college teacher, and a freelance development editor, Richard Lynch spent five years as senior editor and designer for a how-to photography book publisher, learning the ins and outs of book production and image editing. Over those years he designed and edited 40 books on various facets of photography, from the basics of taking pictures and through the nuances of professional lighting, special effects, and infrared photography, gaining an intimate knowledge of the business and art of photography.

Since moving on to a full-time job in communications, information management, and web development, Lynch has written six books on digital imaging, including *The Hidden Power of Photoshop CS* and *The Hidden Power of Photoshop Elements 3*, between being a columnist for *Digital Photography Techniques*, teaching digital art classes at local colleges, and enjoying digital photography. For freelance design work (CDs, books, websites, and other graphics) and writings on digital imaging, he uses Sigma dSLR cameras, LinoHell scanning equipment, and both Mac and PC computers.

Glad to move away from analog equipment that he'd been using since his first experience dabbling in darkroom arts in grade school, Lynch has been working with digital images since 1986 and with Photoshop full time (50+ hours a week) since 1992.

CONTENTS AT A GLANCE

Contents

Foreword

Photoshop Elements has been a runaway best seller for Adobe Systems since it was first introduced in 2001. Who could resist the chance to get so much of the power of Photoshop in an inexpensive, slightly simpler package? But in spite of all the amazing things that Elements can do, lots of people want to be able to do more of the sophisticated kinds of edits and color corrections that aren't easily accomplished in Elements right out of the box.

Richard Lynch's first *Hidden Power of Photoshop Elements* book, for versions 1 and 2 of the program, was a great revelation of what Elements can do with a little help. He introduced tools everyone thought you needed to buy full Photoshop to get, like curves and easy layer masking. Although a whole cottage industry of Elements add-ons has sprung up since then, his *Hidden Power* books remain the best resource for those who want to understand and use Elements at a more advanced level.

With Photoshop Elements 4, Adobe has considerably raised the bar for those who want to expand the program's basic capabilities. They did this by removing the ability to tie into some of the more popular Photoshop features in the program's underlying code, which is how the previous generations of tools worked. Most of the add-on tools designed for earlier versions of Elements no longer work in Elements 4, but Richard has come up with some truly ingenious workarounds to put back a lot of favorite extras, such as the ability to work with individual color channels.

With *The Hidden Power of Photoshop Elements 4*, Richard has not only created new versions of his most popular tools but also offers common-sense discussions of many of the tougher concepts in digital imaging—such as color management—as well as useful advice to keep in mind when taking pictures to make sure you start with the best images possible. Everyone who is at all serious about getting the most out of Photoshop Elements 4 should buy this book.

Barbara Brundage
Author of *Photoshop Elements 4: The Missing Manual*

Introduction

Photoshop Elements is one of the most powerful image editing programs on the planet, bar none. The key to harnessing the power of the program and getting the best results from your images is understanding how the program works, understanding images, and using the inherent capabilities of the program optimally to make the best image adjustments. Getting the most out of your images using Photoshop Elements is what this book is about.

None of the best images are the result of a push-button processes and correction. Computers and computer programs don't think, so expecting that they will make good artistic judgments at the push of a button is an unlikely scenario. As it has been said, beauty is in the eye of the beholder—and that beholder is you. You will need to make artistic judgments that the computer cannot. In the course of the book, you will learn how the program works by learning which tools you really need and how to apply them to make real-world image adjustments. You'll see, step-by-step, how even the most complex image processes work, and then you'll be given automated (and semiautomated) tools (the Hidden Power tools) to compress even hundreds of steps at a time into a single click. These are not fix-it-for-you tools but a means of easily setting up complex scenarios that lead to better corrections. With Hidden Power, you will have the tools to be able to make and understand the most sophisticated image corrections and get better image results globally.

The past five years of working with Photoshop Elements have been a compelling learning experience for me. I have become somewhat of a convert from appreciating the pedestal that Photoshop has been placed on almost unilaterally as the "best" image editing program to appreciating Photoshop Elements as a peer program, on a par with the best. What was initially a challenge to get more from Elements has given me a far deeper understanding of image editing than the previous 10 years I spent as an image editor, digital image technician, and graphic artist using Photoshop. That understanding is what I hope to convey in these pages.

The Goal of This Book

The goal of *The Hidden Power of Photoshop Elements 4* is to take apart the process of correcting images and the images themselves to expose the hidden power Elements has for working with images. You'll learn professional corrections that can be applied with simplicity, and you'll become familiar with the powerful tools you need to know and how they apply to any image. The dissection of process and getting back to fundamentals starts immediately by looking at an essential tool set. The dissection of images starts by looking at tone and separating color into tone components before color correction or editing.

This book is for

- Anyone who wants to get better results from their digital images using Photoshop Elements

- Those who want to understand the process of editing images rather than just making push-button fixes

- Serious hobbyists who want to get more from their investment in Elements or who may feel they are outgrowing the program

- Photographers moving into digital imaging who need powerful tools for image correction

- Graphics hobbyists and professionals who thought their only choice for working with digital images was Photoshop

The focus of the book is on

- Learning a process of approaching images with proven methods and the right tools to make your image corrections

- Learning new tools that Elements supposedly doesn't have to bolster your editing arsenal and expertise

- Working through what you need to do in realistic situations with realistic images by using realistic expectations to get real results

The book is *not* about

- Exploring every last tool in the interface in excruciating detail

- Making crazy effects

The techniques provided here will help you take your corrections to a professional level without hocus-pocus or steps that are impossible to comprehend. It will provide a cache of more than 100 editing tools that provide additional functionality and reveal how to do many things that are generally thought to be impossible using Photoshop Elements alone. The solutions are used right in Photoshop Elements—with no plug-ins, additional investment, or other programs to learn. You'll see what happens behind the scenes in step-by-step procedures, and you'll be given the tools—customized Hidden Power tools created just for this book—to move through those steps quickly. Though created for this book, the tools will work with any image. These tools empower you to make the most out of Photoshop Elements and are available through Hidden Power only.

What Makes a Good Image?

Photoshop Elements gives you the power to alter any pixel in an image. You can technically do anything. Like a bricklayer building a building, you can get in and create your image one pixel at a time to get exactly what you want. If you know what you like and what you don't, it should be easy to improve and create images. Just look at the image or canvas and know what you want to see. Once you know—and can trust—what you want to see on-screen, all you have to do is make whatever changes are necessary so that your image looks the way you imagine it. The whole process should be simple, right? Just click a button and fix it; then print and be done with it.

But it isn't always that easy.

The problem arises because of numbers and possibilities. There can be millions of pixels in an image. Each pixel can be one of millions of colors. Every pixel can be altered with numerous tools and options in groups or separately, with changes based on surrounding pixels or considered on a pixel-by-pixel basis. The color and tone of each pixel have to be orchestrated to make it work with other pixels adjacent to it to form a recognizable whole. When you have finished, that whole has to look as you imagined it. Getting that picture out of your imagination certainly isn't as easy as taking a picture. And building images one pixel at a time overcomplicates the problem of creating what you want to see. Not knowing where to start and what tools to choose just makes the process of working with images that much more difficult.

You have to simplify the approach.

Elements gives you what is potentially a big, heavy toolbox. Some people blindly fall into a trap, thinking they have to understand and use every tool, filter, and effect and strap all those tools to their tool belt in order to be able to use the program efficiently or to do anything the "right" way. There are two things wrong with that idea:

- You don't need to know how to use every tool, filter, or effect; you just need the right ones. There are probably many tools (and shortcuts!) that you will never use.

- There aren't really a right way and a wrong way; there are harder and easier ways and ways that are more and less effective.

In Elements there are numerous tools. Not all are essential; some are essentially redundant; some are merely toys; and some are gimmicky, trendy, or unpredictable. While almost all have their place when you get to know them, the ones that are the most powerful, most useful, and most often used—just like the hammer and screwdriver in a carpenter's tool belt—are often not the most spectacular.

A few others have to be coaxed out of hiding, which is part of what the *Hidden Power* title is all about and some of what the book will do for you.

Not everything that makes an image look better requires a lot of creativity. There are techniques you can use to make an image look better that require very little thinking at all. In fact, much of the initial process of image correction should be nearly automatic. If there is a dust speck in a scan, you'll need to remove it; if there is color correction that needs to be done, you'll need to make the correction. Although there are several ways to approach making any change, if you have a few favorite tools and techniques, the process and correction become much simpler.

In other words, applying a somewhat limited number of tools and techniques can get you most of the effects you will ever need to improve your images. Using what you have in an image and making the most out of that are often key to getting the best results. Some of the most helpful and powerful information in images is hidden or ignored. This book helps reveal that image content and simplifies the tools you will need to use and apply. With fewer tools (and rules) to remember, you can concentrate on what to do with the images rather than pondering options or quizzing yourself as to how to apply the tools. Using image content to leverage selective changes can help target corrections in ways that freehand work nearly never will. It is a fundamental approach. By using fewer tools, you won't be weighed down by the heavy tool belt. Concentrating on a smaller set of tools and using a structured approach will simplify the corrections you make in any image.

But What Corrections Do You Make?

Say you go to the airport to pick up your cousin who has been in the African jungles for a decade. No one has seen him in all that time, let alone seen the talking monkeys he was on the trail of. It sounds like a great photo opportunity, so you grab your camera and head out the door.

You meet him at the airport gate and take some snapshots of him all haggard and weather-beaten from his grueling years living in nature. He looks fresh out of *National Geographic.*

Later, when you open the images on your computer, they seem to have come out pretty well. But the first thing you probably *won't* do in this situation is add an effect that sets his head on fire. Besides occasionally applying a special effect, the biggest wow you can get from your images will usually be achieved by

- Taking a good picture that clearly shows an interesting subject
- Using targeted corrections to make those images look the best you can

Most people viewing your picture will want to see the subject of your image, and you can't get that by burying the subject in flames. Special effects have their time and place, but when the subject and image can be good enough on their own, you can do more to improve the look of your photographic images with good corrections. The idea behind this book is to give you a from-the-ground-up method not only for making better images by correction but also for understanding what makes a better image in the first place. You will find the hidden power not only in Photoshop Elements but also in your subjects and images. The goal of this book is to make people viewing your images say "Wow!" not in response to flames or other effects or magic but because your images look great.

Much of what used to be my standard process in image correction has been rearranged because of my experience with Photoshop Elements. The result is that my process is now simpler and my images have changed for the better. That was a somewhat shocking change to have happen after 10 years of professional experience editing digital images. It was like a carpenter looking at his hammer and suddenly realizing that it actually had two sides and could do more than just bang in the nails. The more shocking thing is that the techniques you'll read about in *The Hidden Power of Photoshop Elements 4* tear down the wall of difference between Photoshop and Elements. I use the same techniques in both programs these days, and—except for a few differences in the interface—I often forget which program I'm using. The most obvious fact is that it doesn't matter, but the hidden fact is that I learned my current techniques from Elements, not from Photoshop. Using the techniques in this book, you won't often be left using Elements limply and apologetically, as if you were banging in screws with your hammer; you'll be using the best tool you have and the only tool you'll need to edit your images and get the best results.

How This Book Is Organized

As you go through the book, you will discover a mixture of practical theory, examples of the types of changes you'll make in images, and projects to work on to help you understand the process as well as why it works. Projects are put together so that you don't just complete an exercise or press a button and ogle the result, but so that you see what goes on behind the scenes to help understand what you have done. When you understand, you can apply that understanding to other images predictably—either by using tools provided to drive a process or by manually applying learned techniques. There are clear goals from the outset of the procedures, and the examples provided ensure that you can see the changes when they have achieved the desired result. This understanding will enable you to apply the techniques you learn to other images so that your images can be improved consistently.

> When following along with the book's step-by-step instructions, use the methods suggested in the steps for accessing the tools, or the procedures may not function correctly. For example, opening Levels with the keyboard shortcut (Command+L/Ctrl+L) will open the Levels dialog box but will *not* produce an adjustment layer, and this can affect the outcome of a procedure that depends on the adjustment layers being created.

You will learn to take apart image color and tone entirely by using several color-separation methods and to isolate color components, image objects, and areas in a number of different ways. When you can isolate colors and image areas, you can correct those areas separately from the rest of the image and exchange, move, and replace elements to make better images. After learning to correct and manipulate images, you will learn about options for output, including making custom separations to CMYK and duotones. Hidden Power tools are introduced throughout to reveal functionality and simplify procedures.

Chapter 1: Resolution: The Cornerstone of Image Detail An essential concept that is a key to getting your images right is having enough resolution in the capture to preserve the details you need. In this chapter we'll look at important basic tenets of using resolution in images and captures to your benefit, from defining and understanding imaging terms for resolution to learning what resolution to set for capturing and working with images.

Chapter 2: Seeing Images as Color, Contrast, and Tone It was no accident that this book was built in black-and-white. The full-color images you see are actually stored as grayscale components that are based in color theories. Learning to see color images as grayscale components rather than as "pretty colors" gives you a better understanding of how to work with images and how they come together on-screen. Here we also look at the slippery subject of color management and setting up your system so that what you see on-screen will be the best representation of what you will get in your output.

Chapter 3: The Image Editing Process Outline Simplifying the process of working with image editing and getting the results you need is a key concept in the book as well. This chapter outlines a core process and explains the tools you'll need to accomplish even the most rigorous imaging objectives. You'll be given a clear outline as to how to proceed in correcting any image, and you'll have in hand a definitive list of tools that you'll want to know and use to achieve the best results.

Chapter 4: Separating and Combining Image Components Understanding images starts with separating image components. In this chapter, you'll see how to split color into simple tonal representations, and then we'll look at how black-and-white tone components can be mixed to become color again. We'll parlay the concept of mixing color and tone by applying color with layered effects over image tones to explore creative hand-coloring of images.

Chapter 5: Correcting Image Tone The ability to manipulate tone is integral to making better images, implementing color, and making effective color changes. Understanding how to work with tone can make a big difference in the final image results. We'll look at effective methods for image cleanup, evaluating and optimizing image tone, making contrast adjustments and sharpening, managing image noise, masking, and shaping images with light and shadow. These basics of adjustment are the core techniques you will use to adjust the color components to achieve the results you want.

Chapter 6: Color and Tone Enhancement Because color components are made of black-and-white representations, we'll show how to apply tonal corrections learned in the previous chapter to adjust color images. We'll look at how corrections for color images parallel correction of image tone and work through specific examples applying each correction technique. Once you've completed general color correction, you'll get into more selective color corrections. Changes can be initiated by special controls inherent in specialized Hidden Power tools or combined to produce highly targeted and effective results. This chapter introduces color range, color-specific masking, and history application to enhance image color.

Chapter 7: Altering Composition Similarly to how you can take apart image color, you can extract image elements from an image and then replace, adjust, or remove them. This gives you control over image composition by giving you control of all the objects in an image. With image elements separated and corrected, you are free to reshape, redesign, and repurpose image parts with a basic understanding of how adjustments affect composition.

Chapter 8: The Image Process in Action In this chapter we put together almost all of what we've looked at thus far to gain experience running an image through the Hidden Power process. We'll take one image from start to finish, opening the RAW camera file and then making adjustments to color and composition to improve the final result just as you will do with most of your other images, in a process that follows the outline in Chapter 3.

Chapter 9: Creating and Using Vectors Vectors provide another way to control image content, which can be valuable in making resolution-independent, scalable artwork (creation of logos) and using printer capabilities to their fullest extent. You'll learn to do more of the impossible with Hidden Power by creating and storing your own custom shapes and applying clipping paths.

Chapter 10: Color Separations for Print Additional separations that target the way a printer works can add some flexibility and power to your image output. This chapter shows how to create your own real, separated duotones that function as they would on press. It then explains the process of making CMYK separations and doing the impossible again by saving the CMYK components to printable files right from Elements.

Chapter 11: Options for Printing More options exist for printing than just working with your inkjet printer at home. In this chapter, we look at how to get the best results at home, in addition to other options that may be more attractive and less costly than you think. You'll learn how to print to the edge of the page with an understanding of how the image information is applied.

Appendix: Other Concepts and References The appendix gathers information that just doesn't seem to fit into the rest of the book. You'll learn how to run Photoshop actions in Photoshop Elements. You'll find out more about the "boring" core information surrounding images, including even more on resolution, file types, bit depth, Camera RAW, 16-bit, and getting your own custom tools.

The Hidden Power Tools

One of the most important parts of this book is the collection of Hidden Power tools provided on the CD. The tools are meant for readers of this book only and should not be shared freely. The tools must be installed into Photoshop Elements to be accessible, and they operate on Windows and Macintosh computers.

To install the tools, first locate the proper Hidden Power installer on the CD. Initiate the installation by double-clicking the installer (for Windows, HPPE4_PC.exe; for Mac OS X, HPPE4_Mac). Target the installation by choosing the Elements program folder if prompted; the installers by default will install the tools into Elements following Adobe's default path. Be sure to carefully read the instructions for the installation as they appear on-screen. You'll need a password for the installation, provided here:

Operating System	Installer	Password
PC/Windows	HPPE4_PC.exe	hiddenpower4
Macintosh	HPPE4_Mac	hiddenpower4

Be aware that the password is all in lowercase and the letter case is important. If you have any trouble with the tool installation, please read the troubleshooting file on the CD, and visit the www.hiddenelements.com website for information that becomes available after publication of this book. If you do not find a solution to your installation problem, please contact me at thebookdoc@aol.com.

Note that custom installations are possible by reading the installer screens and redirecting the installation. On Windows, you can either select a new path using the browse button […] when it appears or install to any folder of your choice and copy the files to appropriate directories in the `Elements` program folder. On a Mac, choose Custom Install from the installation drop-down list when it appears. Tools can be installed to foreign-language versions of the program by following custom installation instructions and copying the resulting files to appropriate folders (the names of the folders should be the translated equivalent).

After you've installed the tools, you'll be able to access them in the Styles and Effects palette. Open the Styles and Effects palette by choosing Styles and Effects from the Window menu (in the Image Editor rather than Organizer). With the Styles and Effects palette on-screen, choose Effects from the drop-down list at the top left of the palette—this will populate the effects categories in the drop-down list on the right. Choose the Power categories (Power_Adjustments, Power_Masking, Power_Extras, Power_Separations, Power_Paths, and Power_Playback) to reveal the power tool listings. The usage of most of the tools is discussed in this book, and all are described in the readme file for the tools on the CD. Please make use of the Hidden Power forum online to discuss the use of any of the tools. Find links for the forums on the website: `www.hiddenelements.com/forums`.

These Hidden Power tools will enable processes and act as helpers for your image processing. They will condense some of the longer step-by-step procedures you'll learn in the book into clicks of the mouse.

I expect to expand on the Hidden Power tools even more after the release of this book. Check the website and newsletter for additions. Subscribe to the newsletter on the website (`www.hiddenelements.com/newsletter`) and check the download area for more tools (`www.hiddenelements.com/downloads`).

Practice Image Files

All images used as practice files in the book are provided on the accompanying CD so that readers can work along with the exercises. They are mostly provided as `.psd` files (Photoshop documents) but may be in other formats as appropriate to a particular exercise.

These images are for educational purposes only and should not be used freely elsewhere. Work with the images by opening them with Elements directly off the CD, and save them as you need them to your hard drive. The images are all compatible with Macintosh and Windows computers.

Mac and PC Compatibility

The tools and images on the CD are completely compatible with Mac and PC platforms. Most of all of the tools in the Photoshop elements program itself work in nearly identical ways on mac or PC. The greatest difference a user will note in these pages is that shortcuts differ between Mac and PC. For example, to open the Levels palette on PC, the user would press the Ctrl+L keys; on Mac the user would press the Command+L keys (Command is sometimes known as the apple or ⌘). Keyboard equivalents on Mac and PC are:

Macintosh	Windows	Example
Shift	Shift	Shift+X
Option	Alt	Option+X/Alt+X
Command	Ctrl	Command+X/Ctrl+X
Control+click	Right-click	Control+click/Right-click

All keystrokes are included in their entirety in the book, first mac, then PC, separated by a slash "/".

Going Further with Hidden Power

There are several ways that you can contact me via the Internet. I am interested in your questions and comments as a means to improve the book in the future, to put frequently asked questions to rest, to develop new tools, and to correct any typos or other errors that may have slipped in when I wasn't looking. Make use of the Hidden Power forums and newsletter for submitting questions (again: www.hiddenelements.com/forums, www.hidden elements.com/newsletter). E-mail rl@ps6.com or thebookdoc@aol.com to contact me directly. Depending on volume, I'll respond personally to e-mail as often as possible, and I look forward to your input. Frequently asked questions will be answered in the *Hidden Power of Photoshop Elements Newsletter*.

The Hidden Power Websites

I've set up a website with more information about the book at www.hiddenelements.com. The site includes information for readers, including links to the newsletter, additional tools, tutorials, a forum, and a contact page where you can enter comments, questions, and other feedback.

Sybex also strives to keep you supplied with the latest tools and information you need for your work. Please check their website at www.sybex.com for additional content and updates that supplement this book. Enter the book's title or ISBN in the Search box (or search for Lynch), and click Go to get to the book's update page.

The Hidden Power Newsletter

The *Hidden Power of Photoshop Elements Newsletter* keeps you up to date on any changes, notifies you of any tools I've made available, and answers frequently asked questions. I send the newsletter to all subscribers; the frequency of the newsletter depends on the volume of questions and my workload. All you have to do to get the newsletter (free) is subscribe by submitting your e-mail address on the subscription page. You can sign up at the Hidden Power site: www.hiddenelements.com/newsletter.html. Subscription is free, and the newsletter is available to anyone who wants to join.

I hope you see from all this that I don't plan to leave readers stranded in deep water. If you have questions about the book, tools, or installation, contact me by e-mail or in the forum rather than posting a review on Amazon or other websites where I have no opportunity to contact you, answer, or even know that the question exists. Too many times people pose questions in other forums or on other web pages where there is no one who can answer their questions. If you have questions, it is likely that other people will have those same ones too, and I'll be glad to answer them as time allows. You'll need to ask me, as it is much more difficult for me to find *you*.

Part I

Essentials for Serious Image Editing

Serious image editing requires preparation and understanding. You have to be prepared with the best source images (the best content, resolution, and color), and you have to understand what corrections you need to make and how best to enhance the images. Problems in your images that you ignore when you are just starting out become more nagging as you gain experience. What you don't want to do when you work on images is waste hours correcting problems that would have taken moments to fix at the time of capture. And you don't want to waste time learning superfluous or redundant tools and techniques. Capturing the best information and getting the best results require understanding the images themselves and how image information is retained and displayed in print or on a monitor. An outline for the tools you should use helps you focus on the right techniques to get the best results with those images from the outset. This part of the book lays the groundwork you'll need for stepping into more advanced concepts later in the book.

Chapter 1

Resolution: The Cornerstone of Image Detail

Your first task in working with images is to always to capture the best image that you can. Starting with the best capture as a photo or scan, instead of one you will just plan to "fix later," will save you time and give you more image to work with. The better the information you start with, the more likely you'll have what you need to make the best result with less effort, in less time.

Images are built around resolution. There is a finite amount of detail in any pixel-based digital image that you get from a digital camera or scanner. *Resolution* is a measure of potential detail; the more resolution you have, the greater amount of potential detail in the image. High resolution suggests that there will be intricate detail; low resolution suggests that detail may be compromised.

While you will want to capture images at high resolution to retain detail, what you really want for images when they are applied is the *correct* resolution. We'll look at how to leverage resolution in this chapter.

In Terms of Resolution

What Image Resolution to Use

Resizing Images

Multipurpose Images

Can You Have Too Much Resolution?

In Terms of Resolution

Pixels are the smallest visual unit in an image. Each pixel (short for *picture element*) represents a single color or tone. The pixels are organized in rows and columns like blocks or tiles to map out the details, one tiny image pixel at a time. The multitude of pixels in an image (numbering more often in the millions for consumer digital cameras) blends together in our vision to create the look and feel of an image in tone (light and dark) and color (hue and saturation). The more pixels you have in an image, the greater potential detail.

This chapter has essential information that you need to know at any level of image editing. If you are a novice, read on. If you are an experienced image editor, you may want to read this chapter for review. If you are experienced and don't want the review, skip on to Chapter 2.

"Potential" detail is mentioned several times. While there is potential to retain more detail with higher pixel counts, limitations of your equipment, poor focus, bad lighting, and bad image handling can all lead to situations where detail is compromised no matter how many pixels you have in your images.

a   b   c

Figure 1.1

This flower is rendered here with the correct resolution for print in this book (a), one-eighth the proper resolution (b), and one-twelfth the resolution (c). Images with less resolution than necessary will appear with too little detail and become blocky.

Image resolution is usually measured in several ways, including the number of total pixels (e.g., a 5 megapixel camera), the size of the image file (number of bytes, kilobytes, or megabytes), the amount of information per inch (ppi, or pixels per inch), and the physical dimension (pixel dimension or ruler sizing). One way of measuring the image resolution is not necessarily better or worse than another, though some are more intuitive. In fact, the measurements serve different purposes, and none of them is sufficient on its own to really define how much detail is in an image. For example, ppi tells how much of the image pixel information should be applied per inch, but it doesn't tell how much information is in the image or the image size. Without those additional defining parameters, it is impossible to determine how big an image will be when applied.

Total pixels is the actual count of pixels (picture elements) in the image. As suggested, digital cameras are commonly rated in pixel count. Pixel count can also be a dimension of the pixel mapping, such as 2100×1500 pixels. An image with a greater pixel dimension or pixel count than another is generally larger in terms of potential detail than an image with fewer pixels. If your camera can shoot images that are 2100×1500 pixels, the images will have more detail than a camera that takes images which are 1600×1200 pixels. The potential for greater resolution (more detail) is why you will generally want to shoot with a higher resolution setting if your camera offers a choice. Images with higher resolution have more pixels and take more space to store, so you will get fewer of them on your camera's memory card, but the images you do get should have greater detail.

Greater pixel count in different cameras using different lenses and sensors can mean different things as far as sharpness in the final image. For example, using alternative technology such as Foveon X3 chips for image capture can render a sharper image than a standard mosaic Bayer chip that has three or more times the resolution in megapixels. The Foveon chip measures RGB for *each pixel,* while a common CCD (charge-coupled device) or CMOS (complementary metal oxide semiconductor) sensor measures color in an array and interpolates the result. Resolution is a good gauge of sharpness but not an infallible one.

Measuring image resolution in file size is probably the least intuitive or useful approach for most people working in Photoshop Elements. File size is used to describe the quantity of information in the source image, independent of how it is to be applied or stored. If you are storing more than one type of image (e.g., RAW and JPEG), file size becomes all but meaningless because different image types store information in different ways (and with different compression schemes). The color mode of the image (grayscale, RGB, etc.) and bit depth (8 or 16 bits) affect the amount of information per pixel. Image attributes (storage of layers, masks, and other image components) can inflate image size without changing the dimension or visual resolution. So file size is really useful only in comparing resolution of like files—those that are uncompressed, the same color mode, and the same file type—and before processing that will add image elements (layers, vectors, alpha channels, etc.). File size is likely the least-used measure of resolution.

Beyond file size, physical pixel dimension, and ppi, there are some interrelated terms for resolution that you will hear from time to time used both correctly and incorrectly (often in the same sentence). For example, *dpi* is a commonly used term, often used casually as a universal term for resolution. However, it is really an output term specific to printing and the number of dots a printer uses in representing an image. Other measures of resolution include spi, ppi, and lpi. The various resolution-related terms can be tricky to use correctly and consistently, but you should know what they mean and use them properly when you mean something specific.

> To simplify with better accuracy, use *spi* when speaking of capture (scan sampling), *ppi* when discussing digital files, *dpi* when considering output resolution, and *lpi* in the context of halftone dot size.

spi (samples per inch) Capture resolution. The number of scanning and digital capture samples per inch.

ppi (pixels per inch) Digital file resolution. The assigned number of digital pixel elements to be used in printing or displaying an image.

dpi (dots per inch) Printer resolution. The number of bitmap dots (smallest printing component) an output can create per inch.

lpi (lines per inch) A measure of halftone dot size. Halftone dots are made of multiple printer dots. The number of rows of halftone dots per inch.

It would seem that you would always want high resolution in your images if you consider detail important. But that's not always the case. Correct resolution depends not only on what size you want the result to be but also on what display or print medium you will be using and how the image information is applied.

For example, if you don't have enough resolution to meet the needs of print output, images won't look as sharp as they could; they might appear a little soft, fuzzy, or blocky (again, have a good look at Figure 1.1). If you have too much resolution in your image, file sizes are unnecessarily large; processing will take longer than it needs to; you'll take up excess storage; and the results will not improve. On the Web, images without enough resolution will be too small; those with too much resolution will be too large and will take longer to download. You can't just guess how much image information you need when applying an image; you have to know the amount you really need and work within those parameters. Understanding what resolution is and how it is used is the only way to use it correctly.

What Image Resolution to Use

Some people generalize and suggest using 300 ppi as a standard resolution for images going to print. For the Web, it is usually accepted that images should be 72 ppi. While these are pretty good as general-purpose guidelines, they don't tell the entire story of what resolution to use. For example, 300 ppi may be more than is necessary for all home printers, but it may actually be too little for demanding output (such as film recorder output). Because monitor resolutions can vary, your 72 ppi image on a 96 dpi screen would actually be about 75 percent of the intended size. Neither choice is likely to totally ruin your output, in most cases, but it can compromise what you expect.

Because output differs in how it applies image information, there is no one universal magic formula to figure out what resolution to use. Each output type has a target range (minimum and maximum), based on its capability to process and use image information. Once you know the range you need, you simply use that range as a target when working on an image. Know what your printing service or printer manufacturer recommends for output on the devices you use. This may require reading the manuals or calling the printing service to find out. The optimal range is the range where the image will perform the best when applied; it is possible to get acceptable results by going outside the range depending on how you implement the image and the results that you expect.

Table 1.1 shows the approximate resolutions to use for your images, depending on how you want to use them. An image sent to a device that uses a specified output resolution should have a specific target ppi. The table shows some real-world examples of output resolution and workable ppi ranges. Formulas used for the calculations are shown in the Calculation Used column; square brackets in the calculations indicate the range of values used to determine the lowest and highest resolution acceptable in that medium.

Note that these resolutions are suggested and not absolute. Images will still print and display at other resolutions, but the results may not be predictable or efficient.

MEDIUM	OUTPUT RESOLUTION	APPROXIMATE IMAGE FILE RESOLUTION	CALCULATION USED
Web	72–96 dpi (monitor)	72–96 ppi	ppi = dpi
Inkjet (stochastic)	720 dpi	180–234 ppi	$[1 \text{ to } 1.3] \times (dpi / 4)$
Inkjet 6 color (stochastic)	1440 dpi	240–312 ppi	$[1 \text{ to } 1.3] \times (dpi / 6)$
Halftone, low resolution	75–100 lpi	116–200 ppi	$[1.55 \text{ to } 2] \times lpi$
Halftone, normal resolution	133–150 lpi	233–350 ppi	$[1.55 \text{ to } 2] \times lpi$
Halftone, high resolution	175–200 lpi	271–400 ppi	$[1.55 \text{ to } 2] \times lpi$
Line art	600–3000 dpi	600–1342 ppi	$(dpi/600)^{1/2} \times 600$
Film recorder	4K (35mm)	2731×4096 pixels	Total pixels
Film recorder	8K (6 × 9cm)	5461×8192 pixels	Total pixels

Table 1.1

Approximate Resolution for Various Media

Actual resolution needs may be somewhat flexible based on circumstances, such as paper and equipment used, original image quality, expected results, and so forth. Be sure to read manufacturer suggestions, and take most of the advice offered by services that offer printing—they should know how to get the best results from their equipment.

> For now, or until you are sure of what to do, set your camera to the highest resolution, and resize images without interpolation (leave the Resample Image box in the Image Size dialog unchecked) to 240 ppi for printing—at least until you read more and have reason to do otherwise. See Chapter 11, the Appendix, and suggestions for resizing in the next section.

Resizing Images

There are two methods of changing the size of an area that a group of pixels occupies: one causes you to resample an image, actually changing the image content (using Bicubic, Bilinear, or Nearest Neighbor interpolation), and the other changes the resolution to redistribute pixels over a smaller or larger area without actually changing the image content.

Redistributing pixels does nothing to actually change the content (mathematics) of the image information that is stored; it just suggests that the content will be applied over a different area. It is a ppi adjustment.

Resampling, on the other hand, actually changes the content of your images and changes it permanently.

The larger the amount of resampling (the greater the percentage increase or decrease), the more it affects the image content. The greater the redistribution, the more it affects image size and efficiency. One of these two things, redistributing or resampling, has to happen each time you either change the size of the whole image (using Image Size, not Canvas Size) or change the size of a selection by stretching or transforming.

When you resample image information (*upsample* or *downsample*), changing the actual count of pixels, Photoshop Elements has to interpret and redistribute tonal and color information, either creating (upsampling) or removing (downsampling) pixels. It does this through *interpolation* (adding image information) or *decimation* (removing image information), which are really fancy names for making an educated guess. Resampling an image to make it larger will never fill in information that is not already there, no matter what you do and which plug-in you use. What resampling will do is estimate and average differences between pixels to make a best guess. Details will tend to soften (upsample) or be lost (downsample). In neither case will it actually increase the captured detail in an image.

That trick you've seen on TV, where a pixilated image gets clearer and clearer as they zoom in, is reverse engineered. You can never enhance image detail that has not been captured. The only thing you can really do to reclaim image detail that you don't already have is reshoot a subject with higher resolution (e.g., using a longer lens, macro setting, or higher pixel dimension to capture more detail) or rescan (assuming that the detail is present in what you are scanning).

Photoshop Elements has three methods of interpolation (methods of figuring out how to insert new pixels or remove existing ones as you change the size of an image) and five interpolation options. Nearest Neighbor, Bilinear, and Bicubic are the methods. Bicubic Smoother and Bicubic Sharper are variations (various levels of sharpening) on the Bicubic method that were added in Elements 3.

Nearest Neighbor When you resize using Nearest Neighbor interpolation, Photoshop Elements adds or removes pixels based on pixel information and color that already exist in the image. Whether upsampling or downsampling, there is no averaging of color and/or tone to create new colors/tones. Nearest Neighbor is useful, for example, for controlled upsampling of screenshots without blurring (quadrupling the pixel count can yield an exact duplication of an image at four times the resolution). Multiply by squares (4, 9, 16, etc.) to achieve controlled upsampling.

Bilinear Bilinear interpolation behaves much like Bicubic and is supposed to be faster, but I've never clocked them. During the sampling, new tones and colors can be introduced between existing colors that are not in the original image. This can blur sampling of hard edges but can provide a smooth transition for tones (Nearest Neighbor might provide a blockier, stepped result). One thing about Bilinear upsampling is that it does simple, true averaging between neighboring tones and adds fewer new qualities to an image than any type of Bicubic resampling. At times these interpolation properties prove to be an advantage in retaining look and feel (when decreasing the image pixel count), and in others they may result in softening (when increasing the image pixel count). Use Bilinear when you want to downsample images.

Bicubic The Bicubic resampling process creates new image information by averaging, like Bilinear, but goes one step further to provide a bit of sharpening to the result. The intensity of the sharpening is stronger depending on the type of Bicubic interpolation selected. The sharpening is intended to counteract the blurring result of averaging when increasing the pixel count. Bicubic resampling changes a greater number of pixels with the same radius setting as Bilinear but may generally give a better visible result in most cases than Bilinear (when upsampling). This type of interpolation is the real workhorse for sizing images. Bicubic Sharper is like Bicubic but with enhanced sharpening; Bicubic Smoother is like Bicubic but with less sharpening. Bicubic resampling can be used for both upsampling and downsampling images.

While making up information and decimating it sound like bad things, each has its purpose. Usually you should avoid upsampling—especially if such options as rescanning or returning to an original camera image exist for gaining more detail. However, images can be upsampled with some success, depending on the desired quality—provided the change isn't huge. Upsampling 10 percent or even 20 percent may not be noticeable if the source image is sharp. Usually you will upsample only to make up small gaps between the resolution you have in an image and what you really need or to adjust borrowed image components (elements you are compositing from other images).

Downsampling, while certainly damaging and compromising to image content, should be less noticeable in your results if you use the right sampling methods. Image information indeed gets averaged or eliminated, but if downsampling is being done for the right reason, any details you lose in resampling would have been lost on output or display anyway. Detail loss is inherent in the process of downsampling, or outputting images at a smaller size. Even if equipment can reproduce detail at a smaller size, eventually details will pass the limit of the human eye's ability to discern them. In other words, at some point you lose the details anyway.

Find even more information on image resizing and interpolation in the Resolution section of the Appendix, under "Interpolation."

Multipurpose Images

Making images that you'll use for more than one purpose (for example, print and Web) can cause a little problem considering the resolution and resizing issues already discussed. Optimally, you'd like to work with images so that you target the result. Doing so ensures that you retain all of the actual image detail rather than relying on interpolation or decimation and your choice of sampling type to interpret detail. However, you can't work on an image at two resolutions or in more than one color mode at the same time. It is a simple fact that an image going to print on a high-resolution printer should have more information than one at the same size used on the Web. This is because of the difference in the way these media use image information. In fact, different printers and printer types will have different optimal utilization of image detail because of their mechanics. You will need to target image information to your output or you will not optimize detail.

You have only two solutions in working with dual-purpose images:

- Create more than one image, each with a specific purpose.
- Create one image and resize it.

Either of these choices poses a trade-off. In creating more than one image, you sacrifice valuable time in repeating processes for correction on different versions of an image. It is often self-defeating to work on two images to produce the same results (even using a detailed script) because the difference in size and volume of information in the image will produce different results with the same application of tools. In creating one image and resizing, you have to allow either interpolation of new image information or decimation, neither of which may be the optimal process. You can't work on small images and resize up because detail will not be present.

The best way to go about working with multipurpose images is usually to work with them at the highest resolution and then resize them smaller. Working at the higher of two or more resolutions retains the details for the higher-resolution presentations and decimates detail that will not be reproducible at lower resolutions. Softening or other ill effects from severe resizing can be countered somewhat by sharpening.

See "(Un)Sharpening and Boosting Contrast" in Chapter 5 for more information on sharpening.

A similar concept in retaining detail holds true when considering color depth. You will want to work in larger color spaces and at greater color depth to retain image detail and then reduce color detail and move to smaller color spaces after making corrections to reduce loss. You will most often use images from your digital camera at full resolution in RGB during corrections before reducing color and resolution for specific purposes.

Can You Have Too Much Resolution?

There are two answers to the question of whether or not you can have too much resolution: yes and no. The answer depends on whether there are other circumstances that make high-resolution images a waste because the information won't ever be used. There does come a point where the amount of image information is simply too much for the purposes of the image as it is being applied, or it gets so fine that more information doesn't really reveal more useful detail.

For the most part, you want all the detail that you can get in your source images from a digital camera. Consumer digital cameras are not so powerful that you will have enormous file sizes that are unwieldy—though you may need to consider alternatives for archiving images and image storage (on camera and off) to make the most of your equipment. Storing your images at high resolution will allow you to return to them for other purposes in the future.

Exceptions to the high-resolution rule happen only when high resolution is absolutely overkill for the purposes that you took the image in the first place. For example, if there are some items that you want to put on eBay that don't require a lot of magnification to see product quality or details, then you may need just enough resolution to show that the item is intact. Taking a full-resolution image may not be necessary, and large image downloads may annoy, rather than attract, potential buyers. If you are taking just a few images of this sort, it may be just as easy to take the high-resolution image and resize the image smaller later (especially if you find you have to look for the camera's manual to figure out how to change the resolution settings). Quality in this case is hardly the issue.

> If you think you might ever use the shot for more than one purpose, grab all the resolution that you can with your digital camera.

Images that you obtain using a scanner or scanning service fall into a similar category. You will want to get as much detail as you can from a scan, but at some point you will be examining the grain of the film or paper in the print rather than extracting detail from the existing image. If you are scanning an image from a newspaper, you can use less resolution (samples) than if you scan from a negative, because the resolution of newspaper printing will be far lower (see Figure 1.2). The detail of your source can dictate the resolution as well as the application.

If you are a casual shooter and only send photos to relatives via e-mail, keep in mind that an image will display at about three times the size in a web browser (72 ppi) than it does in print (240 ppi). So even resolution that seems low can be more than you really need depending on what you do.

When going to print, too much image information can slow down processing and can be overkill. If you have a 5″ × 7″ image at 240 ppi, that will be enough to print at that size for many purposes. That is just 1200 × 1680 pixels, roughly what you get from a 2 megapixel camera. If you envision doing larger prints of the same quality, you will usually need more resolution (depending on the output devices). On the other hand, using that same image without resampling for a 2″ × 2.8″ image in a magazine is overboard: you'll have roughly twice the resolution you really need. That additional resolution taxes computer imaging resources and will not improve your result. Imaging equipment ends up just crunching the image information and decimating detail, likely using a simple averaging technique with no sharpening. What that means is you may even get a better result if you resize the image correctly to a lower resolution on your own and sharpen the result. See the chapters in Part V and the Appendix for more information about printing and resolution.

Figure 1.2

If you're scanning or photographing this image from newsprint, the detail soon runs out, making higher-resolution scans or photos superfluous.

You may want to plan a little for the future; not only may technology improve to demand more resolution from images to make the best prints, but your needs may change and additional resolution may leave you with a little leeway to take advantage of future changes. Use resolution to your advantage, rather than just assuming it is correct. So, can you have too much resolution? Yes, but usually only in applying the images (in print and on the Web). Traditionally, the push has been toward more resolution and greater definition. However, with newer consumer digital cameras capturing larger images, understanding how to apply and use image resolution becomes more important. Get what you can for archiving and storing images, but target that resolution to output and display sizes as needed.

Chapter 2

Seeing Images as Color, Contrast, and Tone

Without light, there would be no images. Light is what shapes the subject of images. It strikes an object that you are photographing, reflects through the camera lens, and is captured in the exposure as color, contrast, and tone. Light shapes the object, because shadows and highlights define object contour. Resolution allows you to capture image detail, but it is the subtle interplay of tones, contrast, and color that gives shape to objects in the image.

Understanding how color, contrast, and tone are captured and how they work together will help you better understand your images and how the corrections you make effect change. Tone and color are more intermeshed than most people think: brightness affects color and intensity throughout the spectrum. Color can be captured with different depth (really, more color resolution) and stored in different file types as color and tone components.

Rendering image color faithfully in print and on screen makes what you see on screen essential to your results. This chapter looks at the relationship between color and tone, bit depth, and displaying images correctly as components of the image editing process.

Tonal Range, Brightness, Contrast, and Image Dynamics

Color as Tone

Types of Color

Gaining Perspective on Color Management

Making What You See What You Get: Monitor Calibration and Color Preferences

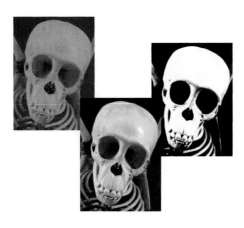

Tonal Range, Brightness, Contrast, and Image Dynamics

Tonal range is the difference between the lightest and darkest image areas. The greater the difference is between the lightest and darkest areas of an image, the greater the tonal range. *Brightness* serves as a measure and limiting factor for both tonal range and contrast. It is a measure of the median luminosity of an image from dark to light. The way light and dark tones play against one another is *contrast.* The more stark the difference is between light and dark image areas, the greater the contrast. If tonal range, brightness, and contrast are not balanced correctly, an image will appear too light, too dark, too flat, or too harsh and contrasty, as illustrated in Figure 2.1.

Creating a dynamic image starts with making the most of the tonal range that exists in the image. Contrast (or lack of contrast) between tones within that range helps define image character. Not every image will naturally have high contrast and a broad tonal range. Some images may be naturally high key (light, usually with moderate to low

Figure 2.1

One image can look many different ways, but the best way usually uses full tonal range and flattering contrast.

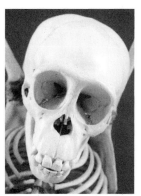
Too light

Too dark

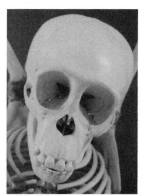
Not enough contrast

Too much contrast

Balanced brightness and contrast

contrast), low key (dark, usually with moderate to low contrast), or simply low contrast. Usually, the goal of correction is to maintain the natural character, or key, of an image while adjusting tone and contrast to enhance and improve dynamics. If there are 255 possible grays for your image, and you use only 100 of those, the image is really only about 40 percent as dynamic as it might be. If you adjust the tonal range, the image can become more visually dynamic; if you adjust with care, you won't lose the natural quality of the image.

Both tone and contrast work in almost the same way in color and black-and-white images: you want to make the most of and expand tonal range and dynamics while maintaining image character. The difference is, when you extend the tonal range in a black-and-white image, you get more potential grays (tones); when you make similar adjustments in color images, you get more potential colors as well as a full range of tone.

Color as Tone

Color is a pretty simple thing to manage if you're picking out clothes, drapes, or upholstery. In those cases it is already mixed and applied for you. If you don't have experience with color mixing, it isn't until the first time you actually try to correct the color of an image that the complexity of color comes alive. If you've never had any training in art and color theory, understanding how color works can be a little confusing. Add to that the existence of different *color modes* (theoretical ways of defining color), and color becomes still more complex. Even more confusion can grow from the fact that color is often stored in your digital images as grayscale components. Because color can be split into simple grayscale components, it is important to understand how grayscale (tone, brightness, and contrast) can also define color. However complex, you have to understand color and how it works in digital images to apply it and achieve the results you want.

For the most part, images that you will work with in color will be in RGB mode. *RGB* stands for red, green, and blue. It is based on an additive light-based color theory: different combinations and intensities of red, green, and blue lights make up the set of available colors. As the red, green, or blue lights are made brighter and applied with more intensity, the resulting color gets brighter, and colors mix in these varying intensities to form other colors. Full intensity of red, green, and blue results in white; lack of red, green, and blue results in black. It is a theory that works great with projection, such as on your monitor and some projection TVs. Breaking images into their component RGB colors is how your monitor displays color, and often RGB color is how image detail is captured by a scanner or digital camera.

Each color you see is made up of these three color components in different combinations. In 8-bit digital images, each of the three components has 256 intensities (Elements does have 16-bit capability, which is discussed more later in this chapter and in the "Bit

Depth" section of the Appendix). The grayscale representations of the intensity of the red, green, and blue are stored as grayscale information in your image files. Light coming into a camera or sensed by a scanner is actually broken into these three components to be stored as intensity of the component color. Later the information is reassembled, allowing your computer to reproduce full-color images from the RGB components.

This theory and practice have been around for quite a while. One of the earliest photographers to create color images did it in Russia in the early 1900s, before there was actual color film. Sergei Mikhailovich Prokudin-Gorskii (1863–1944) made glass plates three at a time when he took pictures with a specially designed camera, filtering for the red, green, and blue components of light to record the strength (tone) of each component on what was essentially grayscale film. The plates would record the captured light as grayscale, and then using a special projector, Prokudin-Gorskii would project the images simultaneously with red, green, and blue filters to reproduce the color images on a projection screen. Figure 2.2 shows one of Prokudin-Gorskii's images; a composited version of this image is also available as Kush-beggi.psd in the Chapter 2 folder on this book's CD. (These plates are from the collection at the U.S. Library of Congress, which can be accessed at `http://lcweb2.loc.gov/pp/prokquery.html`.) A very similar type of light separation is accomplished when shooting color film.

Inside each of your color images are the primary source colors: red, green, and blue. These source colors are stored as grayscale representations and mappings of the intensity of red, green, and blue light in every pixel in your image. When you work on color images, the changes that you make during correction and changes affect all three of the source colors at the same time. Using the right techniques (which we will look at in this book), you can separate out the grayscale representations of all the color components of your images and retrieve them for use in adjusting your image dynamics, tone, contrast, and color.

> Photoshop has a palette called Channels, which is not included with Photoshop Elements. The Channels palette, like the Layers palette, enables you to edit color components and manipulate them separately (in RGB as well as other color modes). This can be a great tool in making complex color corrections. Even though there is no formal Channels palette in Elements, this book shows you how to access and alter channel information easily, just as if you had a Channels palette working for you. For the sake of this book and working with Elements (rather than Photoshop), channels are referred to as *components*.

Breaking down color information into color components may not always be to your advantage when making corrections, but it can often be helpful when trying to isolate damage and perform advanced color correction. The ability to make separations into image components is a key concept of this book. If you understand how to make component separations and how these separations combine to create your images, it opens a world of possibility for improving images.

Blue plate close-up

Figure 2.2

This image by Prokudin-Gorskii (a portrait of Minister of the Interior Kush-Beggi) was taken around 1910 by separating color into grayscale RGB plates. Scans of the glass plates can be composited to achieve a full-color result (as we will do in an exercise in Chapter 4).

Green plate close-up

Original plates

Red plate close-up

As Prokudin-Gorskii did in creating his "color" images, we can re-create representation of color as grayscale components by filtering digital images using functionality in Elements. When the color components are separate, they can be adjusted one at a time, simplifying the way you work with color. This can help when correcting color-specific defects, in simplifying an approach to images and corrections, in developing a better understanding of what happens when you apply a tool to color images, and in doing the most complex color alterations and corrections. Let's look at color types and color management, which affect the way color is stored and represented.

Types of Color

Color in your images can be measured in several ways. Photoshop Elements uses color modes, which as I said earlier are really just different ways of depicting color and tone. The following are the four modes you can use:

- RGB
- Indexed Color
- Grayscale
- Bitmap

> Later in this section and elsewhere in the book we'll look at other color modes, including LAB, CMYK, RGBL, and Duotone. These are not technically working color modes in Elements, but you can achieve separations for these color models and save the separations to files using Elements.

Image color mode and file type are two very different things. Knowing which color modes appear in which file types (and which file types to use with a certain color mode) is often essential for correctly purposing your images.

For the most part, people using Photoshop Elements will be working with 8-bit color images in RGB mode. This mode offers the broadest flexibility for tool use and is the mode most images are in when captured or created. As I have said, RGB refers to the type of color storage; in this case information is stored as red, green, and blue components. *8-bit* refers to the exactitude of the color representation, or the number of variations that can be stored per pixel in a color component. In 8-bit RGB, 256 possible tonal variations in each of the three color components lead to over 16 million different possible color variations ($256 \times 256 \times 256 = 16,777,216$). That's one big box of Crayolas! In fact, it is the largest color set of any of the color modes you will be working with in Elements, except when using 16-bit RGB. A larger number of possible colors in your image allows finer distinction between colors and helps changes that you make to images blend more evenly without noticeable shifts, or banding, between colors.

16-bit is perceived to be an advantage over 8-bit, with 35,184,372,088,832 potential colors. Images can theoretically have better integrity, and changes are less apt to damage image information. The result can be that even dramatic changes may be less damaging. When working with 16-bit images in Elements, however, some important tools and functions are not available for image correction—most notable of these is layers. Other drawbacks to 16-bit include greatly increased file size, greater computer horsepower needed to process the images, and the lack of ability to use output from a 16-bit file (at present, information must be converted to 8-bit for print processing and display).

> Regardless of what you read elsewhere, 8-bit files can be returned to 16-bit in Elements. This will not magically restore 16-bit information that may have been lost or unavailable, but it will enable you to restore the advantage of 16-bit editing to 8-bit images. See the "16-Bit Images" sidebar later in this section.

Generally, you will work in 8-bit RGB for the best access to tools and the most predictable behavior of images. When the image is complete (that is, all changes you are going to make have been made), then you can consider converting the RGB image to other modes as required for your final purpose. You can save RGB files in many formats, but you will probably most often use TIFF (print), Photoshop (archive), JPEG (Web), and PDF (portability).

Indexed Color is a much more limited color mode than RGB and is almost always associated with GIF Web images. This color mode allows a maximum of 256 colors and can include transparent values. The colors are created as a table by using *hex values*: six-character codes that represent specific colors (see the hextable.html Chart in the Chapter 2 folder on the Hidden Power CD). The colors cannot be mixed and must be one or another of the colors in the table. The goal of limiting colors, especially in the case of Web images, is to simplify files and make them smaller. This smaller file size is intended to help enable faster image transfer.

Even without any experience in converting to Indexed Color from RGB, it may be obvious that converting all of your 16 million potential colors from an 8-bit RGB image into a measly set of 256 colors for Indexed Color may not always produce the best results. In converting to Indexed Color from RGB, almost all of your original color will have to change. Of course, the results can be disastrous when imposed on a full-color image. However, there are color tricks (such as dithering) that can make Indexed Color's color sets appear larger than they really are. Because color is applied rather than mixed, Indexed Color is a difficult color mode in which to work. There are no layers, so adjustments are further hampered. Because of the liability of the file type, moving to this color mode will almost always be a last-step conversion and almost always will be done in converting images for display on the Web (when JPEG is not used). Indexed Color files are almost exclusively saved in GIF format.

Grayscale mode is also a limited color mode, but it is limited to no color at all. This "color" mode has 256 levels of gray tones in 8-bit mode that make up all you see in standard black-and-white images (see Figure 2.3) or when working with individual color components (such as color components extracted from RGB images). Generally you will convert images to grayscale when you are seeking to reproduce black-and-white effects. Printing images as grayscale, without color, may also yield the best depiction of tone, by removing the influence of printer inks other than black. Taking the color out of an image can be simple, but it can also be considered an art, because what looks good in color may not look good at all in a straight conversion to black-and-white/grayscale. We will look at various ways to improve your color-to-black-and-white results later in the book. Grayscale images are most often used in black-and-white print jobs, but conversion to black-and-white may also be preparation for making toned images (duotones). Grayscale images can be saved in many file modes, including PSD, PDF, TIFF, and JPEG.

Bitmap images are like grayscale but are more strictly formed in black or white—using no grays, as illustrated in Figure 2.4. For the most part, bitmap images are used with line art (pen-and-ink-type line drawings). Bitmap will probably be the least-used color mode of those available in Elements. You will probably save Bitmap mode images in TIFF or BMP formats. High-resolution bitmap images are sometimes used for line art and other special purposes for print, such as creating dithered drop-shadows for use in layout. If you do not have a need for special purpose images and line art, it is likely that you will never use Bitmap mode.

These BMP bitmap images are different from the color bitmaps used in screen shots and other images as a common file format on Windows computers.

Figure 2.3

Grayscale gradients showing black-to-white gradients in (a) 10 steps (10 percent darker in each), (b) 25 steps (10 levels darker in each), and (c) 255 steps (every level of gray)

CMYK color (depicting images with cyan, magenta, yellow, and black) is a common printing color scheme that is not really available to Elements users as a color mode. It is how color is most often depicted in print. While you will not work in CMYK color mode in Elements, you will usually print with CMYK color. The theory for CMYK color uses a limited set of colors as inks to create the visible color set. At the same time, CMYK is perceptually the opposite of RGB. While RGB is based on additive color (the more light or color you add, the brighter it gets), CMYK is subtractive (the more ink/color you add, the darker it gets, because the light striking the color is absorbed). CMYK ink is most often applied in an array of printer dots; as the dots overlay, the result becomes darker and the ink colors mix. Figure 2.5 shows how two ink halftones combine for a darker result.

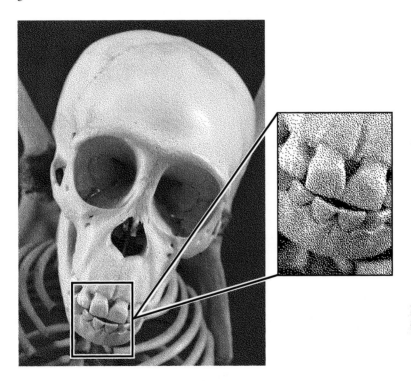

Figure 2.4

The magnification of a portion of the original bitmap image reveals the bitmap patterning.

Figure 2.5

Samples of black (45°, left image) and cyan (108°, middle image) halftone dots as grayscale. When the halftone dots are printed over one another (right), ink colors combine and become denser to absorb more light.

Conversion from RGB to CMYK color representation is often disappointing, because CMYK can portray fewer colors than RGB—even though there is one more color in the CMYK color set. The easiest way to understand this is to consider efficiency. While light is pretty much 100 percent efficient (light is the color), the absorption of light by ink pigments is not (ink attempts to convert light color by absorbing light based on ink color). Pigments are not as efficient as light and do not provide perfect light absorption, so the color they reflect is not perfect in conversion. Black is added to the CMY color set as an attempt to increase the efficiency of absorption. As an additive, it produces only redundant color (color that should have been reproducible in a 100 percent efficient CMY pigment set). Because of the inefficiency in ink absorption, the CMYK color set suffers and results in less dynamic color and tone than RGB overall.

There is a supposition that you cannot work with CMYK images in Elements because it is not a supported color mode, but this is not entirely true. Although the program is not set up to handle CMYK directly, an indirect approach can enable you to make custom CMYK separations and usable CMYK images that can help you improve printed output. The file format used with CMYK is often TIFF, PDF, or Photoshop EPS. Regretfully, none of these will work directly within Elements. However, later in the book we will look at how you can essentially hijack the DCS (Desktop Color Separation) file format to allow saving and manipulating files as CMYK.

16-BIT IMAGES

Some users wonder—and even worry—about using 16-bit mode for image editing. 16-bit images offer more color detail: whereas 8-bit can reproduce "only" 16 million colors per pixel, 16-bit can reproduce more than 35 trillion (based on Photoshop's color handling). While this difference between 16-bit and 8-bit may be significant for archival purposes, for most cases in the real world, it should not make a noticeable difference in your images. You might see the difference if you are making extreme changes to an image or trying to rescue image detail (such as from shadows and highlights). However, most output devices can't handle the additional image information in 16-bit images, and it is questionable whether technology will meet the 16-bit challenge in the near future or whether human perception can really distinguish between the results.

Photoshop Elements supports some 16-bit color adjustment as of version 3. Previously it would convert 16-bit images to 8-bit when opening. The only real gain you have for 16-bit images is in importing original 16-bit information or temporarily extending the usable color space for your images while you work on them (most effectively with RAW file imports). If you have a camera or scanner that creates RAW images, be sure, as suggested, to store copies of the original images before converting them to 8-bit.

When possible, working in 16-bit rather than 8-bit can provide an advantage for grayscale images, arguably more so than for color. The measly 256 colors in the single grayscale component can more easily run out of image room and variation than the 16 million variations per pixel in 8-bit color. While you can't apply all tools in 16-bit (Elements does not, for example, support layers with 16-bit images), you can make some corrections using 16-bit, and you can switch back to 16-bit after making 8-bit modifications using Hidden Power techniques discussed here.

To temporarily switch to 8-bit, do the following:

1. Have a 16-bit image open.

2. Duplicate the image (File → Duplicate).

3. Put your new filename in the As field. For this example, use **Temp_8-Bit**. Click OK.

4. Change the mode of the Temp_8-Bit image to 8-bit (Image → Mode → Convert To 8-Bits/Channel).

5. Make any corrections you want involving layers, and so forth, that you can't do in 16-bit mode.

6. Make a selection of the entire image using Select All (Command+A/Ctrl+A [Mac/PC]), and then choose Copy (Command+C/Ctrl+C) to copy the image.

7. Activate the original 16-bit image and choose Paste (Command+V/Ctrl+V).

When you paste, the image information you have been manipulating in 8-bit will convert to 16-bit. There are, of course, some limitations to the effectiveness of this conversion, but you can return to 16-bit mode and save the manipulation as a 16-bit file.

You can also convert files that were originally 8-bit images to 16-bit:

1. Have a flattened 8-bit image open. Check the Height and Width in pixels by using Image Size (Image → Resize → Image Size) and note the values.

2. Make a selection of the entire image using Select All and Copy.

3. Open the Hidden_16.psd image in the Chapter 2 folder on this book's companion CD.

4. Resize the image (using Image Size again) to the Height and Width noted in step 1. Accept the changes by clicking OK.

5. Paste.

This will paste the 8-bit information into the 16-bit file, converting it during the process. Changes that you make while in 16-bit mode will reflect the advantages of 16-bit files. You can now fluidly move from 8-bit to 16-bit files in Elements.

See the Appendix for more information on 16-bit images.

Gaining Perspective on Color Management

A buzz phrase in image correction is *color management.* If you are not familiar with this term, or if you have heard of it but don't know quite what it is, this section covers most of what you need to know about the topic. Although it is something you should take seriously, color management does not have to be as complex or mysterious as it tends to be. This brief discussion will help you become familiar with it, poke it with a stick, and see that it is dangerous if completely ignored. We'll look at your options and get you set up, and you'll get on with the main course of editing images with confidence as you pass by color management with a better understanding and a knowing grin.

Ill-considered opinions on using color management are common in newsgroups and forums on the Web. Users scoff at other users, abuse innocence and interest, and project ill-gotten conceptual superiority with insistence. If you have questions about this section or about color management, please ask them on the Hidden Power forums: `http://hiddenelements` `.com/forums`. I am also often available for rebuttal and rescue, and I would be glad to discuss the topic with intimidators. Feel free to invite me to a discussion (contact me directly at thebookdoc@aol.com).

Color management is supposed to be a means of helping you get better color consistently. That sounds good, and it is usually the reason why people think it is something they can't do without. By using color management, you stand a better chance of having your images looking the same from a variety of outputs (print and display). Color management uses profiles that describe how your display handles color to help translate what you see to other devices and how those devices handle color (via a common color palette and profiles of those other devices). The profile from your monitor or working color space can be embedded (saved) with your image file to act as the color interpreter for other devices (monitors and printers).

This section deals only with Color Management options for Photoshop Elements. For more information on using printer profiles, see the "Printing with a Profile" section in Chapter 10.

Every device has its own profile. The profiles act as a means to enable interpretation from one device to another, so the devices can speak the same color language and adjust for differences. In other words, color may translate differently to different devices, and color management is meant to improve color use between devices. The key to full color management is that every device has to have a profile to be able to interpret other profiles, so the translation will work reliably. The embedded profile will affect images behind the scenes, both to help represent color correctly on screen and to serve as a translator to other devices. In theory, that results in a better image.

All this talk of automatic translation and better color sounds very appealing, like I'm serving the chocolate cake first. This is all nice in theory, but the sad fact is, it doesn't necessarily work in practice. There are a lot of points in image processing where detours or errors can occur. Your profile can get dropped, changed, or ignored, or it can just plain be wrong. Profiling can occur where you don't expect it, profiling can be compounded, and other profiles can be wrong, causing information in your image to be misinterpreted. Any of these can cause unexpected results.

The first thing that can go wrong is that you are responsible for building yourself a color profile—unless you use a generic one (not recommended). You have to set up the profile correctly, and there is no guarantee that you will (even if you follow instructions) because the process involves your assessment of color by eye (if you don't use a profiling/calibration device). Because your assessment may not be perfect, the resulting profile may not be entirely accurate. Second, every step between saving your image and sending it to the printer has to both respect the color management and process it correctly. This is where the chocolate cake often turns into mud pie.

Although profiling was designed to function behind the scenes and stay with your image, you can't be sure that the results you get are based on the choices you have made to embed your monitor profile in the image—unless you manage each step of the process. You also can't be sure that you really want the process to respect your profile (for example, if it is not correct). Embedding a profile doesn't work consistently because it can't be enforced: even if you embed a profile, some device or person along the way can drop your settings. There are devices that don't recognize color management settings; there are services that don't use them in processing. If your results depend on the color management, and the wrong color profile is embedded or the profile is missing, you are just as likely—or more likely—to get a bad result than you are without depending on color management or embedding color profiles at all.

Your only chance for guaranteed success using embedded color profiles is to make a study of how the profiles work and become intimately knowledgeable about the output types and processes you use. Reading your printer manual is not necessarily intimate knowledge; it goes somewhat deeper than that.

Even with this additional effort, using color management and embedding profiles require testing to be sure the process works as expected and the results look the way they should. Funny thing is, you have another choice: *not* embedding profiles or depending on color management. Not embedding profiles can have pitfalls and also requires testing. It does, however, remove the potential added complexity of using embedded profiles. In the long run, if you set up your system correctly by calibrating your monitor and creating a monitor profile (an ICC profile that describes your monitor), not embedding profiles can often lead to more predictable results. You should not entirely dismiss color management, and you should create a monitor profile—even if you are not embedding profiles in your images. The process of creating the profile helps calibrate your monitor and adjust the view of your screen. Embedding profiles in your images, on the other hand, is like an extra half step in a staircase that can just as likely trip you up as ease your progress up the stairs— depending on how much you are paying attention. My experience is that you are more likely to trip over that half step and swear at it than praise it.

None of this is to say that you can't embed profiles with success! You can, and if you do currently, don't change what you do. My perspective on using or not using embedded profiles and color management is a lot like my perspective on images: don't change what works; change what doesn't. If you currently use embedded profiles and everything works fine, stay with them. If you don't use embedded profiles with success, don't use embedded profiles, have never looked at color management, or don't understand what it is and how to use embedded profiles, then you should practice color management with the following fast, safe, and effective system:

1. Calibrate your monitor and create a monitor profile. (We'll look at how to do this in a moment.)

2. Switch to No Color Management in Color Settings (Command+Shift+K / Ctrl+Shift+K). The shortcut for Color Settings can also be opened from the menus by choosing Edit → Color Settings.

3. Don't embed profiles.

There is really one more step to this equation, and that is being sure that images you introduce to Elements are sRGB or a generic RGB flavor rather than Adobe RGB or other RGB hybrid. If you have a digital camera with options for shooting in Adobe RGB as a color space, don't use it with this method of color management. If you do, images from your camera will look washed out. That is actually an example of how color management can fail. An Adobe RGB image placed in Elements with color management off will be treated like an sRGB image. The broader Adobe RGB color space treated as sRGB will compress the tonal and color range.

> Along with misunderstanding color management, the actual purpose of color profiles is also often incorrectly dispensed. Adobe RGB is said to be a "larger" profile, as if it had more color capability than sRGB. Actually, any 8-bit RGB color space has the same number of colors; the colors themselves are just assigned differently. Although using Adobe RGB may slightly enhance results if used in a strict Adobe RGB workflow, it is not decidedly better than sRGB in achieving color in print. For more information on color spaces, see "Understanding Color Space" in the next section.

To be reasonably successful with color management, the Photoshop Elements user needs to calibrate, create a monitor profile (which Elements uses for image viewing), and choose how to handle profiles by making a selection in Color Settings. Even if you choose No Color Management, you are still using color management—you just choose not to embed profiles in your images or make automated conversions. Calibrating your monitor and creating the monitor's color profile help ensure that you see the best representation of the images on your display. This best representation should show what your image will look like on most other displays—and, for the most part, what it will look like in print. The next few sections present in a little more depth what you should expect to see on your monitor, how to calibrate, and what to do to build an ICC profile for your monitor.

Making What You See What You Get: Monitor Calibration and Color Preferences

One problem with trusting your visual sense is that it assumes that what you see on screen is the right thing. Regrettably, that is not probable without calibration. All monitors are different, they age at different rates, and the settings for display and color will affect what you see. If you haven't calibrated your monitor, colors on your screen might look different from colors on other calibrated monitors—and worse, they might not match or even come close to the color that gets printed.

If you are looking at a screen that is shifted green and you depend on the color to be accurate, a good correction will tone down the greens to make the image look right on screen. This will cause output of any kind to be shifted toward red (the opposite of green). Calibration will help compensate for any uncalibrated color shifts by flattening the response of your screen.

The goal of calibration is simple: you want to be able to trust what you see on your monitor, within reason. If you can trust what you see, you can mostly use your visual sense to correct your images.

I say *mostly* because even if you've calibrated your monitor, you have merely adjusted it for best performance. You are going to get the most out of your monitor, but the monitor itself may have some limitations (poor color display)—and there are inherent limitations in printing, so it is likely that there will be some differences between what you see on screen and the result in print. Although you probably won't reach perfection in matching your monitor and prints, calibrating your monitor gives you a far better chance of at least coming close. With some selective checking, you should be able to feel confident in what you'll get as a result.

Calibrating Your Monitor and Building an ICC Profile

In this section you'll look at how to calibrate your monitor and create a monitor profile. Creating the profile helps your system adjust previews so images on screen appear accurately. Before you begin, you should know several things about the response and performance of your monitor, including the manufacturer-suggested color temperature, gamma, and phosphor settings. These settings should be available from the manufacturer (call tech support for your monitor and ask for an engineer if necessary; support help won't always know phosphor values, but engineers will).

> Monitor manufacturers don't always put monitor specs for phosphors, white point, and gamma in the manuals. You'll likely have to seek out that information. When you obtain the information, write it down. I usually write the settings right on the cover of the monitor manual for easy reference.

Color temperature reflects the monitor display color for the white point, which really is a measure of the color of white on your monitor. It is usually 6500, 7500, or 9300 degrees on the Kelvin scale. The higher the number, the more blue (or cool) the white is; the lower the number, the more red (or warm) the white is. The color temperature is an inherent characteristic of your display and can subtly affect the appearance of color on screen.

Gamma is a measure of tonal response, often a number between 1 and 3 with two decimal places. *Phosphors* are a set of six numbers with x and y coordinates for red, green, and blue; these numbers can have up to three decimal places. These settings vary between monitor brands and models, so don't make assumptions about them or copy someone else's. Find the settings in your manual or contact the manufacturer (via the website or technical support—again, asking for an engineer if necessary).

> What you use for calibration may vary. Adobe provides Adobe Gamma for monitor calibration along with Photoshop Elements on PC, and Macintosh users will have Display Calibrator Assistant provided by Apple. Other utilities are available that you can use to calibrate instead. However, most of these cost money and some are even expensive. Be sure you use calibration software that creates an ICC profile for your monitor so that you get the most out of your calibration.

In the following steps, I describe the sequence (and show the screens) of how to use Adobe Gamma for Windows for calibrating your monitor and creating an ICC profile. Mac users can use Display Calibrator Assistant, and follow the tutorial here, or the specific instructions on the website (see: www.hiddenelements.com/tutorials/mac_calibration, or follow the tutorials link on the hiddenelements.com home page). There are other utilities that you can use. Many of these utilities are similar with respect to what they do, and any will work for purposes of calibration and creating the profile. For the most part, you can simply start them up and read the directions as they appear on screen. If you are lucky enough to have a calibration device (such as the Spyder by ColorVision: `http://aps8.com/ spyder.html`), use that for calibrating your monitor instead of the following procedure; calibration by hardware calibration devices will be more accurate than calibration by eye.

Your monitor should be in an area that will minimize glare, and lighting (except where noted during the steps of the calibration) should be as you will have it when you are most frequently using the computer and monitor. Lighting should generally be subdued and indirect if possible. Changes in lighting within your work area will require recalibrating the monitor. The monitor can be calibrated to different light conditions, but it is easier to maintain consistent room lighting than to add it as a variable in color corrections. Extremely bright or overly dark rooms might cause some problems with calibrations and monitor viewing. Optimally, room lighting should be bright enough that you can read and view materials that are not on the screen, yet not so bright that the light causes glare or washes out the display. After creating your profile, be sure the lighting where you work remains the same as when you calibrated the monitor. You may want to recalibrate semiannually.

Before you begin, you should also locate the monitor's brightness, contrast, and color controls. If your monitor has an option to reset to factory settings, do it now. If there is no reset option, use the monitor controls to normalize the screen by eye. Grays should look flat gray rather than a little warm (red) or cool (blue). After resetting or adjusting color, leave these controls alone and do not change them after calibration. Now you are ready to start calibration.

> Calibration may be slightly different in some operating systems, though the options in various dialog boxes will look and function in a similar way.

Figure 2.6
The initial Adobe Gamma screen

1. Turn on your monitor and system, and let the monitor warm up for at least 30 minutes.

2. If you haven't done it yet, read the owner's manual for the monitor to see if it provides suggestions for calibration.

3. Open Adobe Gamma by double-clicking the Adobe Gamma icon in the `Control Panel` folder. You should see the screen illustrated in Figure 2.6. If Adobe Gamma is not in the `Control Panel` folder, find it on the Photoshop Elements CD.

4. Click Step By Step. This will lead you through the process of calibrating and creating an ICC profile for your monitor. Click the Next button.

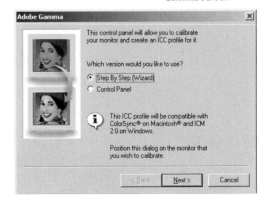

5. In the Description field, type a name for the profile you will be creating (Figure 2.7). You can enter a lot of information here, but it's best to keep it short. I find it handy to name the monitor and add the date, so the profiles are easy to identify. If you use output white point settings (step 12), you may also want to include this value in the name. Click the Next button.

6. Using the monitor controls, set the contrast all the way up and then adjust brightness until the smaller gray box in the center is dark enough that it is just barely discernable from the larger black box surrounding it (see Figure 2.8). If you notice the white frame beginning to darken at any point, stop darkening the screen. If necessary, adjust the brightness setting to lighten the screen a bit until the frame is bright white again. As you fine-tune this adjustment, it may help to squint or use your peripheral vision to get the center square as dark as possible without losing the brightness of the white frame. When you are satisfied with the adjustments, click the Next button.

7. On the screen that appears, select Custom to open the Custom Phosphors screen shown in Figure 2.9.

Figure 2.7

Type the profile name in the Description field.

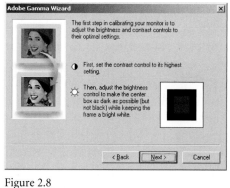

Figure 2.8

Concentric squares in Adobe Gamma help you adjust the screen contrast by observation while making adjustments to the physical monitor settings.

Figure 2.9

Phosphor values describe the monitor's response to color.

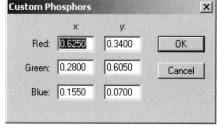

8. Type the six values obtained from the manufacturer of your monitor in the appropriate fields. You don't have to know what each number means, but you do have to place each one correctly. Click the OK button to close the Custom Phosphors screen and accept the changes. This returns you to the Adobe Gamma Wizard dialog box.

9. Click the Next button. The screen that appears (Figure 2.10) enables you to adjust gamma. Select the View Single Gamma Only check box. Using the slider, adjust the appearance of the outer square (the alternating lines of black and white) so that it matches the tone of the 50 percent black center. Adjust the appearance by squinting at the screen (to blur the box slightly in your vision) while moving the slider. The goal is for the entire square to seem to have a uniform tone.

> If you change monitors, you will obviously have to build a new profile. Other less-obvious reasons to build a new profile are monitor aging and changes in response because of use, replacing your system hard drive, and changing room lighting (or computer placement). You should calibrate regularly.

10. In the Gamma field, type the Gamma value you got from the manufacturer. You will be able to enter a two-decimal value, but Adobe Gamma will round the value off when you save the entry.

11. Click the Next button. The screen that appears (shown in Figure 2.11) allows adjustment of the monitor's white point. Set the monitor's white point by choosing the value in the drop-down list that corresponds with the number you got from the manufacturer. If you do not know what value to choose, see the following note on measuring white point.

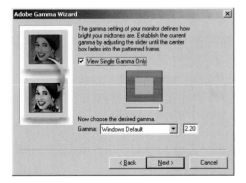

Figure 2.10
Sliders help you visually adjust for the monitor gamma.

Figure 2.11
White point is a measure of the "color" of the brightest parts of your monitor, measured in degrees Kelvin.

A second option on this screen enables you to measure the white point. To do this, dim (or turn off) the lighting in your work area and click the Measure button. A set of three gray squares will appear on a black background. Click the square that seems most flatly gray and repeat until the test closes.

12. Click the Next button. The screen that appears (Figure 2.12) will enable you to select a white point for output. This selection should be based on the color temperature of the intended output media. If you are unsure, or if you are creating images for the Web, use the Same As Hardware setting.

13. Click the Next button. The next screen (Figure 2.13) enables you to compare calibration before and after the adjustments you made in the previous steps. Click to toggle the Before and After buttons several times, comparing the appearance of your screen as you toggle back and forth. Specifically, note the grays in the dialog box and see whether the color appears more neutral before or after adjustment. The more neutral (lacking any color and looking flat gray), the better the calibration.

14. If the before and after results are noticeably different, run through the process again (steps 3 to 13).

15. Click the Finish button to accept the changes.

I never calibrate one time and sit back satisfied—even when using a calibration device. I run through the process a few times to be sure I have the best calibration.

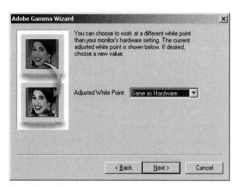

Figure 2.12

Output white point differs from monitor white point. This setting should reflect the color temperature of your output. This may be another monitor, paper, or a projection screen.

Figure 2.13

Compare before and after adjustments by toggling the view with the radio buttons.

What you have just done is calibrated your monitor and created an ICC profile for it. The calibration helps you to be sure the image information you see on-screen is reasonably accurate. The ICC profile is a description of how color appears on your system (notations as to how the monitor needed adjustment in order to appear normal). This information is used by Elements to create previews, and it can be used if you embed profiles in your images to help describe color in your image to other ICC-aware devices.

Although Adobe Gamma is an adequate tool for visual calibration, calibration devices (see the example in Figure 2.14) can measure more accurately than your eye and will measure a greater number of gray levels and create more accurate profiling. The devices take measurements directly from your screen and create a profile based on those measurements. Using such a device can ensure that your monitor is calibrated properly, and it may actually save some time during calibrations.

Figure 2.14

The ColorVision Spyder device attached to a monitor

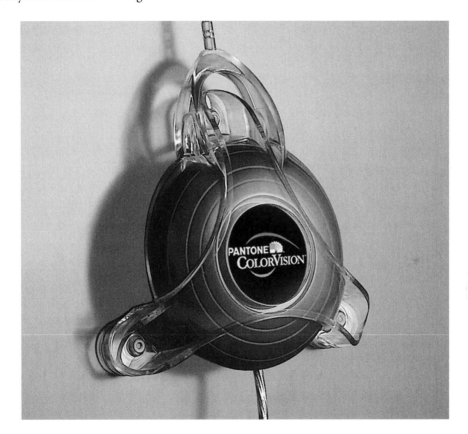

Color Preferences

Most Preferences settings in Photoshop Elements are just a matter of personal preference, and they can be changed at any time as you see fit. However, the one group of settings that you will be better off making a choice about and sticking to it is Color Settings. Color Settings is where you can define how Elements handles images with profiles that you open, what color space you want to work in, and whether profiles get embedded in your images by default. The choice you make can be important to your results and will certainly affect how you work with images. If you are not sure about what to select, or if you are unfamiliar with some of the terminology just used, that's okay. We'll cover your options and explain the terms here. There should be enough information in this section to help you make a choice. If you have questions, feel free to bring them up in the forums (`http://hiddenelements.com/forums`) or send a question to the newsletter (`http://hiddenelements.com/newsletter.html`).

> Before we dive in to selecting color preferences, how much do you really need to know about color management to get results? Actually, not that much—if you use the techniques suggested in this book. The following explanation attempts to clarify why certain suggestions are made and to keep things as simple as possible.

Understanding Color Space

Color space is a defined color set—a mapping of the gamut of colors that are possible in an image when using that color space. Some spaces, such as Adobe RGB, are casually said to be *larger* than others, which makes them sound more attractive. The concept that one RGB color space is described as necessarily larger, bigger, better, or more encompassing isn't technically accurate if it suggests there are more colors. All 8-bit RGB images have the same number of potential colors: 16 million. On the other hand, each different flavor of RGB is mapped to cover a particular range, or gamut, of colors. A different range of color does not mean that a "bigger color space" has more colors; it just maps a broader range, assigning its 16 million values differently. Because different RGB color spaces map to different color sets, all RGB is not the same, though it is born of the same theory.

The difference between one color space and the next is the gamut of colors that the color space covers. In other words, the numbers in two files defined by different color spaces can be exactly the same, as numbers, yet the display or print result would end up different because the numbers in those files represent different colors (however slight the difference). We can see this difference in assigning profiles to an image (see the section on assigning and converting profiles later in this chapter). What you really need to focus on here is what the mappings intend to cover. You can know the name of the color space, but that may not tell you a lot about what you are working with. Two common work-spaces applicable to Photoshop Elements are sRGB and Adobe RGB.

> Each RGB file has the same number of potential colors—no matter what color space you choose to use.

> The difference between color spaces is the range, or gamut, of color in their mapping, not the number of colors.

sRGB is a "limited" RGB color space in that it assumes some limitations of a common RGB monitor to display all RGB colors. Because of inherent limitations in monitor projection, sRGB is mapped to enable you to record color in your files that most any monitor should display correctly. All this really means is that colors are not mapped to the full potential gamut of RGB. The images you make in sRGB color space are more likely to be compatible with what can generally be displayed reliably on other monitors. In other words, it is a generic and friendly color space if you are sharing images for viewing on monitors. This is usually the assumed profile if an image is not tagged (that is, does not have an embedded profile).

Adobe RGB (1998) is a wider-gamut RGB color space than sRGB. It maps to a color set that attempts to better describe colors available on CMYK printers (notably purer cyan). Because it maps a broader range of colors than sRGB, Adobe suggests that it may be a better choice for working with images that are intended for print. The drawback to using Adobe RGB is that you may be manipulating colors that you can't see accurately on screen because they actually extend beyond the range your monitor can display. If color management actually works as designed, however, optimized images for either Adobe RGB or sRGB should appear very nearly the same on monitors or in print, as long as you embed profiles (sometimes known as "tagging" images).

> A third profile you can use for color management in Elements is the custom ICC monitor profile you created for your monitor after calibration. You'll see it as the Embed Color Profile choice in the Save As screen when you are using No Color Management—if you have correctly set up the profile per earlier instructions. This profile attempts to describe the way your monitor handles color. It is used by Elements as a means of attempting to create an accurate preview of colors in conjunction with your working color space.

When you're working with your images and profiles are not embedded, devices using the color file have to make an assumption about the color space. Generally the assumption will be that a generic RGB space was used; that more likely means sRGB rather than Adobe RGB. This is okay for those who use sRGB as a working color space but not for those using Adobe RGB. An untagged Adobe RGB image opened as an sRGB image will desaturate because of the wider gamut numbers being mapped to the smaller gamut color space. The only real choice for getting the right color when using Adobe RGB is to embed the profile (tag the files as Adobe RGB) and ensure, along the route of the image, that the profiles are respected. In other words, using Adobe RGB is a commitment to using embedded profiling for your images and, most likely, color management that respects profiling. Using sRGB will not require embedding profiles for the most part to achieve good results. In other words, the working color space and the preference you have for that will dictate your color preference choice.

The Color Settings Dialog Box

The Color Settings dialog box pops up the first time you open Elements, before you do anything. If you have already dismissed this (or want to change the Color Settings preferences after reading this section of the book), you can revisit the settings by opening the Color Settings dialog box (Edit → Color Settings), which is shown in Figure 2.15. The choices seem straightforward enough, and Adobe has made some effort to clarify what each of the settings means in Elements 4. Still the names may be a little deceiving. While there are descriptions on the screen, we'll go through each choice here and discuss what the options mean so that you can make the best choice for your situation and image use.

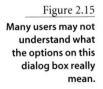

Figure 2.15

Many users may not understand what the options on this dialog box really mean.

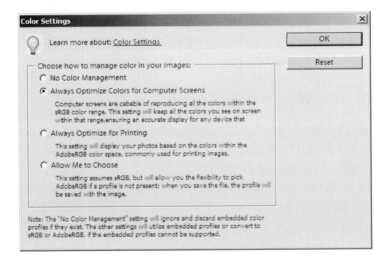

Here are descriptions and some important background information for each choice in the Color Settings screen:

No Color Management This choice ignores any existing profile in an image (if one has been embedded) when you open it. When you save any image, Photoshop Elements will not embed a profile with the image. The option to embed a profile is available by choosing Save As from the File menu; to embed a profile, you simply select (check) the Color, ICC Profile check box in the Save Options panel of the Save As dialog. The profile embedded will be based on the ICC profile you created for your monitor.

Using No Color Management is what I suggest for users who are having trouble with their output and for users who do not want to bother using and learning more about profiling and color management. So long as your digital camera or people with whom you trade images are not using embedded profiles for other color spaces, you should get predictable and reliable results without embedded profiles.

Always Optimize Colors For Computer Screens Selecting this option will convert images to sRGB color space when they are opened using whatever profile is included/embedded in the file. The resulting image will use sRGB as the working color space. On Save, any profile existing in the image will be retained (embedded). The option to embed is available using Save As, and the sRGB profile (sRGB IEC61966-2.1) will be embedded if you choose the option to embed profiles on save and no profile was present when the image was opened.

> In previous versions of Elements, Always Optimize Colors For Computer Screens was called Limited Color Management.

Always Optimize Colors For Computer Screens can be a good choice for those who have selected to shoot images on their camera and embed an Adobe RGB color profile but prefer to work in sRGB in Elements. You will be able to archive the original images with the Adobe RGB profile and still work in a less-worrisome sRGB color space. This color setting selection may solve some problems if you are consistently getting washed-out color from another source (your camera or someone who regularly sends you images). Regardless of the name Adobe chose for this setting, you can use this color management setting for print as well as displaying on computer screens, but the results will be anchored to the sRGB profile.

Always Optimize For Printing This option retains a color profile if it is present in an opened image. On Save, the original profile will be retained with the image. The option to disable embedding the profile can be found in the Save As dialog box. Opening a new image or an image with no existing profile will cause Photoshop Elements to retain the profile with the image based on the color mode.

RGB will have the Adobe RGB (1998) profile.

Indexed Color will have the Adobe RGB (1998) profile.

Grayscale will have a Dot Gain 20% profile.

Bitmap will have no profile.

This selection is for those who want to use a hard-core color management workflow for print. That means every image should have an embedded profile, and all images will be handled by color management—whether or not they originally contain a profile. You would use this setting if, for example, you have the option to embed the Adobe RGB profile with images from your digital camera and you want to work in the Adobe RGB color space during corrections. This is not a good choice for someone who will be casually embedding profiles or someone who is not interested in implementing and learning about color management to its fullest.

Allow Me To Choose This option retains a color profile if it is present in an opened image. On Save, the original profile will be retained with the image. The option to disable embedding the profile can be found in the Save As dialog box. Opening a new image will assume sRGB. Opening an image with no existing profile will cause Photoshop Elements to offer a choice: Leave Image As Is (don't color manage), Optimize Colors For Computer Screen (use sRGB), or Optimize Colors For Print (use Adobe RGB).

If you want to assign a profile or convert your image to the monitor, sRGB, or Adobe RGB profile, you can do that in Elements (no matter who tells you that you can't, and some people will). Assigning a profile means imposing a profile on your image without regard to any previous profile. Converting your image to another profile is a means of making an adjustment between color spaces. Assigning a profile means that Elements uses the colors in the image and maps them according to the profile assigned—the actual content of the image (numbers in the file) does not change, but the look of it very well might (especially if the profile assigned is not the working color space). The intensity of the color change for the image depends on the differences between the original color space and the assigned profile. Converting to a profile should optimally not result in a color change. The content of the image will be converted from one profile to another, and the content of the image (numbers in the file) will change in accordance with the conversion.

> The difference between assigning a profile and converting to one is that the goal of converting to a profile is to retain color as is. Assigning a profile just assumes there is no previous profile and uses the color by numbers.

Making assignments or conversions depends on manipulating Color Settings before and after images are opened to change the program properties. For example, in order to convert from any profile to sRGB or Adobe RGB, do the following:

1. Open the image that you want to convert with Always Optimize For Printing on; this assures that any profile in the image will be respected. You can check for the profile by choosing Save As.

2. Choose either Image → Convert Color Profile → Apply sRGB Profile (to convert to sRGB) or Image → Convert Color Profile → Apply Adobe RGB Profile (to convert to Adobe RGB.

The image content will be converted to the color profile that you have selected. You may see a slight color shift, but the changes should be only because color from the original image was out of gamut for the embedded color space.

To assign the profile, you would do the following:

1. Open the image that you want to assign the profile to with Always Optimize For Printing on.

3. Choose Image → Convert Color Profile → Remove Profile. This strips off the existing profile. You may see an immediate change in the image.

4. Choose either Image → Convert Color Profile → Apply sRGB Profile (to convert to sRGB) or Image → Convert Color Profile → Apply Adobe RGB Profile (to convert to Adobe RGB.

If you try assigning and converting profiles with the `berries.psd` file from the Hidden Power CD, you can compare the results of assigning and converting side by side, and likely you will note a shift in the image where the profile is assigned, converted, or removed. The `berries.psd` file has the Adobe RGB profile embedded.

Converting and assigning profiles is something you probably won't do very often, but it can come in handy when you want to use another color space than the one embedded with the file or if you need to convert to Adobe RGB for output at a service.

It is really a personal decision as to how to manage color. Don't just assume that because a color management option is there that you have to use it, and don't switch to what someone else uses just because you like their results. Good results are part of a good process and determined workflow, not just from color settings in Elements.

The level of complexity and unknowns in working with images seems to rise quite a bit if you choose to embed profiles and use working spaces outside of the more standard sRGB. It is likely that by using optimal techniques for correction (as defined by this book), there should be little difference in your results no matter which color space you use, so long as you are consistent in your approach. This is why I suggest using No Color Management and simplifying the workflow for new users. Personally, I work with color management off until I have a reason to use it for managing profiles. I stick to the workflow I normally use because I can depend on that workflow to get consistent results. I almost never embed a profile unless it is specifically requested or tests have proved it is necessary in getting desired results.

Chapter 3

The Image Editing Process Outline

There are really only a few types of changes that can be made in an image, and these changes all revolve around altering pixel content (tone and color). You choose the tools to use and then work with tone and color in some or all of the pixels in the image to change the composition. That's it. If your process of correcting and enhancing images covers tool selection, color correction, composition changes, and purposing the image, you are doing what you should for every image.

Following a process and understanding the possibilities when making corrections give you a solid foundation from which to work. Although the actual changes for each image may be very different, you can use the same set of tools and the same editing process just about every time. The purpose of this chapter is to outline the process and concepts for you and to give you a set of editing tools on which to concentrate. With this foundation, you can then jump into enhancing your images.

The Image Editing Process

The Tools You'll Need

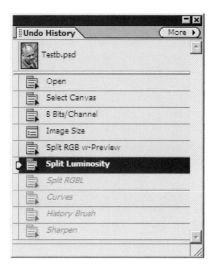

The Image Editing Process

When you go on a vacation, it is a good idea to make a checklist to help you remember everything you have to do before you go and everything you want to bring along. When approaching image correction, a checklist of this type for image correction can help ensure that you've covered all the essentials. The list should cover everything you will have to do to an image. To get to the desired results every time, you'll want to do the steps in a particular order. Until you develop your own preferences and methods, you can use the process that is described over the next sections as your outline for image enhancement.

The image correction process that follows is one that I have developed over many years of working with digital images. The series of steps outlines everything that you will normally need to do in making corrections. The steps are segmented into three distinct parts:

Preparation Be sure your system and program setup are correct and that you know what you want to do with the image.

Correction Take specific steps to achieve your goals in correcting the image.

Purposing Finalize the image to target it to specific output.

The steps in the process will be the same, while what you do at each step will vary from image to image. For some images you may actually skip a step, and for other images you might spend hours indulging one step or another. What you will do depends on the content of the image and what you expect as a result. Procedures that you will use at each step are outlined in detail throughout the rest of the book. Most of the concepts of preparation have already been covered.

Image Correction Checklist

Each set of steps in the image editing process is outlined in the following checklist. Consider this checklist your plan for editing images and use it as a roadmap in making all your image corrections—especially if you do not have your own plan in place. You should cover each step in order.

Preparation

1. Be sure that your monitor is calibrated and that you have set up your preferences and tested your output. Doing so ensures your best chance of getting the results you intend. (See "Gaining Perspective on Color Management," in the previous chapter.)

2. Store the original image file safely and work with a copy to do all of your image editing. If any step in the editing goes awry, you will want to be able to return to the original image to start over. This will also give you the opportunity to repurpose the original in the future.

3. Consider resolution and color. Have in mind a target range for the resolution and a color mode for the final image. You may work at different resolutions and in different color modes throughout, but knowing what you need from the outset can help you work smarter, with fewer color conversions (which you generally want to try to avoid). See "Types of Color" in Chapter 2 and "What Image Resolution to Use" in Chapter 1 .

4. Evaluate the image. This analysis can include looking at color and tone, determining the image type (high key, low key, high contrast), evaluating the extent of work to be done, and considering the composition. The result of the evaluation should be a short list of things you want to improve or change. See "Evaluating Image Tones" in Chapter 5.

Correction

5. Make general color and tonal adjustments. This means do more intensive tonal and color adjustments that will not use selection or masking. Those corrections will come later. See "Redistributing Tone with Levels" and "Snapping and Fading Contrast with Curves" in Chapter 5 and color correction techniques in Chapter 6.

6. Make general damage corrections, such as eliminating dust from scans, fixing cracks and holes in scanned images, and reducing digital noise. See "Techniques for Minor Image Cleanup" in Chapter 5 and "Techniques for Color Image Cleanup" in Chapter 6. Steps 5 and 6 in this checklist may be inverted as appropriate: for example, sometimes you may want to clean up an image to see if it is even worth working with before making color corrections.

7. Make compositional changes including cropping, compositing, and replacing image parts. Some cropping and compositional changes can occur earlier or later in the process. Sometimes early changes help target corrections, and sometimes late changes are final steps in adjusting composition. See Chapters 7 and 8.

8. Make targeted color and tonal corrections to selected parts of the image using selection and masking. You'll use techniques from Chapters 4 through 8.

9. Save the layered RGB version of the image. Be sure to give the file a new name, so you do not save over the original.

Purposing

10. Simplify the image as appropriate. This step may include flattening the image or merging layers, altering the color mode, or removing extraneous image information.

During the process of simplifying, don't delete or merge shape layers that may be important to your output.

11. Optimize the image for output/use. Make color and tonal adjustments, and resize the image to optimize it for output and use. This step can include such changes as setting white and black points and making device-specific color changes. See the suggestions in Chapters 9 to 11.

12. Save the image in output file format.

13. Package the image on proper media for output and use.

This checklist may seem long, but each step will often not be very involved. Some steps you will do naturally, some take just a moment, and some are just reminders for maintaining a positive workflow. Practicing correction by following the steps in the list can ensure that you make all adjustments and corrections that you intend to do in achieving your goals for the image. While this provides a solid process, using the process correctly depends on how well you understand your images. The tools to use in each of these steps are reviewed in the next section. You will look at parts of the process throughout the book, and revisit the process applied to an image from start to finish in Chapter 8.

The Tools You'll Need

In each step of the image editing process, you can use a small subset of the commands in Elements to accomplish your goals. Having a list of these helps you know what tools to concentrate on and master, while leaving others safely behind. Concentrating on the smaller tool set will help streamline your image processing and keep you on target during the editing process.

The tool set listed in Table 3.1 is based on the steps described in the preceding section. Most of these are standard tools you already have in Photoshop Elements; others are add-ins you will find on this book's companion CD. These "Hidden Power tools" can simplify processes or add new functionality to Photoshop Elements. See the "Hidden Power Tools" section of the book's introduction for instructions on how to load and access these additional tools.

You may occasionally reach outside this suggested tool set for a special purpose, but this listing offers a general guideline to simplifying the tools needed to get excellent and consistent results. The choices are based not on which method is easiest to use but on which will provide the best results.

PROCESS STEP	TOOL OR COMMAND	USE THIS TOOL TO DO WHAT?	LOCATION
1. Calibrate the monitor.	Adobe Gamma (PC) or Display Calibrator Assistant (Mac)	Do free, easy monitor calibration and ICC profile generation in one process.	Adobe Gamma calibration software is installed as a separate utility with Elements 4 for PC, found in the Control Panel for Windows; Display Calibrator Assistant comes with the Mac OS, found in the System Preferences, under the Color tab by clicking the Calibrate button.
2. Store the original image.	Save As command	Save your image with a specific name and location.	File → Save As
3. Specify resolution and color settings.	Scanner or digital camera	Set the color, size, and resolution to use for new images.	See camera and scanner user manuals.
	New command	Set the color, size, and resolution to use for new images.	File → New
	Image Size command	Change the size and resolution of an open image.	Image → Resize → Image Size
	Mode command	Change the image color mode of an open image.	Image → Mode
4. Evaluate the image.	Eyedropper	Sample to check color and tone values in specific image areas.	Eyedropper tool in the toolbox. Press I on the keyboard.
	Info palette	Display sampled readouts.	Window → Info
	Histograms	View a chart and statistics showing tonal mapping of the image.	Image → Histograms
	Levels	View image histograms as part of the Levels dialog box display.	Enhance → Adjust Brightness/Contrast → Levels
5. Make general color and tonal corrections.	Levels	Use simple sliders to adjust tonal dynamic range.	Enhance → Adjust Brightness/Contrast → Levels
	Reduce Color Noise	Reduce color noise associated with digital capture.	Hidden Power Tools under Effects on the Styles and Effects palette, in the Power_ Adjustments category
	Basic Color Correction	Adjust tonal levels and balance color as a process.	Hidden Power Tools under Effects on the Styles and Effects palette, in the Power_ Adjustments category
	Luminosity and Color, RGB, and RGBL separations	Split images into component colors and tone (channels) to simplify and target adjustments.	Hidden Power Tools under Effects on the Styles and Effects palette, in the Power_ Separations category

Table 3.1

Tool Set

Continues

Continued

PROCESS STEP	TOOL OR COMMAND	USE THIS TOOL TO DO WHAT?	LOCATION
	Hidden Power Curve Presets	Make multirange adjustments to tone, contrast, and color.	Open the `Hidden_Power_Curves.psd` for drag-and-drop curve presets.
	Gradient Maps	Make custom multirange adjustments to tone, contrast, and color.	Layer → New Adjustment Layer → Gradient Map, or the powerful preset in Hidden Power Tools under Effects on the Styles and Effects palette, in the Power_Adjustments category.
	Hue/Saturation layer	Adjust color by using slider controls to alter hue, increase/decrease saturation, and affect general lightness and darkness.	Layer → New Adjustment Layer → Hue Saturation
	Color Balance	Adjust color by balancing the influence of color opposites.	Hidden Power Tools under Effects on the Styles and Effects palette, in the Power_Adjustments category
	Layer Modes, Layer Opacity, Layer Transparency	Calculate changes in the image using layer properties to target change.	Mode pop-up menu on the Layers palette
6. Make general damage corrections.	Clone Stamp	Make brush-style corrections via sampling of other image areas.	Clone Stamp tool in the toolbox
	Healing Brush	Make smart brush-style corrections via sampling of other image areas.	Healing Brush in the toolbox
	Layer Masking, Blend Mask	Customize selections by using masking.	Hidden Power Tools under Effects on the Styles and Effects palette, in the Power_Masking category
	Copy command	Copy the selected image area to the clipboard.	Edit → Copy
	Paste command	Paste a copied area from the clipboard into a new layer.	Edit → Paste
	Luminosity and Color, RGB, and RGBL separations	Split images into component colors and tone (channels) to simplify and target adjustments.	Hidden Power Tools under Effects on the Styles and Effects palette, in the Power-Separations category
	Layer Modes, Layer Opacity, Layer Transparency	Calculate changes in the image using layer properties to target change.	Mode pop-up menu on the Layers palette

Continues

Continued

PROCESS STEP	TOOL OR COMMAND	USE THIS TOOL TO DO WHAT?	LOCATION
7. Make compositional changes.	Crop	Change the image size by cropping out or adding extra canvas area.	Crop tool in the toolbox. Press C on the keyboard.
	Image Size command	Change the physical dimension and/or number of pixels in an image.	Image → Resize → Image Size
	Marquee and Polygonal Lasso	Select regular and irregularly shaped image objects.	Polygonal Lasso tool in the toolbox. Press L and Shift+L to choose the Lasso tool and scroll the tools.
	Layer Masking, Blend Mask, Highlight Mask, Shadow Mask	Customize the visibility of layered image parts and control the intensity of selections.	Hidden Power Tools under Effects on the Styles and Effects palette, in the Power_ Masking category
	Copy command	Copy a selected image area to the clipboard.	Edit → Copy
	Paste command	Paste a copied area from the clipboard into a new layer.	Edit → Paste
	Transform command	Reshape an isolated object.	Image → Transform
	Add Noise filter	Roughen up tones that are unnaturally smooth.	Filter → Noise → Add Noise
	Gaussian Blur filter	Smooth out tones that are unnaturally rough.	Filter → Blur → Gaussian Blur
	Layer Modes, Layer Opacity	Calculate changes in the image using layer properties to target change.	Mode pop-up menu on the Layers palette
	Layer Transparency	Mask and visualize change with transparent pixels.	Hidden Power Tools under Effects on the Styles and Effects palette, in the Power_ Masking category
8. Make targeted color and tonal corrections and enhancements.	History Brush	Paint in adjustments from filtered results (for example, to target Dodge and Burn).	Hidden Power Tools under Effects on the Styles and Effects palette, in the Power_ Adjustments category
	Gradient Map Layer	Influence specific tones and colors by using gradients.	Layer → New Adjustment Layer → Gradient Map, or the powerful Gradient Map Curve preset in Hidden Power Tools under Effects on the Styles and Effects palette, in the Power_Adjustments category

Continues

Continued

PROCESS STEP	TOOL OR COMMAND	USE THIS TOOL TO DO WHAT?	LOCATION
	Layer Masking, Highlight Mask, Shadow Mask	Customize the visibility of layered image parts and control intensity of selections.	Hidden Power Tools under Effects on the Styles and Effects palette, in the Power_ Masking category
	Blend Mask	Influence specific tones and colors by using tone and color measurement.	Hidden Power Tools under Effects on the Styles and Effects palette, in the Power_ Masking category
	Unsharp Masking	Work with both local and fine contrast in the image to improve edge definition and contrast in color and tone.	Filter → Sharpen → Unsharp Mask
	Hidden Power Sharpen	Complement Unsharp Masking with sharpening that calculates sharpness in a different way, more like darkroom techniques.	Hidden Power Tools under Effects on the Styles and Effects palette, in the Power_ Adjustments category
	Layer Modes, Layer Opacity	Calculate changes in the image using layer properties to target change.	Mode pop-up menu on the Layers palette
	Layer Transparency	Mask and visualize change with transparent pixels.	Hidden Power Tools under Effects on the Styles and Effects palette, in the Power_ Masking category
9. Save the image.	Save As command	Save with a new filename.	File → Save As
10. Simplify as appropriate.	Merge command	Remove extra layers and image content when there are no vector layers to preserve.	Layers → Merge Linked, Layers → Merge Visible, Layers → Merge Down
	Flatten command	Remove extra layers and image content when there are no vector layers to preserve.	Layers → Flatten Image
	Text To Shape	Globalize type handling by converting type to vector layers.	Hidden Power Tools under Effects on the Styles and Effects palette, in the Power_ Paths category
11. Optimize the image for final output and use.	Mode	Convert to final color space.	Image → Mode
	Levels	Make final adjustments to tone.	Enhance → Adjust Brightness/Contrast → Levels
	Blend Mask	Adjust white point.	Hidden Power Tools under Effects on the Styles and Effects palette, in the Power_ Masking category

Continues

Continued

PROCESS STEP	TOOL OR COMMAND	USE THIS TOOL TO DO WHAT?	LOCATION
	Separations (CMYK and Duotone)	Create separations for print ready files.	Hidden Power Tools under Effects on the Styles and Effects palette, in the Power_ Separations category
12. Save in output file format.	Save As	Save with a new filename.	File → Save As
	Save For Web	Save web images with limited color and transparency.	File → Save For Web
	DCS Templates	Use custom files to allow unsupported color modes (CMYK and spot color).	Hidden Power Tools folder included on the book's CD
13. Package the image for output and use.	Permanent and/or temporary storage devices	Assemble the image parts and organize the content to complete purposing and storage.	

We'll explore all the tools mentioned here as part of the exercises in making image corrections. This listing cuts out many native Photoshop Elements tools, most of which provide redundant (and sometimes inferior) means of completing tasks. If you use the tools listed above to follow the methods described in the book, you will find that other tools are seldom necessary. Several other minor tools will sneak in at points during the exercises; while they are not specifically mentioned in the correction tools list, they are mostly related to or substitutes for tools covered in the list.

Adding special effects and noncorrective adjustments can occur during many of the stages, depending on what you are trying to accomplish with the effect. Most of these changes will occur after color and damage correction and before saving the image.

One tool that does not fit into any particular step, but is very useful throughout the correction process, is the History palette, shown in Figure 3.1. When you're doing serious correction and experimentation, it should become a good friend. For example, when you have taken several steps that have not accomplished what you hoped, a single click on the History palette can step you back to an earlier

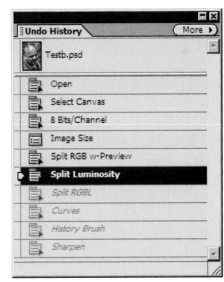

Figure 3.1

The History palette acts like a multiple Undo. Just click a previous state, and the image reverts to the way it looked then.

point in the development of the image so you don't have to start all over again. This lets you undo multiple steps at once or compare before and after changes at a click. It's a real time-saver and a helpful tool.

An entire category of Hidden Power tools not mentioned as part of the list that will help you learn and understand Hidden Power techniques is found in the Power_Playback category for the tools in Styles and Effects. This set of tools will allow you to adjust the speed of tool playback so that you can watch the steps, check your progress, and compare your results to see where things go wrong as you follow the steps. The set contains presets for slowing the playback (Play Slow, Step and Pause, and Step and Long Pause), custom playback (Play Palette), and normal accelerated playback (Play Accelerated).

KNOWING YOUR EQUIPMENT AND IMAGES

Part of working with images on your computer is learning the nuances of systems and software, and having some idea about what you expect to do with the images. You are responsible for knowing your equipment and the purpose of your images. This section cannot help if you are having trouble with your computer system, but it can tell you what to look for and where to get help. Similarly, it doesn't tell you what exactly to do with images but does present some general guidelines for how to proceed.

Knowing Your Equipment

Because all computers and systems are not alike, it is impossible to cover every nuance of every system in every situation in one book. There are innumerable digital cameras on the market, a plethora of ways to get the images off the cameras, and hundreds of home printers to print the result to. Software configurations and utilities can cause fresh problems while solving others, and compatibilities can be an issue with both hardware and software.

If you have trouble getting the images off your camera or have trouble with your printer or computer, the place to find answers is in the user manual for these devices and through technical support from manufacturers. The following is a short checklist of maintenance tasks you should recognize, understand, and perform for your computer, peripherals, and software:

Scanner (and Analog Film) Maintenance

- Calibrate your scanner per manufacturer suggestions.

- Maintain a regimen for cleaning the scanner and scanned objects.

- Be sure to use proper connections and connection settings.

- Consider having important images scanned by scanning services, which may have better equipment and resolution than you may have at home (for example, scan negatives and slides to a Kodak Photo CD rather than on a home flatbed scanner).

Digital Camera Maintenance

- Choose appropriate settings per manufacturer recommendations, and don't change settings if you don't know what they do.

- Learn about special features and settings by reading the manual. This is especially important for resolution and color-management issues.

- Understand image control and exposure.

- Understand how to format camera storage.

- Know how to properly connect a camera to your computer and download images from the camera.

Printer Maintenance

- Use appropriate paper and inks as suggested by the manufacturer.

- Read maintenance and cleaning suggestions, and follow these practices rigorously.

- Don't expect RGB results from a CMYK printer. CMYK is a smaller color space, meaning there are simply fewer colors available.

Computer Software and Hardware Maintenance

- Maintain a firewall if using an open Internet connection.

- Use virus-protection software to minimize problems with infected digital files, especially if you trade a lot of files. Never open a file from an outside source (even a known source) if it has not been scanned for viruses.

- Maintain a schedule of maintenance for data backup, disk error scanning, and associated digital maintenance (such as defragmenting).

- Check manufacturer websites regularly for software updates, bug fixes, and compatibility notices.

- Keep a log of program installations to help locate software conflicts.

- Don't jump to conclusions. Note multiple problems in the operation of your system. If you have problems with more than one program or device, there may be a common link to the real cause.

- Simplify your system whenever possible by detaching chronically unused peripherals and uninstalling unnecessary software.

Know Your Image

Some matters involved in repairing and compositing images are not really judgment calls, and some are. One thing no book or manual can tell you is exactly what you want to do with an image. While I can suggest proven ways of getting good results, learning to evaluate an image's composition and deciding what to do to improve it will be a judgment call. Your judgment will improve over time and with practice.

Don't ever say it is good enough if it isn't good enough. Give up on an image only when it is not worth the effort to improve it. There is almost nothing you can't do with an image if you have the desire. You can also correct the same image from now until doomsday, improving it in increments all the time. Sometimes putting an image aside for a day or two can give you a new perspective: when you come back to it, you may see solutions you hadn't previously considered. Solutions won't always jump out at you, and sometimes you'll have to manufacture them. In trying to stretch your limitations, no matter what you are attempting to do to an image, chances are you will learn from each solution you attempt—whether it succeeds or fails for that particular image.

The more you work with images, the easier and quicker the manipulations will become. Now let's push some pixels.

Part II

Wrestling with Image Tone and Contrast

Understanding correction and adjustment of a digital image starts with separating the image into its components of color and tone. Separating components isn't just an interesting exercise. In the long run, understanding separations empowers you to make image repairs beyond the obvious application of standard tools, ramping up the power of any image editing program. Understanding the basics of separating images into components gives you the power to make other, more complex separations, including working with CMYK in Photoshop Elements. Getting confident with separation empowers you to make targeted changes. If your image shows mottling, uneven color, or some other problem that is color- or tone-specific, taking apart the image elements can help you focus on the real problems in the image. It's like treating a wound with plastic surgery instead of just putting in a bunch of stitches and slapping some gauze over it, where you are almost certain to leave an ugly scar.

Chapter 4

Separating and Combining Image Components

Splitting color images into components helps you leverage existing image information to make changes that would otherwise be either difficult or impossible in Photoshop Elements. For example, a simple use of separations gives you ultimate control over converting images from color to black-and-white. With a little ingenuity, you can use separations to mask specific colors, tones, and image areas to help you target corrections and changes.

Before you master more complex color separation, you need to learn to handle simpler concepts of separation, such as separating luminosity (tone) and color or filtering RGB light components. Once you can make separations, it opens the door to creative image enhancement. We will start by looking at the importance of separation in getting the most out of black-and-white conversions, and we'll also look at how separation is integral to forming color in images.

The Art of Turning Color into Black-and-White

Turning Black-and-White to Color Again

Applying Color: Hand-Coloring

The Art of Turning Color into Black-and-White

Black-and-white images hold a different kind of interest than color images. Sometimes you may want to turn a color image to grayscale to create black-and-white images or duotones (colorized grayscale, such as sepia-toned images). Other times you may want to remove color from an image so you can then colorize it (hand-color, or reapply existing color to revise image tone).

There is more to making a good conversion to black-and-white than just choosing Grayscale from the Mode menu to convert your color to tone. Color images can present about 16 million variations for each pixel, whereas black-and-white is less robust in being able to display only 256 levels of tone in 8-bit. Color adds a layer of distinction between objects in an image: objects can be a similar tone, or darkness/lightness, but distinct in color. So, while objects may be easy to distinguish in a color image, they can appear to merge or become less distinct when the image is converted to black-and-white. In other words, if you take a color image with clearly defined objects and then choose Grayscale to convert to black-and-white, some of the distinct differences might wash away with the color. Usually the result—considering how drastic the change is—is surprisingly not cata-strophic. Except in extreme cases, you'll still be able to distinguish your subject. Different means of handling the conversion can produce better (or worse) results. The key here is that separating the components provides you options not only for making conversions but also for making your conversions better.

The simplest way to convert from color to tone is by either converting the image to Grayscale mode or desaturating the image. For example, instead of just changing to Grayscale mode, you can use Enhance → Adjust Color → Remove Color, or you can desaturate the image by using the Hue/Saturation function (move the Master Saturation slider to −100). These one-step processes each produce the same result, based on combining tonal values in the red, green, and blue channels of an RGB image in specific percentages.

However, the result of the straightforward conversion to tone may not result in the black-and-white image you'd expect to see. The converted image can be rather blah, lack-ing definition and contrast between objects. Looking to other qualities that exist, hidden in the original color of the image, can help provide sources for improving the result.

There are various ways to separate out tones based on color, luminosity/brightness/tone (each of these three terms refer to essentially the same thing), and saturation. Once you learn to make separations, you can use the information to replace, supplement, and com-bine with other tones to produce improved results. Separating tone can also isolate image components for necessary repairs and is often a handy technique to use during image restorations.

In the next exercise we'll be doing the impossible by separating a color image into RGB color components (known as *channels* in Photoshop). It is "impossible" because Photoshop Elements does not have a channels palette that allows you to work with the components.

There is, however, more than one way to coax RGB components out of any image in Elements. In this case, you'll be separating the channel components in the Layers palette. In doing this, you can see how separations work and create at least three sources for working with tone in your image.

Separating RGB Color Components (Creating Channels)

Just because a tool is not in the Photoshop Elements program interface does not mean it can't be mimicked or invoked in another way, and you'll see that we do this throughout the book. In the case of channels and separations, the interface for channels may be formally missing, but the light components of the image that make up the channel content are still there. The red, green, and blue color information exists in your color images or else you wouldn't have color. Just like Prokudin-Gorskii, who took an image and separated it into RGB components to capture on his glass plates (see Chapter 2), you will be able to take any color image and split out the RGB components by filtering for red, green, and blue using copies of the image in the Layers palette. This will enable you to mimic channels and take a better look at the tone information as separate color components.

First, you'll look at how to make RGB separations with a long, but rather simple, step-by-step process. The separation process mimics Prokudin-Gorskii's in that you will take an image and separate out the color components by applying filters, in this case using layer modes and a few simple color properties. There are automated tools to help you do the same thing using the Hidden Power tools included on the book's companion CD. These tools are provided so that you don't have to do the manual steps for the separation each time you need them. However, don't just skip the steps and go right for the automated tools, because you won't learn anything. What you learn here is imperative in preparing you for more difficult concepts of separation and image control challenges to come.

There are actually three methods of accomplishing the complete RGB separation with the Hidden Power tools:

- Using RGB_Separation_Complete
- Using RGB_Separation
- Using the set of five-step tool modules:

  (1) RGB_Separation_Setup

  (2) RGB_Red_Component

  (3) RGB_Green_Component

  (4) RGB_Blue_Component

  (5) RGB_Separation_Color

These methods produce the same results but give you different means of creating the RGB component separation. RGB_Separation_Complete runs through the entire process with comments on screen. RGB_Separation runs through the whole process without on-screen comments. The five-part separation goes through the process in stages to remain true to the process as it is discussed in the book. We'll be looking at the first 4 parts of the RGB separation here.

Because this book is mostly geared to more advanced users, information about the location of basic tools and features is supplied the first time only. Be aware that information is cumulative as you go through the book: especially when it comes to commonly used features, you will most often find references for their use and location early in the book or relevant chapter.

This set of steps was designed to work with a flattened image (one with only a Background layer). Your image can be flattened by choosing Layer → Flatten Image if it is not flattened already (if it is, the option will be grayed-out in the menu). Follow along using the sample image lily.psd (a purple flower) provided on the CD included with this book.

We will approach the separation using the five part separation, but complete only the first four parts here. First, we'll set up the layer-adjustment components that we'll use to filter the separation, and then we'll separate the red, green, and blue color components in the image each one as a separate part of the separation. The final step will be adding back the color to the separated components to re-create the image color, which we will do later in this chapter.

Setup: Create the Adjustment Components

First, let's create several layers that will be used throughout the process to make the color separation for the image:

1. Open the image you want to separate into RGB components.

2. Flatten the image (choose Flatten Image from the Layers menu).

3. Double-click the Background layer in the Layers palette, and rename the layer **Source** when the New Layer dialog appears (using the Name field).

4. Create a Hue/Saturation adjustment layer. To create the layer, choose Hue/Saturation from the Create Adjustment Layer menu on the Layers palette ⬮. Change the name of the Adjustment layer to **Hue Adjustment Template** in the New Layer dialog, and then click OK. Change the Hue setting to **+120** and leave the Lightness and Saturation sliders at 0, as they are (see Figure 4.1). This will shift the color in your image, but don't worry about what the image looks like at this point, since we are setting up for later changes.

To change the name of a layer, double-click the name of the layer in the Layers palette.

5. Create a new layer by clicking the Create a New Layer button on the Layers palette ⬛ . Change the name of the layer to **Color Red**, and set the layer-blending mode to Multiply (see Figure 4.2).

6. Change the foreground color to red. To do this, click the foreground color swatch on the toolbar. Change the RGB settings to R: **255**, G: **0**, B: **0**. Click OK to close the dialog.

7. Fill the layer with the foreground color using the Fill Layer function (Edit → Fill Layer). Set the Fill dialog as pictured in Figure 4.3.

8. Duplicate the Color Red layer. To make the duplicate, click and drag the Color Red thumbnail in the Layers palette to the New Layer button on the Layers palette (see step 5). Name the layer **Color Red Copy**.

9. Duplicate the Hue Adjustment Template layer, and rename the layer **Hue Adjustment**.

10. Move the Hue Adjustment layer to the top of the layer stack by pressing Shift+Command+]/Shift+Ctrl+]. This shifts the color of the Color Red Copy layer 120° on the color wheel to green.

11. Merge the Hue Adjustment layer with the Color Red Copy layer. To do this press Command+E/Ctrl+E. Rename the Color Red Copy layer to **Color Green**.

12. Duplicate the Color Green layer (see step 8). Name the duplicate layer **Color Green Copy**.

13. Duplicate the Hue Adjustment Template layer and rename it **Hue Adjustment**.

14. Move the Hue Adjustment layer to the top of the stack (Shift+Command+]/Shift+Ctrl+]).

15. Merge the Hue Adjustment layer and the Color Green Copy layers (Command+E/Ctrl+E). Name the resulting layer **Color Blue**.

16. Create a new layer and name it **Composite**. Fill the layer with black (Edit → Fill).

Figure 4.1

This Hue/Saturation adjustment layer will be used to help make quick work of color changes in 120° intervals, from green to blue to red and back, around the 360° color wheel.

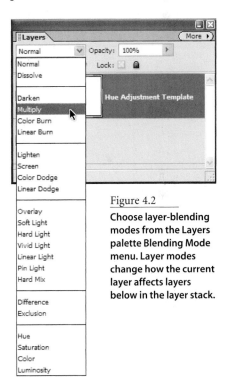

Figure 4.2

Choose layer-blending modes from the Layers palette Blending Mode menu. Layer modes change how the current layer affects layers below in the layer stack.

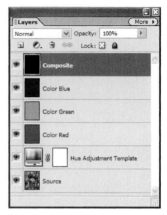

Figure 4.3

The filled color layer will act like a color filter over the lens of your camera when you employ it in making separations of your images in Photoshop Elements.

Figure 4.4

The image layers you have after the 16-step setup should be identical to those pictured here. The image itself will appear black on screen.

At this point you have set up the image elements you will use to calculate the RGB color components. The layers should look like they do in Figure 4.4. Note that these layers retain specific settings for layer mode that will be useful in making the image separation.

The Setup portion of the separation can be created with any image by using the Hidden Power tool: (1) RGB_Separation_Setup. This tool runs through all the steps above and can be used to check your work by slowing action playback with the Power_Playback tools.

Creating the Red Component

The red component will be created following the setup by filtering a copy of the Source layer using the image elements created during the setup:

17. Duplicate the Source layer (Layer → Duplicate Layer). In the dialog box that appears, change the name of the layer to **Red**. Click OK.

18. Move the Red layer to the top of the layer stack.

19. Duplicate the Color Red layer and move that to the top of the layer stack. This layer will be called **Color Red Copy**.

20. Merge the Color Red Copy and the Red layer by pressing Command+E/Ctrl+E. Rename the resulting layer **Red Component**, and set the layer mode to Screen. This is the red component, and it should appear red in the image. We need to convert the layer to grayscale/tone to use it as an RGB component. We do this in the next few steps by adding equal parts of green and blue to neutralize the color.

21. Duplicate the Red Component layer. Change the name to **Red-Green**. This layer will be the equal part of green based on the red component.

22. Duplicate the Hue Adjustment Template layer, and rename it **Hue Adjustment**.

23. Move the Hue Adjustment layer to the top of the layer stack. The color of the image should shift from red to green.

24. Merge the Hue Adjustment and Red-Green layers. This will commit the color change for the Red-Green layer. The image will appear yellow while the thumbnail in the Layers palette shifts from red to green. The yellow color is the result of combining red and green light in equal proportions.

25. Duplicate the Red-Green layer, and rename the duplicate layer **Red-Blue**.

26. Duplicate the Hue Adjustment Template, and rename the duplicate **Hue Adjustment**.

27. Move the Hue Adjustment layer to the top of the layer stack. This will shift the appearance of color in the image to cyan.

28. Merge the Hue Adjustment layer and the Red-Blue layer. This will commit the color change for the Red-Blue layer to blue, and the image will appear in grayscale. Grayscale is the result of adding equal amounts of all three color components.

29. Activate the Red Component, Red-Green, and Red-Blue layers. To activate these layers, with the Red-Blue layer already active in the layer stack, hold down the Shift key on the keyboard, and click the Red Component layer in the Layers palette. This will activate all three layers.

30. Merge the activated layers (press Command+E/Ctrl+E on the keyboard). Rename the resulting layer **Red Component**, and change the mode of the layer to Screen. The appearance of the image will remain the same. This layer represents the red color in the image as a separated grayscale component (Figure 4.5).

Figure 4.5

The image layers you have after step 30 should be identical to those pictured here. The image itself will show the red channel in grayscale.

You can complete the separation of the red component mimicking the steps of this section of the separation by using the Hidden Power tool: (2) RGB_Red_Component. You can run this successfully only after running part 1 of the RGB separation, since it requires the components set up there.

Creating the Green Component

Similar steps to creating the red component will help you extract the green component from the original image source:

31. Duplicate the Source layer (Layer → Duplicate Layer). In the dialog box that appears, change the name of the layer to **Green**. Click OK.

32. Move the Green layer to the top of the layer stack.

33. Duplicate the Color Green layer, and move that to the top of the layer stack. This layer will be called **Color Green Copy**.

34. Merge the Color Green Copy layer and the Green layer by pressing Command+E/
    Ctrl+E. Rename the resulting layer **Green Component**, and set the layer mode to
    Screen. This is the Green component, but we need to convert the layer to grayscale/
    tone. We do this in the next few steps by adding equal parts of blue and red.

35. Duplicate the Green Component layer. Change the name to **Green-Blue**. This layer
    will be the equal part of blue based on the Green component.

36. Duplicate the Hue Adjustment Template layer, and rename it **Hue Adjustment**.

37. Move the Hue Adjustment layer to the top of the layer stack.

38. Merge the Hue Adjustment and Green-Blue layers. This will turn the Green-Blue
    layer blue.

39. Duplicate the Green-Blue layer, and rename the duplicate layer **Green-Red**.

40. Duplicate the Hue Adjustment Template, and rename the duplicate **Hue Adjustment**.

41. Move the Hue Adjustment layer to the top of the layer stack.

Figure 4.6

The image layers you have after step 44 should be identical to those pictured here.

42. Merge the Hue Adjustment layer and the Green-Red
    layer. This will turn the Green-Red layer red.

43. Activate the Green Component, Green-Blue, and Green-
    Red layers. To activate these layers, with the Green-Red
    layer active in the layer stack, hold down the Shift key
    on the keyboard, and click the Green Component layer
    in the Layers palette. (See step 29.)

44. Merge the activated layers (press Command+E/Ctrl+E
    on the keyboard). Rename the resulting layer **Green
    Component**, and change the mode of the layer to
    Screen. This layer represents the Green color in the
    image as a separated grayscale component (Figure 4.6).

The separation of the green component mimicking the steps of this section of the separation can be completed using the Hidden Power tool: (3) RGB_Green_Component. This
can be run successfully only after running part 1 of the RGB separation.

Creating the Blue Component

Separating the blue component follows the same procedure as separating the red or green.
At this point, you should be feeling somewhat familiar with the process.

45. Duplicate the Source layer (Layer → Duplicate Layer). In the dialog box that appears,
    change the name of the layer to **Blue**. Click OK.

46. Move the Blue layer to the top of the layer stack.

47. Duplicate the Color Blue layer, and move that to the top of the layer stack. This layer
    will be called **Color Blue Copy**.

48. Merge the Color Blue Copy layer and the Blue layer by pressing Command+E/ Ctrl+E. Rename the resulting layer **Blue Component**, and set the layer mode to Screen. This is the Blue component, but we need to convert the layer to grayscale/ tone. We do this in the next few steps by adding equal parts of red and green.

49. Duplicate the Blue Component layer. Change the name to **Blue-Red**. This layer will be the equal part of red based on the Blue component.

50. Duplicate the Hue Adjustment Template layer, and rename it **Hue Adjustment**.

51. Move the Hue Adjustment layer to the top of the layer stack.

52. Merge the Hue Adjustment layer and the Blue-Red layer. This will turn the Blue-Red layer red.

53. Duplicate the Blue-Red layer, and rename the duplicate layer **Blue-Green**.

54. Duplicate the Hue Adjustment Template, and rename the duplicate **Hue Adjustment**.

55. Move the Hue Adjustment layer to the top of the layer stack.

56. Merge the Hue Adjustment layer and the Blue-Green layer. This will turn the Blue-Green layer green.

57. Activate the Blue Component, Blue-Red, and Blue-Green layers. To activate these layers, with the Blue-Green layer active in the layer stack, hold down the Shift key on the keyboard, and click the Blue Component layer in the Layers palette. (See step 29.)

58. Merge the activated layers (press Command+E/Ctrl+E on the keyboard). Rename the resulting layer **Blue Component**, and change the mode of the layer to Screen. This layer represents the Blue color in the image as a separated grayscale component (Figure 4.7).

Figure 4.7

The image layers you have after step 58 should be identical to those pictured here.

You can complete the separation of the blue component mimicking the steps of this section of the separation by using the Hidden Power tool: (4) RGB_Blue_Component. You can run this successfully only after running part 1 of the RGB separation.

You have now separated the image into three channels, one for each of the primary light components: red, green, and blue (see Figure 4.8). These components can be looked at as a source for making conversion to black-and-white, as well as a source for learning about the nature of light and RGB theory. These are exactly the same components you would get using the Channels palette in Photoshop. Compare your results to the lily_separated.psd on the CD. There is one more step to the separation process in adding back the color, but we will save that till later when discussing color later in this chapter. Right now we are interested in looking at the separated components.

Take a moment to examine the layers representing the separate light components by viewing them individually. Note the qualitative differences between the red, green, and blue channels. The representations reveal specific qualities about light in each spectrum.

Figure 4.8

These images were created using the separation steps in the previous procedure. Note that the green looks the most like what you might expect as a grayscale conversion.

Red component   Green component   Blue component

As mentioned, you can accomplish the same set of steps in a single click. Just go to the Hidden Power tools on the Styles and Effects palette, open any RGB image, and click the (1-4) RGB_Components in the Power_Separations category of Effects. This will execute the steps for you. Splitting RGB components using this tool should be done on a flattened (single-layer) RGB image—images that are not flattened will be flattened before proceeding.

> If you haven't installed the Hidden Power tools, you can find the tools on the CD and instructions for installing them in the introduction to this book. Supplementary information on installing and troubleshooting can be found on the hiddenelements.com website, the *Hidden Power of Photoshop Elements* forums at retouchpro.com, and APEA (http://www.hiddenelements.com/forums).

Separation is a key concept for grasping everything that follows in the book—it isn't just a neat parlor trick. It is a lossless process based on light theory—lossless in that it won't do any damage to your images. If you can navigate the steps but don't really understand what each is doing, deeper understanding will come, either as you proceed through the book or as you repeat the exercise and learn the process. Right now, let's look at another way to separate component information from your images.

Separating Luminosity

Separating luminosity from your images is another way to extract valuable tonal information and representation of black-and-white. *Luminosity* is a component of Lab color, which is a color model that distinguishes color from tone (lightness). Because this color model considers tone separately from color, the luminosity component is often a good representation of what we would expect to see in black-and-white.

Photoshop Elements does not have Lab as one of the image color modes. However, as with RGB, luminosity and color components can be extracted from an image in more than one way and can easily be represented using layer calculations. As a purer measure of tone, the lightness component is often useful when RGB separations may not provide an advantage. For example, and as you will see, luminosity and color separation is invaluable for color noise reduction (which can be a common problem in low-light digital photography).

Extracting Luminosity from Color

The following steps will enable you to extract luminosity from any RGB image. Use the flower image again (`lily.psd`) with these steps so you can compare the results of the luminosity extraction to the RGB components:

1. Open the `lily.psd` image.

2. Duplicate the Background layer (Layer → Duplicate Layer). Change the layer name to **Luminosity**. Change the layer-blending mode to Luminosity by choosing it from the Blending Mode drop-down list.

3. Activate the Background layer by clicking on it in the Layers palette.

4. Create a new layer (Layer → New → Layer). This creates a new layer between the Background and Luminosity layers. Name the layer **Composite** and click OK.

5. Fill the Composite layer with gray by choosing Edit → Fill and then selecting 50% Gray from the drop-down menu.

6. Duplicate the Composite layer. Name the new layer **Commit 1** and click OK. Your layers should look like this graphic.

7. Activate the Luminosity layer by clicking it in the Layers palette.

8. Merge the Luminosity and the Commit 1 layers (Layer → Merge Down). Rename the resulting layer **Luminosity**.

9. Choose Luminosity from the Blending Mode drop-down list in the upper left of the Layers palette. Your Layers palette should look like the next graphic.

With the layer mode changed to Luminosity, what will display is the lightness (or L channel from the Lab color model). The lightness is a representation of image tone minus the color. You can get this same result as the steps above by using the (A) Luminosity tool from the Hidden Power tool set (in Effects under Power_Separations).Comparing this result to the components of an RGB separation as well as the straight conversion to grayscale by desaturation (as shown in Figure 4.9) should show some distinct differences in quality. Depending on the source of the image (digital capture or analog), the content of the image, and the quality and quantity of light in the capture, these differences will be more—or less—pronounced.

Figure 4.9

The luminosity, or tone, separation for the image (a) shows a somewhat different and often better representation of image tone than simply desaturating the image (b).

a   b

The Luminosity component is a partner to the Color component: the two components work together to create image color and tone. This is similar to the way that RGB color components combine to create image color and tone, but the representations are totally different. We will look at the separation of the color component a little later when talking about color.

Making Black-and-White by Combining Components

Sometimes a simple separation or other conversion (such as desaturating) works just fine for changing a color image to black-and-white. Other times, you have to look around and be more creative to get a good black-and-white result by borrowing and combining the tones from different components. The art of converting an image to black-and-white comes in when you have to have the vision to see what components will combine for an interesting result.

If you look at the components of an RGB separation, the most representative component of what you'd expect to see in black-and-white will often be the green channel. This is because green is more naturally in the center of the visual spectrum and more closely resembles how humans perceive tone. The red channel is toward the infrared spectra, and the blue channel is toward the ultraviolet. Therefore, the red channel more closely represents infrared capture, and blue is more like ultraviolet.

Very often, luminosity will provide an easy source to extract a good black-and-white representation of any image. It is less prone to color noise and at times will look surprisingly smooth, even when RGB separations have strong color noise (again, this color noise generally happens with images shot with a digital camera in low light).

All of the separation possibilities can show you tonal representations that are somewhat different—different from one another and different from straight desaturation. Sometimes a subtle adjustment in any of these three representations can yield greatly improved results in what otherwise would have been a straight conversion. These adjustments may be simple changes in tone using correction tools such as Levels. Or, you can make the changes by using different areas of the image from different components and combining them with isolation, masking, or selection. We will look at methods for making these adjustments throughout the book.

Figure 4.10 shows six possibilities for a simple conversion to black-and-white from a single image, plus one result that combines RGB components and luminosity in a special order. The blue and red can usually be discarded right away as one step conversions

Desaturated

Red Component

Green Component

Blue Component

Luminosity

Custom (Hidden Power)

Figure 4.10

Looking at the six simple conversions of image tone can reveal distinct differences in representing the images in black-and-white.

because they are not often good representations of the way you will perceive image tone. However, red and blue can sometimes be used to make other adjustments (for example, to create selections, create masks, make calculations between components, mix components, or apply using histories—all of these techniques are presented in subsequent chapters). Comparison of the green RGB component, luminosity, and desaturation may reveal different specific advantages as one-step conversions, but none of these may really be the best conversion to black-and-white. Using several of the separated components in a custom calculation may create the best result.

The custom black-and-white conversion in Figure 4.10 uses the luminosity, red, green, and blue components with channel mixing and calculations to achieve the result. We'll look at how to achieve that result and how to use calculations and channel mixing in the next section.

Mixing Components for Calculated Tone Adjustment

In Photoshop, Calculations and Channel Mixer are ways to adjust tone based on separated components. What the two features have in common is that they play components against one another to create a result. The results are usually used for masking or black-and-white conversion, though occasionally they can be used in color correction. Elements 4 has neither a calculations nor channel mixer function standard, but Hidden Power provides a more powerful layer-based solution for each that may well be more intuitive to use. In fact, in the last few sections you used calculations and mixing to create the RGB and Luminosity separations.

Calculations create a result by using components as parts of an equation, much like adding, subtracting, multiplying, and so forth. The simplest calculations can be a way of combining selections to create a different result. For example, say you see a situation where you can easily make two selections separately, but you want to combine the selections by subtracting one from the other. With Calculations in Photoshop, you could make the separate selections, save them as channels (what we are calling components), and then combine them using the Calculation function. In Elements, you will accomplish the same thing, perhaps more intuitively, by combining the components using layer functions. Calculations are usually a means of producing masks based on image color or content.

Channel mixing is an adjustment in which you change components based on combining percentages of other components. Channel mixing is often more suited to black-and-white conversions, though it is sometimes used for color adjustments. For example, say you have an image of a bright red flower appearing over a lush green background. The problem with the image is that in real life, the flower is supposed to be purple. Assuming this is a problem with the image, if you separate and look at the RGB channels, you'll find that the red channel is white (saturated) where the flower is, and the blue channel is dark or black (unsaturated). You could mix some of the red channel into the blue to lighten the blue channel, increasing the blue saturation in the flower. The result will, of course, shade the color of the flower toward purple—although you may have to exercise other control (such as masking) to get the result you want.

The real advantage to calculations and channel mixing is that you use tone that already exists in the image; the tone can act as a complex, natural selection to enhance your image in ways that would be much more difficult if attempting selections manually. The functions allow you to render simple changes, complex image results, and fine adjustments.

What are the most frightening about calculations and channel mixing are the names and the descriptions. If you have followed the concepts behind separations to this point, you have applied some simple calculations. However, how to use calculations and mixing in layers may not be entirely obvious. Once you've taken a look at how to do calculations and channel mixing, they are really easier to control, and they offer more options the Hidden Power way in Photoshop Elements than if you were working with Photoshop. Because you work in layers, the results are visual and immediate, and they simply make more sense to use because you can see exactly what is happening as you make the changes. You are also not limited to using just the few components available in the current color mode: you can mix and match components in any way you find convenient to get your result. The key is the setup in layers.

We'll look at specific examples of calculations first. With some understanding of calculations, understanding channel mixing will fall right in line.

Calculations Setup and Application

Practically the whole challenge in making calculations is deciding what to do—which always depends on your image and purpose—and setting that up. Setting up calculations requires that you have image components (or grayscale representations) that you want to use as a source for creating the desired result. Your source can be selections, masks, and/or separations. All you do is duplicate the parts you want to use for the calculations and use layer properties to create the calculated result. It is easiest and most predictable to use grayscale in the calculations for the best result.

> Layer-blending modes and their functions become important to calculations. Knowing what each layer mode does can help you get the results you want in calculations. There is a listing of the modes and descriptions of what they do in the Appendix for your reference.

It is easiest to see what calculations do through an example:

1. Open a new image 500 pixels × 500 pixels with a black background.

2. Choose the Rectangular Marquee tool (press M), and set the options for the tool to Feather: 0 pixels, Anti-alias: off, Mode: Fixed Size, Width: 300 pixels, Height: 300 pixels.

3. Click the Marquee tool at exactly 100 pixels from the left and 100 pixels from the top of the image. This will create a square marquee selection in the center of the image with a 100-pixel border all the way around between it and the edge of the image. To use the Rulers to measure placement, press Shift+Command+R/Shift+Ctrl+R. Hold down the Shift key just after you click the Marquee tool to move the position of the Marquee before releasing the mouse button.

4. Fill the selection with white. You can do this however you want. If unsure, press D (switch to default colors), X (exchange default colors), and K (choose the Paint Bucket tool), and then click in the selected area of the image. The result is pictured n Figure 4.11.

5. Deselect (press Command+D/Ctrl+D), then duplicate the background layer, and change the name to **Calculation Layer** (you may want to choose layer names specific to your calculations rather than a generic name).

6. Choose Transform (press Command+T/Ctrl+T) and enter **45** in the angle field 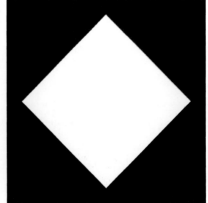. This will rotate the Calculation Layer 45 degrees clockwise. See Figure 4.12.

7. Change the mode of the layer to Darken. At this point, the image will change to look like an octagon (see Figure 4.13).

8. Create a new blank layer at the top of the layer stack, merge a copy of all visible layers to the target layer, and name it **Result**. To merge a copy of all visible layers, press Shift+Command+Option+E/Shift+Ctrl+Alt+E. This commits the calculation as a result that doesn't depend on layer properties.

As a variation, shut off the Result layer and set the mode of the Calculation layer to Lighten. The shape will change to an 8 pointed star. That is just one of many possible variations. Try changing the opacity of the Calculation layer to 50%. Next, change to Normal

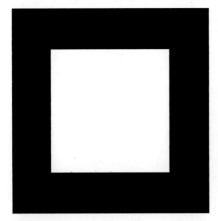

Figure 4.11

Filling the white square selection will make a white square framed by a 100-pixel black border as pictured here.

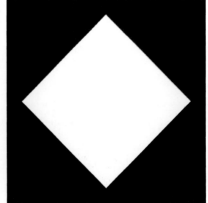

Figure 4.12

Rotating the Calculation layer 45 degrees produces a simple diamond shape.

mode, then change to Multiply mode, then to Difference, and leave difference mode and change back to 100% opacity. The result of the calculation will change as shown in Figure 4.14. This simple concept of calculating results opens numerous possibilities for using layer properties to create an infinite number of different results via calculations.

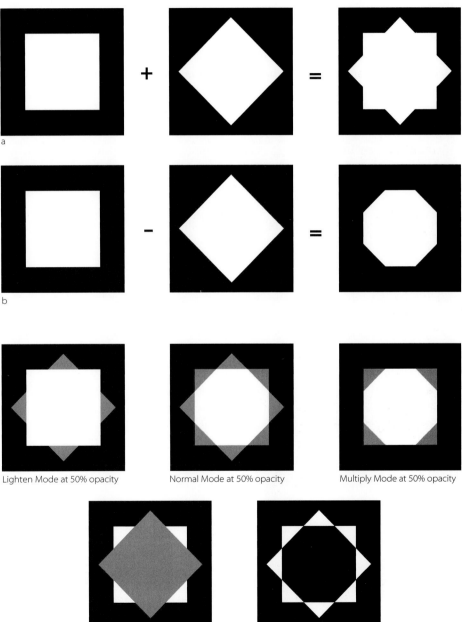

Figure 4.13
Calculations let you add selections together (a) or subtract them (b), but far more complex calculations can occur.

a

b

Lighten Mode at 50% opacity

Normal Mode at 50% opacity

Multiply Mode at 50% opacity

Figure 4.14
Using the same layers from the original 8-step procedure with different mode and opacity can create many different results.

Difference Mode at 50% opacity

Difference Mode at 100% opacity

You can correct calculation results with levels, gradient maps or preset Curves, or you can exercise other correction options while the calculation is being created—all at the same time. You can add masks to the layers in the calculations, invert content, or make selective changes or other tonal adjustments. When you have achieved the results you want, you can use various Hidden Power tools to convert the content into layer-clipping masks, to create selections as a source for filling layer masks, or to make additional conversions and calculations. You can even convert these calculations to vector shapes. We'll look at all of these possibilities in later chapters. This calculation method can be used for masking and selection techniques as well as for making complicated blends for spot colors and other separations (as we'll see in the section on CMYK separation). You will often use the result by loading it as a selection or by using it to create masks, but you can use it as a black-and-white conversion as well.

Because of the complexity of images and their components, how calculations work with images may be less apparent. Here we can look at how to achieve the custom black-and-white result devised for the image in Figure 4.10. The following example makes a calculation using components. The goal here is to make a better black-and-white conversion by calculating a new result. Following this process should help reveal how results are achieved.

1. Once again, open the `lily.psd` image on the CD.

2. Double-click the RGBL_Components_Only tool in the Power_Separations category of Effects. This creates the red, green, blue, and luminosity components for the image.

3. Shut off the view for the Luminosity, Red Component, and Blue Component layers. This leaves the view for the Green Component. The flower petals are dark, but they can easily be lightened using the Red Component, as we will do in the next step.

4. Move the Red Component above the Green Component layer in the layer stack. If you view the Red Component by itself (turn off the view for the Green Component), you will see that it is light in the petal areas but dark in the surrounding greenery. Turn on the view for the Green Component, change the mode of the Red Component layer to Lighten, and lower the opacity to 60%. This will lighten the flower petal area without a significant impact on the surrounding area.

5. To add back in some of the unique dynamics of the Blue Component, turn on the view for that layer, change the mode to Overlay, and reduce the opacity to 16%.

At this point, you have included the three RGB components, and it may not be necessary to make additional changes; however, you can take the following steps to further enhance the conversion:

6. Duplicate the Green Component layer, name the resulting layer **Green Component Screen**, and change the opacity to 70%. This will lighten the area around the petals to create greater contrast.

7. Turn on the Luminosity layer, and change the opacity to 33%. This will mediate some of the extremes that may have been caused by other calculations.

Steps 6 and 7 add some calculations that experience has shown will render a better g eneral conversion for almost any image from RGB to grayscale. You can repeat this whole series by using the Custom Black-and-White power tool in the Power_Adjustments category of Effects.

You can make adjustments to this result by playing around with the opacity of the component layers. This particular adjustment is one developed after fooling with various possibilities and considering light and color theory. You can repeat the separation and calculation using the Custom Black-and-White Hidden Power tool (saving over 100 steps in a single click). As a conversion, it works fairly consistently over a wide variety of images to produce a pretty good black-and-white image. Give it a try on any color RGB image. This is only one of hundreds of possibilities for combining tone. You can fine-tune or completely change the result using layer opacity, additional component layers, and different layer-blending modes.

The previous example was a result derived from experimentation with the Green Component layer because it is similar to how we perceive brightness. If you start with a component other than the Green Component layer, your goals for changing the image and the calculations you make may be very different than those we used above. For example, if you make the separations and start with the Red Component layer, you could go in an entirely different direction and attempt to make the petals lighter than the background.

1. Open the `lily.psd` image on the CD.

2. Double-click the RGBL_Components_Only tool in the Power_Separations category of Effects.

3. Shut off the view for the Luminosity, Green Component, and Blue Component layers. This leaves the view for the Red Component layer. The flower petals are dark but brighter and more contrasty than the background. The background can be darkened, the petals lightened, and the contrast enhanced using the following steps.

4. Activate the Green Component layer, and turn on the view. Invert the layer content (Command+I / Ctrl+I), change the mode to Overlay, and reduce the opacity to 24%. This should darken the background and lighten the petals. Inverting the layer changes the content to a negative of the original, in this case making the petals light and the background dark in the Green Component layer.

5. Activate the Blue Component layer, and turn on the view. Apply a Gaussian Blur of 10 pixels, change the mode to Soft Light, and change the opacity to 60%. This will serve to smooth out the roughness of the blue component and allow it to be applied to enhance the contrast and soften the image, both at the same time. See the result in Figure 4.15.

This calculation will actually not be likely to produce a good black-and-white conversion on many images. The point is that depending on where you start, how you see an image, and how you use the content to make calculations, you can come to very different ends. If you are up to it, try an experiment: start with the Blue Component layer, and see where that leads. See if you can envision the result you want to get and attain it.

In later sections and chapters, we'll look at more examples of how calculations work, both on individual images and in creating standard predictable behaviors—such as building an unsharp mask using traditional darkroom techniques. Now let's look at channel mixing.

Figure 4.15

Using the same components as from the original procedure with different mode and opacity creates a much different result.

Channel Mixing Setup and Application

Channel mixing is just another calculation, offering opportunity for image modification and conversion to black-and-white. The difference with channel mixing is that components are limited to RGB, modes to Linear Burn and Linear Dodge, and varying opacity. The result is based on Photoshop's Channel Mixer function.

You can mix channels directly in the current image with a full-color preview or in grayscale. The color preview lets you see how the change affects the current image; the grayscale enables you to look at the mixing result separate from the current image. The latter is helpful if you are making a mask or other grayscale representation from the mixing. That grayscale result is what we will be looking at here.

To mix channels with a full-image preview of the grayscale result, follow these steps:

1. Separate your image into RGB by using (1-4) RGB_Components in the Power_Separations category of Effects.

2. Throw out the Color Blue, Color Green, Color Red, and Hue Adjustment Template layers.

3. Rename the component layers **Blue Add 1-100**, **Green Add 1-100**, and **Red Add 1-100**. Change the component layer modes to Linear Dodge. Shut off the view for the Green Add 1-100 and Blue Add 1-100 layers.

4. Duplicate the Blue Add 1-100, Green Add 1-100, and Red Add 1-100 component layers, moving each to the top of the layer stack in turn. Rename the layers by substituting **Subtract** for Add, and remove the word Copy (e.g., change Blue Add 1-100 Copy to **Blue Subtract 1-100**). Change the mode to Linear Burn, set the opacity to 0%, and shut off the view for each Subtract layer.

5. (Optional) Add a blank layer between the Add and Subtract layers in the layer stack and name it with dashes ("----------"). This will provide some separation between additive and subtractive layers. Shut off the view for the new layer. The result should look like Figure 4.16.

By default, the setup will show the Red component. To make channel mixing adjustments channels, toggle the view for component layers on or off, and increase/decrease the opacity using the Opacity slider on the Layers palette. Use the Add layers (Blue Add 1-100, Green Add 1-100, and Red Add 1-100) to introduce component content and the Subtract layers (Blue Subtract 1-100, Green Subtract 1-100, and Red Subtract 1-100) to invert component influence.

The result of the mix for each component is the total of the opacity. A simple example of how this works is to turn on the view for the Red Subtract 1-100 layer and increase the opacity. The Red component will gradually fade to black as the Opacity of the Subtract layer increases, and will turn completely black at 100%. This result negates the Red Add 1-100 layer in a simple calculation.

Figure 4.16

The order of the layers should look like this after step 4.

Components set to Linear Burn need to be above the layers set to Linear Dodge, or they will not influence the result.

You can accomplish these steps for setting up the simple monochrome (grayscale) channel mixer by using the Simple Channel Mixer effect provided in the Power_ Adjustments category of the Hidden Power tools. Running the Simple Channel Mixer will separate the components and set up the layers exactly as described above. If you prefer to have the Subtract layers start at 100% opacity rather than 0%, run the Set All Simple Mixer 100% effect after the Simple Channel Mixer effect. To reset adjustments without having to re-run the separation, use the Reset Simple Channel Mixer tool.

A more complex version of the tool is available in the Power_Adjustments as well. The Channel Mixer Hidden Power tool allows users to mix and subtract up to 200% of any component. The capability to mix channels at 200% better approximates the effects that can be achieved by Photoshop's Channel Mixer tool (there are some slight differences when compared side by side).

What Hidden Power channel mixing can do that Photoshop's native tool can't is allow you to change the blend modes of components and allow simultaneous application of a component in more than one blend mode. The result is that you have a far more flexible tool with which to work. The mode and opacity you use depend on what you are trying to accomplish. You will often just use Linear Dodge and Linear Burn as the setup indicates, but other modes can be used, such as Screen or Lighten to brighten the mixed result and Multiply or Darken to darken it.

Channel mixing can be used to make many kinds of corrections. It is useful for creating custom black-and-white conversions (with everything from an infrared to ultraviolet flavor) and creating complex masks based on image color and tone. When it comes to color images, mixing components might allow you to restore image areas that have been ravaged by extreme corrections or distorted or ruined by aging or lighting. You can see a very practical application of calculations and mixing in making custom CMYK separations, as we'll do in chapter 10. Another interesting example of the power of components used in calculations and channel mixing is creating a manual unsharp mask, as we'll see in Chapter 5.

The techniques for masking and combining components are covered in later pages, so we won't look at those techniques here. We will continue to look more at how to specifically make adjustments using components for masking and calculations in topics that arise throughout the book. Right now, let's look at how to make black-and-white into color again.

Turning Black-and-White to Color Again

While separations can be useful for creating black-and-white images, the components are most useful when working with color images if you can make them display color again. Prokudin-Gorskii had a similar problem after capturing his separations on the glass plates: he had the raw components, and he needed to put them together to display the image color. He solved the problem by putting his glass plates in a special projector that could project the three images in near-perfect alignment with appropriate filtering (in the form of color cells) to re-create the color result on a projection screen.

In Photoshop Elements, you can use layer color and blending modes to "project" the separated RGB components to re-create the image color. The result can be achieved without actually combining the separated components. Leaving the components as separate layers is a great benefit during color correction because you can then adjust each component and view how those changes affect the color, immediately as the changes are made. Layered components can be affected by other changes simultaneously, including selection, masking, and adjustment layers.

Projecting Separated RGB Components as a Color Image

The following procedure should be used on an image that has been separated into red, green, and blue layer components by following the steps in the earlier section, "Separating RGB Color Components (Creating Channels)," or by playing the (1-4) RGB Components effect. The steps in the procedure that follows will partially reverse the process of creating the separations by enabling the components to display the full-color result. These steps are essential in letting you see the image as it should appear in color while maintaining the components as separate layers.

This procedure uses the template layers created for the RGB separation to add color filtering to the components.

Changing Separated RGB Tones to Colored Light

This process will convert each of the components of the image back to a color so they can recombine for a full-color result. These steps follow immediately from the last step in "Separating RGB Color Components (Creating Channels)" or immediately after using the (1-4) RGB Components tool (see Figure 4.17 for how the layers should look at the start of this procedure).

1. Move the Color Red layer immediately above the Red Component layer in the layer stack.

2. Group the Color Red and Red Component by pressing Command+G/Ctrl+G (with the Color Red layer active). This makes the Color Red layer act as a filter over the Red Component layer.

Figure 4.17

With component layers set to Screen (view as light) and Color layers set to Multiply (light filter), you are ready to project your color components on the compositing screen to re-create the color image.

3. Move the Color Green layer immediately above the Green Component layer in the layer stack.

4. Group the Color Green and Green Component layers by pressing Command+G/Ctrl+G.

5. Move the Color Blue layer to the top of the layer stack (just above the Blue Component layer).

6. Group the Color Blue and Blue Component layers by pressing Command+G/Ctrl+G.

7. Delete the Hue Adjustment Template layer.

At this point, the image will appear to be as original RGB color in the image window, but the color components will still be available separately in the Layers palette (see Figure 4.18). To make any adjustment to an individual color component, you can create a new adjustment layer (as many as necessary) between the Color layer and the Component layer. You can make any type of adjustment to the component, as long as it adjusts a component layer (Red Component, Green Component, or Blue Component) and not the Color (filter) layers. The result can be converted back to an RGB image, without components, by flattening.

You can accomplish the steps to change the separated RGB components to color layers, adding color to separations you created, in a single click with Hidden Power tools. Just use the (5) RGB_Separation_Color effect to add back color to your image. This effect will work after either using parts 1 through 4 of the RGB separation or using the (1-4) RGB Components tool. To perform both the RGB separation and add the color back in one easy step, click the RGB_Separation or RGB_Separation_Complete tool in the same category of Effects. These Hidden Power tools will be invaluable to you in working through the book and making future image corrections by providing a useful, quick means of creating RGB separations.

Adding Color to Luminosity

Earlier in this chapter, you extracted the tone from the sample image (see the exercise in "Extracting Luminosity from Color"), and the byproduct of completing that separation was a luminosity component. That component represented the tone as separate from the color in the image. The separation didn't address the color component, which can be isolated as well. The *color component* represents the hue and saturation of the image separate from the tone. You can think of *hue* as color (perhaps as picked from a color wheel) and *saturation* as the purity or vibrancy of that color.

Figure 4.18

The separated color components from the image are successfully re-combined to display the color result while being kept separate. This enables you to adjust layered components separately.

Isolating and reapplying original color to tone is pretty simple in a luminosity and color separation—not nearly as complex as re-creating color from RGB separations. When you start with an image from which you have extracted a luminosity component (either following the earlier exercise or by using the (A) Luminosity separation tool), your image should have the following layers from the top down: Luminosity, Composite, and Background (see Figure 4.19). Completing the separation to extract the color is done in a few easy steps:

Figure 4.19

Your image should be separated using techniques for extracting Luminosity from earlier in this chapter before continuing here.

1. Duplicate the Background layer. Name the duplicate layer **Color.**

2. Move the Color layer to the top of the layer stack.

3. Change the mode of the Color layer to Color (see the graphic pictured here).

4. Duplicate the Composite layer. Name the new layer **Commit 1** and click OK.

5. Move the Commit 1 layer just below the Color layer in the layer stack

6. Activate the Color layer by clicking it in the Layers palette.

7. Merge the Color and the Commit 1 layers (Layer → Merge Down). Rename the resulting layer **Color.**

8. Choose Color from the Blending Mode drop-down list in the upper left of the Layers palette.

Figure 4.20

With tonality and color separated, you can effectively control one component without affecting the other. Here Levels are applied to tone, and Hue/Saturation to color.

In completing these few steps, you have added the color back to the image tone by using a separate color component layer. You can then work on the color and lightness (luminosity) components individually. That is, you can adjust the image tone separately from the color and adjust the color independently of the tone. The color component can be extracted, changed, and applied to the original image, it can be applied to the extracted

luminosity component, or it can be applied to other tone variations, such as the tone created by an RGB component. Figure 4.20 shows the result of a completed luminosity and color separation, with a sample of how adjustment layers could be placed for simple alterations to color and tone.

The luminosity and color separations can be achieved in a few different ways. The two-part tool ((A) Luminosity and (B) Color) follows the procedures in two parts as given in this book. Additional tools added for this book, Luminosity Only and Color Only, add a luminosity and a color layer to the top of the layer stack of any image without flattening it (based on the currently visible layers). Finally, the Luminosity and Color tool creates a luminosity and color separation from your image after flattening the layers.

The way color is working in a luminosity and color separation is more like how an artist might mix paint. Color mixes with tone to produce a result. Darker tone results in darker color. If there is no color, the tone is applied in grayscale. If there is no tone (white), there is no color value: because there is no tone in pure white, there is no tone in the applied color. The darker the tone, the darker the applied color, until it turns black. When the image is black, the color layer again shows no effect on the visible result. The brightness/lightness is mixed with hue and saturation (a color) to make the result. This is much more straightforward and intuitive than RGB (when you get used to how it works), encompassing different advantages.

When a color in an image seems wrong, you might need to make a change in the color or tone—or both—to get it right. One or the other won't always work to get you where you want to go. Separating the components gives you more freedom to work with color and tone independently to achieve the desired result.

We'll look much more in depth at adjusting image color in Chapter 6. In the following section, we'll continue exploring adding color to tone by looking at some other ways to add color to black-and-white images.

Applying Color: Hand-Coloring

Separations represent the source components of an image in its original colors. Color can be introduced to your images and enhanced in other ways. Colorizing (or hand-coloring) images is an artistic approach to adding color. It differs from recombining RGB components into color or adding back the color element of a luminosity separation: it is a separate application of color. The color you apply may be a radical change from any original color, may match it, or it can be used as color correction. The tone, color, or components in the image can be used as a canvas on which to paint the color.

Color can be applied to tone in an infinite number of ways, using various Photoshop Elements tools. The color application can be done with simple painting tools or with a more complex color application (for example, gradient mapping and/or blending). We'll take a brief look here at applying original color to tone and applying new color, to further delve into how color and tone work together to create the images you see.

Basic Hand-Coloring

Hand-coloring is the art of applying color by hand to images (usually black-and-white images). The effect can be anything from the addition of a simple color wash to garish additions of color, glitter, and other media. It can be lots of fun, either in attempting to re-create color in an image (in restoration or colorization) or in just replacing color for wild effects. In a way, it can be a better coloring book (for adults or children). For our purposes, hand-coloring is another step in the study of applying color to tone.

The simplest way to add color to a black-and-white image is a method similar to applying the color component in the luminosity and color separation. Try this out:

1. Open any one of the separations you have made for the lily, or create a custom black-and-white separation for any image. You can use any of the techniques discussed earlier for converting a color image to black-and-white.

2. Duplicate the image (File → Duplicate) so you can work on a copy. Check the Duplicate Merged Only checkbox on the Duplicate Image dialog before accepting the changes. This will merge the content of the image to a flattened file.

3. Change to RGB mode if the image is any other color mode (Image → Mode → RGB Color).

4. Create a new layer above the Background layer, and set the new layer mode to Color. Name the layer **Color** (or name it according to the color or area of the image to which you will be applying the color).

5. Change the foreground color to the color you would like to paint in the image (click the Foreground swatch on the toolbar to open the Color Picker, or use the Eyedropper to sample a color from another color image).

6. Choose the Brush tool (press B on the keyboard), and paint over the areas where you would like to apply the color in the new layer.

7. To paint in another color, create a new layer above or below the current layer, change the mode to color, name the layer appropriately, and repeat steps 5 and 6. Your layer setup should look like Figure 4.21.

Figure 4.21

In this technique color gets painted over tone in new layers.

Color

Background

The preceding steps let you paint with whatever colors you like. Colors could be added all in a single layer or directly to the tone, but these options offer less opportunity to adjust the colors later. For more flexibility, add all additional colors and changes to new layers, as shown.

One drawback to this hand-coloring method is that tone tends to get flatly covered with color. Although the color varies as you see it because of the underlying tone, it doesn't always map as you would expect—it can be weaker or stronger in areas because the tone below it varies. To compensate and make more natural-looking results, you can try the following:

- Layer color adjustments.
- Use layer grouping to target adjustments to a specific layer.
- Change the intensity and effect of color application using layer opacity and blending modes.
- Change applied color with Hue/Saturation.
- Use freehand tools, such as Smudge and Eraser, to retouch and blend color application.
- Use Gaussian Blur to feather color edges.
- Use Add Noise to spice up flat colors.
- Use brush dynamics and shape to create effects while painting.

Take a look at the `lily_handcolored.psd` on the CD. This image should give you a few ideas about how you can enhance applied color using layer properties and layer clipping (which will be discussed more later). If nothing else, the example shows that imitating reality may not be the only goal of hand-coloring. Shut off the view for individual layers in the sample image to see what the layer adds to the composition. Some changes are subtle, and some are not.

> When hand-coloring, you will usually want to work with layers so that the colors for the background of the image are at the bottom of the stack, and foreground element colors are at or near the top. This will help dictate a priority as to how the color gets applied.

If you try hand-coloring in an image with people and attempt to replace the skin tones, the flatness of the resulting skin tones will be quite evident and unnatural. Though you can improve this result by adjusting the quality of the color you are applying (see "Managing Image Noise" in chapter 5 where skin tone is adjusted using noise), the color isn't as "smart" as you might expect. A Gradient Map can often be a better choice for hand-coloring in some situations.

EXPLORING COLOR AND TONE THROUGH THE COMPOSITE LAYER

The Composite layer in Hidden Power separations is used as a canvas for applying and mixing separated components. If you fill the Composite layer with white, shut off the view for Luminosity and leave Color viewed. The image will turn white, even though the visibility for the color layer is still on. What many would expect is that the color for the image would be applied to the white composite. This is actually what is happening, and the result is very revealing about the relationship between color and tone. Because there is no tone in white, there is nothing for the color to display.

The point is, the display of color is directly dependent on the tone: if you want color to display differently (lighter or darker), you'll have to manipulate the tone rather than the color. Making the tone darker in an area of color will darken the color; lightening the tone will lighten the color. If you want another hue (for example, if you want to turn green to blue), you can change the color layer from the separation without affecting the tone.

Hand-Coloring with Gradient Maps

Usually, applying flat color is not the best way to hand-color images. Instead, you can use *gradients,* which create a progressive change in color. Gradients can be applied using the Gradient tool or Gradient Map adjustment layers. The *Gradient tool* applies the gradient color according to the pattern selected in the Options bar and in the direction and for the distance that you apply the tool. This tool is more likely to be used in creating effects. *Gradient Map* adjustment layers replace colors and/or tones by using a customized color mapping. When a gradient map is applied, Elements replaces each level of gray with its corresponding gradient color as you've set it up in the gradient mapping.

So, say you have a grayscale image, and you apply a gradient map that has 100% red (R = 255, G = 0, B = 0) at the halfway point on the gradient (50% gray). All of the gray pixels at 50% brightness will display as red. If this gradient blends evenly to black at 0% and white at 100%, the red will fade to pink and then white where tones in the image get lighter; the red will darken to brick and then black where tones in the image get darker. Gradient application of color and tone can be infinitely more complex than this simple example by using more complicated gradients. Simple toning can create duotone effects (again see the `lily_handcolored.psd` image and turn on the Sepia layer).

Remapping color and tone can work well in a limited area of an image. For example, you might use selection or masking to target a specific area of an image for recoloring skin tones. You can combine the effects of two or more different gradient maps in a single image by using different maps with different selections or masks.

To work with gradient maps, you need to be able to create and manipulate gradients. To work with gradients, you will use the Gradient Editor, which you can open from the Gradient Map dialog box. Open the Gradient Map dialog box by applying a gradient map as an adjustment layer (Layer → New Adjustment Layer → Gradient Map, and click OK). When the Gradient Map dialog box opens, click the color bar under Gradient Used For Grayscale Mapping to open the editor.

Once the Gradient Editor is open, you can edit the current gradient and create and save custom gradients for reuse. New gradients are created by adding and removing color and opacity stops to the preview bar, choosing a name, and clicking the New button. The new gradients that you create are stored in the gradient library and are available whenever you choose gradient functions.

Figure 4.22 shows the Gradient Editor dialog box and a breakdown of the major features.

Features in the Gradient Editor include buttons, the Name field, opacity and color stops, and Stops options.

Buttons

- Click More to reveal the Presets panel options menu. You can change the way the swatches are viewed in the Presets panel or change the gradient sets that are viewed.

- Click OK to accept the current values and close the dialog box.

Figure 4.22

The Gradient Editor allows the creation of custom color and tone alterations based on existing image tone.

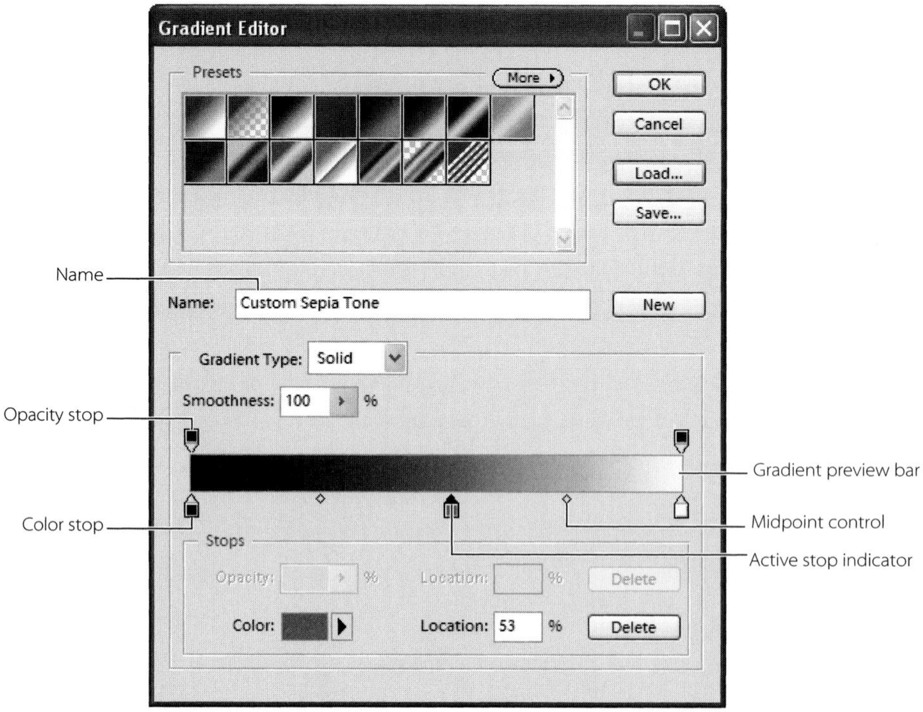

- Click Cancel to close the editor without accepting changes.
- Click Load to load a gradient set.
- Click Save to save the current gradients as a set.
- Press the Alt/Option key to change the Cancel button to a Reset button. Click Reset to eliminate all changes made since the editor was opened and revert to the original values.
- Click New to create a new preset. This will save a swatch with the current settings and name.
- Click Delete to remove an active color or opacity stop. See "Opacity and Color Stops" below for more on stops.

Name

- Enter a name for the current gradient, and then click New to save the gradient (in its current settings) to the Presets list.

Opacity and Color Stops

- Add a stop by clicking above or below the preview bar. Opacity stops are added by clicking above the gradient preview bar; color stops are added by clicking below the gradient preview bar.
- Remove a stop by clicking it, holding down the mouse button, and dragging the stop off the preview bar. Alternatively, you can click the Delete button with the desired stop active.
- Click a stop to activate it. The stop with its triangle colored black is the active stop (the stop whose settings appear in the Stops section of the dialog box).
- Double-click a color stop to open the Color Picker.

Stops Options

- The Stops options on the top row of the Stops section show the values for the active opacity stop. To set Opacity for a stop, activate the desired stop and enter a number or click the arrow to drop down a slider.
- The Stops options on the bottom row apply to the active color stop. The Color swatch provides a preview of the stop's color; click it to open the Color Picker.
- Enter a Location value for either stop type to accurately position the stop (from 0 % at the far left to 100 % at the far right).
- Click the Delete button to remove the active stop.

Editing Your Gradient

Setting up your gradient requires adding color stops to the bottom of the gradient bar to control the application of color to the tones in the image. To add a color stop, click just below the gradient bar and then drag the stop to the position on the gradient bar where you want to locate it. The preview bar will immediately give you a preview of how your mapping will look from black to white (left to right). If the Preview box on the Gradient Map dialog has been checked, the effect of the mapping that you build will also preview directly in the image. You can change the color of the stop in several ways:

- Sample color directly from the image (moving your cursor over the image changes it to the sample tool).
- Double-click the color stop to open the Color Picker, and choose the color you want.
- Make a selection (Foreground, Background, or User Color) from the drop-down menu next to the Color swatch.

You can control the opacity of the color application by the opacity stops set on the top of the gradient bar. If you choose color carefully, the colors you apply should affect simply the color you want to see.

The image to which you will be applying the gradient map can be converted to grayscale if you like, but this isn't necessary; the map will work on the image tonality independently of the current color. In some cases, it may actually be easiest to leave the color in the image so you can use the existing colors as sample color for the enhancement. Different images will require different handling depending on the color that exists and what you want to accomplish. You may want to adjust image tone or separate out image areas before applying gradient maps. You could also use gradient maps for tone adjustment as you would curves or levels.

Applying a Gradient Map for Tone Adjustment

One of the simplest applications of a gradient is to use it to make tone adjustments in a grayscale image. In fact, the Gradient Editor can be used just like a Levels or Curves adjustment (we'll look at how to make Levels and Curves adjustments in the next chapter).

Try this simple Gradient Map application to adjust image tone:

1. Open any flattened black-and-white image (or open a color image, flatten the image, click the Custom Black-and-White Hidden Power tool in the Power_Separations category of Effects, and flatten again). If the image is in Grayscale mode, change it to RGB mode.

2. Press D on the keyboard to reset the Foreground and Background colors on the toolbox.

3. Open a gradient map by choosing Layer → New Adjustment Layer → Gradient Map. Click OK on the New Layer dialog box. This opens the Gradient Map dialog box. Choose the black to white gradient, if it is not already selected, by clicking on it.

4. Click the Gradient Used For Grayscale Mapping preview on the dialog box. This opens the Gradient Editor.

5. Click directly on the whitecolor stop at the right and on the bottom of the gradient preview bar. This reveals a color midpoint (small gray diamond) in the center of the bar at the bottom.

> When you click a stop to activate it, diamond-shaped markers appear on either side of the stop, between it and the next stop. You can adjust these midpoints to affect the application of the gradient. Shifting the midpoint to the left increases the influence of the right stop; shifting the midpoint to the right increases the influence of the left stop. Adjust the color markers while viewing the image to get the best results.

6. Position the Gradient Editor so you can see your image, and move the slider right and then left of center while watching what happens to the image. (You may have to release the slider to see the result). Moving the slider left should lighten the image, and moving it right should darken it.

This simple application remaps the tone of the image based on the position of the slider. You can create far more complex tonal adjustments by adding color and opacity stops to the preview bar. Next, let's use gradient maps to adjust the color in an image.

A Sample Color Adjustment

In the following exercise, you will use painting tools, layer modes, layer masking and gradient maps for adjusting tone and color in our sample image. First you'll want to apply color, and then you'll use that color as a mask to adjust color and tone with variations (hue/color changes, changes in brightness, etc.), remembering that tone and color work together. Once you've applied any color to the image, you can apply changes to get a dramatic color result.

Creating a Manual Color Mask

These steps apply to any image where you want to make a targeted color change. However, it is just one of many methods; this one uses your initial application as a mask for later changes.

1. Open the image you want to adjust. This exercise will again use the lily, but we will start from grayscale. Open `lily_grayscale.psd` from the CD (this is the lily image changed to grayscale using the Custom Black-and-White tool).

2. Create a new layer and call it **Petal Color**. To create the new layer, click the New layer button on the Layers palette. Set the opacity of the layer to 70% and the layer mode to Color.

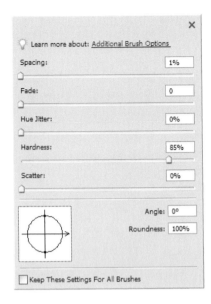

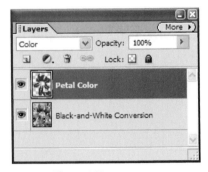

Figure 4.23

The layers should look like this. As you fill in color over the petals, the color of the petals will change but you will still be able to see the tone below.

3. Choose the Brush tool (press B on your keyboard). Adjust the brush options (click the More Options icon on the Options bar at the top of the screen) ✐ so that the brush has 1% Spacing, 0 Fade, 0 Hue Jitter, 85% Hardness, 0 Scatter, and 0 Angle, and 100% Roundness. See the palette here. Before you close out of the More Options dialog, click the Keep These Settings For All Brushes box at the bottom of the menu. Be sure the Size is about 30 pixels (30 px), the Mode is Normal, and Opacity is 100%. These other settings are found in the center of the Options bar. The brush hardness of 85% gives you a little softness at the edge of the brush so your color change will blend better with the background and other color changes.

4. Begin carefully painting color on to the image over the flower in the Petal Color layer. I use red (R: 255, G: 0, B: 0) for the brush color out of habit and because it is very easy to see. Set the brush color by choosing the color you want to apply in the Foreground swatch on the toolbar (just click the box to open the Color Picker). The color you use will ultimately be changed, so it really doesn't matter. You may find it an advantage to use color close to how you envision the result.

You will need to take some time applying the petal color. You want to get as tight as possible to the edge of the petals without going over. You will want to switch back and forth between the Brush tool and the Eraser (press E) to touch up the edges (Brush to add color, Eraser to remove it). Cover the darker part of the petals, and leave other parts clear (stamen, background, buds, and center of the lily; Figure 4.23).

Adding a Gradient Map

At the point where you have covered the petals where you want to apply color, you are ready to add a gradient map.

5. Change the opacity of the Petal Color layer to 100% in the Layers palette. This will intensify the color you have used in painting, but that will change in the following steps.

6. Hold down the Command/Ctrl key and click the Petal Color layer thumbnail in the Layers palette (Figure 4.24). This will create a selection from the solid area of the layer.

7. Create a Gradient Map adjustment layer by choosing Layer → New Adjustment Layer → Gradient Map. Change the Mode to Color in the New Layer dialog before you click OK to create the new layer. This assures the changes will affect only color. The Gradient Map dialog box will open after you click OK.

8. Open the Gradient Editor by clicking the preview bar in the Gradient Used For Grayscale Mapping preview.

9. Create a gradient that you want to apply to the image to color the petals. My settings were as shown here. Yours can be anything you like. It can be adjusted later. Unless you are looking to create some unusual effects, the gradient should be smooth and colors should be darker toward the left of the gradient.

Red	Green	Blue	Location
9	26	151	0
112	11	116	59
232	253	0	100

At this point the Gradient Editor should look something like Figure 4.25 if you used the settings from the table.

10. Click OK on the Gradient Editor to close it and accept the changes to the gradient.

11. Click OK on the Gradient Map dialog box to close it and accept the changes for the new layer.

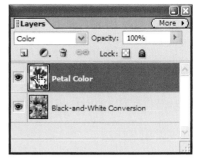

Figure 4.24

Place the cursor directly over the layer thumbnail, hold the Command/Ctrl key and click to load the solid area of the layer as a selection.

Depending on the colors you have selected for the gradient, you will get different effects. You can open the Gradient Editor again to adjust the results (by double-clicking the Gradient Map thumbnail, you will open the Gradient Map dialog). If you'd like, you can add a Hue/Saturation layer to adjust the color some; if you do, group the adjustment to the Gradient Map layer. However, there are a few more steps we will take, so don't bother making too many adjustments just yet. You can revisit the steps and make changes to the layers once you have it all set up.

One of the great advantages of using layered corrections is the ability to adjust them after the fact. Setting color markers is obviously the most involved step in the process—and easily the most arbitrary. It will be useful to go back and experiment by adjusting the color and position of the gradient stops to see the effect each adjustment has on the image. You may want to use additional stops to create other changes you may prefer and to experiment with Gradient Map opacity.

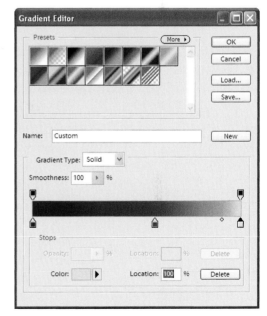

Figure 4.25

The change in the gradient increases the influence of the darker tones.

Adding Fringe Color

Another means of adding in some variation is to make enhancements based on layer clipping. We talk about this in more depth later on, but you don't need to know much about it to see how it works here.

12. Create a new layer above the Gradient Map layer. Name the layer **Petal Fringe**, and group the layer with the Gradient Map layer (if you added a Hue/Saturation adjustment after the last set of steps, group the new layer above the Hue/Saturation layer).

13. Choose a color that you think will complement the current color of the petals by clicking the foreground color swatch on the toolbar. I chose pure red (R: 255, G: 0, B: 0).

14. Hold down the Command/CtrlCtrl key and click on the Petal Color thumbnail in the Layers palette to load the layer as a selection again.

15. Invert the selection by pressing Command+Shift+I/Ctrl+Shift+I.

16. Fill the Petal Fringe layer with the color you chose in step 13. You can do this with the Fill Selection function (Edit → Fill Selection).

17. Deselect (press Command+D/Ctrl+D) and apply a Gaussian Blur. To apply the blur effect, choose Filter → Blur → Gaussian Blur. Move the Radius slider as you preview the image. Adjust the opacity of the Petal Fringe layer. I used a radius of 25 in the sample.

Adjust the color of the Petal Fringe layer using Hue/Saturation. Apply Hue/Saturation directly to the layer (press Command+U/Ctrl+U with the Petal Fringe layer active). The addition of the Petal Fringe layer will allow you to adjust the color at the fringe of the petals separately from the center area of the petals. A general Hue/Saturation above the adjustments you have already made will allow you to adjust all of the color you have applied as a grouping. To do this, load the Petal Color layer as a selection, and then create a Hue/Saturation adjustment layer. Creating the adjustment layer after making the selection will mask the area outside the selection. The result is that this layer does not have to be grouped with any of the previous layers as the mask will target the change to the colored area defined by the Petal Color layer only. You will want to make the adjustment layer Color mode to restrict changes to the color.

You can also adjust tone in a variety of ways. One of the easiest is to add a Levels adjustment layer above the other corrections. To do this, load the Petal Color layer as a selection, and then create the Levels adjustment layer (Layer → New Adjustment Layer → Levels). Again, this creates a masked adjustment layer. You can slide the center slider to the right to darken the area (and darken the color) or left to lighten the area (and lighten the color). Experimenting with these changes can give you flexibility with the color additions and also some experience with the relationship between color and tone. If you have added all the suggested layers, your Layers palette will look like Figure 4.26.

You can revisit the changes in the adjustment layers at any time to fine-tune the color application. To color other parts of the image, you will want to approach the changes as described in this section—first creating the mask and then applying more color based on the mask you created. Take a look at petal_color.psd on the CD to see the complete image shown in Figure 4.26.

By using masking and multiple gradient layers to apply gradients and by working with layer-blending modes and opacity, you can achieve complex colorizing results. Of course, this example is only the tip of the iceberg when it comes to applying color to tone. Combining these techniques with a variety of other tools you will use for enhancing and replacing color (which we will explore in later chapters), your ability to control the result is limitless.

A few points should be clear at this time: The interaction between color and tone is the foundation for what you see in an image. You must be able to control tone as a basis for image color. Targeting areas of change—with separation, layer properties, or masking—can help you confine your correction to specific areas or components of your images so you can achieve better results. In the next chapter, we'll look at further exploiting the color and tone relationship.

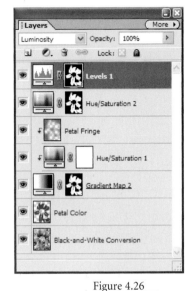

Figure 4.26

With all suggested color adjustments added, your Layers palette should look like this.

Chapter 5

Correcting Image Tone

Manipulating tone with confidence makes all the difference in getting the results you want in black-and-white and color. Adjusting tone starts with evaluating the image to define what you want to do and moves through steps to make changes based on that evaluation. Two points to keep in mind:

- For every action, there is a reaction.
- You might have to break it to fix it.

The first point is an adaptation of one of Newton's laws of physics. Every general adjustment you make will affect what you are adjusting as well as other tones (and colors). The second is based on my experience with "fixing" appliances by disabling broken functions. In images, a fix doesn't always make everything better, but it should improve the appearance of the image. Sometimes you must do something destructive to an image to enable a repair.

Doing Minor Cleanup First

Evaluating Image Tones

Redistributing Tone with Levels

Snapping and Fading Contrast with Curves

(Un)Sharpening and Boosting Contrast

Managing Image NoiseMasking with Image Tone

Soft Focus Effects Using Masking

Shaping Image Elements with Light and Shadow

Doing Minor Cleanup First

Before adjusting an image, it is often good to do a quick once-over to evaluate image problems. This quick evaluation can involve first cropping the image and then removing, or touching up, other obvious problems (tears, dust specks, etc.). Care in touch-up at this point permanently removes unwanted elements so they will not be present later no matter how you use the content of the image.

A simple, direct method of taking care of minor damage is cloning or duplicating existing image areas to cover up problems. With *cloning,* you sample information from one part of an image and then apply that information to another part of the image. In this way, you can patch areas that might be damaged, missing, or undesirable. It can solve any type of minor damage, as long as you have something to clone from that is a close match to the spot you are fixing. Careful cloning can enable you to patch an image seamlessly without creating noticeable patterns or replacing damage with other flaws.

Image areas with tone and color complexities (such as skin tones) require careful selection of replacement areas in order to make unnoticeable repairs. Substitutions can come from within the same image or from another image with similar qualities. All cloning and duplication corrections follow the same basic steps:

1. Define the problem area.
2. Locate a suitable replacement.
3. Sample the replacement.
4. Apply the replacement to the problem area.

DO SOME DAMAGE CONTROL BY PLANNING AHEAD

You can avoid a lot of trouble with your digital images before you create them. Don't get into the habit of just thinking, "I'll clean it up later digitally!" A quick wipe with a clean, lint-free cloth can clear troublesome debris from an image you are scanning, or from the scanner glass, just as you might wipe crumbs from a chair before you sit down. The same idea applies to taking images with a digital camera; be sure your lens and sensor are clean before you point the camera at anything, wipe off dusty or dirty objects that will be in your images, and be sure you take the time to focus so your subject is as crisp and clear as possible (auto-focus doesn't always do what you want). Taking these steps can save a lot of detail work later.

Obviously you can't expect anything to be pristine. Dust and finger smudges can insinuate themselves at any point where the image makes a physical rather than electronic transfer (on the subject, on your lens, on the scanner glass, on the surface of a print or negative, and so forth). But once you've taken the image or scanned it, any minor nagging defects that worked their way into your image will remain until you remove them.

The more time you spend preparing to create an image, the less you may have to worry about correcting incidental problems, which can save lots of time at the computer.

Images can be cropped to remove damage, but also to improve composition. Composition is discussed along with the tools in Chapter 7.

Correcting Problems Using the Clone Stamp Tool

The Clone Stamp tool samples from a spot that you define in the image and copies image information in the shape of the brush you've chosen for the tool. All you do is sample from a clean area of the image that matches (tone, color, and pattern) and then apply the clean sample to the part of the image you want to replace. This tool will help you take care of dust, flecked dirt, scratches, and many other image problems.

The Clone Stamp tool lets you do simple copying and pasting from one area of your image to another in the shape of the currently selected brush and using brush dynamics. Let's start with a simple cloning and look at options for other variations.

1. Open the image you want to apply the Clone Stamp to in order to make a correction. For a sample of an image that this type of correction might work on, see `icecream_spots` `.psd` in the Chapter 5 folder on the CD.

2. Choose the Clone Stamp tool (press S on the keyboard; press Shift+S to toggle to the Clone Stamp from the Pattern Stamp if necessary) and make sure the settings are as follows in the Options bar:

Brush characteristics (hardness, spacing, fade, jitter, etc.) can be set only when using the Brush tools (including Healing Brushes below). To create the brush you want for cloning, choose the Brush tool, set the options (by clicking More Options on the Options bar), and then save the brush by clicking the brush preview menu and choosing Save Brush from the pop-up menu. After the brush is saved, you can use it with other tools.

- Clone Stamp tool icon selected (the left tool)
- A soft or custom brush selected in the Presets menu. The selected brush should be semi-soft (80%–90% hardness). A softer brush will help your clones blend into the surroundings.
- Mode: Normal
- Opacity: 100%
- Aligned: Checked
- Use All Layers: Checked

3. Create a new, blank layer and name it **Clone**. In multilayered images, you would move this Clone layer to the top of the layer stack.

4. Take a good look at the image, determine what needs to be replaced, and locate suitable sample areas.

5. Sample a replacement area. This should be an area that is clear of other damage or detail (e.g., clothing seams, as in this example). To make the sample, hold down the Option/Alt key and click the spot in the image that you want to use as the sample area.

6. Apply the sample by releasing the Option/Alt key, moving the cursor over the area where the clone will be applied, and then clicking in that area.

Steps 5 and 6 will apply the clone to cover the target area by copying the sampled area and painting it into the application area (see Figure 5.1).

Optimally, the size of the brush should be just slightly larger than the area you are hoping to remove. You will usually use a slightly soft brush so that the changes blend into the background. Too soft a brush can lead to corrections that look blurred. For best results, be sure that the color and tone are similar in the clone-from and clone-to areas and that the area you are cloning from is already clear of defects. Checking the tone may require using the Eyedropper and Info palette; failing to use a clean sample area will replicate defects to the new area. It is a good idea to zoom in close and clean up with a small brush first, picking up little bits of damage before moving on to larger patches. This will help clear sample areas for larger cloning.

During application you can increase and decrease the size of the brush using the bracket keys: [and]. The left bracket will decrease the size of the brush, the right bracket will increase the size of the brush.

Figure 5.1

Using the Clone Stamp tool is just a fancy, but convenient, way of applying copy/paste.

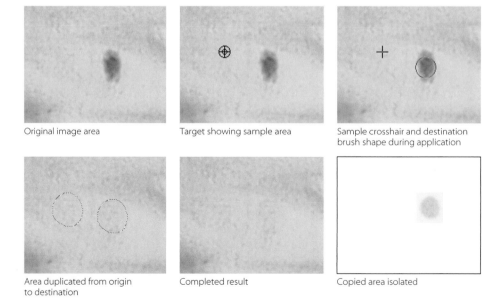

Original image area

Target showing sample area

Sample crosshair and destination brush shape during application

Area duplicated from origin to destination

Completed result

Copied area isolated

For the most part, the areas you should target with the Clone Stamp are the smaller spots. It isn't the best tool for cloning a subject's head from one image to another, for example. For larger areas, you will want to use patching (as we do in the following section), as long as there is a reasonable replacement area.

When you apply the Clone Stamp tool, click and move rather than holding down the mouse button and blowing away large areas of the image. You'll want to resample often, changing angles and position of the sample so you clone from different areas (you'll do this far more often than changing the brush). This will reduce the chances of creating undesirable patterns.

You will most often use the Clone Stamp tool in Normal mode, but in some instances other modes can serve a purpose. For example, to correct black specks, use Lighten mode and stamp from a slightly darker portion of the image. This will lighten the specks without darkening lighter areas. If you are trying to fix light specks, clone from an area a little lighter than the area you are cloning to using Darken mode. The corrections will tend to affect only the specks while keeping the general tone of the area unchanged. At times, you'll switch modes to Color or Luminosity to help move only the color or lightness component of the sample area rather than both. For example, you may want to sample the tone from one area and the color from another to get a good match to the original.

Figure 5.2
This image offers many obvious areas that will require correction.

Making corrections is easier and more flexible if you apply the changes to another layer as suggested in the steps. You can view the image before and after the changes by toggling on and off the view for the layer. You can also erase cloning that you have done or make other adjustments such as applying filters or changing layer modes while preserving your original image. If you want to adjust only color or tone, you can set the layer to the appropriate mode (and use the brush in Normal mode).

A practice image called icecream_tone.psd is supplied in the Chapter 5 folder on the CD. It is a black-and-white conversion for a picture of a young child on the playground (see Figure 5.2). She's had an altercation with a chocolate ice cream cone, and her light clothes became quite spotted. It is a great image to practice Clone Stamp corrections on, and we will be using it in the next few sections.

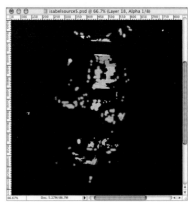

The Mess   Touched Up   The Corrections

Figure 5.3

Correct only the smaller spots and details as shown, leaving some of the larger problems to techniques that follow.

Open the image and do your best to make corrections to the spotty mess using the Clone Stamp. Pay close attention to the patterning and shading. This will be especially important around the seams and stitching. Try and get the image to about the point shown in Figure 5.3.

Take a better look at the many corrections made with this tool by opening the `icecream_fixes.psd` on the CD. Turn on the Clone Stamp layer to see the suggested corrections.

Using Healing Tools

The Healing Brush tool and Spot Healing Brush tool are "smarter" cloning tools that help users make changes by "intelligent" substitution between the sample and target areas. The key difference between the tools is that the Healing Brush enables the user to choose the sample area, and the Spot Healing Brush decides for the user where the sample will come from. Especially with smaller corrections, these tools can help you swiftly correct damage without a lot of fuss in matching tone and pattern.

> While it is true these healing tools can help users make corrections, over-reliance on them can damage images and create undesirable results. Don't always reach for the Healing Brush tool before the Clone Stamp or before considering manual patching.

The Healing Brush

The Healing Brush is a very close relative of the Clone Stamp tool. You have to define a sample area to clone from and then apply the tool to make the repair. The better your selection of the clone-from area, the better your result will be. The real difference between the Clone Stamp and Healing Brush is that when you release the mouse button, the healing function takes over, compares the sample with the target, and attempts to make the best correction. This automates many steps of blending, comparison, and blurring that achieve the final result—and it all happens in a blink.

If you want to know more about how the Healing tool works, you can explore using the Hidden Power Mend tool at slower playback speeds. The Mend tool was made as a Healing substitute before Elements had a healing tool. While it is no longer necessary for Elements 4, it is a great learning tool. Find it on the Hidden Power website: `http://www.hiddenelements.com/downloads.html`.

The Healing Brush is great for some types of damage (such as dust) and for minor repairs (such as removing wrinkles from a forehead). There are several limitations to how and where the healing tools can be applied. To avoid any problems using the Healing Brush tool, use the following guidelines:

- Use a hard brush; the tool takes care of blending.
- Use a single application of the tool to cover the whole area that is to be replaced with a little to spare (use a brush that is 1.5 to 2 times the width of the damage).
- Use the tools on isolated damage only; avoid application of the tool near object edges. Remove a stray eyelash fallen on a cheek rather than stray hairs at a hairline.
- Be sure the source can replace the tone/texture of the target area—color isn't a primary consideration in choosing a replacement area.

The application of the tool is almost identical to the Clone Stamp tool. Just select the tool (press J; toggle the Healing Brush and Spot Healing Brush tools using Shift+J), choose a brush size, choose the clone-from (or sample) area, and apply the tool to cover the damage. Application of the tool can be made to a separate blank layer by creating the new layer and choosing Use All Layers in the Options bar. You will almost always use this tool in Normal mode with the Sampled option selected instead of the Pattern option. Pattern will be used in repairs only if you have created a source to use for repair or if you are doing more creative enhancement.

Continuing on with the sample image, you can make a few corrections with the Healing tool. Open `icecream_fixes.psd`, and turn on the Healing layer to see what corrections are suggested (see Figure 5.4).

The Spot Healing Brush

The Spot Healing Brush, a variation on the Healing Brush, attempts to make it easier to make spot corrections quickly. The tool decides for the user where the sample will be taken from (with the Proximity Match option selected for Type) or synthesizes the sample

Identify Problems

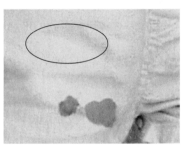

Identify Solutions

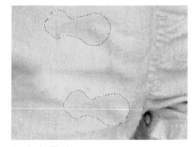

Apply the Tool

Figure 5.4

Healing can handle select details, so long as they are matched. The closer you work with tone and detail, the better.

(with the Create Texture option selected for Type), automatically replacing the area of the image that you select by using the brush. It is meant to be used for spot correction—ergo the name—meaning that you should consider it for tasks such as picking dust out of scans rather than making larger damage corrections. It should be used only for quick corrections that are not critical.

Because the Create Texture option synthesizes replacement information by some form of averaging, you will most likely get better results by using the Proximity Match option. However, unless the sample selection doesn't matter, even the Proximity Match option is somewhat suspect because the randomized behavior of the tool makes the result impossible to predict. Unless you are using the tool in an area of flat color and tone (a sky) or where patterns will blend in (grass), the Healing Brush, Clone Stamp, and manual patching techniques discussed elsewhere will almost always produce a better result than using the Spot Healing Brush.

Using Spot Healing is similar to using the Healing Brush, except that you do not have to define a sample spot. It is as simple as selecting the tool and clicking on areas that you want to replace in the image. The same suggestions as for the Healing Brush apply.

CHOOSING A DISPLAY CURSOR

Your setting for Painting Cursors on the Display & Cursors preferences (Edit → Preferences → Display & Cursors) will determine the way the Clone Stamp tool appears on your screen. Make your selection under Painting Cursors. Standard shows the tool icon ✐ during application, Precise shows a crosshair -¦-, Normal Brush Tip shows the shape of the brush being applied where it is 50% or more opaque (when using a soft brush this will display a smaller area than is affected by the brush) ◯, and Full Size Brush Tip shows the shape of the absolute size of brush being applied ◯. All display options use the sample icon ⊕ when you hold down the Option/Alt key to sample the image. Checking the box will place a crosshair inside the brush shape for either the normal or full brush size ⊕.

Correcting by Duplication (Patching)

It is sometimes advantageous to make corrections by copying and pasting larger areas of an image rather than painstakingly removing each spot or speck of dust one at a time with the Clone Stamp tool. This section looks at an option for patching an image that will work on tears, holes, and other broad-area damage.

Start making the patch by preselecting the damaged area. This will define the shape and size of the damage that you want to correct. Making a selection of the damaged area will enable you to find the best available replacement. The order of your approach and some basic techniques will be similar to cloning with the Clone Stamp tool:

1. Identify the problem area in the image and the intended replacement.

2. Choose the Lasso tool. It is often a good choice for patching because it will make irregular selections, and irregular patches tend to blend in less noticeably. Set the tool to feather several pixels (2–10); this will soften the edge of the sample. In general, you will want to use more feathering with images that have higher resolution.

3. Make a selection with the Lasso around the general area of the image you want to replace. Making this selection will ensure that you get a patch that is sized to cover the damage—like a template. Make the selection a bit larger than the damage so you can have some leeway in blending pasted areas. See Figure 5.5.

4. Move the selection tool over the selection created in step 3, and the icon will change to the Selection Move icon ▸⁞⁞. Click and drag the selection over to the area of the image to be used as a replacement. Choosing exactly where to place the selection can require rotating, flipping, or carefully sizing the selection. Note any changes you make so you can reverse them after you paste the replacement in step 6. The options bar will show these changes. See Figure 5.6 for the sample area.

5. Copy the selected area.

6. Paste. This creates a new layer containing the image area you are using as a patch. Because the patch is on its own layer, you can size and position it (by reversing the changes made in step 4), use the Eraser tool and a slightly soft brush to blend the patch with the area being covered, or transform the replacement (see Figure 5.7). Layer modes can also be employed (for example, Lighten and Darken) as you might use them with the Clone Stamp tool.

7. Repeat steps 1 through 6 as needed to create more patches and repair the image.

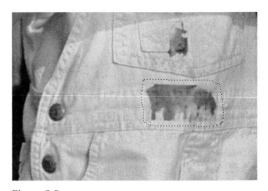

Figure 5.5

Make a selection around the area to be replaced.

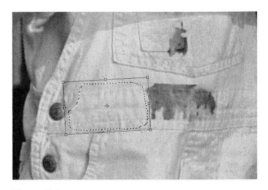

Figure 5.6

Move the selection around the area to be used as a replacement.

Figure 5.7

In this case, the patch area is transformed to fit in as a solution. For more on transforming image areas, see the section on "Transformations and Distortions" in Chapter 7.

You may have more than one option for making the correction in any given image; you might want to try several different solutions for the same problem area—especially if the area that you are patching is large or important to the image. To compare, make the first patch and then turn off the visibility for its layer. After making the next patch, you can compare the two by turning the layer views on or off. Don't be afraid to mix manual patches—use more than one, if that improves the result. This patching technique can be combined with Clone Stamp and Healing tool corrections (switch between tools using the J and S shortcuts)—and with other techniques we have yet to look at.

> When it comes to repairs, unlike general tone or color correction, it is often best to work on removing smaller problems and then working up to larger ones. By first removing minor problems, you can then use those corrected areas to repair larger areas without duplicating old damage and problems.

If you take a look at the `icecream_fixes.psd` image and turn on the Manual Patch layer, you'll see how the correction for this image works. It leaves only a few more spots to clean up, which you can take care of with your choice of methods. You can see the final cleanup of spots by turning on the Pocket Patches layer.

There is still more to do in the image, as discussed earlier in the chapter. If you turn on the Leg Patches layer, you'll see the pant leg straightens out, the sock straightens out, and the tone and color of the leg even out. These changes were made using cloning techniques—mostly patching. Attempting to make some of these corrections before going on to other techniques may help give you some valuable experience.

Evaluating Image Tones

Evaluating the tone of an image can help you make better corrections. At times you'll need to make precise measurements of image information, and at others you'll have to evaluate the general appearance of the image. The Eyedropper tool (used in conjunction with the Info palette) and the Histogram feature can provide just about all the image information you'll need to make sensible adjustments.

Using the Eyedropper for Tone Evaluation

The Eyedropper, located in the toolbox, makes it easy to gather information about individual pixels or small pixel groupings. Simply click the Eyedropper tool and put the cursor over the image area you want to measure, and the Eyedropper will sample the composite of the visible layers and display the information in the Info palette (Figure 5.8). Such measurements can be helpful in evaluating an image periodically throughout the correction process. For example, comparing grayscale values for sample and target areas before cloning or duplicating can give you a good idea whether those areas are a good match (similar tone) before you make the clone or patch.

Figure 5.8

The Palette Options pop-up menu on the Info palette enables you to choose color references: Grayscale (luminosity), RGB Color, Web Color, and HSB Color.

From the drop-down list on the Options bar, you can select a sample size: Point Sample (samples the pixel at the tip of the tool icon), 3 By 3 Average, and 5 By 5 Average. These options are also available by pointing the Eyedropper at an image and clicking the right mouse button. The Average options look at a square of pixels (with the tip of the tool icon as the center pixel) and then average those to determine the result. If tone is noisy—for example, as it is in skin tones—it is better to use a broader sample size to get a better average reading of the tones you are measuring. If you use a sample size that is too small when measuring a noisy area, it might make for confusing samples: values between one pixel and the next might change too rapidly to make sense or provide anything meaningful in the way of a reading.

To make a sample measurement, follow these steps:

1. Select the Eyedropper tool (I).

2. Choose the sample size from the drop-down list on the options bar.

3. Bring the Info palette to the front by selecting it from the Window menu or by revealing it in the Palette Bin.

4. Choose a color mode in the palette pop-up menus.

5. Spot-check with the Eyedropper by passing the cursor over various areas of the image while noting the values in the Info palette.

If you're using this in conjunction with the Clone Stamp tool, for example, you could sample the target area to determine the tone and then use the eyedropper to locate a donor area that has very similar tone. In this way you can make better, less detectible, corrections.

Evaluating Images with Histograms

The Histogram feature (Window → Histogram) displays a graph of image information. The height of each column in the graph represents the number of pixels with a particular luminescence throughout the entire tonal range of the image. If a specific component is selected in the Channels drop list, the graph displays only information for that component. A histogram is also available in the Levels dialog box (Enhance → Adjust Lighting → Levels). A histogram can help describe the tonality and integrity of an image, pointing out both image qualities and abnormalities that may need to be corrected.

For example, a histogram graph can tell you whether an image is naturally bright (high-key) or dark (low-key), whether the contrast is neutral or high. If the qualities are desirable, histograms can help you maintain those qualities by reevaluating the image later in the correction process. Although image qualities such as high- or low-key may be apparent to the naked eye, histograms also help you determine whether an image has been damaged in processing or whether it shows some other limitation, such as not taking full advantage of tonal range.

Aberrations in the image information can present themselves as uncharacteristic shifts, lack of balance, or gaps in the graph. A histogram that contains many peaks and valleys, gaps in information, and/or *clipping* (spikes in information that bunch up at either end or run off the chart) may represent some form of image damage, limitation, or loss of image information. If the damage appears extreme, the image might need correction or be essentially beyond repair. The graph can show insufficient tonal range for manipulation, correction, and use.

Evaluating a histogram is as easy as looking at it. Characteristics become obvious in a quick visual evaluation of the graph. The following examples show a basic blueprint for specific image types, such as high-key, low-key, high contrast, low contrast, and images with damaged information.

> You can evaluate a section of an image by selecting it with the selection tools and then looking at the histogram. The histogram charts results for only the active or selected portion of an image.

A histogram that is weighted toward the black or dark end of the graph—and that does not show gaps in tonality at the light end of the graph—represents a low-key (dark) image. These are often images taken in low light, such as around a campfire or birthday cake. Figure 5.9 shows an example of a low-key image and the histogram that represents it.

A histogram that is skewed to the light (right) end of the graph represents a high-key (light) image, such as the one in Figure 5.10. Beach shots with lots of light sand or snowy winter scenes are good examples of high-key images.

Figure 5.9

A low-key image

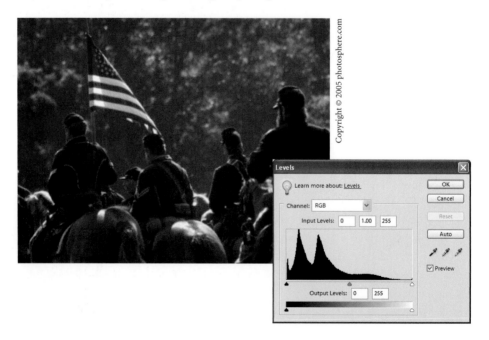

Copyright © 2005 photosphere.com

A histogram that peaks in the dark and light areas while having lower pixel density in the middle of the graph (like the one in Figure 5.11) represents a high-contrast image. Harsh lighting in direct sunlight can create a chasm between lights and darks, which is a typical example of high contrast—although not necessarily a desirable one. A silhouette, in which a figure is shown lit from behind, is another example of high contrast.

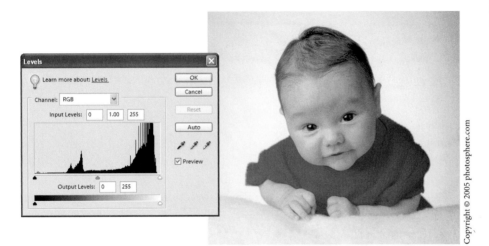

Figure 5.10

A high-key image

Figure 5.11

A high-contrast image

A histogram that shows a peak in the center (Figure 5.12) is low contrast and medium-key. These images are dominated by midtones. Images shot on an overcast day can often have a low-contrast appearance.

An image with a mix of global and local contrast displays as a flattened graph in a histogram with few peaks and valleys; see Figure 5.13 for an example. Images with full tonal range can have quite a bit of local contrast as opposed to high total contrast.

The histograms in Figure 5.14 represent an image that has been altered by limiting the number of tones it contains (for example, by using the Indexed Color mode). Gaps between tones and a spiky appearance on the histogram suggest that the image has limitations. These types of gaps can be symptomatic of other damage, such as poor scanning or extreme handling during corrections.

Figure 5.12

A low-contrast, medium-key image

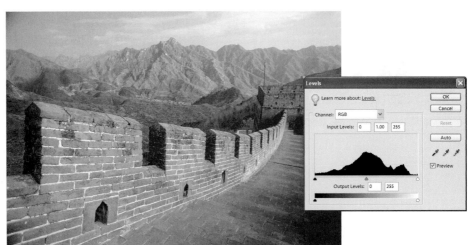

Copyright © 2005 photosphere.com

Figure 5.13

A full-toned image

Copyright © 2005 photosphere.com

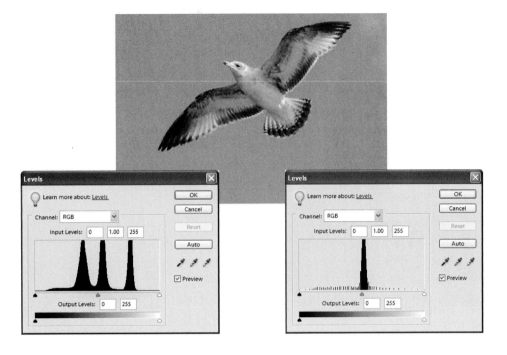

Figure 5.14

These histograms represent the original tone and a conversion to 64 grays.

Histogram graphs should have some information for every level from the right to the left of the graphing, or else the tonality is not covering the potential dynamic range. Abnormalities might not always represent problems, but they are certainly good indications of unusual conditions and potential problems. If the histogram shows a gap, it suggests that image information is missing or damaged. Intermittent gaps (like those in the histogram created by reducing the colors in Figure 5.15) can suggest a cause or origin of the image damage. Anomalies can result from capture problems, such as bad scanning (faulty techniques or equipment), incorrect image exposure, filter use, or unusual lighting conditions. Anomalies can also be the result of image processing: color mode conversions, color-management issues, corrections, poorly applied filters, and so forth. While it is possible for gaps in tone to be a natural state for the image, it is unlikely.

The most common tendencies in image histograms that help identify an image that can be improved are shortened tonal ranges and clipping.

Shortened tonal range is represented by a histogram that does not have information across the entire range of the graph, with a gap at either the light or dark end of the graph or both. A shortened tonal range indicates that the image is not taking full advantage of the shades of gray available (0% to 100% black) in individual color components or brightness (depending, again, on the information being displayed—which is based on channel selection).

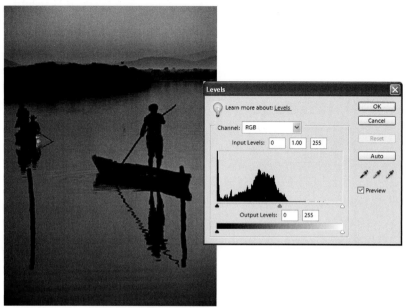

Copyright © 2005 photosphere.com

The image in Figure 5.15 is a good example of shortened tonal range. The image shows some potential for stronger contrast. The histogram displays a shortened tonal range, confirming the visual inspection. The tonality of the image could be adjusted to make the image more dynamic.

Clipping occurs when image detail gets combined. For example, this can happen when an image is overexposed and a range of highlight detail gets recorded in an image as pure white, or when an image is underexposed and a range of shadow details is recorded as pure black. Wedding images, for instance—in which the groom is in black and the bride in white—can easily be prone to over- or underexposure problems and a resulting loss of detail in either shadows or highlights. Some of the extreme highlights or shadow details may be lost, and this is reflected in the histogram by a spike at the extreme right or left of the graph. Clipping may be caused by any number of processes that occur in obtaining, opening, or resaving an image.

The key to using histograms is knowing that, when the histogram confirms image damage, it may point toward a course of correction. In the case of clipping, the histogram may suggest that you have to retake or rescan an image to capture the detail that was clipped.

You should never look at only the histogram, shout "Aha!" and make an image correction regardless of how the image appears on-screen. Be sure to visually assess the image as well, and use the two assessments (visual and measured) in tandem. The visual assessment should override the digital one, especially if you get good results in tests and can trust the view of your monitor.

Even if you evaluate an image, and feel you need to make corrections, that doesn't tell you where to begin or how to make the corrections. The next task is to define what you want to do and how to accomplish your ends.

Although drastically altering tonal range is sometimes a mistake, shifting the range—even radically—can work to the benefit of the image by improving contrast and dynamic range. While correction may temporarily skew an image's key and/or contrast, several corrections can be made in succession to achieve the desired result, or corrections can be blended between the original and corrected versions. In the following sections, you'll look at making specific corrections to images by using Levels and Curves, and you'll evaluate how each of these tools affects tonal correction.

Redistributing Tone with Levels

Tonal correction will often give black-and-white images broader tonal range and stronger overall contrast. After you correct minor flaws and evaluate the image both visually and with histograms, the next step in correction will often be to open the Levels dialog box to make a general tonal correction. Proper use of levels can quickly fix tonal range and the general brightness and contrast of an image. First, we'll look at the steps, and then we'll show how these steps might apply to a particular image:

1. Open an image. It should be black-and-white, or you should convert the image (you can use the Custom Black-and-White tool included with the Hidden Power tools).

2. Complete dust corrections, cropping, and minor alterations.

3. Create an adjustment layer for adjusting levels (Layer → New Adjustment Layer → Levels).

4. Inspect the image both visually (on the monitor) and by using the histogram in the Levels palette, noting the image qualities (the image key, contrast, and potential damage). If you have no concerns about the histogram and image damage, skip to step 6.

5. If the histogram seems out of character with the image or shows hints of damage, consider rescanning, replacing the image, or weeding out the source of the trouble.

6. Correct shortened tonal range by adjusting the Levels sliders.

7. Adjust the midtone slider on the Levels graph to manipulate the overall brightness of the image.

Of these steps, all but steps 6 and 7 have been covered previously. To understand the effects such changes have on an image, it will be best to look at an example. Look back at the image and histogram in Figure 5.15. The image was originally in color, and the warm tones in the color made the low-key appearance interesting. However, once converted to black-and-white, the image became dark and murky. This is confirmed by the histogram, which shows a decided skew toward the dark end of the graph and a gap between midtones and highlights.

Moving the Levels sliders to the left lightens the image; moving them to the right darkens the image. Where exactly to place each slider is a matter of what you want to accomplish. Changes can be conservative or quite radical. To correct a shortened tonal range, move the end slider on the outer side of the gap in toward the graph, and keep repositioning it until the graph information becomes solid (see Figure 5.16). Open the `silhouette.psd` image on the CD and try this to see how it works on this image.

When you commit your changes by clicking OK, Photoshop Elements redistributes the tones over the total available range (0 to 255 levels of gray, from black to white). Redistribution of the tonal information in an image from a thinner to a broader range will necessarily create some gaps in the presentation of the image information (see Figure 5.17).

Figure 5.16

The Levels sliders let you quickly redefine the white and black points in an image and redistribute the tone.

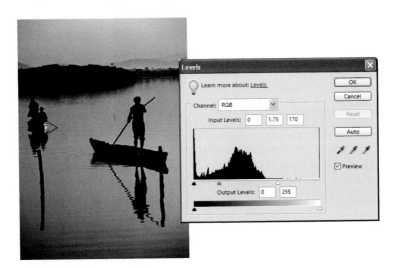

Figure 5.17

Gaps can suggest that image information is adjusted, but can also signify damage (or just that you have the Use Cache For Histograms preference selected in the Image Cache preferences).

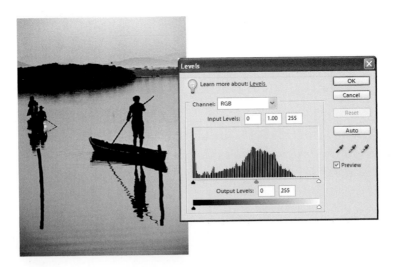

This Levels change is one you can make strictly by looking at the appearance of the histogram and adjusting it accordingly. The purpose is to take full advantage of the tonal range. The change will intensify overall contrast and broaden the dynamic range of the image. It may affect the apparent key of the image.

One possible means of smoothing inconsistent tonality caused by redistribution is to apply a slight (less than 1-pixel radius) Blur or Sharpen filter to the image. This will, however, change fine detail and distort edges depending on the severity of the application of either filter. In most cases, you will want to leave well enough alone and not blur the picture just to enhance the histogram graph. It isn't worth sacrificing the content of the image to make the histogram look better.

It may be possible and desirable to go even further with this Levels correction. When a histogram presents a tail toward the shadows or highlights (see Figure 5.18), it can often be clipped in part or whole. *Tails* on the histogram often represent scattered highlight or shadow information—generally attributable to image noise rather than image detail. Snipping the information turns it to absolute white for a highlight or absolute black for a shadow. Generally, you will want to cut an entire tail when the graph represents scattered pixels; however, it is sometimes desirable to eliminate none, some, or all of a solid tail, depending on the image and the length of the tail.

As a general rule, the longer the tail, the less (proportionally) you should cut off. For example, whereas you may completely remove a tail that covers 15 levels, you might trim half or less of a tail that covers 50 levels or 33 percent of one that covers 100 levels. Cutting proportionally in this way will help retain image integrity and character.

Don't feel that you have to crop a tail in an image just because it is there. If the results seem too drastic after cutting a tail, then they are. Put simply: do crop a tail that improves the image; don't crop a tail that compromises the image.

After adjusting tonal range, images can be adjusted for overall brightness as well by using Levels. A black-and-white image that appears too dark or light can be corrected by using the middle slider in the Levels dialog box. Moving the slider to the left lightens midtones, whereas moving it to the right darkens them (see Figure 5.19). This may seem slightly counterintuitive, because you might think that moving the midtone slider toward the light range would lighten the image and moving it toward the dark would darken it. However, the results

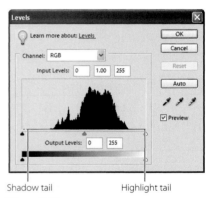

Shadow tail   Highlight tail

Figure 5.18

The Levels sliders let you quickly redefine the white and black points in an image and redistribute tone.

Lighten Darken

Figure 5.19

The middle Levels slider lets you quickly redefine the black and white points in an image and adjust overall brightness.

actually make a lot of sense. The idea is that you are moving the median of the graph representation and not the tone of the image. In moving the median of the graph, more levels of tone fall within the lighter or darker half of the tonal range. If more tones are shifted to fall in the lighter half, more tones are light, so the image brightens; if more tones are shifted to fall in the darker half, more tones are dark, so the image darkens.

Be careful not to abuse the middle slider on the Levels palette—there are other, and perhaps better, ways of controlling the midtones (such as using Curves, as described in the next section, or Gradient Maps). As a guide, try not to move the midtone slider more than 25 levels in any direction when making corrections. This keeps the redistribution small and more forgiving. You can always come back and lighten or darken an image later.

> Although Levels adjustments can be made automatically, automated tools will not often make your best corrections. Automated tools may get it right sometimes, but for many images, personal judgment should prevail. Auto-corrections have no means to determine what "looks good."

Snapping and Fading Contrast with Curves

Another means of adjusting tone in your images is with curves. The Curves tool is the ideal tool to help fine-tune and reshape the tonal distribution of an image. Whereas Levels has only three slider points to change, Curves can have many, and those additional points allow you more control and the ability to control different levels of tone separately. Curves is both a more versatile correction tool and a more dangerous one than Levels because of its power. However, using Curves can help remove steps in corrections because you can make numerous corrections to various parts of image tone in one application.

While Adobe has chosen to remove curves (even the hidden ones) from the interface for version 4 of Photoshop Elements, you can still use curve presets to make some adjustments. These presets are available in the Hidden Power Curve Presets image in the Chapter 5 folder on the CD. We'll also consider an option for using Gradient Map layers for multipoint tone adjustment that mimics curves. If you want more flexibility with curves, plug-in options are available from third-party manufacturers through the hiddenelements.com website that offer familiar Curve flexibility (see www.hiddenelements.com/downloads.html).

Because the Curves tool is powerful, applying it requires a little savvy. You should have specific goals in mind before applying it, and these goals should be at least partially derived from your visual and measured image evaluations. For example, you may want to increase or decrease image contrast or brighten the shadows. Specific Hidden Power Curve Presets are available for a variety of purposes, as outlined in Table 5.1.

Table 5.1

**Hidden Power
Curve Presets**

NAME	DESCRIPTION	USE
Contrast increase 20%	Increases general contrast of the image 20% (10% lighter highlights; 10% darker shadows).	General correction.
Contrast increase 10%	Increases general contrast of the image 10% (5% lighter highlights; 5% darker shadows).	General correction.
Contrast decrease 10%	Decreases general contrast of the image 10% (5% darker highlights; 5% lighter shadows).	General correction.
Contrast decrease 20%	Decreases general contrast of the image 20% (10% darker highlights; 10% lighter shadows).	General correction.
Highlights 10% darker	Decreases brightness of highlights by 10%, while anchoring midtones and shadows.	General correction.
Highlights 5% darker	Decreases brightness of highlights by 5%, while anchoring midtones and shadows.	General correction.
Highlights 5% lighter	Increases brightness of highlights by 5%, while anchoring midtones and shadows.	General correction.
Highlights 10% lighter	Increases brightness of highlights by 10%, while anchoring midtones and shadows.	General correction.
Midtones 25% darker	Decreases brightness of midtones by 25%. Results in increased contrast in highlights and decreased contrast in shadows.	General correction.
Midtones 10% darker	Decreases brightness of midtones by 10%. Results in increased contrast in highlights and decreased contrast in shadows.	General correction.
Midtones 5% darker	Decreases brightness of midtones by 5%. Results in increased contrast in highlights and decreased contrast in shadows.	General correction.
Midtones 5% lighter	Increases brightness of midtones by 5%. Results in decreased contrast in highlights and increased contrast in shadows.	General correction.
Midtones 10% lighter	Increases brightness of midtones by 10%. Results in decreased contrast in highlights and increased contrast in shadows.	General correction.
Midtones 25% lighter	Increases brightness of midtones by 25%. Results in decreased contrast in highlights and increased contrast in shadows.	General correction.
Shadows 10% darker	Darkens shadows by 10%, while anchoring midtones and highlights.	General correction.
Shadows 5% darker	Darkens shadows by 5%, while anchoring midtones and highlights.	General correction.
Shadows 5% lighter	Lightens shadows by 5%, while anchoring midtones and highlights.	General correction.
Shadows 10% lighter	Lightens shadows by 10%, while anchoring midtones and highlights.	General correction.
Mask absolute shadows	Turns all tone in the 75%–100% black range to 100% black. All other tone becomes white.	Mask creation. Isolate absolute shadows from change.
Mask shadows	Uses a bell curve to shift shadows toward black and lighten midtones and highlights.	Mask creation. Isolate shadows from change.

Continues

Continued

NAME	DESCRIPTION	USE
Mask absolute midtones	Turns all tone in the 25%–75% black range to black. All other tones become white.	Mask creation. Isolate absolute midtones from change.
Mask highlights & shadows	Uses a bell curve to make highlights and shadows black, while lightening midtones to white.	Mask creation. Isolate midtones for change.
Mask midtones	Uses a bell curve to make highlights and shadows white, while darkening midtones to black.	Mask creation. Isolate midtones from change.
Mask highlights	Uses a bell curve to shift highlights toward black and lighten midtones and shadows.	Mask creation. Isolate highlights from change.
Mask absolute highlights	Turns all tone in the 0%–25% black range to black. All other tones become white.	Mask creation. Isolate absolute highlights from change.
Chrome wave (2-peak)	Uses a wave form with 4 peaks, evenly spaced.	Special effects.
Chrome wave (3-peak)	Uses a wave form with 6 peaks, evenly spaced.	Special effects.
Chrome wave (4-peak)	Uses a wave form with 8 peaks, evenly spaced.	Special effects.
Invert	Inverts an image from black to white; creates a negative.	Special effects and mask adjustment.

Let's take a look at how to apply Hidden Power Curve Presets:

1. Open an image, and determine through inspection and measurement what needs to be altered.

2. Click the uppermost layer on the image to activate it. If there is only one layer (e.g., Background), it will already be activated.

3. Open the Hidden Power Curve Presets image in the Chapter 5 folder on the Hidden Power CD. The file will open with the appearance of the Curves interface.

4. Locate the curve you would like to apply in the layer stack on the Layers palette by name.

5. Click the thumbnail for the curve next to the preset you would like to apply, and drag the curve layer to the image where you wish to apply the correction.

The curve you choose to apply should be directly related to your evaluation. For example, if you want to brighten the highlights, apply either the Highlights 10% lighter or the Highlights 5% lighter preset. You will not be able to manipulate the curve directly in a Curves interface; the change will be applied to the image immediately. You can adjust the intensity of the change using the opacity for the Curve layer to decrease the effect, or you can add other curve adjustments by dragging in more layers to intensify it. Shutting off the view for the layer temporarily shuts off the curve and allows comparison of before and after.

While this offers significantly less control than a free-form Curves interface, the curves provided with the presets are carefully constructed to cover all of what should be the most common corrections. Nearly any curves adjustment can be achieved using a combination of these. For the most part, you will want to use only those curves that are described as being for general corrections, unless you are trying to achieve a special effect. Again for more Curves interface options, see the website (`http://hiddenelements.com/downloads.html`). The clear advantage of presets is that you don't even have to set points on the curve; it is all done for you, with the ease of a drag-and-drop application.

PRESET CURVES FOR COLOR CORRECTION

You can use these same curves to make corrections for individual components in RGB images, if desired. After making an RGB separation of any image, add a curve preset by dragging it to a position just above the grayscale component layer and below the associated color layer. The curve should be grouped as a clipping layer along with the color layer. In this way, you are adjusting the tone for the component. You can apply as many curves as necessary to achieve your results, and you can adjust the opacity or mode as described.

While this is a viable method for making corrections to individual components, we will be discussing a more flexible substitute for this method in the color-correction section that involves Gradient Maps, simply because they provide the flexibility that presets do not.

I welcome requests for other curve settings that may be valuable for users that may not be included here. I will gladly make these available on the Hidden Power website—www.hidden elements.com—for no charge if they are valuable for all users. Contact me by e-mail at thebookdoc@aol.com to make your requests. Please use the subject line New Curve Preset.

(Un)Sharpening and Boosting Contrast

Sharpening filters in Photoshop Elements are sometimes thought to be a means of actually refocusing an image. The filters strengthen local contrast in an image based on the difference between adjacent tones and the filter settings you select (Amount, Radius, and Threshold). The filters are quite capable of enhancing edges that already exist, making reasonably sharp images even sharper. Regretfully, they will not take a wildly out-of-focus image and snap it back into focus or replace detail in an image that is lost by poor focus or camera or subject movement. If you have seen that on TV, it is an effect that was reverse-engineered.

The goal of sharpening is to improve the local contrast in an image, not reclaim it from being out of focus. Sharpening will be more or less effective depending on the content of the image and how sharply it was captured—the sharper the capture, the sharper it can be. You should not expect a miraculous recovery of any image if it is just a poor image—no matter what method you use, what plug-ins you buy, or how intense the settings you choose.

Sharpening tools can help the appearance of sharpness in the image, but they are actually often even more useful for enhancing local contrast in your images and making tone adjustments. By playing one tone against another in a sophisticated calculation, they can actually add some dramatic difference between objects to improve images.

Sharpening is also used as an adjustment tool to enhance images that are going to print, in an attempt to offset dot gain and ink absorption, which can change the definition in an image. In other words, although the filter can help with sharpening, it can also be used as an "intelligent" tool for enhancing image contrast and improving the appearance of images.

Although other sharpening tools are included with Elements besides Unsharp Mask (the freehand Sharpen tool, and the Sharpen, Sharpen Edges, and Sharpen More filters), I find them somewhat less valuable because they lack controls, and they do nothing that you can't do using the Unsharp Mask filter. We'll look exclusively at the Unsharp Mask as your standard sharpening and tone adjustment solution in the next section.

The Unsharp Mask Dialog Box

The Unsharp Mask dialog box (Filter → Sharpen → Unsharp Mask) has three sliders: Amount, Radius, and Threshold (see Figure 5.20).

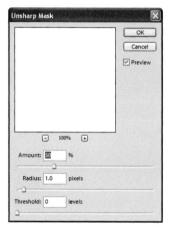

Figure 5.20

The Unsharp Mask dialog box (Filter → Sharpen → Unsharp Mask)

Amount The Amount can be between 1% and 500%. It determines how much neighboring pixels will influence one another. The setting is affected by choices for Radius and Threshold: the higher the percentage entered as Amount, the greater the sharpening.

Radius The Radius can be from 0.1 to 250 pixels. Radius works similarly to a feather radius: the farther out from the center of the radius, the weaker the effect. The distance affected in the image is actually greater than the Radius (about 2.55 times), because the radius value is plugged into a calculation rather than limiting the range to the specific radius. The intensity decreases over the range.

Threshold The Threshold option controls the way pixels work against one another based on their relative difference. The threshold notes the number of levels by which neighboring pixels must differ to be included in the calculation. For example, a low threshold (0) would allow neighboring pixels to freely influence one another if there is a difference; a high threshold (255) keeps pixels from influencing one another.

The Unsharp Mask filter dialog box offers a preview option and zoom buttons for the preview in addition to the sliders. Use the zoom to get a better look at what is going on with the details in your image. If you move the cursor over the image, the cursor will change ◼ to help you target an area of the image for the preview.

Generally, you will want to choose a setting with a low threshold, which is measured in levels. This means Photoshop Elements will look at the number of levels of difference in the surrounding pixels, and if the number of levels is greater than the threshold, it will apply sharpening based on the settings for Radius and Amount.

> The name *Unsharp Mask* comes from the traditional darkroom process in which an inverted, blurred (unsharp) duplicate of the original image was sandwiched to mask the exposure during printing. This helped target and adjust (sharpen) contrast differences.

You should usually keep the Threshold setting between 0 and 5 levels—toward the lower end of this range. In fact, you will often want to use zero tolerance. Low tolerance levels (1 or 2) can keep Photoshop Elements from sharpening what is otherwise image noise. Sharpening noise will only make the image noisier. With that in mind, a good rule of thumb is to raise the threshold more for images with more image noise. This will keep you from enhancing image noise. The only time you will set the threshold higher than 5 is when you want to limit the filter's effect to high-contrast areas of the image to play up existing contrast and separation of image elements.

Radius and Amount might be set quite differently depending on what you are trying to achieve and the ppi and content of the image. In many cases, you might apply the filter twice: once with a low radius for general sharpening and once with a higher radius for broader enhancement of image contrast. The following sections cover these techniques.

Affecting Sharpness with the Unsharp Mask Filter

Sharpening an image with the Unsharp Mask filter depends on Elements recognizing and enhancing existing edges in an image. In other words, if the image is too soft or blurry to have defined edges, the filter can't tell where the edge is, so it can't tell what to enhance. This is why the filter works best to sharpen images that are already characteristically sharp.

Although settings can vary depending on the type of image, the size of the image, and the desired result, you will normally maintain the following settings in 300 ppi, 5 × 7″ images that have average busyness and contrast:

Radius: 0.5 pixels to 3 pixels

Amount: 50% to 100%

Threshold: 0 levels

Note that these are rough guidelines, but they work for a variety of situations. If the content of the image is not busy, lacks focus, and/or is lower contrast, you can tend toward the high end of the ranges; if the image is busier, is relatively sharp, and has high contrast, you would probably tend toward the low end. If the image has more resolution, you would tend toward the higher end of these ranges; less resolution, tend toward the lower.

Figure 5.21 shows an image before and after sharpening. Before sharpening, the image appears slightly soft and perhaps a bit lacking in contrast. A single application of the Unsharp Mask filter in the midpoint for the suggested range increases the contrast and boosts the sharpness (see Figure 5.21).

A *halo effect* occurs when the Unsharp Mask is applied too strongly over areas where flatly dark portions of an image meet flatly light portions, forming a high-contrast edge (see Figure 5.22). Often, a halo effect is more apparent when the applied Radius is short— or not long enough to dissipate the edge of the sharpening effect without being obvious. Not only will the halo tend to blow out (or clip) areas of images, but the image will also distort, and the effect will become unpleasant.

You can reduce the halo effect by first undoing the Unsharp treatment and then reapplying it with either a broader Radius, a lower Amount, or a combination of these or by blending the result. Methods of blending are discussed in later parts of the book. One quick method of blending is to flatten the image (Layer → Flatten Image), duplicate the Background (Layer → Duplicate Layer), apply the Unsharp Mask filter, and reduce the Opacity of the Background copy layer in the Layers palette.

Figure 5.21

Sharpness and contrast in this image improve with an application of Unsharp Mask.

Figure 5.22

The original image and an oversharpened counterpart: Although some sharpening may be desirable, a halo effect probably will not be.

Another option for blending the sharpening effect is to use the Fade tool in the Hidden Power tool set. You can find the Fade tool in the Power_Extras category under Effects on the Styles and Effects palette. Just undo the sharpening (press Command+Z/Ctrl+Z) and double-click the Fade tool. Instructions will appear on-screen.

Staying within the guidelines helps you avoid oversharpening and creating halos in high-contrast areas of your images. Better to sharpen a little several times, sharpen a duplicated layer, or try other measures than to sharpen hastily and heavily and damage the image.

Raising Local Contrast with Sharpening

Adjusting contrast with the Unsharp Mask filter has a much different effect on an image than applying Curves or Levels, because the effect actually compares adjacent pixels rather than adjusting based on a more predictable scheme. The results of the application will be unique as they are dependent on the differences that already exist in the image. Applying Unsharp Mask to increase contrast works well with low-contrast images or images that seem to lack dynamics that increasing dynamic range (with Levels) or contrast (with Curves or Gradient Maps) doesn't fix.

When you are adjusting local contrast with the Unsharp Mask, the Radius might be much higher than suggested for sharpening (50 pixels or more) and the Amount much lower (between 10% and 50%). Again, these are just suggested ranges. The goal of these broad settings is to increase the radius beyond the distance where a halo is noticeable and to force objects in the image to play against one another.

Figure 5.23 shows a somewhat low-contrast image of a boat (a) and corrections using the Unsharp Mask filter (b and c). Although it looks okay in color, the image lacks a little pop in black-and-white. By using Unsharp Mask to raise the local contrast, the image elements have more separation from one another. Two applications of Unsharp Mask—one to build local contrast (b) and one to sharpen (c)—make quick work of what would otherwise be an arduous task in masking to separate this boat from its surroundings, creating a result based on existing image differences.

The third image (c) includes slight Levels and Curve preset adjustments. Curve presets were used to enhance the contrast that Unsharp Mask brought out, and Levels was used to adjust the final brightness. Some tone was replaced quickly by duplicating the original, moving it to the top of the stack, setting it to darken, and lowering the Opacity to 10%; this filled in areas that sharpening had forced to clip (go to 0% gray). So you see that techniques of using Levels, Curves, and Unsharp Mask work together—rather than separately—to produce enhanced results.

Figure 5.23

The original boat is a little dull (a). After raising the local contrast with the Unsharp Mask (using a broad radius and low percentage), the boat stands out better from the surroundings (b). The filter is then applied again (c), but this time to sharpen the image (using a short radius and higher percentage).

Copyright © 2005 photosphere.com

a

b

c

Manual Unsharp Masking: Calculations in Action

While calculations were briefly introduced in the last chapter, they have many creative and interesting uses, most of which are not immediately obvious. One of the first really useful layer calculations I worked with was manually creating unsharp masking effects. Unsharp masking, as mentioned earlier, was a darkroom process before it was a filter. The photographer doing the developing would sandwich a blurred film negative copy of the image with the original to burn in (increase exposure of) the image shadows. The blur would target the contrasty edges, and the result after the application would be increased shadow detail and a sharper look to the image. This Hidden Power application of unsharp is a little different but builds on the same concept.

Imitate a modified version of the darkroom sharpening effect by using the following steps:

1. Open a flattened image to which you'd like to apply an unsharp mask calculation.

2. Duplicate the Background layer.

3. Invert the Background Copy layer (press Command+I/Ctrl+I or choose Filter → Adjustments → Invert), and rename the layer **Unsharp Mask**.

4. Blur the Unsharp Mask layer using Gaussian Blur. The size of the blur will depend on the resolution of the image and the amount of detail. The more detailed the image, the less blur; the higher the resolution, the greater the blur. Start with 5 pixels for a $3 \times 5''$ image at 300 ppi; use more pixels in the radius for larger images.

5. Change the Layer mode of the Unsharp Mask layer to Overlay.

6. Reduce the opacity of the duplicate layer to 50%; adjust the opacity as desired.

The result of these steps is a sophisticated mask based on the content of your image. The Unsharp Mask layer you have created ends up working much like the sandwiched negative in the darkroom process, in pretty much the opposite way than the unsharp mask filter does, reducing image contrast and pulling details from shadows and highlights. Because the effect is nearly the opposite of the Unsharp Mask filter, the two sharpening effects can often be used together to greatly intensify image sharpness. Alternately, you can apply curves or other adjustments to increase contrast to offset the manual unsharpening.

The best results for the unsharp masking will often be had by applying the change just to the image tone (or separated Luminosity). If you apply the changes to the color as well, the change will enhance color noise. By targeting tone, color won't be altered, and you may achieve better results than applying sharpening to tone and color at the same time. A means of doing this in reverse is to add back the color from the original image, which you could do by duplicating the Unsharp Mask layer before making any changes and setting that layer to Color mode. Other adjustments, such as increasing saturation and making a tone adjustment, may be necessary to compensate for alterations that the Unsharp Mask inflicts.

The Hidden Power Sharpen tool included with the Hidden Power tools (in Power_ Adjustments) will go through the simple sharpening process described above in steps 1 to 6, allowing you to select the intensity of the blur. The tool goes several steps further, to include the option for Hue/Saturation and Levels corrections, apply the Unsharp Mask filter to tone, and group all of these corrections into a clipping mask. To use this tool, open the image on which you want to use the tool, and double-click the Hidden Power Sharpen tool. You will be able to adjust the intensity of the separate sharpening applications by using layer opacity after the tool runs you through the process. You can view Before and After images of the effect by toggling the view for the Snapshot Composite layer, and you can adjust the whole effect by lowering the Opacity for the Snapshot Composite.

This is layer masking and calculations working together to create a powerful tool and repeatable result.

Managing Image Noise

Management of noise in your images is another way to adjust tone. Having noise in an image can mean a number of things, from having many objects in an image to something more akin to random digitized information—like you might get when turning on your TV without a cable connection or antenna. The concepts in this section deal mostly with the latter and will help you to reduce or eliminate undesirable patterning, digital image noise, and texture in an image by controlling image noise.

At times you may want to edit out, reduce, or even add image noise to achieve particular results in your images. To do this, you will use Blur and Add Noise filters, often in conjunction with other image editing functions, such as layer blending, selection, masking, and perhaps a few Hidden Power tools.

The Gaussian Blur filter (Filter → Blur → Gaussian Blur) can blur images or image areas. It does this by averaging the effects of pixels over a radius, which you define by using a slider on the dialog box: the greater the radius, the more intense the blur. As a result of averaging pixels, blurring removes or lessens image noise by lowering the contrast of adjacent pixels. This averaging softens image edges, smoothing hard lines between areas of contrast, and can mitigate or obliterate image details. Essentially, this is the opposite of sharpening, which enhances existing contrast.

The Add Noise filter (Filter → Noise → Add Noise) generates image noise by randomizing color assignments for pixels. There are several choices in the Add Noise dialog box for controlling the filter. The Amount is related to Percentage, and it defines the range of variation possible in creating the noise distribution. As the Amount goes up, the application of the noise is potentially more radical. Very strong applications of noise, like blur, can obliterate detail—in this case by wiping it out with random behavior rather than averaging. Noise applications can swiftly become something of a special effect, depending on the ppi of the image. An image with a higher ppi, containing more pixels and resolved detail, will be able to withstand stronger applications of the filter.

Generation of noise is affected by the Distribution Type. A *Uniform* distribution changes the values of individual pixels by selecting a random number within the range defined by the Amount. This number can be the original value plus or minus the amount for each color component. For example, applying an Amount of 25 to a 50% gray image (128 levels) in Grayscale will result in values between 103 and 153 levels of gray for any pixel, each value generated at random. You can see this effect by creating a new image, filling with a 50% gray background, and applying the Add Noise filter.

A *Gaussian* distribution changes the values of individual pixels by selecting a random number based on a Gaussian function. The function creates a tendency to select from the center of the range, but the results can also deviate more strongly from that norm. While the quantitative effects to each pixel can extend beyond what is dictated by Amount, the total effect is the same as uniform distribution—just with greater peaks and valleys in the deviation. Because deviations can be broader, Gaussian noise can appear to be a stronger effect than the Uniform distribution with the same Amount setting, as shown in Figure 5.24. Compare this to the Uniform effect by creating another gray image of the same size, applying the Add Noise filter using the Gaussian setting, and comparing the images side by side.

The *Monochromatic* option applies the filter to only the tonal elements in the image without changing the color. For example, this would keep an RGB image that has been desaturated from generating color noise when the filter is run.

So far, neither adding noise nor blurring may sound desirable, because either could be damaging (or at least compromising) to an image. However, used in a controlled fashion, both can enhance an image and make the results look more realistic. For example, an image or image area that is damaged by JPEG compression can be restored, somewhat, by selective blurring. In this case, blurring could potentially dissipate artifacts generated by compression. In a similar way, some types of digital noise can be lessened or removed, as might be effects of film grain, halftone printing, and paper texture. Selective blurring can also help in isolating image subjects by imitating effects of focus, such as depth of field.

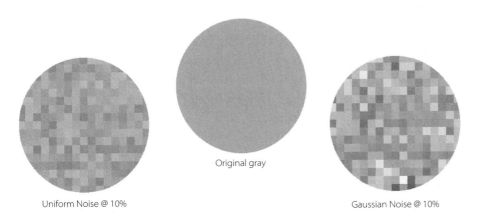

Original gray

Figure 5.24

A magnification of a 25% gray area shown with Uniform and Gaussian noise distributions of 10% The histograms show the flat application of noise in the Uniform distribution and the bell-shaped application in Gaussian distribution.

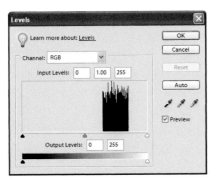

Uniform Noise @ 10%

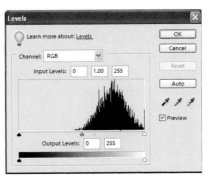

Gaussian Noise @ 10%

On the other side of the coin, most image tones that look natural in an image are not completely flat when you look at them close up. When you attempt to add new objects or elements to an image, such as by painting them in with flat tones or creating an area with blends (for example, to replace a sky), the elements can tend to look *too* perfect. The result is that the repair will look like a repair: skin tones will look more like a mannequin or caricature; a replaced sky will look like a fill or gradient. Applying noise can mimic a more natural look by randomizing and effectively dithering image information. In addition, you can use Add Noise to create texture or graininess (for example, to mimic film grain).

As strange as it may seem, sometimes when blurring won't solve a problem that you may have thought required noise reduction, applying noise can. Even more often, applying both blur and noise can do the job, adding variation while mediating extremes.

Blur and Add Noise filters can be used along with other functions to produce the best results. For example, you might make a selection of a particularly noisy area of an image to isolate it before applying a blur. After using Blur, you may need to use the Add Noise filter to fix the blurred areas so that they don't seem flat. You also might use a layer mode, mask, or other features to isolate the application so the fix is applied only to the areas where it is intended.

Both Add Noise and Blur are best when applied lightly and in combination. Figure 5.25 shows a repair in which noise was used to make an image correction blend better after a blur was applied. The skin on the subject is not bad in the original, but it could appear much more youthful with smaller pores.

A selection was made of the subject's face (mostly using the red channel as a mask—a technique we will look at more later). With the selection loaded, the area of the subject's skin was copied and pasted to its own layer to isolate it. Once isolated, the copied skin was blurred. The results smoothed the skin, but left it too flat. Noise was added, using Uniform distribution with the Monochromatic check box selected. This returned some of the texture to the skin without leaving it looking too flat and fake. The appearance of the pores was softened first, using the Blur filter to remove noise. Next, the Add Noise filter was used to gently replace some of what was lost in the texture. The result is much smoother skin and a somewhat more youthful smile.

Several techniques, including erasing information on the new layer or masking, could have been used to bring back the details that were getting covered. However, Blend Mask, a Hidden Power tool, was applied to the layer to enable the character of wrinkles to blend through based on tone. Again, combinations of tool applications and functions generally work best in achieving goals in an image because no one tool can do it all. You'll see more of Blend Mask in the following section. We'll also talk more about noise reduction in Chapter 6 in a section called "Quelling Color Noise."

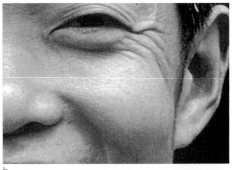

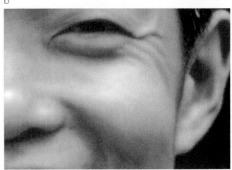

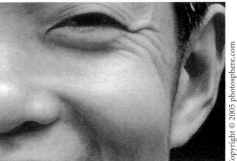

Masking with Image Tone

Masks are very much like selections, in that they can help you isolate image areas and work on them without changing other parts of the image. Masks can be based on tone (as we will look at in this section), color, saturation, manual selection, or other calculated results. Masking is quite flexible. The greatest advantage of masking is that it is not permanent; masking allows you to temporarily hide parts of specific layers in the image rather than erasing or otherwise permanently altering the layers. If you want, you can adjust the masking to add and subtract layer content at will by adjusting the layer masks to reveal or hide more of the layer.

Figure 5.25

Original image(a) is shown closeup (b). Blur is added (c), and then noise for texture (d).

One frustration with using Photoshop Elements is that it natively uses masks only in conjunction with adjustment layers, and it does not freely allow you to mask any layer in an image. It also doesn't allow you to work fluidly with alpha channels, which is where Photoshop can store masks and selections. Although you can save a selection in Elements 4, you still can't attach a mask to any old layer—that is, you can't unless you have Hidden Power.

The Hidden Power tool set can help by offering several tools for working with masks. We'll explore native possibilities and the Hidden Power enhancements for masking in the next few sections.

Native Layer Masking

Layer masks are available natively when you are using Adjustment layers (such as Levels or Gradient Maps, found on the Layer → New Adjustment Layer submenu). A layer mask is a

mask attached to a specific layer that applies to that layer only. All this means is that the content of that layer will be targeted at the areas that remain unmasked. Masks created with adjustment layers reveal all the content of the layer by default. However, you can control layer masking of adjustment layers by making a selection before you create the layer. Instead of trying to explain this technique, it is best shown in an example.

Figure 5.26

The layer mask for the adjustment layer is represented in the Layers palette by the thumbnail to the right of the layer thumbnail. In this case there is nothing masked, so the thumbnail is white.

1. Open a new image at 500 pixels × 500 pixels, 72 ppi, RGB, and use a white background.

2. Change the foreground color to red (R: 255, G: 0, B: 0).

3. Fill the Background layer with red. Use the Paint Bucket tool (press K).

4. Create a new Hue/Saturation Adjustment layer (Layer → New Adjustment Layer → Hue/Saturation).

5. Shift the Hue slider to −120 and choose OK. This should turn the image blue. The Layer palette should look like Figure 5.26.

6. Choose the brush tool, and make the foreground color black (press D to set default colors, and then press X to exchange the foreground and background swatches). The foreground color should be black. Change the brush to 100 pixels in diameter using the Options bar.

7. Paint in an *M* shape (for "mask") over your image. As you paint, the black will be applied to the layer mask for the adjustment layer, and you will reveal red from the layer below. See the thumbnail change in Figure 5.27.

If you want, you can adjust the Hue/Saturation sliders (double-click the Hue/Saturation layer icon to open the Hue/Saturation palette) to see how the image is affected. The black

Figure 5.27

The mask for the adjustment layer will now have a black M. The image will show a red M surrounded by blue. Black masks out the effect of the layer.

portion of the mask will block the corresponding portion of the layer with which it is associated.

While masking is a neat trick, it actually has many interesting applications. Open any image, and then double-click the Highlight Mask tool from the Power_Masking category of the Hidden Power tools. This will make a selection of the shadow areas in the image. Now make a Levels adjustment layer

(Layer → New Adjustment Layer → Levels). The selection will be automatically transferred to the mask for the layer, and corrections you make with the Levels sliders will apply to the shadows in the image. If you wanted to darken the highlights in the current image, now is your chance! Just move that middle slider to the right. That's just one simple example of how masking can help you accurately target corrections.

As far as what you can mask, you are really limited only by your imagination. As long as you can envision the result and create a selection to target an area, you can convert it into a layer mask. You might, for example, mask a layer with a separation component, or a specific area of one of the components by altering the component with curves presets or calculations. We'll look more specifically at this type of targeting in creating the CMYK separation in Chapter 10.

Adding Layer Masks to Any Layer with Hidden Power

It is nice that Adobe provides layer masking for the adjustment layers, but you may find it comes in handy to apply masking directly to other layers as well. Elements 4 doesn't allow you to do this directly with the standard Elements tools, but Hidden Power provides more than one solution. In the Power_Masking category of the Hidden Power tools, you will find the Layer Mask tool and the Selection to Layer Mask tool. The Layer Mask tool allows you to apply a blank layer mask to any layer in your image. Just choose the layer where you want to apply the mask, and double-click the Hidden Power tool. If you have a selection that you want to apply as a layer mask, use the Selection to Layer Mask Hidden Power tool rather than Layer Mask. The Selection to Layer Mask tool will take care of converting the selection to mask content for you.

One thing to note about the layer masks applied via the Hidden Power Layer Mask tool is that selections will not be converted into masks as a matter of course as they are with adjustment layers. You will have to manually apply selections, adjust mask content with other tools (such as painting in black or white on the mask to hide or reveal layer content), or use the Selection to Layer Mask tool. To apply a selection as a mask manually, just make your selection, invert it, create the layer mask, and fill with black. That is what the Selection to Layer Mask tool does for you.

Hidden Power Blend Mask

The Blend Mask Hidden Power tool is a unique solution to masking based on layer clipping and layer transparency. Essentially, it does the same thing as a layer mask, but does it in a different way. It was originally included in the Hidden Power tools as a workaround to layer masks in earlier versions of the program (when it seemed likely Adobe would eliminate masking entirely). It is included here to provide another masking technique that can be used in conjunction with or instead of layer masks.

Blend Mask converts a layer into semitransparent pixels based on the brightness of each pixel. The darker the pixel, the more opaque the result will be when converted to a mask. These Blend Mask layers can then be grouped with other image content to be used as high-tech cookie cutters to isolate the masked area in a separate layer. This allows you to make changes either to the masked area or to all other areas of the image separately.

Figure 5.28 shows an image that could benefit from correction in just the shadow area. To mask just the shadow, you can use the Blend Mask Hidden Power tools. Several power tools converge in this exercise to create your image editing advantage.

1. Open the sample image (`horsehead.psd`) from the CD.

2. Create a Blend Mask layer that includes the tone on which you want to base the mask. In this case, we will use a curve preset adjustment to isolate shadows. Double-click the Luminosity Only tool in the Power_Separations to separate out the luminosity for the image. Change the Luminosity layer mode to Normal. Open the `Hidden Power Curve Presets` file, drag the Mask Shadows layer to the Horsehead image, merge the Mask Shadows layer with the Luminosity layer, and then change the layer name to **Blend Mask**. The image should look like that shown in Figure 5.29.

> The content of the layer created in step 2 can be anything, from a shape-based fill to an image component or a calculated result/black-and-white conversion. You want to shift the area you are interested in masking toward white and darken or even make black the rest of the image. Remember that this is a mask—not a permanent adjustment to the image.

3. Double-click the Blend Mask tool in the Power_Masking category of Effects. This will convert the layer created in step 2 to a transparency mask and make a clipping layer from that with a copy of the original image. Nothing on-screen will change, but the highlights will be masked off from the shadows. See Figure 5.30.

Figure 5.28

This image of a giant bronze horse was taken with the sun as a backlight, without compensation, leaving the detail of the shadow flat and dark.

Figure 5.29

After step 2, the image should look like the original except in black-and-white with the contrast greatly enhanced, as shown here. This is a template for the shadow mask. Alternatively, you could mask the highlights for a very similar (but opposite) effect.

If you toggle the visibility for the Background layer at this point, the shadows will show without the shadow portions of the image. You can adjust the color or tone in the shadow area by applying changes—either grouped layer adjustments or changes directly to the layer content—to the Mask Content layer. Commit the changes by flattening the image.

To quickly create masks that are based on shadows, you can use the Transparent Grayscale Hidden Power tool. Some users may find this more straightforward because you are creating the transparency mask first. Just double-click Transparent Grayscale in the Power_Masking tools, and a new layer will be created as a transparent mapping based on the image grayscale. To base the mask on highlights, use the Inverted Transparent Grayscale tool. Each of these tools will run through the process and create a Transparent Grayscale layer (like the Mask layer) and the Mask Content layer. The only difference with Blend Mask is the ability to further define what component/grayscale you want to use with the mask.

Figure 5.30

When steps 1 to 3 are complete, your Layers palette should have just three layers (as shown) and the image should look like the original. Make changes to the Mask Content layer to adjust the isolated area of the image.

If you tried to make a transparency mask on your own in Elements without Hidden Power tools, you would indeed have a problem. That is because the Hidden Power tools make use of conditional blending (Blend If in Photoshop), which is a feature that is not accessible in the Elements interface. I have included several tools in the Power_Masking category that allow you to control layer visibility based on conditional blending. These are listed in Table 5.2. Some will be discussed and used later in the book. All can be found in the Power_Masking category of Effects.

NAME	DESCRIPTION	USE
Clear White	Makes pixels that are absolute white (0% black) transparent.	View conditional transparency.
Clear Black	Makes pixels that are absolute black (100% black) transparent.	View conditional transparency.
Clear Grayscale	Makes pixels in a layer transparent based on brightness. White pixels (0% black) become transparent, and black pixels (100% black) remain opaque. 50% gray (50% black) become 50% opaque.	View conditional transparency.
Drop Black	Makes absolute black pixels transparent and pixels between 87% and 99% black increasingly opaque.	View conditional transparency.
Commit Transparency	Changes the content of the layer so that transparency is applied to the pixels.	Commit any conditional transparency.
Remove Transparency	Changes layer properties to remove conditional blending that has not already been applied.	Revert transparency of a layer where the Clear White, Clear Black, Clear Grayscale, or Drop Black tools have been used.

While the content of a conditional blend will become transparent, you can still apply changes to the content of the layer. When you apply changes, all of the content of the layer will change, even if you can't see it, and transparency will change accordingly. Try this quick experiment:

1. Create a new image 400 pixels × 400 pixels, RGB color mode with a white background.

2. Create a new layer and fill it with a black-to-white gradient using the Gradient tool.

3. Apply the Clear Black tool to the gradient layer. The absolute black area of the gradient will become white, while the content of a conditional blend will become transparent, you can still apply changes to the content of the layer. When you apply changes, all of the content of the layer will change, even if you can't see it, and transparency will change accordingly. Try this quick experiment.

4. Create a Levels Adjustment layer (Layer → New Adjustment Layer → Levels). When the New Layer dialog appears, check the Group With Previous Layer button before clicking OK.

5. Move the middle, gray Input Levels slider on the Levels dialog to the right while watching the image. An increasing amount of the black area should become white as you move the slider.

If you move the slider back to the left, the area that became white should gradually become black again. Just because you can't see it doesn't mean it's gone and isn't affected—effectively, it is masked. When you get used to using conditional blending, it ends up functioning just like another mask, but a fluid one that will change according to changes in content.

This is just a little trick and by far not what you will generally do with masking. We'll take a quick look at a tone-based masking effect for soft focus in the next section.

Soft Focus Effects Using Masking

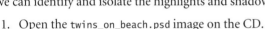

An interesting effect that is easily achieved using masking in more than one way is soft focus. Soft focus effects usually attribute a sort of glamour glow to an image, reducing the appearance of wrinkles and flaws in portraits and imparting a dreamy quality. Soft Focus is traditionally done during the capture, using a soft focus filter. Soft focus filters diffuse light. The more light, or the brighter an image area, the more the light becomes diffused and glows, softening edges; the less light, the darker and sharper the image area. Because we can identify and isolate the highlights and shadows, we can mimic the effect.

1. Open the twins_on_beach.psd image on the CD.

2. Isolate the highlights in the image using the Shadow Mask tool in the Power_Masking category of Effects.

3. Copy and paste to place the highlights on their own layer, and name the layer **Glow**. This effectively masks the highlights into their own layer.

4. Adjust the highlights to be brighter by opening the Levels (press Command+L/Ctrl+L; if you use an adjustment layer, group it with the Glow layer), and shift the black Output Levels slider to the right. See Figure 5.31.

5. Apply a Gaussian Blur to the Glow layer using a radius of 30 pixels. You will immediately see the glow effect.

6. Create a new layer at the top of the stack, and name it **Sharpen**. Merge all to the Sharpen layer (press Shift+Command+ Option+E / Shift+Ctrl+Alt+E).

7. Apply the Shadow Mask tool to the Sharpen layer. This masks the shadows from change.

8. Create a layer mask for the Sharpen layer using the Layer Mask tool.

9. Fill the layer mask for the Sharpen layer with black. This will fill the highlight area with black and mask the highlights in the layer.

10. Apply a Levels correction to the mask to enhance the tonal range. See Figure 5.32.

11. Apply the Unsharp Mask filter to the content of the Sharpen layer. Be sure you are

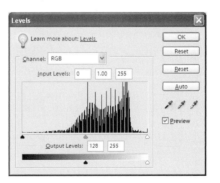

Figure 5.31

This Levels adjustment will shorten the range of tones in the Glow layer so that everything is 50% gray or lighter.

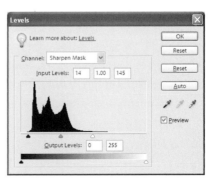

Figure 5.32

This Levels adjustment to the mask will make sure that darker portions of the image in the masked layer appear in the image.

applying the sharpening to the content of the layer and not the mask by clicking the content thumbnail in the Layers palette to activate it. Use an Amount of 140% and a Radius of 2, while leaving Threshold at 0.

When you are all done, the layers should look like they do in Figure 5.33. Compare before and after by toggling the views for the Glow and Sharpen layer simultaneously. You will see a marked increase in the softness of the image, without losing a lot of detail. This is because the masking dissipates the highlights, and masks sharpening to target the shadows.

You can do many variations of this effect, including simply changing the Glow layer to Screen mode, which leaves a more contrasty result. You can add and adjust in many different ways, using different types of masks, but the key to this effect is that the highlights get blurred or dispersed while the shadow detail remains intact to hold the shape of objects in the image.

Shaping Image Elements with Light and Shadow

As you just saw in the previous section, light and shadow affect the shape of objects and how they appear relative to one another. You can use shading and highlighting to provide separation between objects, for example, by adding a slight drop shadow or glow behind an object to create separation. It is light and shadow that affect depth and texture in an image and light that gives shape and color to everything in your image.

The following provides a good, simple example of how light and shadow can create shape. The following steps will turn a flat gray square into a shaped button that appears to be elevated from the background:

1. Create a new grayscale image (File → New) that is 500 × 500 pixels.

2. Make a marquee by using the Fixed Size option for the Marquee tool on the options bar. Set the size to 300 × 300 pixels and click the tool at 100,100 (x,y). If you click exactly on that point (use the rulers; if the rulers are set to inches, change the preferences to pixels), the selection will be centered exactly on the image. In this case, it doesn't matter if you are off by a few pixels.

3. Create a new layer named **Button**, and fill the selection made in the previous step with 50% gray.

4. Select the Background layer. Create a new layer named **Drop Shadow**, and set the mode to Multiply. Creating the new layer just above the Background in the layer stack will keep the drop shadow behind/below the button.

5. Feather the current selection 20 pixels, and fill the selection with black. Change the layer Opacity to 75%.

6. Deselect by pressing Command+D/Ctrl+D.

7. Offset the shadow layer down 20 pixels and right 20 pixels. To do this, choose the Move tool, hold down the Shift key, and press the Right arrow and Down arrow keys on your keyboard two times each.

8. Activate the Button layer by clicking it in the Layers palette.

9. Create a new layer, and name it **Highlight**. Check the Group With Previous check box, set the layer mode to Screen, and change the Opacity to 50%.

10. Reload the previous selection by pressing Shift+Command+D / Shift+Ctrl+D. Invert the selection (Shift+Command+I / Shift+Ctrl+I), and fill it with white.

11. Create a new layer, and name it **Shadow**. Check the Group With Previous check box, set the layer mode to Multiply, fill the layer with black, and change the Opacity to 50%.

12. Choose Select → Deselect.

13. Activate the Highlight layer, choose the Move tool, and offset the layer down 20 pixels and right 20 pixels. To do this, hold down the Shift key and press the Right arrow and Down arrow keys two times each.

14. Activate the Shadow layer, and offset it up 20 pixels and left 20 pixels. To do this, hold down the Shift key, and press the Left arrow and Up arrow keys two times each.

This leaves you with a square button that appears to be slightly raised and separate from the background. Figure 5.34 shows the results: the flat square is transformed into a shaped button with apparent contour. The drop shadow between the button and the background creates distance between those objects; the Highlight and Shadow layers create object shape by mimicking how a raised button might look if a light were coming from the upper-left corner of the image. The more extreme the offset effects, the greater the depth or distance appears.

Simple highlight and shadow creation of this sort happens when using layer effects. The way you choose to handle shadows and highlights controls the shape of the object, but the final image has to show some consistency with the scene to portray the desired result and the direction of the light. All this is to say you can create some cool effects with light and shadow, but you can't just drop a shadow into an image willy-nilly and have it look correct. You have to take existing lighting into account and adjust for angle and direction. You also have to adjust the landscape to make the shadow fall correctly. This attention to the direction of light becomes imperative when you want to composite objects from different images.

Figure 5.34

A flat area of flat tone can be both raised from the background and shaped with simple application for highlights and shadows.

Other uses for adjusting highlights and shadows are dodging and burning effects where you brighten or darken areas of an image to add or reduce emphasis, create framing, etc. Try the following:

1. Open Twins_on_beach2.psd.

2. Create a new layer at the top of the layer stack and name it **Vignette**.

3. Select All (press Command+A/Ctrl+A).

4. Modify the selection, and make it a Border (Select → Modify → Border). Use a Radius of 150 pixels.

5. Fill the resulting selection with black.

6. Deselect (Command+D/Ctrl+D) and apply a Gaussian Blur using a Radius of 100.

7. Reduce the Opacity for the Vignette layer to 15%.

While the character of the image may not seem to change a lot, toggle the view for the Vignette layer to compare before and after images. Similar framing vignettes have often been used in the darkroom to make subtle frames around images. In this case, it may also imitate vignetting of the image frame. These are the types of subtle changes and corrections you may want to make in your images to keep the viewers' focus on the subject.

There are many, many more ways to use masking, selection, and transparency to effect change in image tone, and we will discover some of those as we move through the remaining exercises. At this point, it is time to look at adjustments to color.

Part III
Serious Image Correction

The term *color correction* suggests that there is a correct color in your images to shoot for in the first place. You may consider "correct" to be what you saw with your eyes when capturing an image, but what you see isn't a measure that you can duplicate. However, what looks best won't necessarily match the original color, and in some cases matching color will not be what you'll want to do at all. In a similar way you may want to take control of your image composition and alter it to make improvements.. In this part of the book you'll look at ways to apply color correction for both technical and artistic success by using techniques that expand on those you learned in earlier chapters. We'll also take a look at making purposeful changes to composition. Finally, we'll wrap up this part by taking a good look at using the image correction checklist to process an image.

Chapter 6

Color and Tone Enhancement

If you look at RGB components as the basis for image color, color is just a slightly more complex version of black-and-white. The difference ends up being that three grayscale images are sandwiched together to make a color representation. It is interesting to note that if you consider the three black-and-white RGB components of your color image separately, and make basic correction to the tones, correction for color follows.

This chapter looks at all manner of color-specific correction that you will do in Elements. Most of the tools used in working with tone from manipulations and techniques in earlier chapters can be applied to the RGB components of a color image in order to adjust image color. Correcting color using the techniques learned for correcting tone can solve many color saturation and brightness problems and balance color to compensate for color shifts. In this chapter, we'll look at the techniques for performing color correction and color adjustment, and we'll learn why the techniques work.

Minor Cleanup for Color Images

Levels Correction for Color

Gradient Map Corrections for Accurate Color

Using Hue/Saturation for Color Adjustment

Color Masking with Hue/Saturation

Adjusting Color Balance

Painting in Changes: History Brush Application

Minor Cleanup for Color Images

The place to start in doing minor cleanup of your color image is to get rid of what absolutely should not be in the image. Cleanup for color images is similar to the techniques already described for cleaning tone and black-and-white images. For example, you will still use the Clone Stamp tool to clear out spots and minor debris by stamping over them with good replacements. But, because you are trying to match red, green, and blue tones all at the same time, you have to be a little more careful in selecting the source for replacement color so that it matches color as well as tone. Making the corrections in a new layer can help you make better corrections by enabling you to fine-tune any changes. The Use All Layers option for the Clone Stamp tool should remain turned on. You may want to experiment with other modes for the Clone Stamp tool, such as using Color or Luminosity instead of Normal mode to adjust color or tone separately.

Other options for cleanup can present themselves in separated components, in some instances more readily than on a color composite. Looking at RGB tones or Luminosity and Color separations may reveal color-specific noise or other damage (such as stains on scanned prints). All you have to do is split the components by using Hidden Power tools, examine the separations individually to see whether there is any damage to specific components, and then repair that damage as black-and-white.

To view the grayscale for a specific component in a separation, make the separation and then turn off the visibility for the other components and the color fill associated with the component, if any (see Figure 6.1).

Figure 6.1

To view the blue channel, turn off the visibility for the red and green channels as well as the blue color fill.

The Prokudin-Gorskii images (see `kush-beggi_sep_rgb.psd`) are a great example of how correcting in separated tones may be useful. The glass plates in Gorskii's images have unique information because they were taken as distinct captures through different lenses to occupy distinct areas of the film. Because they are distinct captures, each color plate has unique damage from dust and scratches, as the red plate shows in Figure 6.2. In that case (certainly a rare one), it is better and easier to correct much of the damage in the separated tones as RGB because the damage will stand out more clearly than it will in the full-color preview.

> Splitting out the channels is often useful for removing color-related problems, such as stains on scanned prints or colored blemishes. We'll see additional advantages when looking at more-intensive color correction later in this chapter.

Once you have stamped out damage in the components—and as long as you have made each correction carefully, so it is undetectable in each of the individual tones—the result should appear undetectable in the composite image as well. When the changes are complete, you can merge the separated components back to a single layer by flattening the image before moving on to other corrections. Although you can switch back and forth between working with the separations and the composite without harming the image, you should avoid making a lot of separation changes at this point because it wastes time. This stage of cleanup should usually be simple and quick before getting on to the main course of correcting color.

Figure 6.2

Defects in the components show up prominently in the original scan of the Gorskii image.

Before correction

After correction

Quelling Color Noise

Digital noise can be a problem in images and is something else that you might want to clean up at this point, before moving on to other corrections.

Figure 6.3 shows a close-up of an image that was taken in conditions that were not the best. JPEG compression settings were not high, but they were high enough to accentuate the color noise that accumulated in a low-light exposure. Although the image isn't bad, it could be much better. The separation into RGB and luminosity (use the RGBL Components Only tool) for this image shows noisy red, green, and blue components but a much smoother-looking luminosity. The smooth luminosity (see Figure 6.4) clearly indicates that you have mostly color noise on your hands. You can see the original image as vince.psd on the CD, as well as before and after results in vince_corrections.psd.

> Although you might want to clean up or improve such obvious problems as color noise, you might instead wait to do it after making Levels correction (in the following section). Doing too much before making basic corrections can potentially cause even greater problems later.

There are many more things that you can do in addition to the few steps we will present here for correcting the color noise. For example, you might mask skin tone areas to apply smoothing to some of the tone or sharpen the image. But that type of complex correction is a good example of one that might be better accomplished later, after initial color correction

Figure 6.3

The color noise in the vince.psd image is most obvious in this close-up of the blue channel.

Figure 6.4

Looking at the luminosity, you can see that the tone is relatively smooth. Smooth tone and rough RGB channels are telling of color noise.

with Levels. You will be able to better judge when to flip-flop your basic correction steps as you gain additional experience with correction.

1. Open vince.psd from the CD.

2. Split the luminosity and color components by double-clicking the Luminosity and Color Hidden Power tool in the Power_Separations category of Effects.

3. Activate the Color layer by clicking it in the Layers palette.

4. Apply a Gaussian Blur (Filter → Blur → Gaussian Blur). For this image, try about a 10-pixel radius for the blur.

These few steps have a dramatic impact on the RGB components of the test image. These steps blur the color information in the image while keeping the tone intact. If you separate the RGB components for this image again after completing the steps (just flatten the image and use the RGB Components Only tool), you'll see a marked change in the image. Figure 6.5 shows the result of the content of the Blue component after flattening the image and re-separating into RGB.

Because the tone holds the detail in place, the color can be smoothed out—often dramatically—without softening the appearance of the image. When you are finished, flatten the image and save it with a different name before continuing any other corrections. This will keep you from saving over the original if it turns out that you want to go back and see what happens if you don't correct the noise first.

You can use other filters to reduce the noise after the color is separated. You may want to experiment with the advantages of applying the Median filter, Dust and Scratches, or the Reduce Noise filter to the Color layer. Each will handle the color adjustment in a somewhat different fashion.

There is a Hidden Power tool that will perform the noise-reduction steps for you while enabling you to choose how much Gaussian Blur or Median filter to apply. Just click Reduce Color Noise under the Power_Adjustments category in Effects. This tool will automatically flatten and commit the changes in the image so that you will be ready for additional corrections. To use only Gaussian Blur or only Median Filter, use the dedicated Color Noise Reduction Blur or Color Noise Reduction Median tool.

Figure 6.5

You'll see a great improvement in the color channels if you flatten the image again and separate the RGB. Note the dramatic change in the blue channel. Surprisingly, you lose almost nothing in sharpness or detail.

Levels Correction for Color

Object color is a result of light. Brightness of 100% indicates a 100 percent intensity of red, green, and blue light components. Brightness of 0% indicates a 0 percent intensity of red, green, and blue. If the color in a scene runs from white to black (a full dynamic range), all of the components must have a full range as well. Levels corrections for each component of RGB will optimize the dynamic range of your image and simultaneously balance your images for the quality of color lighting during capture.

If you followed the discussion of correcting tonality with Levels in Chapter 5, making the leap to correcting color with Levels is a small step. It brings together the concept of components and separations with the corrective steps for Levels. In making the Levels correction for color images, you want to apply Levels corrections to the separate red, green, and blue components, treating each component as you would a black-and-white image. This extends the range of each color component to render greater image dynamics and more balanced color.

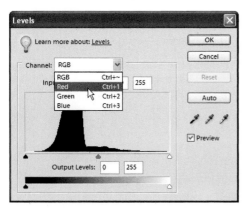

Figure 6.6

Selecting a channel from the drop-down list in the Levels dialog box reveals the histogram specific to that channel and confines the effects of your adjustments to that component without making separations.

The Levels dialog box makes it easy to apply corrections to the separate components and saves you the step of separating the colors into tone. All you have to do is open the Levels dialog box and separately correct the red, green, and blue components—as selected from the Channel drop-down list (see Figure 6.6). Select the components one at a time from the Channel drop-down list, make the correction according to the histogram just like you would for black-and-white, and then choose the next channel. After adjusting each component, click OK to accept the changes. Don't bother correcting the RGB composite; this will be taken care of by properly completing the Levels correction for each of the components.

To apply Levels corrections to color images, follow these steps:

1. Open the image you want to correct.

   In most cases you will complete minor cleanup before advancing to other corrections.

2. Choose Enhance → Adjust Lighting → Levels. This opens the Levels dialog box.

3. Select Red from the Channel drop-down list. This reveals the histogram for the red component.

4. Make a Levels correction for the component by using the guidelines provided in Chapter 5 for making grayscale corrections with Levels for tone. Do this correction by evaluating the histogram.

5. Repeat steps 4 and 5 for the green and blue components. Do this by selecting Green and then Blue from the Channel drop-down list, instead of Red.

6. Accept the changes in the Levels dialog by clicking OK. This closes the dialog box.

When the correction is complete, the image should show increased dynamic range, stronger saturation, and a better likeness to realistic color (color balance)—as long as there was something to correct. Again, this correction may not get you entirely where you want to be, but it will often do quite a lot to improve an image that needs a little help. Even so, you'll probably have additional corrections to make.

When making a Levels correction for color, you must remember the following:

- Making a correction might remove a desired color shift.

- To retain existing color characteristics, make similar adjustments to histogram tails in the red, green, and blue components.

At times, this type of Levels correction doesn't improve an image. Examples include extreme lighting conditions or intentional/expected shifts—such as in a sunset or when an effect was achieved by color filtering (to purposely shift color in the image at the time it was taken).

If you apply a levels correction to the boat.psd from the CD, adjustments for the Levels would probably look something like the sets of screens shown in Figure 6.7. The Levels correction in RGB will also improve the result when making conversions from color to black-and-white: increasing the dynamic range for color extends the dynamic range for the image, and the extended dynamic range enhances the image contrast. Make the corrections to the image yourself using the boat.psd file included on the CD, and compare the results before and after by undoing (Command+Z/Ctrl+Z) and redoing (Command+Y/Ctrl+Y) the Levels change.

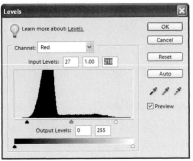
Red Component

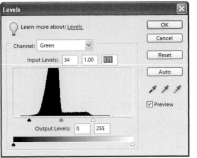
Green Component

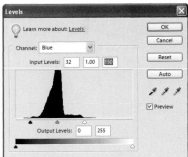
Blue Component

Figure 6.7

The corrections shown here remove the entire tail. Color balance results from using a consistent approach to correcting image components.

If you make a Levels correction by using the guidelines for correcting tone in Chapter 5, the color in this image will spring to life on your screen, from a hazy image with a yellowish tint to something more striking and blue. All you have done is redistribute the black-and-white tones in the red, green, and blue components to achieve better dynamic range and color balance. Because light in the most dynamic image will run from white to black, your correction in Levels is just enabling the image to look its most dynamic. In the corrections for Figure 6.7, the rules for the adjustment are pretty clear-cut: because the image doesn't have a decided skew, and there is a reasonable similarity in the quality of the histograms for red, green, and blue, the common rules hold.

In Figure 6.8, however, the histograms for the RGB channels differ from one another dramatically and require some unusual treatment. The image, a close-up of a rose, is decidedly skewed toward reds. If you apply the Levels as just a straight cut of the histogram tails, some of the detail in the highlights blows out—or becomes too extreme. You can achieve a better result by clipping only half of the very long tails in the Green and Blue components and doing an additional adjustment to the midtones in RGB. The first part of the adjustment makes the shadows in the image seem pale, but adding a shift in the midtones compensates—pushing more image information toward the shadows. Once that's accomplished, the tone of the image seems more natural and balanced. See the result of these Levels applications in the color section. Use the image `rose.psd` on the CD to work out the results for yourself.

Levels adjustments can be used to manipulate tones in your images, as well as the balance of color and brightness. Coupled with other functions in Elements, Levels can be a powerful tool for correction and change. For example, if you mask areas of the image or components, you can target Levels redistributions to those areas and create specific changes, such as lightening midtones while leaving highlights and shadows unchanged. If you want to correct for accurate color, you can use Gradient Maps, which we'll look at in the next section.

Gradient Map Corrections for Accurate Color

Color casts in an image can result in flatness or unnatural color. A cast might be the result of poor image processing, varied lighting conditions (photos taken under fluorescent bulbs, for example), aging of the original medium (such as paper yellowing), or any number of other factors. Basic color correction with Levels often takes care of a lot of these problems. However, color casts and shifts between the lightest and darkest parts of an image are often a little more complex than looking at a histogram or doing a linear color correction in Levels. It is difficult to look at an image and envision how a correction should appear to fix problems in the image. While it may be easy to determine what looks wrong, correcting it can remain a puzzle.

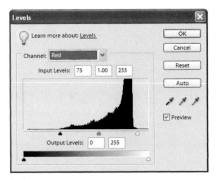

Red Component

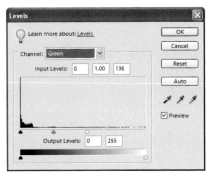

Green Component

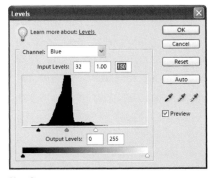

Blue Component

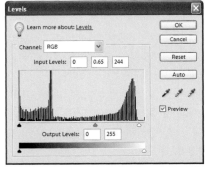

Composite RGB

Figure 6.8

Visual evaluation of the results suggests an additional change in the composite level.

Before

After

For example, say you are looking at an image, and the color of the subject's skin just looks wrong. If the skin tone looks wrong, the image will look wrong. If there were a reference that you could use to correct skin tone perfectly, everything else in the image would also fall in line. However, there is no absolute reference for skin tone. There are ways to estimate and approximate, but if approximations were good, you could just put your trust in the image you have on-screen and correct completely by eye. The difference in skin tones is vast. Not only does skin tone have many colors and shades in general, but the same person can have different skin tones at different times (for example, when the person has a tan or when looking pale or flushed). This being the case, there is no value that can be used as an accurate reference for skin tone, no matter what chart you look at.

The best references to use in your image when you are considering correcting color are grays. Grays can act as references because they are easy to measure: any gray has even amounts of red, green, and blue. When you measure with the Eyedropper, the R, G, and B values displayed in the Info palette should all be the same—or very nearly so.

In a perfect world, you could find areas of your image that would be grays of exactly 25 percent (RGB: 64, 64, 64), 50 percent (RGB: 128, 128, 128), and 75 percent (RGB: 192, 192, 192) black when corrected. You could then take measurements from these areas of your digital image to use as references for correction. All you'd have to do is set accurate white and black points (which you will usually do with a Levels correction) and then correct the areas that should be gray by manipulating them. As a result, your images would color-balance nicely. However, it usually isn't too easy to find gray references unless you place them in your image. Although you can do this using a reference card (a gray card, usually 18 percent gray, but anything of a standard flat tone will work), it is not something that everyone will take the time to do.

In many cases, grays that already exist in the image can be used as reasonable substitutes for a reference card. If you look closely, you may find something that should be a flat shade of gray, such as a steel flagpole, chrome on a car, cement, asphalt—anything that should be flat gray can be useful for color evaluation. White and black objects (such as paper or car tires) can work, too, as long as they are not drastically over- or underexposed, respectively. While objects that you expect to be gray can vary in color to some degree (such as the mossy side of a tree), they will be easier to judge and correct for than skin tones. Your choice in the selection of a gray reference is important to the outcome of your color correction. For example, if you choose a gray that in reality is supposed to be slightly green and you don't allow for that in the correction, your final corrections will end up somewhat warm as a result. Again, visual inspection must work hand in hand with the numbers to achieve the best result. Once you determine a target gray in your image, Gradient Maps can help you easily manipulate the targeted areas. All you have to do is measure the RGB values of the gray object and then adjust the mapping to flatten the color response. Flattening the color response can be done by shifting the markers to correct the sample toward gray while ignoring everything else in the image. When the changes are complete, the image color will be fixed as a by-product of normalizing the grays.

First, we will look at single sample manipulation and then at multiple point samples.

Single Sample Gradient Map Adjustment

Basing a Gradient Map adjustment to balance grays on a single sample is similar to what happens when you use the Gray Point tool ✐ with the Levels dialog to balance an image. The idea is that you take a sample from what should be a gray image area and then make a mapping adjustment to balance the color. To balance the color, you will adjust the tone of each of the RGB color components, based on your measurement.

To determine the values for a gray object to use in correcting an image, do the following:

Figure 6.9

Sample each of the gray swatches, and note the B value from HSB.

1. Examine the image to locate an object that should be gray.

2. Be sure the Info palette is visible and that one of the sample types is set to HSB Color (HSB).

3. Select the Eyedropper from the toolbox. Select a sample option from the Sample Size drop-down list on the Options bar. Choose either 3 By 3 Average or 5 By 5 Average, depending on the size and resolution of the image. Larger images with more resolution can usually stand broader sample areas.

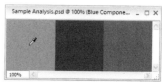

4. Point the tip of the Eyedropper at the gray reference area in the image, and click to sample the color.

5. Double-click the Sample Analysis tool in the Power_Extras category of Effects. This will create a new image from the color sample separate from the RGB and leave a swatch of each of the component layers in RGB order.

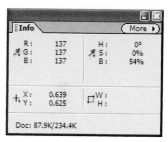

6. Sample each of the tones in the Sample Analysis image, and note the B value of each (see Figure 6.9). Write them down, and average them. Close the Sample Analysis image without saving it.

7. Make an RGB separation of the original image (using RGB Separation in the Power_Separations category of Effects).

At this point, you are ready to make adjustments to the Red, Green, and Blue layers with Gradient Maps using the measurements taken in step 6. The corrections will be easier to understand using a concrete example. Say there is a flagpole in your image, and you will be using it to make your color correction. You sample the pole and run the Sample Analysis tool. You measure the B values of the three swatches and determine the values to be 54 for red, 26 for green, and 36 for blue. To get the gray to be flat (no color) in that zone, you'll want to make the B values for each of the components equal. Because you want the gray to be flat, you can average the B values to find a target (54 + 26 + 36 = 116; 116 / 3 = 39). Once you have the average of the components, you are ready to make adjustments. To make the correction, you will add gradient maps—one at a time, grouped to the split and layered RGB components.

Color	Original Value	Target Value
Red	54	39
Green	26	39
Blue	36	39

Just to be clear, these are hypothetical values that we will carry through here to see how it works; then we'll use the process in a real example later. Continuing from step 7 above, do the following:

8. Activate the Composite layer and create a new Gradient Map layer by selecting Gradient Map from the Create Adjustment Layer menu ⬤..

9. On the Gradient Map dialog, click the Gradient Used For Grayscale Mapping preview bar. This will open the Gradient Editor.

10. Choose the Black, White gradient or create a black to white gradient by placing a black (RGB: 0, 0, 0) color stop at the 0% Location and a white (RGB: 255, 255, 255) color stop at the 100% Location.

11. Add a new color stop at the Location that corresponds to the averaged value (in the example above, 39%), and change the color of the stop to the same value (in the example, HSB: 0, 0, 39).

12. Accept the changes by clicking OK on the Gradient Editor and Gradient Map dialogs.

13. Change the name of the Gradient map layer to **Gradient Map Template**.

14. Duplicate the Gradient Map Template, and drag the copy above the Red Component. Change the name to **Red Map Adjustment**.

15. Duplicate the Gradient Map Template, and drag the copy above the Green Component. Change the name to **Green Map Adjustment**.

16. Duplicate the Gradient Map Template, and drag the copy above the Blue Component. Change the name to **Blue Map Adjustment**.

17. Throw out the Gradient Map Template. Your layers should look like Figure 6.10.

18. Activate the Red Map Adjustment layer, and click the Gradient Map thumbnail. This will reopen the Gradient Map dialog. Click on the preview to open the Gradient Editor. Slide the color stop to the original value measured for the Red component (in the example, this is Location 54%).

19. Activate the Green Map Adjustment layer, and click the Gradient Map thumbnail. This will reopen the Gradient Map dialog. Click on the preview to open the Gradient Editor. Slide the color stop to the original value measured for the Green component (in the example, this is Location 26%).

20. Activate the Blue Map Adjustment layer, and click the Gradient Map thumbnail. This will reopen the Gradient Map dialog. Click on the preview to open the Gradient Editor. Slide the color stop to the original value measured for the Blue component (in the example, this is Location 36%).

At this point, the adjustment is complete. The target value replaces the original value, simply by moving the color stop.

We've taken a look at how this works for a single sample to get familiar with the process. You can make corrections similarly to this procedure, as suggested earlier, using just Levels. If you open your image, open Levels, and then click the Gray Point tool 🖋, you can click any place in the image, and Levels will balance to that sample point as if it were gray—quick and easy. What Levels does not offer, however, is multiple sample correction. We'll see in a moment that the multiple-sample variation of this technique offers a lot more flexibility and potential accuracy. However, first let's look at a variation of single point sampling using only a percentage of the sampled change.

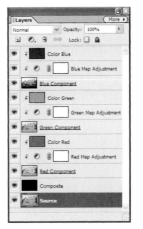

Figure 6.10

Gradient Map adjustment layers should be placed between the component tone and its associated color layer.

Using a Percentage of a Single Sample for Gradient Map Application

Because you are making an assumption about the gray (that it is indeed a flat gray rather than one with a slight tone), you may want to make an adjustment by using only a percentage of the change. This concept is similar to not cropping off all of a large tail in Levels. If the difference in the colors is broad or skewed to one of the channels, it may be preferable to average 50 or 75 percent of the difference. The more positive you are that the value you are measuring should be gray, the stronger the percentage of change you should apply. If you are positive the object is gray, make the change 100 percent of the difference (as we did in the original example above). Scaling back to 50 or 75 percent respects some of the color measured in sampling the gray area of the image.

To scale back your adjustment and respect color in the original image, you will arbitrarily choose how much to deviate from that color. If you are going to make a 75 percent change according to your measurement, you will keep 25 percent of the original color influence. Using the previous example, take the difference between the measured and average value, multiply that figure by the percentage you will deviate from the strict average, and add the result to the average value.

new target value = average value + ([measured value − average value] × deviation percentage)

In the example, the average value is still 39 (54+26+36/3). Using the red channel, which measures 54, your equation would look like the following if you were applying 75 percent of the change:

new target value = 39 + ([54 − 39] × 0.25), or 39 + 4 = 43

Using an Output value of 43 makes the red change only 75 percent of the way, leaving some respect for the value you originally measured in the image. The following list shows the target values for making the change with 75 percent strength (deviating 25 percent from the original measurement of color in the image):

Color	Original Value	Target Value
Red	54	43
Green	26	36
Blue	36	38

In this case, you would take the same steps as for the adjustment made earlier, the only difference being that you would need to target the variable target value. Instead of using the Gradient Map Template, you would have to create gradient maps for each of the targets individually, aligning each of those with the related component color.

Choosing to make only a percentage of the change is a bit more complicated mathematically, but it may render a better result if the image capture is rendered with some accuracy. It could actually be replicated by making the 100 percent change and then reducing the opacity of the Gradient Map layer. It is clinically similar to making a Levels Gray Point adjustment layer and reducing the opacity. Knowing how the math works will help if you want to adjust the highlights differently than the shadows or midtones based on the range of the sample(s). Again, the real strength in using Gradient Maps is having the option for multiple samples, and we'll look at optimizing color correction using Gradient Maps in the next section.

Multiple Sample Gradient Map Adjustment

The more gray points you measure in your image, the more potentially accurate your balance in the resulting color corrections will be. If you measure several key gray spots to sample from, you can make the corrections all at once and improve accuracy in your image color balance.

When measuring one gray sample, you should try to make it a midtone; if you are measuring two, use a lighter and darker gray; if you are measuring three, it is optimal to use quartertones (25 percent, 50 percent, and 75 percent, or 63, 128, and 191 levels). The more evenly you divide the gray levels used for the correction, the better. The more levels of gray you correct for, the more accurate your correction will appear—so long as you are correcting accurately for objects that should appear gray.

Really, the only way to be sure you are correcting accurately for a gray is to place it in your image. The following example uses the image from Figure 6.11 that was photographed by including a homemade 25 percent, 50 percent, 75 percent gray card in the image. The image was opened as a digital image and corrected for Levels. The gray card was then measured, and those measured results were applied as curves to make a correction. Use the bleedingheart.psd file on the CD to follow along.

Figure 6.11

The gray card (shown to the right) can help balance color at three levels of gray.

You can make your own gray card by making an image with scaled tones (for example, 25, 50, and 75 percent gray) and then printing that image with black ink only on your printer. This won't be entirely accurate, since black ink can have color and color can be influenced by the whiteness of the paper, but it can certainly work well in many situations—better than guessing what should be gray in your image. You could try experimenting with paint swatch samples from a hardware or paint store as well.

Use the following steps to adjust the gradient maps according to your gray selection:

1. Open the bleedingheart.psd image on the Hidden Power CD.

2. Be sure the Info palette is visible and that one of the sample types is set to HSB Color (HSB).

3. Select the Eyedropper from the toolbox. Select a sample option from the Sample Size drop-down list on the Options bar. Choose either 3 By 3 Average or 5 By 5 Average, depending on the size and resolution of the image.

4. Point the tip of the Eyedropper at the light gray reference area in the image, and click to sample the color.

5. Double-click the Sample Analysis tool in the Power_Extras category of Effects. This will create a new image from the color sample separate from the RGB and leave a swatch of each of the component layers in RGB order.

6. Sample each of the tones in the Sample Analysis image, and note the B value of each. Write them down, and average them. Close the Sample Analysis image without saving it.

7. Repeat steps 4 to 6 for the medium gray and dark gray swatches in the image. Your results should be similar to those noted here.

Color (as B from HSB)	75%	50%	25%
Red	89	51	22
Green	82	59	35
Blue	82	56	30

8. Make an RGB separation of the original image (using RGB Separation in the Power_Separations category of Effects).

9. Activate the Composite layer, and create a new Gradient Map layer by selecting Gradient Map from the Create Adjustment Layer menu ⬤.

10. On the Gradient Map dialog, click the Gradient Used For Grayscale Mapping preview bar. This will open the Gradient Editor.

11. Choose the Black, White gradient or create a black-to-white gradient by placing a black (RGB: 0, 0, 0) color stop at the 0% Location and a white (RGB: 255, 255, 255) color stop at the 100% Location.

12. Add a new color stop for each sample at the Location that corresponds to the B values in the card, and change the color of the stop to the same value. Since there are three samples, you will create three stops as shown.

Location	75%	50%	25%
HSB value	0, 0, 75	0, 0, 50	0, 0, 25

13. Accept the changes by clicking OK on the Gradient Editor and Gradient Map dialogs.

14. Change the name of the Gradient map layer to **Gradient Map Template**.

15. Duplicate the Gradient Map Template, and drag the copy above the Red Component. Change the name to **Red Map Adjustment**.

16. Duplicate the Gradient Map Template, and drag the copy above the Green Component. Change the name to **Green Map Adjustment**.

17. Duplicate the Gradient Map Template, and drag the copy above the Blue Component. Change the name to **Blue Map Adjustment**.

18. Throw out the Gradient Map Template. Your layers should look like Figure 6.12.

19. Activate the Red Map Adjustment, and click the Gradient Map thumbnail. This will reopen the Gradient Map dialog. Click on the preview to open the Gradient Editor. Slide the color stops to the original values measured for the Red components. In the example, move the 75% Location stop to 89%, the 50% Location stop to 51%, and the 25% Location stop to 22%.

20. Activate the Green Map Adjustment, and click the Gradient Map thumbnail. This will reopen the Gradient Map dialog. Click on the preview to open the Gradient Editor. Slide the color stops to the original values measured for the Green components. In the example, move the 75% Location stop to 82%, the 50% Location stop to 59%, and the 25% Location stop to 35%.

21. Activate the Blue Map Adjustment, and click the Gradient Map thumbnail. This will reopen the Gradient Map dialog. Click on the preview to open the Gradient Editor. Slide the color stops to the original values measured for the Blue components. In the example, move the 75% Location stop to 82%, the 50% Location stop to 56%, and the 25% Location stop to 30%.

After you have performed all the corrections using the card, you will have corrected for white and black, as well as 25 percent, 50 percent, and 75 percent gray. The colors of the card should appear to be flat grays, and associated changes to color will take place throughout the image. This adjustment gives you five reference points that should result in some pretty accurate color. This technique should be more accurate than using just one sample reference point and can account for complex lighting. For example, if you take a picture in a royal blue room where there is incandescent lighting, ambient light (reflected) might tend to be blue, while direct light would be warm (or a little red). Highlights would tend toward red, while shadows would tend toward blue. Making multipoint corrections enables you to compensate for color difference and shifts at more points, leading to color that is more correct overall.

Although Levels and Gradient Maps are excellent correction tools, and making corrections absolutely by the numbers may seem pretty accurate, it may not produce the most pleasing color. If you have no idea where to start your correction, the techniques described here for basic color correction are definitely a fine start that will get you moving in the right direction. Curve presets can also be used to make these adjustments based on the discussion in the previous chapter, but they will not be as accurate for correcting to specific values.

Figure 6.12

The setup here is identical to the single sample adjustment, just with a different image and templates.

Because of other considerations (such as the limitations of the CMYK color space), you may get better color by replacing colors and tones, by making corrections not so strictly tied to measurements, or in some cases by altering color completely. Making targeted and selective tone and color corrections can help with these additional changes, and we'll look at those approaches in the following sections. Let's start by using Hue/Saturation, a dedicated color tool.

Using Hue/Saturation for Color Adjustment

Hue/Saturation (Enhance → Adjust Color → Adjust Hue/Saturation, Layer → New Adjustment Layer → Hue/Saturation, or press Command+U/Ctrl+U) is a powerful but easy-to-use color-correction tool. It enables you to adjust color based on hue, saturation, and brightness (HSB). HSB measurements are used on the Color Picker along with RGB. We used the B value (brightness) in the previous section to help target changes in tone with Gradient Maps. The HSB color model is used to mix color—often in painting. *Hue* adjusts colors as if you were selecting color from a 360-degree color wheel. *Saturation* controls the density of the color; greater saturation means that the color in an image has the potential to be richer (the actual appearance of color is influenced by tone). *Brightness* (or lightness) affects the tone in the image. Hue/Saturation can affect all the color in the image or it can be confined to affecting only a specific range of color, using the Edit drop-down list in the Hue/Saturation dialog box (see Figure 6.13).

The Hue/Saturation feature can help with color corrections by providing visual feedback and a relatively easy interface. When using the Hue/Saturation dialog box, all you have to do is adjust the sliders and use the image on-screen as a preview to watch what happens as a result of your adjustments. For the most part, as long as you have made proper Levels corrections, you won't have many additional color changes to bother with because Levels adjustments will have corrected for some issues of saturation, hue, and lightness (brightness).

Figure 6.13

The Hue/Saturation dialog

Although it may not be the best use of the feature, you can open the Hue/Saturation dialog box and play with the sliders to see if you happen to stumble on an adjustment that improves the image. Testing adjustments by using Hue/Saturation can yield pleasant surprises. Unless you use selection or masking to target a color change, global adjustments to hue, saturation, and brightness will tend to require only a slight movement of any of the sliders—unless you are looking to achieve a special effect. You might be a little wilder with your experimentation if the subject in the image is something like a flower that may not have a specific color reference (unlike, for example, skin tone—skin has real-world limits and can't be, say, green or purple unless painted).

In making straightforward changes with Hue/Saturation, adjusting Hue will often throw the color out of balance swiftly, and adjusting Lightness may provide too drastic and primitive a change in tone for color correction (it has other uses, as we will see). Lightness is the least attractive adjustment for most images when used by itself: it's far better to make these types of changes in brightness with Levels, Curves presets, and/or Gradient Maps. However, you can occasionally get some pleasant results from increasing Saturation in some images.

To make a correction using Hue/Saturation, follow these steps:

1. Select the appropriate portion of the image to target your corrections. You can do one of the following:

   Target the whole image. Flatten your image (choose Layer→ Flatten Image) or select the top layer in the stack if you're adjusting the whole image (press Option+Shift+] / Alt+Shift+] to activate the top layer, or just click it).

   Target a layer. Activate the layer you want to correct by clicking it in the Layers palette, if you're making a selective change based on layer content.

   Target a specific image area. Create a selection or mask to define a specific area of the image. This targeting can be done by using selection tools or masking techniques or by making a selection from the Edit drop-down list in the dialog box. Any active selection will become a layer mask for the Hue/Saturation layer, masking areas outside the selection.

2. Open the Hue/Saturation dialog box by creating a Hue/Saturation adjustment layer (choose Layer → New Adjustment Layer → Hue/Saturation). If you're targeting a specific layer for change, be sure the Group With The Previous Box option is checked in the New Layer dialog box.

3. When the Hue/Saturation dialog box is open, attempt to adjust the Saturation by moving the slider a few points to the right of the center position to see if greater saturation improves the color dynamic.

Admittedly, this procedure isn't terribly exciting. The result is that you will get more saturated color, and you'll either prefer it or not. One other option on Hue/Saturation is Colorize. Using the Colorize option is like applying a layer filled with a single color set to Overlay mode (at 50 percent Opacity). The difference is that you can adjust the Color, Saturation, and Lightness sliders on the Hue/Saturation dialog box to achieve the color effect you want rather than selecting a color from the Color Picker.

You needed this brief introduction to the Hue/Saturation function because the tool also offers some unique opportunities for selective correction when used in combination with other features and tools. Several Hidden Power tools help make selective corrections, and selective correction is where the real power of Hue/Saturation lies. That's what we'll look at in the next section while making a color-based mask.

Color Masking with Hue/Saturation

If you want to make a selective color change (if you have a specific color or color range that you want to change or isolate from change in a shot), you can target those colors by using Hue/Saturation to help in creating a mask. You can make more drastic changes after targeting than you could with general adjustments because the rest of the image won't change. Clever use of the Saturation slider in the Hue/Saturation dialog box can help you quickly create masks based on hue. These masks can help you target image areas based on color so you can make corrections and changes by using other features and tools.

The image in Figure 6.14 has several distinct colors that might be adjusted independently. The image (balloons.psd) is provided on the CD for your experimentation and so you can see the color detail and follow along with the masking procedure. In the example,

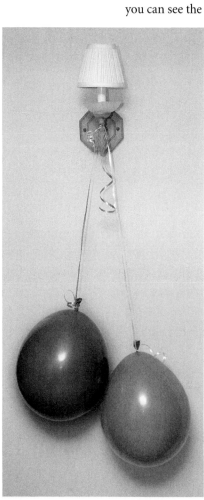

the balloons are red and blue. If you want to keep it that way while making other changes, you can target other areas by freezing (masking out) the color of one of the balloons. This will enable you to alter color in the other parts of the image without changing the color in the masked balloon. Just a warning: as we go along, this image will look quite awful before it begins to get better. This is a normal result of what you will do to build the mask.

The process of creating a mask based on color and saturation is basically the same for any image. You have three tasks to complete in order to make the saturation mask:

1. Prepare the image for making a color range choice by adding some key layers that help you create the mask.

2. Choose a color range. Select the color range you want to either change or keep from changing by using Hue/Saturation functions.

3. Use the color range selection and preparations to create a useful color mask.

The following three sections expand on the details for each step in the process.

Preparing the Image

To prepare this image, you'll need to set up a few layers that will help you make the mask. You create these layers for the sole purpose of being able to commit changes you make when using layer-blending options. Some of the layers depend on modes or calculations for the result that is displayed. Until you commit the changes by merging

Figure 6.14

This image offers several opportunities for hue-based color isolation.

layers, the changes are only an appearance. You need to commit the changes in order
to use them.

1. Open a flattened image, or flatten an open one. For this example, use `balloons.psd`,
   found on the Hidden Power CD.

2. Duplicate the background. You'll use this layer to select the target colors for masking
   and to create the mask. Name the layer **Saturated Colors**.

3. Activate the background (press Option+Shift+[/ Alt+Shift+[).

4. Create a new layer. Name it **Mask**. This layer should remain transparent until the
   final steps of the exercise, and then it will become the mask.

5. Create another new layer, and fill it with gray. To create the gray fill, choose Edit → Fill
   Layer. When the dialog box opens, set the Contents to 50 percent Gray, Blending
   Mode to Normal, and Opacity to 100 percent (Mode and Opacity are set to these by
   default, so you may not need to change them). Name this layer **Commit Mode 2**.

6. Duplicate the Commit Mode 2 layer created in step 5. Name this **Commit Mode 1**.
   There are two changes to commit using layer modes, and this upper layer will be the
   first in line, even though you created it second.

Choosing a Color Range

Now that you have prepared the image, you can choose the colors to be excluded, or
masked out, and made safe from change. You will temporarily desaturate the area of the
image that you want to keep as it is, leaving only the color that you plan to change visible.
The remaining saturated colors will be used to create your mask.

7. Activate the Saturated Colors layer by clicking it in the Layers palette.

8. Choose Layer → New Adjustment Layer → Hue/Saturation. This initiates the creation of
   a Hue/Saturation adjustment layer at the top of the layer stack. Select the Group With
   Previous check box in the New Layer dialog
   box when it appears, and click OK to continue.
   The Hue/Saturation dialog box opens.

9. Select a color from the Edit drop-down menu
   that most resembles the color of the object or
   image area you would like to mask (see Figure 6.15). Choosing from the list enables the
   color sliders at the bottom of the Hue/Satura-
   tion dialog box and the eyedropper buttons.
   The sliders on the color bar represent the
   color range that will be affected by changes

Figure 6.15

**When the selection
is made for the target
range, the sliders
automatically set to
that range. Here
Blues is selected, but
you should choose
the color according
to your target in the
image.**

made to the Hue, Saturation, and Lightness. The eyedropper buttons enable sampling modes that help you adjust the range to your image. Select Blues for this example, because it is closest to our target range for masking the blue balloon.

10. Drag the Saturation slider in the Hue/Saturation dialog box all the way to the left. If you have selected a good representation of the color you want to work with, the color you have targeted will desaturate. You are actually starting to build your mask, which will be based on desaturated areas of the image.

11. Adjust the color range so that all the color that you want to keep from change becomes desaturated. To do this, use the Add To Sample eyedropper 🖊, and click on anything in the image that is in the target area. If you make a mistake, you can clean it up by changing to the Subtract From Sample eyedropper 🖊, adjusting the sliders on the preview bar manually by clicking and dragging them, or just starting over using the Reset button. All color that you add to the color range will appear to desaturate in the image; any colors removed from the range will turn back to the original color. Color range adjustment can be accomplished in any of the following ways:

Use the Add To Sample eyedropper. Click the plus eyedropper icon 🖊, and use that to sample colors from the image that you want to add to the range.

Use the Subtract From Sample eyedropper. Click the minus eyedropper icon 🖊, and use that to sample colors from the image that you want to remove from the range.

Use the Eyedropper. Click the eyedropper 🖊, and use that to sample a color to use as the target for the current range. If you have made adjustments to the range, the grouping will shift, keeping the breadth of the range change.

Adjust the sliders manually. Click directly on the slider or slider components at the bottom of the dialog box, and drag them to adjust the range. The close-up of the color range slider in Figure 6.16 shows some details of the slider.

Reset the range. Press the Option/Alt key on the keyboard, and click the Reset button when it appears. The Cancel button toggles to Reset as the Option/Alt key is pressed.

Figure 6.16

Close-up of the parts of the Hue/Saturation color range sliders

The color bar above the slider at the bottom of the dialog shows the range of color being affected, and the color bar below the slider shows the resulting color spectrum. The slider itself (see Figure 6.16) is a font of information about the range being affected. The dark gray area between the absolute markers (the rectangular markers on the inside) shows the range that will be affected 100 percent by changes. The gray area between the absolute markers and the fade point markers (the triangular markers on the outside) shows where the color range will be affected in decreasing intensity (100 percent to 0 percent). Everything

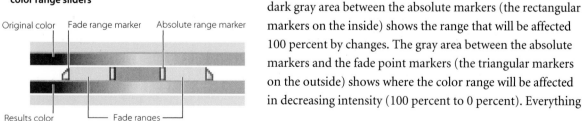

Original color   Fade range marker   Absolute range marker

Results color   Fade ranges

outside the range of the markers will not be affected by Hue/Saturation changes to this color selection.

12. After the range is set and the colors you want to mask are desaturated, accept the changes for the dialog box by clicking OK.

The key to the process at this point is that the color area that you want to mask should be desaturated. Be aware that it may at times be difficult to target areas or a range without selecting additional colors. Where this technique may be useful for isolating solid-color balloons from a background (distinctly colored objects), it will be less useful for adjusting the skin tone of one face in a crowd and for making corrections in busy images in general.

Creating the Mask

With the color range you want to mask desaturated, you can use the color that is left to create a mask.

13. Merge the Hue/Saturation change with the Saturated Colors layer below by activating the Hue/Saturation layer (if it isn't already) and pressing Command+E/Ctrl+E. This commits the changes and shows the original image with the selected color range as desaturated.

14. Change the mode of the Saturated Colors layer to Color (select Color from the drop-down mode list at the top of the Layers palette). This shows image color saturation against a 50 percent gray background. The flat gray represents unsaturated image areas and image areas you want to mask, as well as other areas of the image that previously were not saturated (white, gray, and black).

15. Merge the Saturated Colors and Commit Mode 1 layers by pressing Command+E/Ctrl+E. This commits the changes. The name of the layer should be **Commit Mode 1**.

16. Change the mode of the Commit Mode 1 layer to Difference. Difference mode compares the pixels in the current layer with the pixels below. If there is no difference, the result will be black. The greater the difference, the lighter the result will be. The desaturated areas of the image and the blue balloon will appear as black; anything that is not completely black means there is some saturation in that area—the lighter and brighter the result, the greater the saturation.

17. Merge the Commit Mode 1 and Commit Mode 2 layers to commit the changes. To do this, activate Commit Mode 1 and press Command+E/Ctrl+E. The resulting layer should be named **Commit Mode 2**.

18. Open the Levels dialog box (Enhance → Adjust Lighting → Levels, or Command+L/Ctrl+L), and make a Levels adjustment by pushing the white RGB Input slider to 128. This intensifies the brightness of the saturated areas (everything that isn't absolute black).

19. Double-click the Drop Black Hidden Power tool in the Power_Masking category of Effects. This function makes shadows in the current layer transparent, revealing the blue from the balloon and other unsaturated areas of the image below.

> The Drop Black function makes pixels between 0 and 2 levels (or 100 percent to 99 percent black) completely transparent and then fades the opacity of dark pixels between 3 and 31 levels (or 99 percent to 90 percent black). This helps blend the masking.

20. Merge the Mask layer and the Commit Mode 2 layer by activating the Commit Mode 2 layer and pressing Command+E/Ctrl+E. This commits the Drop Black changes and leaves part of the mask layer transparent. The resulting layer should be named **Mask**.

21. Duplicate the Background layer. Change the name to **Mask Content**.

22. Move the Unmasked Color layer to the top of the layer stack.

23. Group the Unmasked Color layer with the Mask layer by pressing Command+G/ Ctrl+G.

At the end of this procedure, the Layers palette should look like Figure 6.17. The last few steps recolor the masked image area. It will look like the original image, but you have successfully masked your target area, as we'll see in a moment.

If you turn off the visibility for the background at this point, you will see the area that you have isolated in original color with a hole where the color portions of the masked area were. The complexity of the area is nothing you would have wanted to select manually. You can make changes to the areas outside the blue balloon freely by grouping any new adjustment layers that appear above the Mask Content layer in the Layers palette. This targets change to everything but the blue balloon. You can make changes to the blue balloon isolated from the rest of the image by grouping changes with the Background layer.

For example, if you want to make a Hue/Saturation adjustment layer change to the masked area and a Levels change to the rest of the image (Mask Content), the placement for these adjustment layers is shown in Figure 6.18.

Color masking enables you to mask any distinct areas of color in any image so you can work on those areas separately. This technique uses image color as a means of selection, masking, and targeting a specific area of the image for change. Color masking is different from working with separated color as you do when separating RGB tones, because with color masks you

Figure 6.17

Many changes result in just these few layers. The mask result is very powerful and useful.

Figure 6.18

This Layers palette shows how to set up Hue/Saturation adjustments made to the masked color range and Levels for the Mask Content.

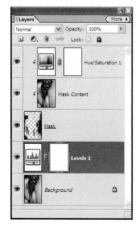

are isolating colors that may have information in red, green, and blue components all at the same time. Not only can this method be used to isolate specific colors, but it can also be used to make selections of objects based on color—or lack of it. You can use this same image and practice by masking off the red balloon, background, and sconce.

Masks you create can be loaded as selections by pressing the Command/Ctrl key and clicking the Mask layer. If the mask is loaded as a selection when you create an adjustment layer, changes in the layer will be reflected in the layer mask for the adjustment layer. This offers an additional option for targeting change based on the mask you have created.

A function is provided in the Hidden Power tools to quickly work through the previous procedures and create a color-based mask. Just double-click the Color Masking tool under the Power_Masking category of Effects, and you will be walked through all the steps. Although this tool enables you to make color masks with the click of a button, you should practice this manual technique first and work through it several times in different variations by trying to isolate different color areas in your images. Understanding how color masking works is invaluable when working on images that need isolated color corrections or when working on complex separations such as creating the K (black) component in CMYK (which we'll be doing in the next chapter). You can do a lot more with the concepts that are being mined here than just make color masks.

Adjusting Color Balance

Color balance refers to the balance between color opposites. For example, green and magenta are opposites; in order for image color to look right (not too magenta and not too green), these colors have to be in balance. Color balance tools enable you to shift the balance between these opposites to realign the color. Adjusting image color balance allows you to compensate for color shifts that may have occurred in capture or correction or to add shifts that create a pleasing look.

The one problem with Color Balance is that, like Curves, the built-in interface is missing from Photoshop Elements, and hidden access to the tool in the interface has been removed for the release of Elements 4. The Hidden Power tools included on the CD allow you to mimic Color Balance as a layered process by double-clicking Simple Color Balance from the Power_Adjustments category in Effects. This will create a number of layers that can be used for color balance adjustments.

Balancing color is often more effective than using Hue/Saturation at bringing out pleasing color in your images. It does this by removing counter colors—or colors that effectively work against one another in your images that can make them look dull or lifeless. For example, if yellowish highlights have been tainted by blue, they flatten and muddy toward green. Shifting the color back can make the color seem more vibrant. You work at balancing color to finesse, rather than manhandle, color elements as you might do with color masking.

To make color balance adjustments, you will use the Hidden Power Simple Color Balance tool, which mimics and restores color balance functionality to Photoshop Elements using another layer setup. As you drag opacity sliders back and forth for color controller layers, you will note the image tints to extremes; your goal in these changes is to find the point where these extremes balance (ergo the name *color balance*) and leave the slider at that juncture.

Figure 6.19

The setup for Simple Color Balance involves making color adjustment layers for each component color (red, green and blue), and a converter layer that enhances or inverts the color.

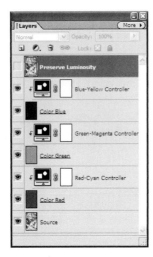

1. Open the image you wish to correct.

2. Double-click the Simple Color Balance tool in the Power_Adjustments category under Effects. This will run through a number of steps to set up the color balance adjustment. The resulting layers will look like Figure 6.19.

3. Start your adjustment by activating the Controller layer for the color set you want to balance. You can choose the Red-Cyan Controller, Green-Magenta Controller, or Blue-Yellow controller layer. You should visit each of these in turn over the course of this procedure to make your correction. For the example, start with the Red-Cyan Controller.

4. Click on the arrow to the right of the opacity button to open the opacity slider and make a slow sweeping, but radical, shift in the position of the slider from right to left (0 to 100), and watch the effect on the image. This big movement gives you an idea as to how the change in color balance between red and cyan will affect the image overall. It is unlikely that an extreme will look balanced. Don't expect to make a monumental change; you may make a slight change, or even none at all.

> Note that the starting, or balanced, position is at 50% opacity. This is because the controller is an Invert adjustment layer. When applied to each of the color components, 50% inversion is a balanced, or neutral, color: 50% gray. If you want to neutralize the effect of any adjustment, return the opacity of the controller layer to 50%.

5. As you push the opacity slider back and forth a few times, pick a position that seems the most pleasing. Compare the results as many times as you need to by sliding the slider left to right while looking at the image to make the decision.

6. When you have selected the slider position that seems most pleasing, toggle the view for the Color Red layer to compare before and after application of the change.

7. Open the opacity slider for the Red-Cyan Controller layer again, and fine-tune the adjustment by swinging the slider +/– 5% from the spot you left it. See Figure 6.20.

> Experiment with the Preserve Luminosity layer at the top of the layer stack. When it is visible, Elements will keep luminosity/tone from changing while you adjust the color.

8. Repeat steps 3 through 7 for the other controller layers, adjusting the sliders for each.

9. To be reasonably sure you've made the best choices, run through steps 3 through 8 a second time. This will help you to adjust for balance changes you made first.

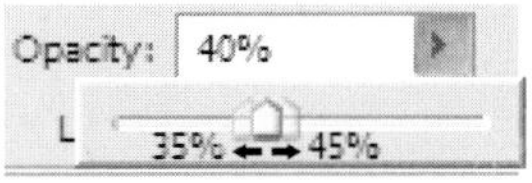

While the application here may seem conceptually simp-listic, as long as your monitor can be reasonably trusted, you will find that this trial-and-error method can greatly improve your images—in tone, contrast, and color. You'll also get good rather quickly in determining the best slider positions and will spend little time doing comparisons and cutting down your options. Once you gain confidence, you'll just watch the image change as you move the sliders.

Figure 6.20

Reconsidering a smaller change allows you to fine-tune the adjustment.

An interesting byproduct of the adjustment is taking a look at the result of the change. If you shut off the Source and Preserve Luminosity layers after making the correction, you will be left with a flat color appearance to the image, as if you filled the image with color. You can also simplify the result. Try this:

1. Complete the color balance adjustment for any image as described in the last procedure.

2. Shut off the view for the Preserve Luminosity layer and the Source layer. This reveals your color balance color.

3. Create a new, blank layer at the top of the layer stack. Name it **Color Balance 1**. Set the mode to Overlay.

4. Press Command+Shift+Option+E / Ctrl+Shift+Alt+E to merge the visible layers to your Color Balance 1 layer.

5. Shut off the visibility for the Color Red, Color Green, and Color Blue layers.

6. Press Command+[/Ctrl+[to move the Color Balance 1 layer below the Lumi-nosity layer.

7. Turn on the Source and Preserve Luminosity layers.

The Simplify Color Balance Layers tool will do this set of steps for you (it will leave the visibility toggle for the Preserve Luminosity layer off by default). You will see that the Color Balance composite layer can be used separately from the layers that make up the correction. This adjustment layer can be used in conjunction with other tools to achieve targeted results as well. For example, color balancing can be masked to balance highlights, shadows, and midtones separately for cyan/red, magenta/green, and yellow/blue. In fact, there are additional color balance tools to target color balance to shadows (Shadow Color Balance), midtones (Midtone Color Balance), and highlights (Highlight Color Balance). There are also tools to simplify each of these adjustments into portable layers (Simplify Color Balance, Simplify Midtone Balance, Simplify Highlight Balance, and Simplify Shadow Balance). This ability for selective range changes provides an advantage when colors have gotten out of balance in different ways over those tonal ranges for whatever reason. These types of combinations of tools and masking give you infinite control over targeting image color results.

There is somewhat of a difference between the handling of the ranges for color balance in the Simple Color Balance tool and the range-specific tools, and again between how Hidden Power handles these corrections and how Photoshop does. Range-specific color balance tools in the Hidden Power set (highlight, midtone, and shadow) leave the Preserve Luminosity layer turned on by default to help retain image integrity. They also apply each color at one-third the strength (Red Color, Green Color, and Blue Color layers are at 33 percent opacity) because there are three ranges of change. The ranges chosen for Hidden Power tools are more specific than Photoshop's tools, which amble across the entire gamut of the image whether they are selected for shadows, highlights, or midtones. This difference will lead to subtle variations in results if you compare the results of using color balance in Elements with Hidden Power and of using Color Balance in Photoshop side-by-side. These differences are intentional.

Something that Hidden Power's layer-based correction model allows that Photoshop's more rigid interface controls do not is the ability to play openly with various layer modes, opacities, layer order, and means of combining pixels. We will take another angle on combining image content in the next section.

Painting in Color Changes: History Brush Application

Sometimes it is easiest to get the color you want in different portions of an image by combining different corrections of the same image. You may find that making one part of an image look good comes at the expense of absolutely ruining the color in the rest of your image. This little dilemma might make it seem that there is no way to make a compromise between the two without damaging the image color or making complicated selections.

As it turns out, you don't have to settle for a compromise. There is a way to make changes to your image—even drastic ones—and store those changes so you can use them later. Using techniques and Hidden Power tools, you can imitate what is called Snapshots in Photoshop and store different versions of your image in layers. Later, you can use these layers to paint back in only a portion of the color.

Photoshop allows you to do what is described here with something called the History Brush. The History Brush lets you select a *snapshot* (a stored state of your image) as the source for painting so you can apply that version of the image back into your present image by using a brush. It enables you to do all sorts of things such as making color changes or a spot application of filters (apply the filter, take a snapshot to use as a source, and then jump back to the original image and paint changes in as desired). This Hidden Power workaround can do all the things the History Brush and snapshots do together.

Using Hidden Power tools, you can store a version of your image in a way similar to taking snapshots by double-clicking the Snapshot tool found in the Power_Adjustments category of Effects. The stored versions (or snapshots) are saved in layers, and the visibility is turned off so that you can return to them as needed. Using layer masking will allow you to easily imitate the History Brush: you can group the snapshot to an empty layer, turn on the visibility for the snapshot, and use brushes to fill in the mask. As the mask layer becomes solid, it paints back changes stored in the snapshot.

To take a snapshot of your image, be sure it looks like you want it to, and then double-click the Snapshot tool. When you take a snapshot, several things will happen in the image. Whatever you see on-screen will be merged into a single layer (retaining transparency, if any), and a copy of that will be stored in the image as a Snapshot layer. The Snapshot layer will be stored at the top of the layer stack, above and grouped with a Snapshot Mask layer. The snapshot content will be hidden because it is grouped to the mask, and the mask is empty. Leave the snapshots in storage until you want to apply them. The rest of the image will be left exactly as it was when you made the snapshot. See Figure 6.21.

After making a snapshot, you have several options for continuing to work and make changes and corrections:

- Leave everything as it is and just keep making changes.

- Throw out the changes you made to achieve the snapshot by deleting those layers (leaving the snapshot, of course) and then make new changes.

- Retain the changes and start with the original background.

- Retain the changes and start from the snapshot.

In any of these instances, you may want to duplicate the image before taking more steps (your choice depends on how much information you really want to keep and how you like to work). If you just keep going from where you are, you can retain information in layers you might want to use later. On the other hand, if you are sure there is nothing you want to retain, tossing out the changes will keep the important information in the snapshot and make your image a little leaner.

Figure 6.21

After you take a snapshot of an image after making layered adjustments (Tone Adjustment, Highlight Color Adjustment, Levels 1, and Levels 2), the layers look like this. You can have multiple snapshots.

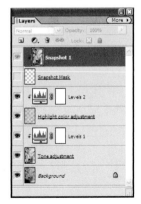

Saving snapshots is something even Photoshop doesn't allow. When you work in Photoshop, snapshots are good for your current session only. The method shown here will allow you to keep snapshots and save them with the image.

You may want to retain some or all of the layers used in making the changes that lead up to creating the snapshot so that you can make adjustments (for instance, if you want to reshoot Snapshot 1 with additional changes or in a different style). You might also want to retain the layers if you just aren't finished with the image yet (if you can't complete what you are working on right then). To retain the layers used in making the changes, just leave them there. Use a duplicate of the Background or Snapshot layer, and drag it just under the Snapshot layer at the top of the layer stack. Duplicate the Background layer so you will be able to return to the original image, or duplicate the Snapshot layer to continue working from where you were.

Technically, you can save the image with all the layers and changes by using this snapshot method. You may want to thin out the layers as you go along to keep the file size small. Although retaining snapshots and layers can be an important time-saver, it can also fatten your image heartily. Be sure you need what you save.

The purpose and application of this type of change may be best looked at in an example. We will run through an application of the tools in context, and you can see how they work.

Figure 6.22 shows a butterfly. This butterfly landed on an object that was nearly the same color as itself. While the color is interesting, you may prefer a little more variety to make the butterfly stand out. Because the color of the background is similar to that of the butterfly, Hue/Saturation masking wouldn't accomplish the change, because it would select both the color in the butterfly and the background. And while you could make some sort of complicated selection, there are much easier ways.

Start by making a general correction to the image to be sure you are starting with the best representation of tone and color. With that complete, it is time to start exploring opportunities to change the image. In this case, we'll change the color of the butterfly; you could change the background by using the same technique.

The process of making the change occurs in two stages: preparation and application.

Preparation First, do some exploring and experimenting. Instead of working with complicated selections, you can simply adjust different versions of your image to create sources for the color you'd rather see in specific areas of the image. Taking snapshots will store the changes; then you can later use the snapshots to recall and apply the changes to your original image.

Application Once the source color is all set up in the original image, you just paint the color back into the original image by using brushes.

We'll explore the preparation and application in more detail in the following sections.

Figure 6.22

A blue butterfly rests on a blue back-ground, but you might want a more interesting color distinction.

Preparation

To prepare for changes to the butterfly, you will make some corrections to separate areas of color and freeze those changes by taking snapshots. Each snapshot can focus on a different color or element that you will want to work back in later. The corrections here are specific to this image, but the use of snapshots and the idea of storing image sources for later changes can be used with any image.

1. Open the butterfly image (`butterfly.psd` on the Hidden Power CD).

2. Adjust the color of the image so that the dark portion of the butterfly looks how you want it to look. Don't worry at all about what you do to the blue—or any other color, for that matter. Don't bother to use selection or other masking; just change the color/tone. You should work on duplicates of the source image. Leaving the Background layer alone will allow you to return to the original content later to adjust for different colors. You can use any tools or filters that you want, but for this example start with the Shadow Color Balance Hidden Power tool (you'll find Shadow Color Balance on the Styles and Effects palette under Effects in the Power_Adjustments category). Try adding yellows and reds to warm up the black.

3. Once the dark portion of the butterfly looks how you want it to look, take a snapshot by double-clicking Snapshot from the Hidden Power tools (also found under the Power_Adjustments category in Effects). This will be your source for the dark portion of the butterfly. Name the snapshot **Dark Portion**. It will appear at the top of the layer stack.

4. Make changes to adjust the butterfly's wing color to however you would like to see it. This may require deleting and enhancing other changes that you made to create the Dark Portion snapshot—and that is okay because you have achieved the objective of those changes and stored them as the snapshot. Duplicate the Background layer, and drag it below the Snapshot Mask layer to give you a fresh starting point. This is a good time to use Hue/Saturation to make the change, editing the default Master color set. Again, adjust the color on the wings and ignore everything else. It should be relatively easy to make the wings look a vibrant green using the Hue slider.

5. Make a snapshot of the image when you have completed the change for the wing color. Name the snapshot layer **Wings**.

6. Make changes to the image to target just the color of the spots on the bottom of the wings. Again you can duplicate the Background layer and remove other color changes. If you use Hue/Saturation, selected Red from the Edit menu, and fiddle with the sliders, you can achieve a brighter, more saturated red.

7. Make a snapshot of the image when you have completed the change for the spots on the wing. Name the snapshot layer **Spots**.

You could continue to make changes for other elements in the image, but these three changes are enough to give you an idea of what you can do during application of the snapshots you have stored.

Application

Now that the snapshots are created, you are ready to apply them to make changes to the butterfly.

8. View the original image Background layer. This may require turning off visibility for other layers you have created. As an option, you can duplicate the Background layer and bring it up below the snapshot layers.

9. Click the Snapshot Mask layer for the snapshot source you want to apply. This activates the visibility for the Snapshot Mask. Start with the Wings snapshot, because the resulting change will be the most dramatic.

10. Choose a painting tool (the Airbrush is a personal favorite) and a brush for the application. For this part of the example, chose a brush size of 200 pixels that is fairly soft (30 percent hardness).

Brush selection and dynamics in step 10 matter, and they should make sense for your application. If you are going to be painting back image areas that are large and mostly open, select a large brush; if you will be painting back smaller areas, choose a smaller brush. Solidity also matters: an opaque brush will create an opaque mask, and a brush that is soft and/or applied with less than 100 percent opacity will only partially apply the snapshot content.

11. Although it doesn't really matter, choose white for the foreground color. Any color will work, but the idea of masking is usually based on black-and-white, where white represents unmasked areas.

12. Paint over the wing area in the Snapshot Mask layer you selected by clicking and dragging the paintbrush. The content from your snapshot source will fill in as you go. To compare the change before and after, toggle the visibility of the Snapshot Mask layer for the snapshot with which you are working.

13. Choose the next source by clicking the Snapshot Mask for the snapshot that you want to apply. Repeat steps 10 through 12, choosing an appropriate brush size for the changes you want to make, and painting, in turn, on the Snapshot Mask layer for the Dark Portion and Spots snapshots to fill in the desired color changes.

After you have painted in information from the Dark Portion, Wings, and Spots snapshots, your butterfly should look significantly different. By the time you are finished, you should have painted in some interesting color that you have from each snapshot source. This is eons easier than making complex color selections and often a lot more fun. The layer stack should look like Figure 6.23.

You can adjust the results of applying any of the snapshots at any time by using the Eraser tool to touch up the mask and by changing layer modes and opacity. When you do, make the changes on the *Snapshot Mask* layer, not the snapshot itself. If you change the snapshot, it will permanently change the content of the snapshot and/or reveal the content of the mask (which would be white, if you took the suggestion I made previously). If you really botch the application of a snapshot and want to start over, just activate the Snapshot Mask layer for the snapshot you want to redo, select All (press Command+A/Ctrl+A), and press Delete on the keyboard. This will clear any painting you have done in the layer so you can start over with a clean slate.

Snapshots are simple in concept: all they do is store an image state and enable you to apply that information later by using layer-masking properties. Although they are simple, snapshots can enable you to paint in filter applications and

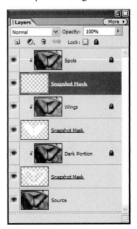

Figure 6.23
The blue butterfly is now green and a little brighter and more dynamic because of the snapshots.

make other color corrections and changes with the flexibility of a changeable layer mask. A snapshot can be used to spot-apply any change and is a versatile tool for spot corrections.

In this chapter, we have covered a wealth of color-specific possibilities that can literally keep you occupied for years. Using these techniques on any image starts with a vision or the will to experiment, while following the guidelines for tool application should keep your experimentation constructive.

In the previous sections and chapters, we have mostly been concerned with working on your image color and tone. However, other possibilities come into play when considering the look of an image. In the next chapter we'll begin to look at composition and composition adjustments that will give you even more control of the look of your images.

Chapter 7

Altering Composition

The next area of attack is the objects in your images. While the title of this chapter may sound like we're going to discuss image overhauls and sweeping changes, such as transposing heads, that isn't quite the point. The idea is just as it is with color: to work with what exists in an image and improve it as much as possible. We won't be swapping faces here, but you will certainly learn the tools to use to accomplish that. What we will be doing mostly is concentrating on making alterations that can almost unilaterally improve your images.

Understanding a little about composition can give you a good idea as to what you will want to do to improve an image. Once you're able to separate color and separate objects in a scene, you have more or less ultimate control over how an image looks. Compositional rules are just sensible guidelines, and rules were made to be broken. But in this chapter, guidelines serve as a structure for making compositional choices and changes and as an outline for additional techniques.

Problems in Composition (Ten Tips for Better Images)

Cropping as a Tool for Composition

Isolating Image Elements

Compositing Image Elements

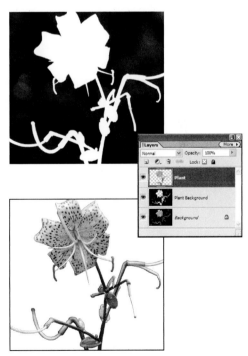

Problems in Composition (Ten Tips for Better Images)

Before just changing around parts of your images, you need a plan. An image can become infected with a lot of simple composition problems. If you treat the infection, the image will improve. Composition problems come in three types:

- Problems inherent in an image

- Problems born of careless composition

- Personal vendettas

Problems inherent in the image are those that just couldn't be fixed when taking the image. Careless composition results when something sneaks into the frame unnoticed or when you haven't paid enough attention to what is there. The vendetta category consists of making certain changes to things you simply like or dislike; you might want to change a perfectly good image. There's no accounting for taste. There are guidelines to better composition, but the rules aren't rock solid. Understanding composition can help you achieve better images both with your camera and by making better corrections.

All good images have at least one thing in common: they usually flatter and enhance the subject. Chances are when you look at a good image, the subject stands out in a pleasing way. Good images also always start in the camera (or in your scanner), but you do have the opportunity to fix problems and make compositional alterations later in Photoshop Elements. The changes you make can be simplified by the understanding of color and masking that you've gained thus far, and they can be mastered by fixing what is "broken" in the image.

You've probably seen some of the most ridiculous composition faux pas in images you shoot—regrettably this usually happens after you've taken them and you are looking at the image result. The problems in composition almost always have to do with placement of objects in an image, image clutter, lighting, and the perspective on the subject.

For example, say you are at an awards ceremony where the governor comes to make an award presentation at a local Moose lodge. You try to get a picture at the climax of the evening, just as the award is handed to the recipient. You've never stopped to look at the background, and you've never considered another perspective but standing and shooting flat-footed from wherever you happened to get placed in the seating lottery. Later when you look at the image, you see the massive horns in the background. The mounted moose head on the wall in the background and the placement of the horns in your image make the person getting the award look more like Bullwinkle than a hero.

You could have prevented the need for correction by doing a little more to anticipate the image. Such planning could have included trying to position yourself for a better angle. By doing so, you probably could have avoided the moose head, and maybe you'd

Figure 7.1

This chair can be framed to fill the entire image or moved to another position in the frame so the image includes more of the setting and objects of potential interest.

have found a slightly more interesting angle on the subject as well. Don't forget to consider portrait and landscape options for framing.

- Look at every object in the viewfinder when framing your images, and eliminate what you don't need or want before taking the image, whenever possible.

- Take advantage of different angles, framing, and distance from your subject that may reveal interesting perspectives on your subject if it is appropriate, as shown in Figure 7.1.

Figure 7.2

The natural shadows in this image are complicated by unnatural shade. The result will be nearly impossible to save without editing heroics.

Another common problem with composition is that it is often just boring. When you take a portrait of friends who have come to visit from overseas, you line them up like cattle and take pictures only slightly more interesting than mug shots. And the only reason they are slightly more interesting is that you've again forgotten the moose head on the wall—which they probably don't have in the police station's booking room.

If you take an image with an on-camera flash of three static people standing and smiling—perhaps even at the ultimate moment as they chorus the smiley phrase "cheese"—no matter what you do, you are going to have three static people smiling flatly lit smiles. They may be washed out in the exposure and in various stages of blinking, sneezing, scratching, and so forth. For the next shot, you could move them to the shade of a leafless tree, where the branches cast a pattern of shadows that weave a complexity on their faces that you'll never remove (similar to the child in Figure 7.2). It won't matter if you change the backdrop to something interesting—Egyptian tombs, the Eiffel tower, or a moose head—the result will be about the same: an unflattering image of the main subject.

In the same vein, don't consider a flash as a tool to be used only in situations where it is otherwise too dark to shoot. A flash can fill in shadows and help offset harsh shadows caused by direct light (such as the sun). A portable reflector, foam-core board, white walls, and sheer curtains can all help you adjust lighting and get better results without much effort.

- Pay attention to sources of light and shadow—both artificial and natural. Use light to your advantage.
- Use reflectors, flash, and positioning to enhance lighting on subjects.
- Avoid the temptation to stagnate shots with posing, and avoid always shooting with the subject at the center of the frame.
- Consider taking multiple shots of a subject even if you think you got a good one; this can give you more image data to mine if you need to make corrections later.

Many times, composition problems—such as bird droppings on a statue—are just part of the "ambiance" of an image. Images can have clutter and debris that is no more attractive than minor dust and dirt that you'd get in a scan, and there is no way to anticipate or avoid it without missing the shot. Taking an image of a play on a ball field with a $2,000 lens will still capture the garbage caught in the swirling wind behind as the play unfolds—it just might get a better picture of it.

"Zoom lenses, aperture, shutter speed—who needs that stuff? Just about any camera on the shelf can be set to an auto mode that will correct the exposure. The catch phrase is 'point and shoot': all you have to do is follow orders, right? The gizmo does something, and the thingamajig does something else, and what the heck—you get a picture when it's all done." If you have that attitude toward taking pictures, your understanding of photography, and your control of the results, will never improve. Read your manuals and maybe a book or two on photography. Being good at editing images alone won't always get the job done.

- No equipment will always or automatically take a better picture just because it costs more.
- Don't depend on auto mode to know what you want. Read your manuals. Know how to use shutter speed, lens length, aperture, and exposure to control movement and depth of field when you need it. See Figure 7.3.

Certain things *can't* happen when you edit an image. You won't ever take a picture of the back of someone's head and flip it horizontally and see their face. That may sound ridiculous, but in a similar way, select objects can't often just be flipped right to left: you may be somewhat frozen in orientations because of lighting, perspective, and content. A stop sign flipped will not say *POTS*, it will say *STOP*, backward—that is, with all the letters reversed and in reverse order. In a similar way, an object captured with the light falling from the left will look odd if flipped the other way because it will be the only object in the scene where the light is striking from a different direction.

- Consider the image you are taking as the final product, even if you know you'll be editing it later. Always start with the best images you can.

- Be realistic in the results you expect from editing your images. When flipping the orientation of objects, be sure that the lighting, shadows, and content all make sense.

So if you take all of these steps to make good images, why is it that you need Photoshop Elements to fix your photos at all?

If you do advanced work with Photoshop Elements, you probably aren't taking images intending to spend a lot of time in front of the computer fixing them. Although there are certain things you can do to your images in the computer that you can't do in the heat of a flashbulb, you want to be going to the computer to enhance and flatter the content of your captures, just as good composition flatters a subject. Unless you are doing restoration, you will generally want to start with good images to make them even better, rather than spending a lot of time editing bad images to make them okay.

Whether you are taking an image by looking through the camera's viewfinder or evaluating it for corrections, the same questions of composition can come to mind. Even with your best effort on every image, there will often be compositional elements to adjust. The trick to correcting problems is not always so much finessing the image as recognizing what you consider a problem—then calmly stalking the problem like a hunter.

Figure 7.3

Lack of a more extreme depth of field and lighting conditions in this image provide only moderate separation from the background. Different settings would bring more or less of the background in focus.

TEN TIPS REVIEWED

1. Look at every object in the viewfinder when framing your images, and eliminate what you don't need or want before taking the image, whenever possible.

2. Take advantage of different angles, framing, and distance from your subject that may reveal interesting perspectives on your subject if it is appropriate.

3. Pay attention to sources of light and shadow—both artificial and natural. Use light to your advantage.

4. Use reflectors, flash, and positioning to enhance lighting on subjects.

5. Avoid the temptation to stagnate shots with posing, and avoid always shooting with the subject at the center of the frame.

6. Consider taking multiple shots of a subject even if you think you got a good one; this can give you more image data to mine if you need to make corrections later.

7. No equipment will always or automatically take a better picture just because it costs more.

8. Don't depend on auto mode to know what you want. Read your manuals. Know how to use shutter speed, lens length, aperture, and exposure to control movement and depth of field when you need it.

9. Consider the image you are taking as the final product, even if you know you'll be editing it later. Always start with the best images you can.

10. Be realistic in the results you expect from editing your images. When flipping the orientation of objects, be sure that the lighting, shadows, and content all make sense.

Now let's take a look at the tools you use for correcting and altering composition in your best captures.

Cropping as a Tool for Composition

Cropping entails cutting away the edges of your image; you choose what to keep or eliminate in the image while adjusting the orientation. You can crop to snip away image areas that don't matter or are distracting, to get the viewers' attention back to whatever it is that you want them to see. You can also use cropping to reorient images so the horizon is straight or so the composition is more interesting. Cropping is usually the first adjustment you will make in a digital edit when it comes to composition: it reduces the image area that you have to work on and helps focus the rest of your changes. Reshaping an image by cropping can result in a significant change in composition and in the feel of an image.

Figure 7.4

Cropping can correct perspective, remove unwanted image area, and help the viewer focus on the image.

OK

Cancel

Figure 7.5

Set the color of the cropped area to contrast with your image or as gray (or black) so it behaves as an image matte. Use the Opacity to block out any image area that you will crop, to give a good view of the result.

You can access the Crop tool by pressing C on the keyboard or by clicking its icon ⬛ in the toolbox. To use it, all you have to do is click on the image and drag a cropping box. Once the box is on the image, you can resize and rotate it by using the handles. Figure 7.4 shows two examples of how cropping can improve composition.

Color and Opacity options for the Crop tool found on the Options bar (see Figure 7.5) can help you visualize the result of your crops before you commit them. You can change the color of the area outside the crop area to give you an idea of what the image looks like cropped. I often use a 50 percent gray background at 90 percent opacity so I can barely see the image area I am removing and can get a good idea of the result. Too little opacity gives you very little idea of the final result as a preview; too much, and you can't really see what you are cropping out. Changing the color to white rather than the black default can help you see what the crop will look like on white paper. You can change to other colors as a preference or to preview how a crop will look with colored matting.

> You can commit the crop by clicking the OK button on the tool options bar, by pressing Enter, or by double-clicking within the boundaries of the cropping box over the image. Once you've accepted the crop, you can undo it by clicking Undo, pressing Command+Z/Ctrl+Z, or stepping back in the Undo history.

You can practice cropping these examples by using the Crop1.psd and Crop2.psd files included on the book's companion CD. These are simple examples of images that could use some cropping. At times, you may want to crop an image more than once: the first time to change the orientation on the object and the next to restore the framing. Cropping outside the image boundary (see Figure 7.6) will leave you with image areas filled with the background color.

Transformations and Distortions

One step away from cropping is using transformation and distortion to reshape an image or image objects. Transformations and distortions are casually looked at as a means of bending an image or making something look, well, demented. People tend to have fun with tools such as Transform or Liquify, and that is all well and good, but distortion tools can be used for repair as well. You may well need to distort your images using transformations to make them look more natural. So long as this is done with consideration (for resolution and the purpose of the image), you can sometimes use it to adjust composition. It can be useful for adjusting objects to "fit" them into a new image.

Figure 7.6

The cropping boundary has crossed over the image frame. It will take some concentrated effort to fix the missing corners of the image.

For example, images taken with a wide-angle lens may exaggerate the size of objects at the center of the image; if you take pictures of tall objects looking up at them, they can show an exaggerated perspective. Sometimes you will want to enhance these effects, and at other times you may want to minimize them. You may simply want to display some creativity and change the appearance of an object or reshape it to make it fit where you want it to appear in an image.

Take a look at the example image in Figure 7.7. There's nothing really wrong with this image; however, there are some things you might want to improve or change. For example, the window seems a bit skewed, and the wall does, too. The horizon (where the wall meets the floor) isn't flat, and the tree is a little tilted. The image looks as though the picture was taken somehow to distort the whole scene. It can be considered art—or something you want to adjust.

Say you are a perfectionist and just need to have all the objects in your image squared up. You can use the Transform command (Image → Transform) to bend and stretch the image until the window looks right— or has the perspective that you'd prefer. However, in some images like the sample pictured here, no one correction will fix all the problems, but several corrections using both the whole image and isolated areas will get much of the job done.

Figure 7.7

This original image shows a lot of distortion in perspective that can be adjusted with Transform.

If you want to reshape an entire image, you can flatten and duplicate the background or merge the content of the image to a new layer (merging to a new layer is two steps):

1. Create the new layer.

2. Use the Merge Visible command (Command+Option+Shift+E / Ctrl+Alt+Shift+E) to stamp the visible image to the new layer.

To isolate corrections, isolate image parts by moving them to their own layer. To move objects to their own layer, make a selection around what you want to reshape (in this case, the window), copy and paste it to its own layer, and use the Transform function to reshape the content of that selection.

In transforming layers or the whole image, you'll want to zoom out from the image to give you a little room to make adjustments. To zoom out from the image, use the

Command+-/Ctrl+- shortcut, and then pull open the image window using the image-sizing control at the lower right of the image window. Just click and drag the control to change the image window shape (see Figure 7.8).

Click and drag the handles on the bounding box to reshape the image. The image information inside the box changes to fit the new shape of the box. Pressing the Enter key or clicking the OK button on the Options bar commits the changes. Pressing the Esc (Escape) key will undo the transformation before it is committed. The modes for Transform are described in Table 7.1 and are demonstrated in Figure 7.9.

Starting with the image from Figure 7.7, you can go through a series of adjustments using Transform to adjust the image perspective for the sidewalk (Figure 7.10), the tree (Figure 7.11), and the window (Figure 7.12 and Figure 7.13). To make the changes, you can use multiple layers to adjust parts of the image separately and take advantage of some of the lack of detail in the wall area.

Figure 7.8

Moving the image window controller will adjust the size and shape of the image window without affecting zoom.

Figure 7.9

The Transform options can skew, rotate, scale, distort, and change perspective of your selection. Note that the cursor changes for different actions.

The original selection

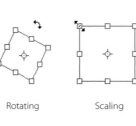

Rotating

Scaling

Skewing down

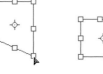

Skewing right

Skewing on center

Skewing a center handle

Distorting

Changing perspective

MODE	DESCRIPTION	
Free Transform	Enables you to rotate, scale, skew, distort, or change perspective without having to switch tool modes via the menu. Move the cursor outside the bounding box to rotate. Click any handle and move to scale the box; hold down the Shift key to scale proportionally; hold down Option+Shift / Alt+Shift to scale proportionally on center. Hold down Command+Shift / Ctrl+Shift to skew; hold down Command/Ctrl to distort; hold down Command+Option+Shift / Ctrl+Alt+Shift to change perspective.	**Table 7.1** **Transform Modes**
Skew	Enables you to reshape the bounding box by moving any handle along a current axis (side). Hold down the Shift key to switch the tool to Perspective; hold down Option/Alt to skew opposite handles (corners or sides) on center.	
Distort	Enables you to reshape the bounding box by moving any point freely. Hold down the Shift key to restrict movement to a current axis (side).	
Perspective	Enables you to skew or reshape the bounding box by moving handles. Moving the center handle skews the box along any axis (side). Moving a corner handle resizes the box in sync with the opposite corner: corners on the same axis (side) move in the opposite direction from one another.	

Transformations that you make should often be slight and as simple as possible to prevent distorting and resampling image areas excessively. Larger changes will compromise sharpness in a way similar to resampling.

The image is available on the CD (`perspectives.psd`). You should attempt to make the adjustments to the image just to practice a little with transformations. On your way through the corrections, you'll probably want to work with a few more Hidden Power tools: Guide Horizontal, Guide Vertical, and Delete Guide. These will enable you to place one-pixel-wide lines in your image to help with alignment—so you don't have to guess if things are aligned in the image. You can add as many guides as you want to an image, but you should probably remove them before storing the image, as they will add bulk to the file size. Guides will be added either 100 pixels from the top of the image (Guide Horizontal) or 100 pixels from the left of the image (Guide Vertical). The tools will select the Shape Select tool for you so you can move the guides into place. Holding down the Shift key as you move the guides will keep them fit to the image.

When using Hidden Power Guides, it's best to be working at 100% zoom. At lower percentages, these guides may disappear from view, though they will remain in the image.

To adjust the sidewalk, you want to level the horizon line where the wall meets the sidewalk. You do this with a simple movement of the Transform function and align to a guide that you place as a visual cue.

1. Open the `perspectives.psd` file on the Hidden Power CD.
2. Duplicate the Background layer, and rename the layer **Level Sidewalk**.

Figure 7.10

Tugging down the lower-left corner of this image helps straighten the sidewalk.

Figure 7.11

Pushing in the upper-right corner of the image easily straightens the tree.

3. Make a new horizontal guide by double-clicking the Guide Horizontal tool in the Power_Extras category of Effects.

4. Hold down the Shift key, and drag the guide into place so the right end of the guide aligns to the spot where the sidewalk meets the wall at the right of the image.

5. Activate the Level Sidewalk layer.

6. Open the Transform function by pressing Command+T/Ctrl+T. This will create the bounding box for transform around the image.

7. Hold down the Command+Shift/Ctrl+Shift key, click and drag the controller at the lower-left corner of the bounding box down until the sidewalk is aligned with or parallel to the guide created in step 2, and release the mouse button. Pressing the Command+Shift/Ctrl+Shift key will shift to Skew mode.

8. Accept the changes by clicking the Commit Transform button ✔ on the Options bar.

9. Delete the guide by double-clicking the Delete Guide tool in the Power_Extras category of Effects.

With the horizon straightened, the next area of attack is the tree, which you can adjust using a duplicate of the Level Sidewalk layer and a guide to help you determine what is vertical.

10. Duplicate the Level Sidewalk layer, and rename the layer **Straighten Tree**.

11. Make a new vertical guide by double-clicking the Guide Vertical tool in the Power_Extras category of Effects.

12. Hold down the Shift key, and drag the guide into place so the lower end of the guide aligns with the middle of the base of the tree.

13. Activate the Straighten Tree layer.

14. Open the Transform function by pressing Command+T/Ctrl+T. This will create the bounding box for transforming around the image.

15. Hold down the Command+Shift/Ctrl+Shift key, click and drag the controller at the upper-right corner of the bounding box to the left until the tree is aligned with or parallel to the guide created in step 11, and release the mouse button.

16. Accept the changes by clicking the Commit Transform button on the Options bar.

At this point, there is a gap to the right of the image where the lower layers show through. You can adjust that area now or wait till the end of the perspective adjustments. We'll discuss the patching adjustments more at the end of the step-by-step. Right now, we will go through the steps for adjusting the window, which will include adjusting both the inside and the outside of the frame.

17. Duplicate the Background layer, rename the layer **Window Adjustment**, and drag the layer to the top of the layer stack.

18. Choose the Rectangular Marquee tool, set the Feather to 20 pixels, and make a generous selection around the window. Select the inverse (Command+Shift+I / Ctrl+Shift+I), and press Delete. This will leave the original window on its own layer.

19. Make a new vertical guide by double-clicking the Guide Vertical tool in the Power_Extras category of Effects.

20. Hold down the Shift key, and drag the guide into place so the guide aligns with the lower-left corner of the window frame base.

21. Activate the vertical guide that you used to straighten the tree, and then hold down the Shift key and drag the guide so it aligns with the lower-right corner of the window frame.

Figure 7.12
This first part of the adjustment straightens the outside of the window frame.

22. Create a new horizontal guide using the Guide Horizontal tool, and then hold down the Shift key and drag the guide so it aligns with the upper-right corner of the window frame.

23. Create a new horizontal guide using the Guide Horizontal tool, and then hold down the Shift key and drag the guide so it aligns with the lower-left corner of the window frame. This will complete a frame of guides around the window.

24. Activate the Window Adjustment layer.

25. Open the Transform function by pressing Command+T/Ctrl+T. This will create the bounding box for transforming around the window area isolated in step 18.

26. Hold down the Command/Ctrl key, and click and drag the corner controllers at each corner of the bounding box to align the sides of the window to the guides you have placed (steps 19–23).

27. Accept the changes by clicking the Commit Transform button on the Options bar.

Adjustments to the outside of the window frame will leave the inside of the frame seeming a little skewed.

28. Duplicate the Window Adjustment layer, and name the duplicate layer **Sash Adjustment**.

29. Choose the Rectangular Marquee tool, set the Feather to 2 pixels, and make a selection around the window a few pixels in from the edge of the frame on all sides. Select the inverse (Command+Shift+I / Ctrl+Shift+I), and press Delete. This will leave the selected area isolated on its own layer.

Figure 7.13

This second adjustment to the window is fine-tuning for the inside of the window frame.

30. Choose the Shape Selection tool, and activate the layer with the vertical guide to the right (this should be the topmost Guide layer in the Layers palette). Hold down the Shift key, and move the guide in to align with the lower-right corner of the inside of the window frame.

31. Activate the left vertical guide (this should be the second Guide layer from the top in the Layers palette), and then hold down the Shift key and drag the guide so it aligns with the lower-left corner of the inside of the window frame.

32. Activate the upper horizontal guide (this should be the third Guide layer from the top in the Layers palette), and then hold down the Shift key and drag the guide so it aligns with the upper-left corner of the inside of the window frame.

33. Activate the lower horizontal guide (this should be the bottom-most Guide layer in the Layers palette), and then hold down the Shift key and drag the guide so it aligns with the lower-left corner of the window frame. This will complete a frame of guides around the inside of the window frame.

34. Activate the Sash Adjustment layer.

35. Open the Transform function by pressing Command+T/Ctrl+T. This will create the bounding box for transforming around the isolated area.

36. Hold down the Command/Ctrl key, and click and drag the corner controllers at each corner of the bounding box to align the sides of the window with the guides you have placed.

37. Accept the changes by clicking the Commit Transform button on the Options bar.

38. Delete the guides by double-clicking the Delete Guide tool in the Power_Extras category of Effects four times.

While this seems like a long series of steps, it allows you to go through a good variety of transformations to see how they work. These examples show that you can manipulate whole images or attack objects that you want to fix separately. You can make selections using simple selection tools, or you can use other Hidden Power techniques.

After adjusting the tree, the right-hand side of the image will expose the layer below. To patch the area, create a new layer and call it **Patch Wall and Shadow**. Use the layer to patch the area that is exposed. You can use more than one layer, if desired. For information about patching the image, see the techniques for repairing black-and-white and color images in Chapters 5 and 6, and see the layered corrections in the perspectives_corrected.psd image on the CD. Patching can include using the Clone Stamp tool, the Healing tool, and other patching techniques.

When you use transform functions, you might be looking to make a fine-tuning adjustment to an object or image, or you may want to radically reshape an image element, in essence re-creating the image or object in a form that didn't exist before. Either type of adjustment may require isolating elements based on color or tone and then altering the shape of the element itself. We'll look at some techniques for isolating image elements in the next section.

Isolating Image Elements

Flattering the subject can mean complementing or isolating it in some way so the object is clear in the image. Isolation is really a three-step process. First, you isolate an image area by using selection or masking. This can be an involved process in which you use many of the techniques that have been discussed prior to this point in the book (separations, masking, calculations, channel/component mixing, and so forth). Once you've selected your elements, you can cut and paste them to a new layer to isolate them from other image areas. With the area isolated, you can apply effects focused on just that isolated area of the image. The digital isolation of the image element is technical, and the image alteration that completes the visible separation is more artistic. We'll look at a few different solutions as we jump into an example.

> Keep in mind that it will sometimes take a variety of methods to get a good outline of any object in your images that you can use to create a selection, and you may well have to combine manual, calculated, and other techniques. Selection and masking are not always easy, and sometimes they require meticulous effort. It is often the case that newer users expect tools to essentially read their mind. While it may be obvious in looking at an image that you want to select a particular object, the mathematics that controls tool functions never sees the image. Don't feel you are doing something wrong just because it takes a long time.

The `tigerlily.psd` file (included on the CD) looks like Figure 7.14. When you first open the image in Photoshop Elements, the background and foreground will show some difference, but there could be more separation between this object and the background. Also, the background is riddled with color noise and looks uneven. We'll strengthen that separation by using different effects, such as placing a drop shadow, blurring the background, and even replacing the background. Blurring will further obscure detail in the background, and the drop shadow will serve to burn in (or darken) the area around whatever selection you make. Each of these things is easy to do once you have separated the "keeper" part of the image into its own layer.

We'll expand on the three basic steps below over the next few sections as we go through the exercise.

Select the object You have a lot of options for making selections of the plant and flower, from making a manual outline of them, to selecting with the assistance of calculations, to making a selection with the Hidden Power Blend Mask tool. We'll look at more than one way to do this and save the selection.

Use the selection to isolate the object Once the selection is made, you have the run of the house. You can manipulate the elements separately—including color, tone, and any other adjustment you can think of. All you have to do is get the image object(s) on their own layer(s), which we'll do in short order by using the selection in conjunction with the Copy and Paste commands.

Make separation changes We'll use some effects on the background to reduce the detail there, and then create a drop shadow from the isolated flower to add some separation between the plant and the background.

Making a Selection of the Object (Manual)

One way to make your selection is by manually defining the selection area. There are many ways that you can do this, including using the Lasso or Magnetic Lasso tool or converting a stencil that you make by painting on a new layer. Here we'll use the Selection

Brush tool. The section that follows, "Making a Selection of the Object (Calculations)," presents an alternative set of steps for accomplishing a similar selection with far less manual intervention.

1. Open the `tigerlily.psd` file included on the CD.

2. Choose the Selection Brush tool (press A). Set the options for the tool as follows: Size = 20 Pixels, Mode = Mask, Hardness = 95%, Overlay Opacity = 60%, Overlay Color = red (R = 255, G = 0, B = 0).

> The Selection Brush can be used in either Mask or Selection mode. We used Mask mode for this example. You can switch back and forth between modes by changing the mode while using the tool.

3. Change the colors on the toolbar to the default colors by pressing D on the keyboard.

4. Zoom in to 200%–300%. This will ensure that you can see all the pixels in the image.

> The percentage displayed at the bottom left and title bar of the image in Elements refers to the percentage of pixels that you are viewing rather than print size. Any time you view at greater than 100%—regardless of image resolution—you will be able to make out pixilization to a greater or lesser degree.

5. Using the Selection Brush, trace the outline of the flower (outside), staying as close as possible to the edge of the petals and stems. If you hold down the Shift key and click, you can create short line segments; using a series of these line segments when drawing around the edge of the petals will work on all but the toughest curves, and it is easier than trying to draw the whole outline freehand. After outlining with a larger brush, you can change the brush size to get into tight areas. Hold down the Option/Alt key to erase. Complete the circuit of the selection, making an edge all the way around the lily. Be sure to get the areas between the flowers. The completed outline will look something like Figure 7.15 but will be in red on your screen. You could continue to use the Selection Brush here to fill in all the areas of the image that you don't want to select, but we'll speed this up and make it more accurate by combining a stenciling technique using layers.

> There is a difference between input devices. Mice, tablets, and trackballs all have their advantages and disadvantages. I have used a trackball for more than 10 years (see http://aps8.com/trackball.html) because it suits the way I work and gives me unparalleled control. If you are having trouble with freehand movements in Photoshop, you might try another input device.

Figure 7.15

The outline surrounds the entire plant with solid color.

6. When the outline is complete, choose the Magic Wand tool (press W). The mask you have created will turn into a selection. Invert the selection by pressing Command+Shift+I / Ctrl+Shift+I. Set the Magic Wand to 0 Tolerance, Contiguous, and uncheck the Use All Layers option.

7. Create a new layer (Command+Shift+N / Ctrl+Shift+N), and fill the selection with black (Edit → Fill Selection; use the Foreground Color, Normal Mode, and 100% Opacity). Name the layer **Plant Selection**.

8. Deselect (Command+D / Ctrl+D).

9. Using the Magic Wand, hold down the Shift key, and click in each of the areas that you have not painted red that lie outside the areas of the plant. This will add those areas to the selection. You should only have to click in five places for this image.

10. Expand the selection (Select → Modify → Expand) by half the diameter of the brush created in step 2 (in this case, 10 pixels). Expanding the selection compensates for any softness at the edge of the area you filled previously (step 7). This should make the selection fall across the center of the outline created in steps 5–7.

11. Fill with the foreground color. At this point, you have completed the basic shape for the selection of the flowers. Figure 7.16 shows the result.

12. Change the Opacity of the layer to 0% or shut off the view. No kidding. This will hide the layer whether the visibility is on or off and will essentially store the selection. It is just another way to temporarily hide a selection in your image.

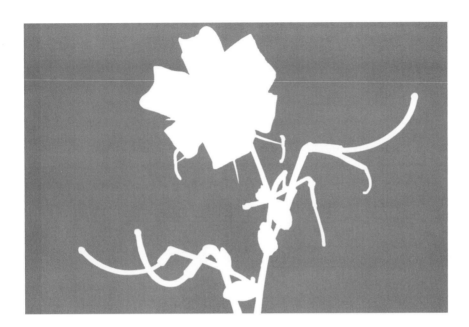

Figure 7.16

The gray area of this figure shows the area that should be filled when you have completed step 11.

The black fill in the Plant Selection layer should not cover any of the flowers, and it should have a slightly soft edge. Later we will use this content to load a selection and make short work of the image adjustment.

Making a Selection of the Object (Calculations)

A second way to select the lily is by helping to define the selection of the shape with calculations. This section does not follow from the previous one but substitutes for it. You may find a number of ways to do something similar to what is suggested here using calculations. The idea is to take whatever advantages you see in the image, successfully make an enhancement to get the result you need, and lessen the amount of work you have to do manually.

The lily is the brightest element in the image, and that generally makes it a pretty easy target for this kind of selection and open to a lot of other possibilities. For example, you might just be able to use the Threshold tool to define most of your selection. In a similar way, the darkest, most saturated, least saturated, or most color-defined image areas can all provide the information you need to make a calculated selection—depending on the separations you choose to make, the image you are working on, and what you want to achieve. We'll look to a calculation to bring out your result in a way that is partially specific to this image.

1. Starting with the `tigerlily.psd` image, make an RGB separation by using the RGBL Components Only tool under the Power_Separations category in Effects.

2. View all the components, and then delete the Blue component layer. You won't need it for this calculation, because it offers very little practical distinction in the object you are trying to separate. However, take a look at it to see why it isn't helpful.

Figure 7.17

The basic image components split out as shown here. The Blue component offers few advantages, but Red, Green, and Luminosity do.

Red

Green

Blue

Luminosity

3. Leave the Green and Luminosity components visible; then set the Luminosity component layer to Linear Dodge mode. Doing this will emphasize the bright information in the Green component. Light areas will get much lighter. Most of the flower will turn pure white.

4. Move the Red component layer to the top of the layer stack, and set it to Multiply mode. Other options that produce similar results are Overlay and Hard Light. The red is more consistently dark around the flower, and setting it to one of these modes uses the natural contrast of the Red component to darken the perimeter area outside the flower. This should help darken the area around the flower to black, while leaving the flower itself pure white. This will result in a pretty good outline of the petals in black-and-white. See Figure 7.18.

5. Merge the layers used in the calculation (Green, Luminosity, and Red) to a new layer, and name the layer **Plant Selection**. It is not yet a selection, but you will use this layer just like the Plant Selection layer in the manual technique.

6. Get a brush and touch up the rough outline of the flowers made with the calculation. To touch up, either fill in any areas you don't need to select by painting over those areas with black, or paint with white to remove black areas to add to the selected part

Figure 7.18

While this outline is not perfect, it uses existing image information to enhance the image content to make manual adjustment easier and quicker than using manual selection alone.

of the mask. Once you have either the black or white part of the mask complete, you can use it to finish the job (use the Magic Wand with 0 Tolerance to select the area you have completed, and then invert the selection and fill with the opposite color). While touching up, you will want to use a larger brush (50–70 pixels diameter) that is 90%–95% hard. Press D to get default colors, and switch between those colors using X to exchange foreground and background colors.

As an alternative to painting, you could use a selection tool such as the lasso to select larger areas of the image to fill with black or white. Other options include doing a levels correction to emphasize content or making other calculations.

7. When you have finished with the touch-up, double-click Clear Grayscale and then double-click Commit Transparency, both found in the Power_Masking category of Effects in the Hidden Power tools. This will first create the appearance of the mask and then commit the transparency. It creates a mask based on the black-and-white content of the Plant Selection layer. The white areas will be transparent.

8. Change the Opacity of the Plant Selection layer to 0 percent, and/or turn off the Visibility.

9. Delete the Green, Red, Luminosity, and Composite layers by dragging them to the trash icon in the Layers palette.

10. Change the Source layer back to the Background by activating the Source layer and choosing Layer → New → Background From Layer.

This series of steps should create a layer filled with black that is nearly identical to the manual selection made in the previous set of steps.

SELECTING FLYAWAY HAIR?

A common request in user forums on the Internet is the ability to quickly select a subject's flyaway hair. This can be challenging: there is no guaranteed way to make that kind of selection and no one-size-fits-all methodology. If the hair is photographed against a distinct color (such as a blue or green screen), it may be a better idea to apply the advantage posed by the background color to create a mask rather than attempting to make an absolutely nutty selection based on the thin wisps of hair. Similarly to the techniques used in "Making a Selection of the Object (Calculations)," you might build a color range mask either using Hue/Saturation or Blend Mask. If you target the mask correctly to the color range of the background, you can use it to drop in whatever background replacement you want or use it to create a selection that enables you to isolate the wisps to their own layer.

Alpha Channels in Elements Images

Since each of the previous sections talks about storing a selection as a layer, this seems like a good spot to discuss saving selections as alpha channels. An *alpha channel* is like a hidden layer and acts as a means of storing a selection, only you can't see it in the Layers palette; it is stored in the same way color is stored (as a component), but the alphas don't affect image color. When the alpha channels are loaded, they re-create the selection that was stored—exactly. You can use the alphas to store and resurrect selections of the objects.

One of the improvements made to Photoshop Elements in version 2 was the ability to save, load, and delete alpha channels by choosing the Save Selection, Load Selection, and Delete Selection functions, respectively. (For those using Photoshop Elements 1, the Hidden Power tools include a way to work with alphas.) To save a selection, you should have the selection active and choose Save Selection from the bottom of the Selection menu. Later, after saving the selection, you can load it again at any time by choosing Load Selection from the Selection menu.

The only problem with saving and loading selections in Elements is that you can't see alpha channels, so you have to work a little blind and partly from memory. If you store a lot of selections in any one image, there isn't a quick way to purge them from your images.

(If you're still using either version 1 or 2, see my website, `www.hiddenelements.com`, for information about procuring the appropriate Hidden Power tools.)

For version 4 of Elements, I've provided two Hidden Power tools to help you work with selections: Del Selections And Alphas, and Preview Selection found in the Power_Extras category of Effects. Del Selections and Alphas will help you purge selections from your image without having to delete them one at a time, or it can help you separate out selections into separate documents. Removing the alphas will help keep your images trim in file size. Preview Selection will provide a brief preview of any of the saved selections you choose. You'll work with alphas to save and load your selections, so we'll look at how to save and load in the following procedures.

To store a selection, you have to have one active. You can use the selection layer you created to load a selection and then save that as an alpha channel.

1. Hold down the Command/Ctrl key and click on the Plant Selection layer in the Layers palette.

2. Choose Save Selection from the Select menu.

3. Type a name for your selection/alpha channel in the field provided in the dialog for the name. For this example, enter **Plant Selection**.

4. Click OK to accept the changes and save the selection by the name you entered.

That is all there is to saving a selection. Once it is saved, you can actually go ahead and delete the Plant Selection layer. Before you do, try loading the selection so you can be sure you have it all working right. Just choose Load Selection on the Select menu. When the dialog box appears, select the name you entered in step 3 above from the Selection drop-down list (it will be selected for you if it is the only alpha in the image). If a selection shows up around the plant, you have successfully stored the selection. Go ahead and delete the Plant selection layer. To Delete an alpha channel and permanently remove a stored selection from you image, just choose Delete Selection from the Select menu. When the dialog box appears, choose the name of the alpha channel that you want to delete, and click OK to accept the change. Do not delete the Plant Selection, as you will be using it in the next section.

If you have an image where you've saved a bunch of selections and you want to purge them all, the Del Selections And Alphas tool in the Power_Extras category in Effects can help you out. All you have to do is double-click Del Selections And Alphas, and the Hidden Power tool will separate all the channels in the image and then ask you which you want to combine to re-create your image. If the image was RGB, you would choose RGB from the drop-down list in the dialog to tell Elements what type of file it should make; then choose the color channels. In an RGB image, the RGB channels will be separated into `filename.red`, `filename.green`, and `filename.blue` (where `filename` stands for the name of the image before you split it; if you are splitting a file you hadn't saved, the filename will be `Untitled` with a number: `Untitled-#`). The image will be reassembled from the sources you choose.

A selection is represented on-screen by the selection outline. This selection outline tells only part of the story about what is actually selected. The outline shows only where the selection is at least 50 percent effective. If there is grayscale in your selection or feathering, the only way you'll know exactly what total area will be affected is by previewing the selection. Hidden Power provides the Preview Selection tool to preview any saved selection.

To preview a selection as grayscale, be sure you've saved the selection you want to preview in the current image, and then double-click Preview Selection in the Power_Extras category of the Hidden Power tools on the Effects palette. This tool will prompt you to select a saved alpha. When you have made the choice, the selection will preview automatically and then fade. When the preview disappears, a message will appear telling you the preview is complete. Do not interrupt the process. Try it out by running the tool and choosing the Plant Selection alpha.

These few tools should add powerful selection-storage and selection-management features to your repertoire. The method that you use for storing the selection is not as critical as the result. You can use the layer-storage method or the alpha storage and garner the same result. Storing the selection as an alpha assures you won't lose it by flattening the image, and it keeps the Layers palette free of clutter. We will use the stored alpha with the process in the next section.

Using Stored Selections to Isolate an Object

Whether you made your selection manually or with the help of calculations, should now have stored the Plant Selection layer as an alpha channel that will enable you to manipulate elements in the image.

1. Load the Plant Selection layer as a selection by choosing Load Selection from the Selection menu and choosing the Plant Selection alpha from the channel drop-down list.

2. Activate the Background layer.

3. Copy and paste (Command+J / Ctrl+J). This will paste the plant into a new layer. Change the layer name to **Plant**.

4. Load the selection again by choosing Reselect from the Selection menu or pressing Command+Shift+D / Ctrl+Shift+D. Choose Select → Invert (Command+Shift+I / Ctrl+Shift +I) to invert the selection.

5. Activate the Background layer.

6. Copy and paste the background to create a new layer. Name the layer **Plant Background**. Figure 7.19 shows a breakdown of the layers in detail and in the Layers palette.

Your layers should be in the exact order shown in the figure. Isolating the background might have taken you one step further than you expected to go. However, you may need the plant background on its own layer. The reason for this is that the color from the plant could bleed into the background when you make certain adjustments to the layer if the objects aren't separate. Treating them as separate objects keeps the reactions separate. We'll look at some instances where that can be an issue in the next section, where we use the layers that have been created for changes to improve the image.

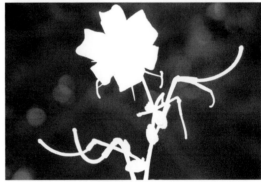

Making the Isolated Changes

Now that the image elements have been isolated into their own layers, you can edit them individually. By adding layered changes over the background, such as a manual drop shadow, or even replacing the background, you can improve separation or change the entire image. First, let's place the drop shadow and blur the background to see how that improves the image.

1. Activate the Plant Background layer.

2. Apply a Gaussian Blur (Filter → Blur → Gaussian Blur). The radius should be broad enough to significantly blur the background, but the setting is your choice (probably 5–10 pixels in radius is enough). If you click the Lock Transparent Pixels option ▣ for the layer on the Layers palette before the blur, solid pixels on the layer will remain solid. The result should be a smoother look to the background.

3. Load the Plant layer as a selection by Command+ clicking it / Ctrl+clicking it in the Layers palette. Create a new layer, and drag it below the Plant layer (between the Plant layer and the Plant Background layer). Name the layer **Drop Shadow**. The selection will be used to create a drop shadow on the new layer.

4. Adjust the selection. For this example we will both Expand and Feather the selection (find these tools on the Select menu). Expanding will give you a broader base

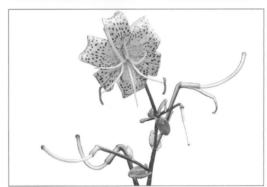

Figure 7.19

The layers you have left will be the original Background, the Plant Background, and the Plant neatly stacked from the bottom up in the Layers palette.

around the area of the plant, and Feathering will blend in the effect of the shadow at the edges and into the background. The stronger you want the effect to be, the broader you should make both. Try Expand and Feather settings of 10 pixels.

5. Fill the selection with black. Set the layer mode to Multiply to ensure that areas of the image below the shadow darken. You can control the intensity of the effect by using layer opacity. Figure 7.20 shows the original, the drop shadow, and the result.

Blurring the background does several things, including smoothing out the image noise rather handily and making the depth of field seem that much greater (a blurrier background adds an appearance of distance from the background). Placing the drop shadow increases the local contrast around the plant and enhances the separation from the background.

At this point, you may want to try painting in some highlights or working with other effects and correction, but the basic purpose of isolating these image objects has been accomplished. You can replace the background entirely (Figure 7.21) or work to enhance the background and control the effects (Figure 7.22). The point is that isolation of objects gives you the control to do so.

Figure 7.20

This example shows shadowing to enhance separation. Other options, such as using white for the shadow, could add separation between a dark object and its dark background.

Original

Drop Shadow

Result

Figure 7.21

A popular replacement for background could be a sky, a tree trunk, a background with some effects, or something shot specifically for the purpose. In any case (as is the case here), shadowing or glow can be added to keep the objects distinct.

Figure 7.22

Working with the background to enhance the interesting parts and blackwashing the rest creates a more natural and effective background.

Along the line of working with isolated elements in your images is working with separate elements and images that you may want to composite. We'll look at how to work with those situations in the next few sections.

Compositing Image Elements

In times of image trouble, one of the greatest options to have is the availability of more than one source image with which to work. If you take several shots of the same scene, you are really safeguarding yourself for any corrections you might have to make. For example, if you are taking one of those artificially posed group shots (we all do it at some time or another), and you take one shot, you may find that Bessy blinked and Billy had a finger up his nose. If you pause a moment and take another shot, Billy and Bessy might be fine while Uncle Dom is fending off a bee and one of the twins has run off. Neither of the shots is good by itself, but since they were taken at the same time, you can use elements from each to create one good image. It is probably more time-efficient to go find the twin and try one more shot, but in a pinch, you have the information you need for the completed image. Just composite a shot including Bessy without the blink and the more flattering pose for Billy from the second shot to fix the first.

This same philosophy works to help you fix any number of other problems. Say you go out and shoot a great picture of a balloon race starting off in the early morning as they float up the hillside at the peak of fall foliage. The image is perfect, except for one balloon basket that is partially in the image and seems like a mistake, or the billboard ad you can't crop out, or the electrical wires, or a water tower.... If you wait a moment and snap another image, the balloons will have moved and you'll have a different view of the background—and perhaps a different way to crop the image. If you wait till the balloons are above the hillside, you can take a clean shot of the hill by itself, revealing a whole fresh set of autumn leaves, and then place the balloons wherever you want. If you take a shot of the balloons against the sky, you gain the advantage of easily isolating them to later mix and match the positions of the balloons as you'd prefer. More source material in the same light, from the same angle, can be far better than having to repeat information in the image that is cloned from one place to another. As long as the images are good, you'll have more freedom to use different parts of different images to create the image you were looking for in the first place.

This type of multi-image thinking can be turned right on its head to help you make better shots and solve creative problems. You may set up shots that you take in parts *on purpose* to get a better result.

For example, say you are taking a product shot of the teapot in Figure 7.23 to sell on a website. There is a little more than meets the eye because there are several internal parts, and you'd like to show them all in one image. Lighting multiple objects in a scene can get tricky: objects in close proximity can block lighting and cast shadows over one another—not always in a flattering way. One way to rid yourself of the lighting problem is to shoot each part that you want to include and then assemble the shots into one final image. This enables you to make the best of each part and simplifies the process: you make one lighting setup, shoot each of the parts so you can easily extract it from the background—perhaps even take a picture of just the background—and then make a composite of the parts. This is similar to isolating objects in your images as we did in the previous section, but because you are shooting objects with the intent to isolate them later, your work in selecting and isolating the objects can be much easier.

If you take pictures of the parts of the teapot separately, all you have to do is compile them in a single image. Simple, right? You may have to create a background, unless you take an image to use for that separately. You can spend a lot of time with this one depending on how meticulous you are. The results will be much different than if you had just placed all the objects together in a clump and shot a lot of pictures trying to get the right one.

At this point, a detailed step-by-step procedure that walks you through the process would really be superfluous and counterproductive, and it would thwart your creativity. If you have followed the idea of the previous sections, now it is time to put that understanding

Figure 7.23

This teapot contains several different pieces.

to work for you and apply the process. Here is an outline of the steps to take in creating an image composite:

1. Collect the Image Parts I've already shot the image parts for you, and the files are included on the CD in a folder called Teapot. There are five: the glass, the harness, the insert holder, the top, and the basket. Open all the images.

2. Extract the Image Parts Isolate the objects in each image, and copy and paste each element into a new layer. Use whatever method you want to use to make the selection prior to isolating the parts—you may even want to mix techniques. The previous section with the plant may provide some guidelines for accomplishing selection and isolation. In some instances, calculations can prove to be pretty easy because the blue parts of the pot will provide an easy target. However, the glass and basket have highlights and a lack of color, which may be a bit more challenging. To make this a little more interesting, the separate shots are not all color-correct, so you might want to fix that (see suggestions for color correction in chapter 6). You can match the color across the pieces either by making an adjustment to each image according to the background or by correcting the background to gray. I'm not sure how it happened, but one of these darned objects got shot in slightly different light. See how even the best-planned images can easily go awry?

3. Create/Obtain the Background Image You can use a totally flat background, or you can add a little interest and make it seem more realistic with a slight gradient—perhaps multiple gradients—and a touch of noise. Make a background large enough to hold all the objects, and create the content for the background. Suggestions include borrowing the background from a public domain website (please be careful of copyright restrictions) or quickly making up your own. I have included a grayscale version of the background pictured in Figure 7.24 on the CD (Background.psd), but it may need to be colored, and I encourage you to make your own. The background you create is up to you, but it should be at least twice as wide as the widest object and twice as tall as the tallest, with the same ppi. You'll have to remember one additional challenge: that glass on the pot is supposed to be transparent, so whatever you end up with as a background has to somehow make sense with what you can see through the glass. You might want to take care of that with color masking.

4. Combine the Image Parts Move all the objects into the background image you have chosen to use, and arrange the objects in positions roughly as you want them to appear. This may require not only moving positions of the objects but ordering the layers as well so objects appear in front of and behind other objects as desired. You can arrange the objects however you want to within the image, either following the example or creating your own order.

5. Make the Image Parts Work Together Make adjustments to the objects in the image to make them work in concert. Now that all of the objects are in one place, it will be easier to see what looks unnatural. For the most part, this will be because there are no shadows. Create drop shadows for each of the objects individually, and link the object layers to their shadows (to link, highlight both layers and click the Link icon 👄 on the Layers palette). Often, just a simple, soft, semiopaque shadow outlining the base of the object will do. This helps to blend the elements and make them interact—rather than seeming like disparate pieces of a puzzle that were pasted into an image. You may want to create these shadows manually by using black, a feathered brush, and a layer with the mode set to Multiply just below the object (similar to what we did with the plant, but applying the effect manually). Be conscious also of areas where elements cross. For example, if you overlap the glass onto the harness, part of that harness should probably show through the glass. Your adjustments will have to reflect that.

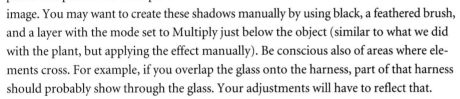

Figure 7.24
This light gradient background was made entirely from simple applications of the Gradient tool and should serve as a fine place to insert the objects. You can try to imitate this, or you can just make your own background.

When you are finished compositing the elements, the image might look something like Figure 7.25.

While this may seem like a lot of trouble to go through, if the results you are looking for are that the image is clear and the objects are rendered well, this may be a good solution. Your other choice would be obtaining lighting equipment that can help you light objects and reduce shadows (such as a light box). However, the real point is that compositing elements is possible—and sometimes even desirable. And the process always uses the same steps:

1. Collect the image parts.
2. Extract the image parts.
3. Create/obtain the background image.
4. Combine the image parts.
5. Make the image parts work together.

Let's look at one more example of compositing in creating a panorama and the advantages it poses for interesting image composition.

Figure 7.25

The composite of the parts will show a clear rendering of each component without the trouble you'd otherwise have with shadows in trying to light all the parts at once.

Creating a Panorama

Similar to the exercises in the last few sections—and with elements of each—is creating a panorama by stitching together consecutive shots taken in a horizontal or vertical plain. Images shot for a panorama are taken in a series—usually in quick succession—and the series of images is connected to create a continuous landscape. The photos are usually taken in a vertical or horizontal pan to capture a broader or taller area than you would normally get in a single frame with whatever camera and lens you are using. Because you take several overlapping images shot in succession (perhaps using a tilt [vertical movement] or pan [horizontal movement] of a tripod), your resulting image will have more image information once stitched together and can be enlarged more than a single frame of the same scene.

Good panoramas are a little tricky to shoot and often tricky to stitch together seamlessly. Lighting conditions change as you pivot the camera, and cameras in any type of auto-exposure mode will try to compensate for that between shots. This leaves you with a lot of tone and color changes to correct in post-processing. Taking some care while shooting the source images for the panorama will help simplify processing. Instead of looking forward to corrections, you can avoid some of them by switch the camera to a manual mode first—before shooting any of the images. This will keep the exposure setting the same for each frame in your panorama and will make matching the exposure of the individual frames similar and your work at the computer a lot easier later. Setting up your camera on a tripod for the movement can also help by keeping the frames mostly aligned. When you shoot the frames, you will want 30–50 percent overlap to give yourself plenty of room to blend one image into the next as you stitch them together.

A good way to see how panoramas go together is to try an example. Instead of sending you out to shoot some source images, the shots for this exercise are included on the CD. The panorama shots are shown in Figure 7.26.

Figure 7.26

The composite of the parts will show a clear rendering of each component without the trouble you'd otherwise have with shadows in trying to light all the parts at once.

Left.psd

Middle-Left.psd

Middle-Right.psd

Right.psd

Panorama_Sample.psd

During editing to make these images stitch together smoothly, you will likely have to pull out all the stops and use almost all we've done so far to get a good result. If you open the source images (`left.psd`, `middle-left.psd`, `middle-right.psd`, and `right.psd`), you will notice some noise in the images, and the color may need a little correction—though it is possible to forgo most of these corrections until after the images are stitched together, as long as you keep them in their own layers.

Photoshop Elements provides a tool for helping you work with panoramas. Now is a good time to test it out, though we will explore an entirely manual method. To take a look

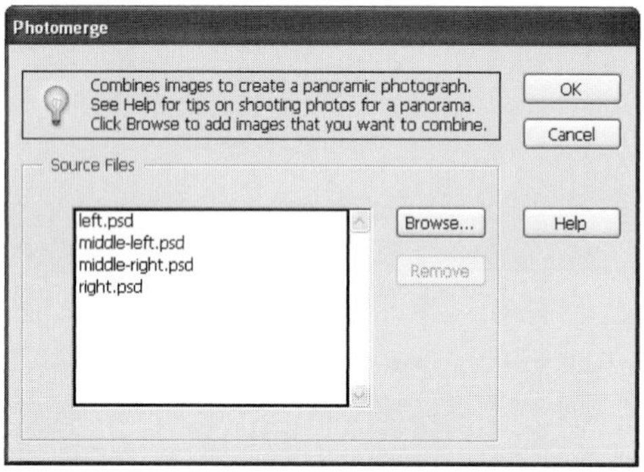

Figure 7.27

The initial dialog for Photomerge allows you to select the images you will be using for the panorama, either from images that are already open or images accessible by your computer.

at what the panorama tool does, with the four source images open, choose File → New → Photomerge Panorama. The Photomerge dialog will appear with a listing of the files you have open (see Figure 7.27). If there are images that you have open that you don't want in the panorama, eliminate them from the list at this time by selecting them and then using the Remove button; then accept the changes by clicking OK. The program will attempt to align the shots for you, and while it will make a valiant effort, I have never quite found it to be right on the money.

In the case of our example images, you may find that the tool actually gives up and places only two or three of the images in the workspace, leaving some of the source in the thumbnail bar at the top of the screen. Your results will often vary if you close the Photomerge dialog and try the process again. With the dialog open and the images in it, you can click on and drag the source components out of and into the thumbnail bar (Lightbox) and adjust positions of the images in the main preview panel. As you move the source images, note that the angle of blending between the images changes as they overlap.

You can zoom into or out from the image using the Zoom tool 🔍 or Navigator slider. You can rotate individual source images by selecting the Rotation tool ⟳ (you will likely not have to use this if you shot your image series using a tripod). You can view other previews by using the Perspective tool ✳ (change to Perspective mode in the Settings panel, and click on one of the source images with the tool) and by clicking Advanced Blending. While all these tools are interesting, the one I find most useful is the Keep As Layers check box. Check this box to be sure the images are compiled in a new image in separate layers so you will have the ability to adjust and move them using all of the tools you are familiar with in Elements. In other words, I find that Photomerge is most useful for helping you set up and rough in the panorama, rather than completing it.

With this brief introduction to the panorama tool, we will use it in the steps below to set up your panorama, and then we'll complete the adjustment of parts manually to achieve the final result:

1. Close all the images you currently have open.

2. Choose Photomerge Panorama from the New submenu on the File menu.

3. Browse for the images you want to use in the panorama by clicking the Browse button and selecting them from the Hidden Power CD. For this example (and your first attempt), open the trimmed images in the `Trimmed` folder (`left_trimmed.psd`, `middle-left_trimmed.psd`, `middle-right_trimmed.psd`, and `right_trimmed.psd`). For later attempts, you might try the untrimmed images for more of a challenge. When you have selected the images, click the OK button to accept the changes; the images will open and will be added to the main Photomerge dialog.

4. When the images are all in the Photomerge dialog, make adjustments as desired by moving the images in relationship to one another, adjusting the overlaps and positions for a best rough fitting.

5. Check the Keep As Layers box on the Photomerge dialog, and click OK to accept the changes. The images will be collected in a new image with the layers named according to the filenames you have incorporated. See Figure 7.28.

6. Adjust the layer order so the layers are stacked right_trimmed.psd, middle-right_ trimmed.psd, middle-left_trimmed.psd, and left_trimmed.psd, from bottom to top as pictured in Figure 7.28.

7. Add a layer mask to the top three layers using the Hidden Power Layer Mask tool in the Power_Masking category of Effects. This will place a blank layer mask in the Layers palette next to each of the source images.

8. Activate the Middle-right_trimmed.psd layer in the Layers palette, and click on the mask thumbnail.

9. Choose the Gradient tool, and set the gradient to black-to-white (left to right). Set the gradient options to Linear Gradient, Normal mode, 100% Opacity, and check Reverse, Dither, and Opacity.

10. Apply a gradient from about 2 inches to the left of where middle-right_trimmed.psd falls off into right_trimmed.psd, to about 1/4″ to the left of that same edge. Apply the tool left to right. The mask should erase the right edge of middle-right_trimmed.psd, revealing right_trimmed.psd below.

11. Activate the middle-left_trimmed.psd layer, and apply a gradient to the mask in the same way you applied the mask in the previous step, starting about 2 inches from the left of where the middle-left_trimmed.psd layer falls off into the middle-right_ trimmed.psd layer and ending about 1/4″ before the edge.

Figure 7.28

The layers in the new image reflect the positioning accepted in the Photomerge dialog. No blending will be incorporated.

12. Activate the left_trimmed.psd layer, and apply a gradient to the mask in the same way you applied the mask in the previous step, starting about 2 inches from the left of where the left_trimmed.psd layer falls off into the middle-left_trimmed.psd layer and ending about $1/4''$ before the edge. Once you have completed this step, the layers should look like they do in Figure 7.29.

13. Touch up the masks to smooth out the transitions between the image layers. You can use the brush tool to paint in black to remove areas from view or paint in white to reveal them again. You can adjust the gradient tool opacity and apply that over a broader range to feather transitions better. You can also dodge/burn. Take a look at the adjustments made in the panorama sample by viewing only one of the source layers at a time.

> The sample image panorama_sample.psd shows an example of dodging where the dodging is done using layers instead of the dodging tool. A new layer is created and set to Screen mode, and then white is painted in over areas that are to be brightened. Opacity of the layer is then used to temper the effect.

14. Once you have blended the image to your satisfaction, you may want to do some color correction. Color Balance, Levels, Curves Presets and Hue/Saturation were all used in the sample to brighten the result and shift the image to more of a sunrise color. See previous chapters and specifically the chapter on color correction for more information on using these tools.

After the image has been blended and color corrected, it is a good time to crop and reshape the image. This image provides some interesting challenges. The horizon is not straight, and there is an osprey far off in the distance to the upper left of the image—almost out of the frame. You will find that just trying to adjust the horizon using transform will distort the pelican unpleasantly and may result in cropping out the osprey. The solution is to get the pelican on its own layer. Take the following steps:

Figure 7.29

After applying the Gradient tool, masks for the layers should all be white to the left and black to the right, as shown here.

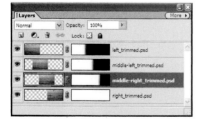

15. Create a new layer at the top of the stack and copy the content of the image to it. Name the layer **Composite**. This gives you a fresh source to work from that compiles all the changes you have made thus far.

16. Select the pelican and copy it to its own layer (label the layer **Pelican**). Use a feathered selection so the bird blends into the background. Separating the pelican also allows you to move it in the image to adjust the composition if desired.

17. Duplicate the Composite layer, and use the transform tool to straighten the horizon by pulling down the right-bottom controller, as pictured in Figure 7.30. Name the layer **Tone**. You'll see why in a moment.

18. With the horizon straight, you may want to try some noise reduction. You will note that the low light has riddled the image with color noise. Duplicate the Tone layer and name the new layer **Color**. Change the mode to Color, and apply a Motion blur of 7–10 pixels. Because of the horizontal feel of the image (the horizon, clouds, and waves are all mostly horizontal), the color will tend to blend in more naturally than using a Gaussian or other nondirectional blur. You can also make a selection of the sky and apply a few pixels of blurring to the tone there to smooth out the spottiness.

Figure 7.30

Pulling down this one controller leaves the osprey virtually untouched but straightens the ocean horizon.

You see that this project has run through a gamut of things discussed in this chapter to make both small and grand adjustments to the image to improve the composition. The main key to getting good results with this image is in keeping objects separate and attacking problem areas one at a time. We will continue to look at taking images through the entire process of correction and enhancement in the next chapter.

Chapter 8

The Image Process in Action

We've looked at multiple facets of image correction and adjustment, and now it is time to put them all together. Using a sample image supplied on the CD, we will step through the process of correction and adjustment from start to finish to show how the process works in practice.

The base process used for the image will follow suggested Hidden Power procedures, and it may go a step further than you would expect to embellish images. You don't have to agree with or even like the embellishments, but you should understand the procedures and how they fit into the process of getting to the image result. We will take a critical look at the photo before stepping through the procedures so that we can outline the goals for the image.

The goal of this chapter is to have you see how the procedures outlined in the previous chapters work together on a real-world image, so you can apply the steps and concepts to your own images.

The Wild Stallion

The image in Figure 8.1 was taken on the outer banks of North Carolina on a private guided tour of a remote coastal area—likely the only major existing coastal area in the continental U.S. that has not been developed. The image is available on the Hidden Power CD (`wildstallion.X3F`). Note that the `.X3F` filename extension, which you may never have seen before, is the proprietary extension for "raw" files from Sigma cameras. Elements will recognize this file as a Camera RAW file when you attempt to open it.

This particular area of the Outer Banks is accessible only by taking a half-hour off-road ride down ocean beaches in a four-wheel-drive vehicle that can navigate beach sands—it is an area literally beyond where the road ends. The reason to make the trek is that the area is one of the few remaining places where there are actually wild mustangs—and certainly the only place on the Outer Banks where the advertised "wild horses" actually run free.

Since the image was taken on an excursion that likely won't be repeated, it is a keeper almost regardless of quality. This handsome stallion struck a pose just as the wind was tossing his mane. While it is an interesting image, there are a few ways that it can be improved. For example, the image is, admittedly, a little soft, though it was shot with a fairly fast shutter speed in daylight (see the "EXIF Metadata" sidebar). Let's review our image-processing checklist (from Chapter 3) before getting together a specific outline of changes to perform.

Figure 8.1

We'll use this image (`wildstallion.X3F`) from the CD to run through the correction process.

EXIF METADATA

Your camera captures EXIF (Exchangeable Image File) information at the time of exposure. You can use this data to track exposure information at the time of capture. You can find it in Photoshop Elements by choosing File Info from the File menu. The following data was listed for the example image under the Camera Data 1 category.

Camera Make/Model: Sigma SD9

Date and Time: 7/13/05, 2:38 PM

Shutter Speed: 1/350 sec

Aperture: 6.7

ISO: 200

Lens: Sigma 70–300mm DL

This information can both track what you did to capture the image and give hints as to the quality of the capture. For example, the 70–300 DL lens performs better with a smaller aperture, so this image is apt to be a little soft.

General Image Editing Steps Review

The following list of steps was taken from the list of steps suggested in Chapter 3. We'll follow this editing checklist in processing the `wildstallion.X3F` image in the next section.

1. Be sure that your monitor is calibrated and that you have set up your preferences and tested your output.

2. Store the original image file safely and work with a copy to do all of your image editing.

3. Have in mind a target range for the resolution and a color mode for the final image.

4. Evaluate the image.

5. Make general color and tonal corrections.

6. Make general damage corrections.

7. Make compositional changes, including cropping, compositing, and replacing image parts.

8. Make targeted color and tonal corrections to selected parts of the image.

9. Save the layered RGB version of the image.

10. Simplify the image.

11. Optimize the image for output and use.

12. Save the image in output file format.

13. Package the image on proper media for output and use.

Applying the Image Editing Checklist to a Specific Image

We will assume at this point that you have taken the initiative to calibrate your monitor and build the ICC profile you need for properly viewing your images on screen (checklist step 1). Image storage (checklist step 2) is taken care of by providing the RAW file on the CD. The image on the CD cannot be overwritten, so it is safely archived. We will be processing the image using full resolution, which will allow a 9.5″ × 6.3″ photo-quality printout of the result (checklist step 3).

> The odd size is simply due to the capture resolution of the camera, which is 2268 × 1512 pixels. At 240 ppi, which is optimal for most photo-quality printers, the size works out to 9.5″ × 6.3.″

Now we are ready to evaluate the image (checklist step 4).

Open the image in Photoshop Elements. We'll attempt to coax out the best source to work with by opening the .X3F image. This RAW file format will provide the opportunity to make some adjustments to the image that may not be possible otherwise because you will be manipulating the preprocessed image source. Opening the image will kick off the Camera RAW plug-in, where you will be able to adjust the image initially to your preference using the raw captured data. The settings used for this example are pictured in Figure 8.2.

After you accept the RAW file conversion, the image will open in Elements. Despite adjustments, the color seems a little wanting. While the horse is a brilliant chestnut color, the greenery seems a bit washed out. Overall, the image may appear a little dark, but that is by design (and preference). We'll make both general (checklist step 5) and selective (checklist step 8) color corrections in order to solve these problems. General corrections will follow standard Hidden Power suggestions for Levels correction and Color Balance. Selective corrections might occur before or after compositional correction, but they will likely include shifting the color of the greenery with Hue/Saturation and perhaps adjusting the color of the horse and its mane.

While there isn't really any damage that needs correction (checklist step 6), there are some potential distractions, such as the fence pillar just above and to the left of the mane and the white bird droppings at the left edge of the photo on the stallion's back. Perhaps we can even address the white spot on the horse's forehead and the flat coloring on the ear (to the viewer's left). We can remove the pillar by careful cloning/healing, and we can eliminate the droppings with a quick cropping that will also move the horse's head to a slightly more dramatic position toward the center of the photo. Once we've made all these changes, we'll add a few additional effects to adjust the sharpness/softness of the image. Then it will be time to save the working version of the image (checklist step 9) and then simplify (checklist step 10) and save it again as optimized output (checklist steps 11 and 12). The assumption is that you will save the result to your hard drive for output (checklist step 13).

Figure 8.2

This RAW conversion can be different if you don't plan to follow the example exactly; however, the settings must be exactly as they are here to resemble the later dialogs and changes.

The summary above takes care of all the points in the editing checklist, so we are ready to go. Assuming you have opened the image and made the Camera RAW adjustments pictured in Figure 8.2, let's move on to the corrections. The following procedure steps concentrate on

Figure 8.3

The separations for this image reveal three drastically different appearances for the main subject.

checklist steps 5–8 in the correction process where you make color, damage, and compositional changes to the image. Later chapters will get into more specifics covering targeted output.

Convert the color mode This could really be taken care of as part of the RAW conversion by choosing 8-bit in the Depth drop-down list in the lower-left corner of the Camera RAW dialog. However, opening the file in 16-bit gives you the opportunity to make some changes in 16-bit if desired—we just won't be doing it for this image. To change the image to 8 bits per channel so we can take advantage of layered corrections, choose Image → Mode → 8 Bits/Channel.

Make an RGB separation While this is really only a curiosity for this image, make an RGB separation for the image using the RGB_Separation tool in the Power_Separations category of Effects. Take a look at the separate components by shutting off the Color layers and viewing the Component layers one at a time. These reveal possibilities for converting to very different black-and-white images where the horse could be either nearly black (blue component), gray (green component) or almost white (red component). These are potential variations you could use in converting the image for duotoning at the end of the process, and they may be useful for creating selections and masks. See Figure 8.3 for the separated components.

Make general color corrections with Levels Turn on all the layers for the separation, and flatten the image. Open Levels, and make the standard Hidden Power Levels adjustment (as described in Chapter 5) by clipping the graph tails in each of the drop-down list channels. Figure 8.4 shows the Levels changes that are suggested for this image. If you open the image with different RAW settings than suggested, or if you make other changes before using Levels, your graphs and associated changes will be different. Graphs can also be affected by color settings.

Make general color corrections with Hidden Power Color Balance Use the Hidden Power Color Balance tools (in Power_Adjustments) to adjust the color in the image. For this image, the Simple Color Balance tool may prove a bit too rudimentary. Use the Midtone

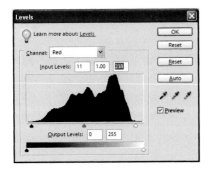 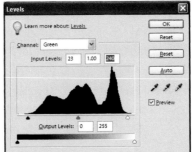 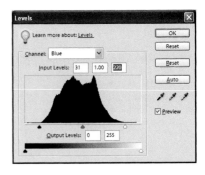

Figure 8.4

If you have made the RAW conversion using the settings shown in Figure 8.2, all of the component channels will require a Levels adjustment, as pictured here.

Color Balance, Highlight Color Balance, and Shadow Color Balance tools in that order. The adjustments used here were as defined in the table below. You can use different settings according to your preference. Go right from one color balance range to the next in order (Midtone, Highlight, Shadow), without bothering to flatten the image in between— the tools will flatten the stages as you move forward. Flatten the image after making the Shadow adjustment. If you compare the original to the current changes (in the Undo History, click the original snapshot at the top of the palette to undo all that you have done so far, and then redo by clicking the last step), the image should be more contrasty and less red. To retain the changes made with the individual color balance tools separately, duplicate the flattened image to a new document, apply the color balance, and then flatten the result and drag it back to the original image while holding down the Shift key to align the dragged layer. Rename the layer as appropriate.

	MIDTONE	HIGHLIGHT	SHADOW
Blue-Yellow	42	53	60
Green-Magenta	41	46	47
Red-Cyan	54	54	55

Make selective changes to objects Get to work on removing the pillar from its position near the mane. To do this, you will have to work carefully between the wisps of the mane, probably using both the Clone Stamp and Healing tools. The method used in the sample was to create a new layer named Clone Stamp Normal and use the Clone Stamp to stamp in a careful repair. First, use a large brush (about 60 pixels) to patch areas away from the hair. The tool settings should be Sample All Layers, Aligned, Normal, and 100% Opacity. Work carefully as if this were to be the final fix, and try to blend areas well. Resample often. When the base patch is made, switch to a smaller brush (about 5 pixels), and create a new layer named **Clone Stamp Darken**. Painting with the clone stamp on this layer will help shade in the lighter areas between the hairs without obliterating the hairs. Moving the brush in the direction of adjacent hairs can help blend in the changes. You can experiment with varying the opacity for the tool when applying it to this layer. Next, create a new layer above the Clone Stamp Normal layer, call it **Healing Normal**, group it with the Clone

Figure 8.5

If you did this correction 100 times, it would come out differently each time. If you are not satisfied, toss the layers (or hide them) and try it again.

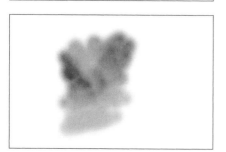

Stamp Normal layer, and go over the patched area with the Healing brush to adjust and smooth tone and texture (you may need to set the tool to lighten in tight spots so as not to distribute the darker hair color into the patched area). You can apply the Healing tool over a broad area or spot correct where patches seem problematic. In this layer setup, the Clone Stamp layer acts like a clipping mask for the Healing application, so it will not cover the stray hairs. Figure 8.5 shows the layer setup and corrections made for the sample. These adjustments are included on the wildstallion_process.psd image on the CD. You can clean up some additional areas if you want.

Adjust composition with cropping Crop the image to remove the bird dung and to bring the horse's head closer to the center of the image. The vertical orientation of the image is already pretty straight, so there is no reason to tilt the cropping box. You will need to crop only the left edge of the image.

Make selective color changes Open Hue/Saturation to make a quick adjustment to the color of the image greenery. To do this, choose Greens from the Edit drop-down list, and then click the Add To Sample icon. Click and drag in the green parts of the image. To be sure you are sampling the right areas, push the saturation slider all the way to the left. As you sample the image, it will desaturate in the green zone you have sampled. Use the Subtract From Sample icon to remove colors from the selected range. Watch out for selecting too much of the gray/blue areas of the background near the horse's ears, as this can lead to a patchy-looking color change. Adjust more than one range if desired. Use the Hue/Saturation mask to remove areas of change that fall over the horse. Figure 8.6 shows the range and settings for the adjustment used in the sample, as well as the masking. As an alternative, and with the advantage of being able to use other masking and blending techniques, you can use the Hidden Power Blend Mask tool.

Adjust image sharpness With basic color correction and composition changes in the book, it is time to take a look at the sharpness of the image. Consideration of sharpness is not in the sharpening alone but in adding blurs and soft-focus effects as well—and possibly for print considerations (though the latter are usually considered later when optimizing for print).

Figure 8.6

Hue/Saturation can make a quick and painless adjustment to greenery in one fell swoop. Adjust the mask with a large, soft black brush.

As stated, this image is a little soft, and it is better to go with that quality rather than fight it. It is also subject to considerations of depth of field—notably that the horse is far sharper than the background. To this end, we will apply some sharpening, but adding a softening glow and targeting the sharpening to the foreground. Be sure to keep the layers in the exact order you create them in the steps below. If in doubt, check the CD file `wildstallion_process .psd` for the layer order.

a. First, lock all the current changes to this point by creating a new layer and stamping the visible image to that layer (press Command+Option+Shift+E / Ctrl+Alt+Shift+E). Name the layer **New Source.**

b. Duplicate the layer four more times, and name the duplicates **Unsharp Mask Filter**, **Hidden Power Sharpen**, **Soft Focus**, and **Color**. Set the Color layer to Color mode, and drag it to the top of the stack. This will lock in the color over the subsequent changes.

c. Make a masking layer for the sharpening, and define the mask content. To do this, create a rough selection around the horse. Any method that you prefer from making a lasso selection to making a more sophisticated selection using calculations is viable. Be sure the edge of the selection is significantly soft (say 50 pixels) so the changes will blend. For the sample, we used the technique used to isolate the flower in Chapter 7. When the selection is created, create a layer mask using the Hidden Power Layer Mask tool in the Power_Masking category of Effects for both the Hidden Power Sharpen and the Unsharp Mask Filter layers, and then fill the area outside the horse in the masks with black. This will confine the changes to the horse.

d. Shut off the view for the Hidden Power Sharpen and Soft Focus layers, and activate the Unsharp Mask Filter layer.

e. Launch the Unsharp Mask filter, and apply the filter two times using the settings pictured in Figure 8.7.

f. Activate and view the Hidden Power Sharpen layer. Apply a Gaussian Blur with a 20-pixel radius, invert the layer (Command+I/Ctrl+I), change the mode to Overlay, and set the Opacity to about 20%. This will apply sharpening that lowers contrast.

g. Activate and view the Soft Focus layer. Open Threshold (Filter → Adjustments → Threshold), set the slider to about 190, and click OK. Choose the Magic Wand, set the tool options to 0 Tolerance, and shut off Anti-alias, Contiguous, and Sample All Layers. Click in the black area, and press Delete to clear it. Deselect, and then use Gaussian Blur with the Radius set to about 70 pixels. Change the layer mode to Soft Light. For added glow, duplicate the Soft Focus layer, if desired.

Figure 8.7

Sharpening gets applied twice, once to enhance local contrast (top) and a second time to sharpen details (bottom).

Targeting the sharpening to the horse in the foreground will keep you from enhancing details of the blurry background that are better left out of focus. Using more than one technique to sharpen will heighten the visibility of the detail that you do have. Applying a soft-focus glow adds a slightly dreamy quality to the image where absolute sharpness might be unexpected and serves to enhance the quality of the image.

At this point, you may want to consider other corrections and changes, or even repeat some of the adjustments to fine-tune, but for the purpose of this exercise we have completed the image correction. For example, you may want to look at other cropping, run Color Balance again, or even do another Levels correction. Save the image in RGB with the correction layers intact before making any additional changes. You can then flatten the image and continue working or print the image. For comparison, open the original without changes, and print that as well. With the two side by side, you should see some significant differences in the image. If you make additional changes that you want to save, copy them to the layered version.

> Be careful when continuing to make changes that you do not save over your original layered version of the image, or you will lose the corrections. Change the filename between saves. It is easy to do using a simple numbering system to indicate saved versions (e.g., `wildstallion1.psd`, `wildstallion2.psd`, etc.).

Of course, you can do more with this image, and experimentation is encouraged. In the following chapters, you will find additional techniques that will affect your output/printing. An interesting experiment will be to convert your corrected wild stallion to a duotone or tritone image and print the components, as suggested in Chapter 10.

Part IV

Controlling and Enhancing Images in Print

Once you've spent a whole bunch of time making an image look just how you want it, selecting Print and sending the image to your home printer may not always achieve the results you want. Printing images to get the most out of them may require just a little bit more fancy dancing.

You may need to consider using some special tools such as vectors to control the sharpness of text, artwork, and the shape of your images during output. Additional color work in preparing images for print may require making separations into CMYK or for printing genuine duotones using spot colors and ink. Understanding your printing options (for hardware, software, and images) and how those options control output can help you achieve better results.

Chapter 9

Creating and Using Vectors

For the most part, Photoshop Elements is a pixel-based image editor, and we have concentrated on that aspect of working with images. Vectors are another means of controlling image content, usually associated with adding illustrative elements or text to images. You may have seen vectors in action if you've used Shape tools in Elements, and the Hidden Power Guides tool uses them as well. *Vectors* define image areas as mathematical outlines, independently of the pixels and resolution of the image. They have a number of different (shall we say *hidden*?) uses, mostly associated with controlling your images in print. Vectors can be used to make shapes, sure, but they can also be used to redefine the actual boundaries of an image. They can be used to store hard-edged selections. They can be used as clipping layers in order to shape image layer content. They also can be used to create artwork (such as logos) that can be scaled infinitely. We'll look at all these possibilities in this chapter.

Making Vectors

Making Custom Shapes

Creating Scalable Vector Art

Applying a Clipping Path

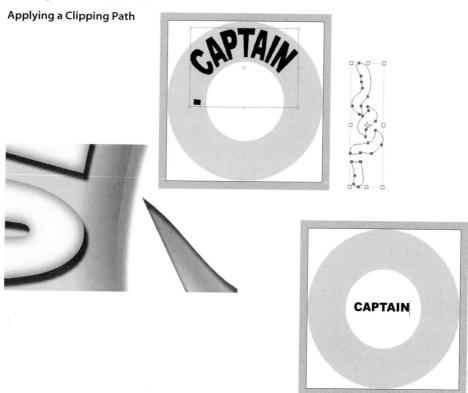

Making Vectors

The basic way to make vectors in Photoshop Elements is to select any one of the Shape tools, select a shape, and apply it to your image. Shape tools include the Shape Selection tool, Rectangle tool, Rounded Rectangle tool, Ellipse tool, Polygon tool, Line tool, and Custom Shape tool. You can access the Shape tools by clicking the Shape tool icon in the toolbox; this icon will vary depending on which of the Shape tools you used last. After you select the tool, numerous options for selecting shapes appear on the Options bar (see Figure 9.1), including custom shapes 💬. You apply the shape by clicking and dragging the Shape tool cursor ⬆ on the image. When applying the tool, Elements responds by creating a new layer for your shape. That's that. Descriptions of the various Shape tool options are in Table 9.1.

Figure 9.1

The Options bar offers possibilities for selecting different Shape tools and controlling how they combine. Shown here are the seven modes. Modes are controlled by tool selection (as per the icon at the left of the bar).

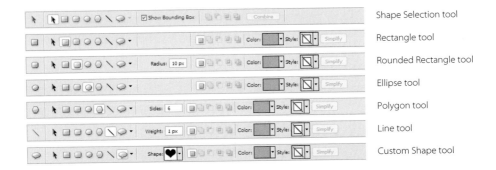

Shape Selection tool
Rectangle tool
Rounded Rectangle tool
Ellipse tool
Polygon tool
Line tool
Custom Shape tool

Table 9.1

Shape tool options

OPTION	TOOL	USE
Show Bounding Box	Shape Selection tool	Displays/hides (checked/unchecked) box that can be used for shape distortion/sizing.
Radius	Rounded Rectangle tool	Allows user input of the radius of the arc in rectangle corners.
Sides	Polygon tool	Allows user input of the number of sides a new polygon will have.
Weight	Line tool	Allows user input of the number of pixels wide a new line will be.
Shape	Custom Shape tool	Allows user selection of custom shape from a drop-down menu.
Color	Rectangle, Rounded Rectangle, Ellipse, Polygon, Line, and Custom Shape tools	Allows user selection of colors from a swatch menu or the Color Picker.
Style	Rectangle, Rounded Rectangle, Ellipse, Polygon, Line, and Custom Shape tools	Allows user to assign a style to new shape layers based on the presets stored in Layer Styles (part of the Styles and Effects palette).

Custom shapes are limited to the sets you have available in the `Presets/Custom Shapes` folder in Elements. There are many predefined shape sets to choose from if you explore the Shape menu on the Options bar (available only when the Custom Shape tool is active). Just click the current shape in the Options bar preview, and the Shape menu will open. Then click the submenu pop-up button, and you will see a long list of categorized shapes to choose from. See Figure 9.2.

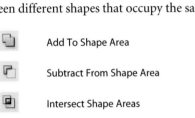

It's possible to create more complex shapes than those provided by using shape modes to combine shapes. These shape modes are Add To Shape Area, Subtract From Shape Area, Intersect Shape Areas, and Exclude Overlapping Shape Areas. They are used like calculations between different shapes that occupy the same layer.

Figure 9.2

There are many predefined shape options provided with Elements to help you add creative vectors to your images. Just choose a category from the submenu to view the associated shapes.

Add To Shape Area

Subtract From Shape Area

Intersect Shape Areas

Exclude Overlapping Shape Areas

Using just these standard shape modes, you can make some interesting and complex shapes. Try the following:

1. Create a new image (File → New) with a white background that is 1000 × 1000 pixels.

2. Make a new shape layer. To do this, choose the Shape tool, select the custom shape option on the Options bar, choose a custom shape from the drop-down list on the Options bar, choose any color other than white, and begin drawing the shape by clicking and dragging on the image.

> Press the spacebar as you draw to move the position of the shape you are drawing.

3. Choose a shape mode from the Options bar (Add, Subtract, Intersect, Exclude). This mode choice will determine how the next shape that you draw interacts in the image.

4. Change the custom shape you have selected (if desired), and draw the next shape.

The vector component that you add in step 4 is introduced on the layer that you created in step 2. The shapes combine to display a result based on the mode(s) you have selected for *each* component. That result is displayed in the color selected in step 2.

To take a look at the effect shape modes have on the result, highlight the second shape that you drew using the Shape Selection tool, and change the mode on the Options bar. The result should change in the image based on the mode you select. You can add more shapes to the layer by repeating steps 3 and 4. See Figure 9.3 for an example.

You can join the shape components that you have drawn in your layer into a single, complex vector shape:

- To combine shapes into a single-vector component, create the shape components and then double-click the Combine button on the Options bar. The button appears only when the Shape Selection tool is selected.

> After you combine or simplify your shapes, you will no longer be able to adjust the positions of component shapes individually. You may want to duplicate the shape layer and hide it (shut off the view for the duplicate) before combining components so the components will be available separately without having to redraw them.

- To join shapes into a single non-vector shape in its own layer, create the shape components and then double-click the Simplify button on the Options bar. This option will drop vector advantages.

- To join shapes that you have created on separate layers, you will have to move them to a single shape layer using cut and paste. Use the Shape Selection tool to highlight the component shape(s) you want, and then cut and paste shape(s) to the target layer. Once they're in the same layer, you can join the shapes by changing the combining mode.

- To highlight a component, just click it with the Shape Selection tool (click right on the vector line).

- To highlight more than one component on the same layer, you can click and drag the Shape Selection tool over multiple shapes, or hold the Shift key while clicking individual shapes.

This covers the basics of shape creation and joining shape components. You can also create your own custom shapes in Elements, with a little help from some Hidden Power tools. We'll look at custom shape creation in the next section.

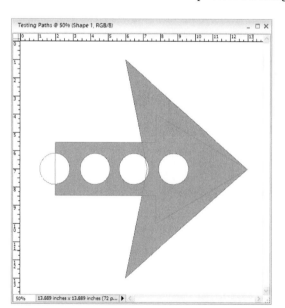

Figure 9.3

Several shapes mesh here to make a far more complicated result than drawing a single shape. First the arrow was drawn in Add mode, then a new tip was drawn in Add mode, and then circles were drawn in Subtract mode.

Making Custom Shapes

Say for some reason you want to make a custom shape—for example, a fishhook—that you can't find in the shape libraries, and you can't imagine how to construct it by joining shapes from these libraries. One task you can't do with standard Photoshop Elements Shape tools is to make freehand shapes. You could spend most of the day using the existing shapes that are supplied—adding, subtracting, and combining—but creating a custom shape this way will probably prove a little tough, will take lots of time, and can be frustrating.

Hidden Power tools add some functionality that can help you change any selection to a shape, and this gives you the power to make any custom shape you need.

All you have to do is make a selection (any shape or size, using tools you have), and then double-click Shape From Selection in the Power_Paths category of the Hidden Power tools on the Effects palette. This will turn the selection you made into a custom shape on its own shape layer. Once the selection is a shape, you can use it just like any other shape created with the Shape tool: copy and paste the shape to other shape layers, and size, mix, and combine the shape with other shapes. The difference is that the shape you make can be your own, unique from the limitations of the provided libraries.

> Tolerance settings on the Make Work Path dialog that appears after you click the Shape From Selection tool allow you to choose how closely you want the vector to conform to the pixels. Higher numbers simplify and smooth the vector while sacrificing accuracy; lower numbers add vector anchors and may produce a blockier result. Shooting for a balance between the two extremes will get the best results. It is sometimes best to increase the image size (upsample the image) to create the vector if you want to retain smooth vector results.

Using this Hidden Power tool, you can create shapes from any selection, even highly complex ones. One way to create custom shapes is by making a rough sketch of the shape you want with a painting tool and then converting that shape to a selection (Command+click the layer / Ctrl+click the layer where you have drawn the shape to load it as a selection). You can even refine the selection before conversion using other selection tools (the Lasso tools are a favorite).

Figure 9.4 shows how a very rough sketch of a fishhook made in its own layer is turned into the final fishhook illustration. The shape is roughed in with a painting tool and loaded as a selection; the selection is refined with the Lasso tool and made into a new filled object. Once the object is refined, the object is blurred to smooth out the curvature and edges, and then a final selection is made and converted to a shape using the Hidden Power tool.

Figure 9.4

A very rough sketch (a) is used as a simple guide for creating a more refined selection (b) made with the Polygonal Lasso tool. The polygon selection is refined and smoothed by filling with black (c) and using Gaussian Blur (d) and then Threshold (e). Additional selections (f) are used to make alterations (g), and the final selection (h) is converted to a shape (i). Once the shape is in a layer, layer effects can be applied (j).

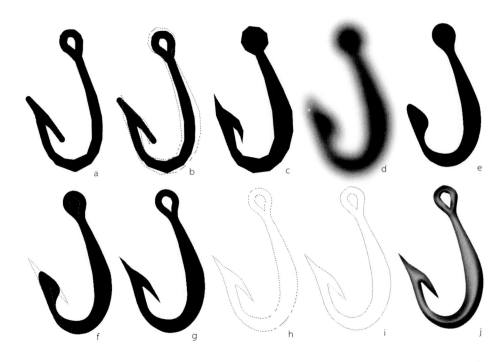

Shapes can be created from loaded selections, selections made with any selection tool, selections made from layer transparency, and selections made with any combination thereof. Once you have made the selection and converted it to a custom shape, you can store the shape and use it as you might use one of the shapes from the shape libraries. The process for storing your custom shapes is a little different from using shapes in the library in that you will not save the shapes you create to a shape set for display in the submenu. You will save the shape to a dedicated image where you can store the shapes as a library. When you need a shape you have created, you just open the library image and then copy and paste the shape from it as needed. The ability to store and reuse shapes that you create gives you much greater flexibility with vectors than using shape libraries alone. For an example of how to store shapes in a library image, see `hiddenlibrary.psd` on the CD. If you have shapes that you want to store, follow these steps:

1. Have the image open in which you created the shape you want to store (e.g., the custom fishhook shape created from a selection).

2. Open the `hiddenlibrary_template.psd` file on the Hidden Power CD, or you can create your own library file. The file can be any size, but 500 × 500 pixels at 72 ppi will cover what you need the file for, even if the original shape is larger than that size. The advantage of using the Hidden Power template is that it will have a template layer for use in step 8.

3. Save the image file with a name that reflects the shape types you expect to save there (in other words, name your shape library what this image will contain). If you will have only one shape library, you might name it something simple, like My Shape Library.

4. Choose the Shape Selection tool.

5. Click on (highlight) the shape you want to store from the image in step 1 to activate it. The shape can be from any open image.

6. Copy the shape (Command+C / Ctrl+C).

7. Activate the library image that you opened or created in step 2.

8. Create a new shape layer. If you're using the template image provided, just duplicate the template layer.

If you use another image, you will have to create a new layer using one of the shape tools, draw a shape, follow steps 9 and 10, and then delete the shape. Elements will not allow you to create a shape layer that does not contain a vector.

9. Paste in the shape copied in step 6.

10. Name the layer something meaningful so you will know what it is from the description. When you need to use the shape, you can just locate it by name and copy it to the image in which you want to use it.

An alternative to the steps above would be to drag layers from the image that you want to copy to the library. With both images in view on the screen, locate the shape you want to copy in the source image in the Layers palette, click on it, hold down the Shift key, and drag it to the library image window. This will copy any effects you have applied as well.

Shapes can be resized to fit the 500 × 500 pixel image you are using as a library, because vector shapes do not change as they are scaled. If you have pasted or dragged and dropped a path and you do not see the shape, zoom out from the image, be sure the layer is active, and choose Free Transform. If you can see the outline of the path and the bounding box (the Show Bounding Box option must be checked), hold down the Shift key and fit the bounding box to the image. Holding down the Shift key will retain the ratio of height to width for the path.

Another way to store shapes in a library is to save all the shapes as separate files in a directory (for example, named MyShapes) and then use Photoshop Elements' Create Web Photo Gallery function (see Photoshop Elements 4 Help) to create a preview of all the shapes in the folder. This will be easy to update and will enable you to scan previews of many shapes quickly in your web browser or in the Elements File Browser, rather than having to remember the names or search through various library files.

> Shapes can be another means of storing selections—as long as you want to store the selection without anti-aliasing, feathering, or other grayscale manipulations. Such hard selections can be converted to shapes by using the Hidden Power tools, and the visibility can be turned off. To create a selection from the stored shape, Command+click the layer / Ctrl+click the layer where the shape is stored.

Another handy tool provided with the Hidden Power tools is one that will make a shape from any text you've created. The Shape From Text tool is located in the Power_ Paths category of the Hidden Power tools on the Effects palette.

Converting text to vectors may not seem to be much of an advantage when I tell you that you won't be able to edit the text anymore. However, converting text to vectors can save you from having to worry about transferring fonts with your Elements images; vectorized fonts will show up correctly even on computers that don't have the same fonts you used to create the text, and the vectors will render the result without softening (as would happen if you rasterized the text by converting it to pixels). Changing the fonts to vectors locks the shape of the font and makes it a graphical part of the image, while still allowing you to scale the image and not have a fuzzy font result. Vectors will produce sharper text results than rasterized text when used correctly. Converting to vectors also puts to rest some potentially annoying font errors.

The application of these Hidden Power vector-conversion tools should become clearer in the following example, where we'll use shapes to create scalable vector art.

Creating Scalable Vector Art

Pixel images are normally trapped by their content in that pixel content is inflexible and must be interpolated to be resized. Interpolation can cause softening or loss of detail. Using vectors can help you create art that can be scaled to any size while retaining sharpness in the shape of objects. Although you can't turn all elements of a standard photograph into vectors, you can create artwork as vectors so it can be scaled to suit your needs.

Captain Hook's Bait & Tackle is the name of an imaginary tackle shop. Let's say the owner wants a logo and asks you to make it. He wants to use the logo on his letterhead, business card, and website and on promotional items such as caps and T-shirts. One other thing the logo will be used for is a 10 foot × 16 foot billboard next to the Fishingtown exit from the I-1000 freeway. The only answer you get when you ask how big the logo will be on the billboard is "Big." So it's safe to assume that the logo will run about 9 feet tall.

A 9-foot-tall image in Photoshop Elements at 100 ppi would be almost 11,000 pixels square. That's about 333 MB. It isn't a file that you'll want to transfer over the Internet even if you have a fast connection. Interestingly, if you are careful, you can probably create the file you need and do it in less than 1000 pixels square (technically, even smaller than that!) and satisfy all of the client's needs with one image.

Follow these steps to create the logo:

1. Open a new, blank 1000-pixel-square image. Set the resolution to 72 ppi.

2. Click the Shape tool on the toolbar. Then on the Options bar choose the Ellipse Shape tool. Create a new shape layer by drawing a circle to fill the square image. Start drawing at the center. You can find this center of the image by opening the Info palette, setting the measure to pixels, and then watching the coordinates change as you move your cursor in the image window. The center will be at 500,500. When you have located the center, hold down the Shift+Option / Shift+Alt keys and drag your shape; the shape will constrain to a circle and draw from the center point, where you first clicked. Leave 100 pixels or more at the edge of the image all the way around—you may need some space to maneuver your shapes and artwork.

3. Click the Subtract From Shape Area ⬚ button on the Options bar, locate the center of the image again, and then draw a second circle from the center, about half the diameter of the first. This will give you a torus—a donut shape—as a result of the two shapes you created that inhabit the same layer. You should not have to adjust this, but if you do, use the Shape Selection tool to click on the shape component you want to move. When the component is highlighted, you can move it freehand by using the Shape Selection tool, or you can change to the Move tool and use the keyboard arrows to position the shape.

4. Create a hook using the technique described earlier in "Making Custom Shapes." Alternatively, you can copy in the hook you made during that exercise, if you'd like.

5. Create the text to be placed in the donut. This is the toughest part of the exercise, because Elements does not offer a lot of type controls. Fitting the text to the donut will take some experimentation. All you really have to work with are the Create Warped Text function 𝐼 , point size, and Transform. It might be easiest to set one word or phrase at a time.

To use the Create Warped Text function, type out your words and then click the icon on the Options bar. Results in the example were achieved by setting the Arc at 100% for the top text and –100% for the bottom text with about 30% Vertical Distortion. Add spaces before and after the text evenly to shorten the arc and control horizontal distortion caused by the arc. To add spaces at the beginning of the text, you have to add an extra junk character (use a period) before the spaces, or the spaces will just move the text to the right—but don't forget later that the junk character is there, or it will show up in your final image. Once the text is close using Arc and spaces, use Transform to fit it in place if it still needs adjustment. See Figure 9.5 for a quick approximation of these steps.

Figure 9.5

Make the arc on the bottom of the text match the hole of the donut, and then rotate the text into place. You may have to make other tweaks to the position.

6. Convert the text to shape layers by using Shape From Text on the Hidden Power tools, found in the Power_Paths category of Effects. You may want to duplicate these text layers and hide them before the conversion, in case you need to come back and make changes.

7. Create the worm. Roughly sketch in its shape as it would appear wrapped around the hook, using a soft brush (0% hardness) on a new layer. Merge with a new white layer (created below the worm), and use Threshold to tighten up the edge. Load the hook as a selection by Command+clicking the Hook layer / Ctrl+clicking the Hook layer (created earlier). Use the selection to erase areas of the worm that would wrap around the hook by using a hard brush (100%). You can't just hit Delete because you would remove the parts of the worm that appear in front of the hook as well. See Figure 9.6.

Figure 9.6

Sketch the worm roughly, and remove parts you don't need by using the hook as a selection and guide.

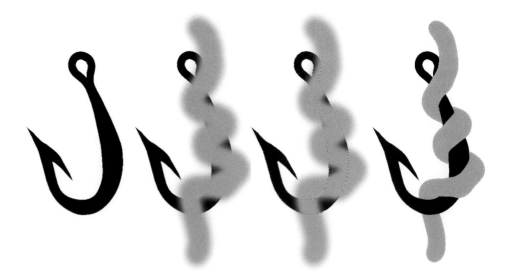

8. Convert the worm to a shape layer. To do this, make a selection from the worm you drew (Command+click the Worm / Ctrl+click the Worm layer), and then double-click the Shape From Selection tool in the Hidden Power tools under the Power_Paths category of Effects.

9. With all the elements in place, apply layer effects and color to achieve the desired depth and effects. You can apply manual effects as long as you want the edges blurred in the result. If you need a tight edge on any effect (such as a hard drop shadow), you can duplicate a shape layer and adjust the color or effects. I used strong bevels on the worm, hook, and donut, along with inner shadows and drop shadows.

At the end of this exercise, you should have something that looks like Figure 9.7. Keep the layered version of the image, and store it safely. It is possible to change the size of the image as necessary and correctly target the file for different types of output. Because your image is essentially composed of all vectors, you can retain sharpness in your image at any size. You can also temporarily shrink the image for moving it from one place to another; as long as the person receiving the file has Photoshop Elements (or Photoshop), they can expand the image again. The important edges remain defined by vectors. Any blends and/or effects you used for coloring and shading will simply blur more without damaging the result so long as you resize by using Bicubic or Bilinear interpolation. There will be some difference between these two interpolation types depending on the content of the image.

Figure 9.7

Separate layers were used for each effect by duplicating the shape to which the effect was to be applied. See `captainhook.psd` **on the CD.**

If you wanted to add other details (for example, to define the worm segments), you would have to do so by using an additional shape layer so that the effects would not blur during resizing. When you resize, you will probably need to adjust layer effects to re-create what you had. This is far easier than re-creating the entire image—and far better than just resizing an image by upsampling dramatically.

"Oh, what's the difference in using vectors?" you say! The difference is a quality image rather than a soft one. Look at the comparison in Figure 9.8; these are depictions of the same image. Image A was created at 1000×1000 pixels, flattened, and then resized to fit our billboard. Image B was created at 1000×1000 pixels and then resized to fit the billboard by taking advantage of vectors: the image was resized with layers and vectors intact and then flattened.

It should be apparent from the comparison that the vector image can be resized without losing image quality, whereas pixel images will lose some definition. You can now take your vector logo and happily resize the image for use on a billboard or business card with equal success. You can use similar techniques and custom shapes to define your own unique logos (for example, for use in watermarking your images, business cards, flyers, letterhead, etc.).

Vectors not only shape the content of layers, they can actually harness the shape of your entire image. Read on about applying clipping paths that you create from vector shapes that adjust your image boundaries.

Applying a Clipping Path

Say you want to create an image that isn't constricted to the rectangular shape of your standard digital image. Suppose you want the image itself, and not just a layer, to be star-shaped or circular. An easy way to do this is to make a selection of what you want to keep, and then invert the selection and delete the area of the image that you don't want. As long as the background color is set to white, the image shape will appear to be a shape other than a rectangle when printed. White areas of images don't print with color (unless you are printing with a spot white ink, and you'd know if you were doing that).

Figure 9.8

This small segment of the billboard was magnified. Note the softness, pixelation, and lack of definition in the upsampled image (a) compared to the vectors (b).

a   b

This easy solution is okay if you don't have anything in the background below the image. If you are printing your easy-shaped image over another image or other content in the background of the digital file, using white won't work. One thing a white background will do in your rectangular image is whitewash anything behind it. If your image is like our Captain Hook logo, and you want to bring it into a layout program to print over a background image, you might want to import just the shape of the logo rather than the whole image. What you really want to do to the image is clip it out of the background and paste it into the layout—as though you were making a collage.

Clipping paths do exactly what you want. These are vector shapes that redefine the boundary of your images. They enable you to "float" an image over a background in layout programs and clip the edge of the image with vector accuracy, just as if you'd used scissors. This technique can work best with images that you create with shapes in mind (such as the Captain Hook logo) and that contain text. All you have to do is save a vector in the image as a path and then assign that path as the image-clipping path.

Again, the problem with clipping paths in Photoshop Elements is that the program doesn't let you work with them. You can't save a path, and you can't assign a clipping path, because there are no tools in Elements that allow you to do those things. However, the Hidden Power tools will allow you to create clipping paths from active paths or shapes in your image.

To use a clipping path with our Captain Hook logo, follow these steps:

1. Prepare the image by creating the shape that you want to use for the clipping path. This requires combining the separate paths for the hook, the worm, and the donut. Use *one* of these two ways to do this:

   - Make a merged selection by holding down Command+Shift / Ctrl+Shift while clicking each shape layer in turn on the Layers palette (Figure 9.9). This will merge the selections of each shape as you go.

   - Copy all the shapes to a single shape layer, change the shape modes of each component to Add, and then double-click Combine Vectors in the Power_Paths category of Effects, or click the Simplify button on the Options bar (Figure 9.10).

Figure 9.9
You can multiple-select your shape layers...

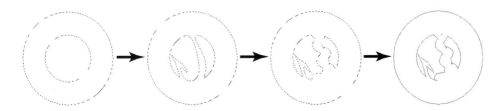

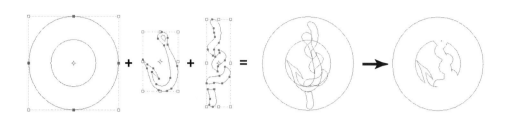

To copy the shapes onto one layer, you'll need to use the Shape Selection tool ![pointer] (part of the Shape tool set) and the Copy and Paste commands. First, duplicate any one of the shape layers you have created, and then get the components you created in the other layers one at a time by copying and pasting them to the duplicate layer. When all the shapes are copied to the duplicate layer, highlight them by clicking and dragging with the Selection tool. Once the shapes are highlighted, add the components by clicking the Add option on the Options bar.

2. Assign the clipping path by double-clicking Make Clipping Path from the Power_Paths category of Effects in the Hidden Power tools.

At this point, you'll be ready to place your Elements image in the layout program. Figure 9.11 shows what your Captain Hook billboard might look like. Be sure to save your file in a format that is compatible with clipping paths, such as EPS or TIFF.

Figure 9.11

The clipping path
cuts away the white
portion of the logo
when the image
goes to print by
considering the clip-
ping path as the
absolute boundary
of the image.

You may have noticed that this will remove your drop shadow in the printed result because the shadow lies outside the boundary of the clipping path; even though you can still see it in the image, it won't show up in the result. If you want the shadow, you can create it by using a little trick that will also enable you to place the shadow manually in the layout.

1. Copy the clipping path to a new grayscale image that is the same size and resolution as the final print file.

2. Make it a fill layer—filled with 75% black. (You may need to increase or decrease the percentage of black to get the results you desire. The greater the percentage, the darker the shadow result.)

3. Change the image to a bitmap by selecting Bitmap from the Color Mode menu. When prompted, change the resolution to the output/printer dpi. Use the maximum capability of the printer.

4. Save the file as a bitmap (BMP) file by using Save As.

You can place this file in your layout program below the clipped image (how you do this depends on the layout program you use). You will be able to manually move it separately from the clipped image. It may not look very pretty in the layout preview, but the result should look just fine on a high-resolution image setter or PostScript printer.

The success of printing images that have clipping paths depends on two other factors: you have to save the file in a format that will respect the clipping path, and you have to print in PostScript. The problem here is that most home printers are not PostScript. We'll look at a solution for testing PostScript output without a PostScript printer in Chapter 11.

The techniques you have learned here are essential for getting sharp text and graphics in high-resolution PostScript printing. If you don't need to create reusable shapes and will not be printing with a device that respects PostScript encoding, you may never have to use the techniques you've learned here. However, if you like to use illustration and text in your photos, you can get results that surpass any pixel-based image with vectors. Next we'll look at converting color for printing.

Chapter 10

Color Separations for Print

Up until this point, we have looked at working with images from the vantage of making the image appear better on-screen by adjusting color, tone, contrast, and composition. This often translates into better images in print, but there are special possibilities that arise in the conversion to print colors that you may employ to improve printed results.

Images in print will require a conversion from light-based display to ink-based (unless you will be using CRT or LED technologies discussed in Chapter 11) at some point during the process of getting them on paper. This conversion can be conceptually simple, but in reality it has a number of problems that often lead to choices as to how to best represent color. In this chapter we will look at how to best handle color and color separation for print.

Making Duotones

Separating CMYK Color

Using CMYK Components

Making Duotones

A *duotone* is an image in which two ink colors are applied as tone to create a colored effect. The idea behind using two tones of ink is often to create a richer feel for black-and-white images, perhaps to add a little color and maybe even increase the dynamic range of the printed result. Duotone effects for photographic images have traditionally been achieved by chemical processes that add tone to black-and-white prints (e.g., sepia toning). On the printing press, true duotones are created by applying two or more inks based on image tone rather than to reconstruct natural color. We'll look at how to control duotone results digitally and in print.

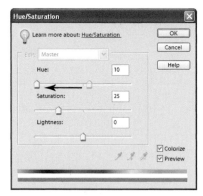

Figure 10.1

The default position for the Hue slider after clicking the Colorize checkbox is 204. Changing the Hue setting to about 10 will give a decent sepia tone to any black-and-white image.

Creating a duotone effect digitally in Photoshop Elements can be done a number of ways. For example, you can rather quickly emulate a sepia tone by opening Hue/Saturation, clicking the Colorize option, and shifting the slider to achieve a duotone effect (see the Hue/Saturation palette in Figure 10.1). When you print to an inkjet printer, the result will often be satisfactory—though not at all optimized for print or taking advantage of using duotone inks.

You could apply a color in a fill layer that is set to Color mode, or you could experiment with colorizing by using the Gradient Map function. Each of these methods may achieve the effect of duotone color, and the image might print out and look just fine on your home inkjet printer, but the methods do not produce a true duotone and may not be the best solution. Certainly duotones can simply be pleasing to the eye, but true duotones offer specific advantages in printing. Using more than one ink to print halftone images on a press can take advantage of ink-screening angles and can produce a better richness and depth in the result. Other advantages to using duotone over black ink alone in prints include lessening the appearance of printer dots and increasing ink coverage on the page. Duotone effects can also help to correct and emphasize subtle tonal detail where colorizing likely will not.

> When printing halftones with two or more inks, using two black inks can improve a printed image because the two sets of dots will be screened differently (the rows of dots applied at different angles). The increased number of halftone dots can result in a better application of inks.

When duotone images are used in spot-color print jobs, the purpose is often to limit color because of budget constraints. To create effective duotones for this purpose, you have to be able to control the color separation for two inks (such as black and a spot color). If not, you will have to pay a technician to do the separation for you, or worse, you'll have to pay for four-color work (CMYK printing) on a two-color job. Because there is no built-in duotone handling in Photoshop Elements, there is really no direct way to save the separate plates for duotone colors. Add to the difficulty the fact that there really isn't a means to handle spot color in Elements in the first place, and you have a problem. Luckily, it is another problem that you can solve with Hidden Power tools.

Solving the problem and understanding the application require a little knowledge of duotoning as well as working with separations and spot color. We'll take a look at the whole process, from how to break down and apply spot-color inks in preview to how to get actual duotone print effects on your inkjet printer and on a press by using Photoshop Elements alone.

Understanding Duotones

When you create a duotone, you replace the existing tone of an image with two tones. A key to the difference between duotone color and four-color printing (CMYK) is that CMYK color printing attempts to imitate natural color that already exists in the image or a scene. Duotoning is different because it is often a means of adding color and richness to black-and-white images to enhance the tone. Inks in a duotone are applied variations of existing image tonality. The original tone is duplicated and altered to represent the density of ink color components—something like using red, green, and blue components to represent color in RGB. The effect of duotoning a black-and-white image is more of a creative endeavor in that the tone of the image is influenced by color rather than an attempt to represent realistic color. The mix of the inks is controlled in Photoshop using Curves. Since Elements 4 is limited to the Hidden Power Curve presets, we will create duotone effects using Gradient Map to adjust tone components. In some cases, you may want to experiment and use other adjustments, such as the Curve presets, Levels, and perhaps even selection or masking. These latter possibilities come into play when you want to adjust the inks not solely based on image tone.

The duotone effect is controlled by selecting and mixing colors successfully. Interplay between the colors is often a subtle shift rather than a radical application. While other tools can be used for creating the interplay between colors, Gradient Map will give you the most control.

A third-party plug-in called Booster Elements is available from the Hidden Power website that will allow users to work with Curves to make duotone adjustments (see the download page: http://hiddenelements.com/downloads.html). Other solutions will be posted there as they become available. However, Gradient Map can do the job.

Setting the mapping without some sort of technique, method, or understanding of what you are trying to achieve might prove quite fruitless and frustrating. Likewise, problems can result if you pick color you like rather than color that will be effective. Your plan should be as follows:

1. Select inks that are compatible and that can accomplish your goal in duotoning.

2. Set up the image and apply a gradient map to make the most of the inks you have chosen with consideration for the tonal qualities of the image.

Although there is a little art to experimenting with color selection and application, there is some pretty straightforward science as well. A 25 percent gray ink at 100 percent strength will be 25 percent gray when printed; it just covers 100 percent of the paper (see Figure 10.2). It can never get darker than 25 percent gray unless mixed with another color. With this in mind, any color affects an image mostly in tonal areas that are lighter than the 100 percent strength of the color. That is, a 25 percent gray ink will be able to more effectively influence tonality in 1 percent–25 percent grays—although it will affect darker colors that it mixes with, it will be less effective in manipulating the image over that tonal range. A dark color can represent lighter tones, but the opposite can never happen. A rule of thumb should be to use at least one dark color or black for your duotone so you can maintain the dynamic range in the image.

When choosing color, opt for color that is harmonious and sensible. Select color that can blend effectively to produce a smooth white-to-black tonal gradient (see Figure 10.3). You will most often want to use colors with distinct tone rather than all dark or all medium-toned inks. In a simplistic view, the lighter colors you use will emphasize the contrast and tone in the brighter or highlight/midtone range of the image, and the darker colors will emphasize the shadow details. If you select a light color and a dark color for a duotone, the light color can be run with a greater density in the lighter image areas and the dark color in the shadows. This will help you to most effectively work with (rather than against) image tone. For example, for a straightforward duotone you might choose black and light orange (for something resembling a sepia) or black and sky blue (for a cool tone).

Figure 10.2

Magnification shows black ink—100 percent black— printed at 25 percent gray (left), and gray ink— 25 percent black—printed at 100 percent strength in halftone printing (right)

Figure 10.3

Unrealistic expectations in color selection and application can yield bad results in your duotones. You want blended tones to be able to flow evenly from light to dark (a). Bad choices can limit tonal range (b) or lead to color being applied inappropriately (c).

Whatever colors you choose, the emphasis of the colors in the duotone should be in the tonal range where the ink is most effective. Harmony between colors will make it easier to set up blends that work with the image tones. If you choose difficult color combinations or have unrealistic expectations, you can make much more work for yourself than necessary in getting the blends to work—or you may simply make it impossible to get a good result.

> The colors used in duotones are often called *spot colors*, although commercial color book names are also used (such as PANTONE, TRUMATCH, Focoltone, and so on). These colors are standards and can be matched by your printing service. To use specific colors for duotones that we will create in Elements, you'll have to get an RGB equivalent to spot colors from a color book or a printing service, or you can just eyeball the color using the Color Picker.

Gradient maps serve as translators for how ink is to be applied. The mappings are used to influence the tone of an image to increase or decrease the strength of an ink applied in a specific range. Throughout the tonal range, the inks blend to form colors and tones, which you finesse to the advantage of the image and your vision for it. A rule of thumb is that if you want to apply a 25 percent gray ink, the application should show high intensity at 25 percent for that ink (as shown in Figure 10.4).

Deciding how to set the mapping is part art and part science. Darker inks are often steeply graded in the shadow tones, whereas lighter inks are more steeply graded in the highlights. This will use the ink optimally in its most effective area and help it to render the tone dynamically. Steep gradation over a short range will enhance the image contrast. See Figure 10.5.

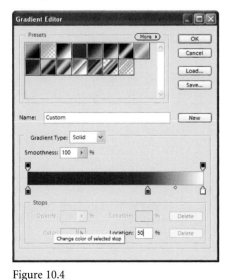

Figure 10.4

Depending on the color, desired effect, and image, the gradient map can be even more radical than shown here.

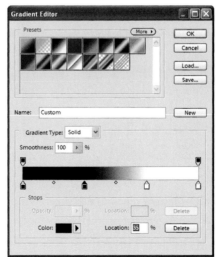

Figure 10.5

The map for this ink goes from full strength to about 2 percent over the image midtones.

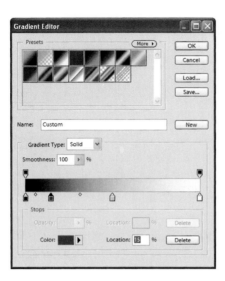
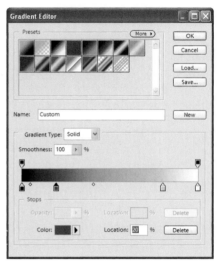

If you use two shades of black or two dark inks, you will want to de-emphasize the density of the inks (especially in the midtones), or you will darken the image. The effect would
be similar to taking a flattened black-and-white image, duplicating the background, and
setting the upper layer to Multiply mode. However, when using two dark inks, setting both
gradient maps the same way may not always take full advantage of potential dynamics in
the image. Figure 10.6 shows a sample of gradient map settings used in an actual scenario
with two dark inks.

Experimenting with gradient maps for application of inks can yield some pleasant and
subtle toning effects. Using some of the ideas here can help you apply the colors in a way
that makes sense. Now let's look at creating a duotone effect in Elements.

Applying Duotone Effects

To build a separation-ready duotone in Photoshop Elements, you have to use an image's
tonality along with some tricks; we've seen hints of both in using gradient maps and in
making RGB separations. Gradient maps are used to enhance the tone for the separate
inks, and preview techniques such as those used for RGB separations are used to look at
the results of how inks will combine. When the preview appears the way you want it to
look, you can provide separations to your printing service as grayscale images, or you can
print actual duotones on your home printer.

Follow these steps to create a duotone in Elements:

1. Open a black-and-white image or convert a color image to black-and-white by the
   methods described in Chapter 4, and flatten the image. See the sample image shown
   in Figure 10.7. This image is available on the CD (`duotoning.psd`).

Figure 10.7
People are often good subjects for duotones.

Be sure the image tone is corrected before you move through the setup process. You won't want to make corrections afterward because it will change the look of the duotone and will be more cumbersome to manage since you will be replicating the source. The source should be the same for each ink you plan to use.

2. Create a new blank layer, name it **Composite**, and fill it with white. This layer will act like white paper to which you will be applying inks.

3. Duplicate the Background layer once for each ink you will use. If you were creating a tritone (three inks) or quadtone (four inks), you would duplicate the layer three or four times, respectively. For this example, just use two inks and two layer duplicates.

4. Move the duplicate layers above the Composite layer in the layer stack.

5. Rename the layers to identify the colors/tones you expect to apply. In this example we will use the layer names **Black** and **Spot 1**.

6. Change the mode of the Black and Spot 1 layers to Multiply. This will make the layer content act like ink, darkening the composite layer below, as ink would when applied to paper when printing.

7. Create a new layer above the Spot 1 layer, fill it with the color you want to apply, and group it as a clipping layer (press Command+G / Ctrl+G). Name the layer according to the color you are applying. In the example, to create something of a sepia tone I used an orangey-brown color (R = 175, G = 100, B = 0). This layer will be used to apply a color to the Spot 1 layer.

8. Change the mode of the color layer to Screen. Using Screen mode will lighten the Spot 1 tone layer in accordance with the color you have selected. Because your source is black, any color you use will be lighter, and Screen mode can only lighten the result.

When stacking colors, arrange them from darkest at the bottom to lightest at the top. This will help your organization and the application of color as well.

9. Activate the Black layer by clicking it in the layers palette.

10. Double-click Gradient Map Curve in the Power_Adjustments category of Effects to initiate the creation of a gradient map adjustment layer with preset color tabs. Be sure the Group With The Previous Layer check box is checked in the New Layer dialog box before continuing.

11. Adjust the gradient map to manipulate the toning results. You will have to remove stops (just drag them off the preview bar) and adjust colors and positions of the remaining stops. See Figure 10.8 for the mapping used in the example for the black ink. The idea here is to lower the influence of the black overall, while using it to emphasize contrast in the darker half of the image. The table below with the Color Stop Position column represents the color stops, and the table with the Median Markers column represents the position of the color midpoints.

Color Stop Position Tone (%)	Color
0%	0%
33%	50%
65%	80%
100%	100%

Median Markers	Position
0%–33%	40%
33%–65%	50%
65%–100%	50%

12. Activate the Spot 1 layer by clicking on it in the Layers palette.

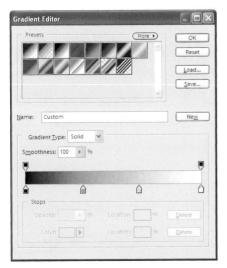

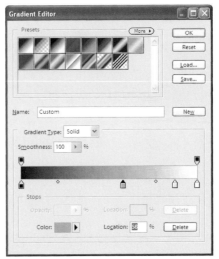

Figure 10.8

The mapping for the dark ink enhances contrast in mid and darker tones.

Figure 10.9

This mapping for the light ink strengthens the influence in the lighter tones.

13. Double-click Gradient Map Curves in the Power_Adjustments category of Effects to initiate the creation of another adjustment layer. The Group With Previous Layer check box should be checked already.

14. Adjust the gradient map to manipulate the toning results. The lighter ink should have stronger influence and contrast in the lighter tones, and this is reflected in the use of the mapping pictured in Figure 10.9.

Color Stop Position Tone (% Black)	Color
0%	0%
58%	60%
87%	90%
100%	100%

Median Markers	Position
0%–-58%	36%
58%–87%	64%
87%–100%	60%

Your Layers palette should look like Figure 10.10 when you are finished. As far as layer order goes, the gradient maps should be immediately above the tone they are adjusting and beneath its associated color layer. Should you need more adjustments, you can insert adjustments between the spot color tone layer and its color. You can add as many adjustments as you want and test different combinations by toggling the visibility for any of the

Figure 10.10

**The result of the
example should look
like this in Layers.**

adjustment layers. If you want more spot colors (to create a tri-tone or quadtone), duplicate the setup for Spot 1. If you want black to be a spot color, add a color layer above the gradient map for the Black layer (you may want to change the name for the Black layer as well). The adjustments may require some fiddling before they look just right.

Again, this type of work on individual color separations can serve many purposes: achieving the effect of adding color to a black-and-white image, working within the limitations of a two-color print job, enhancing printed results by using two inks and screens rather than one, and gaining the opportunity to enhance image tone by influencing ink coverage and ink contrasts. If you are colorizing an image just to get a duotone effect, you probably won't have to go through the trouble; if you want a true duotone that can be separated into specific inks, this is the way to go.

Hidden Power tools provide functions for creating duotone images. Just start with a flattened RGB image, and double-click the Basic Duotone Setup in the Power_Separations category of Effects. The power tool will lead you through the process of setting up the layer stack and creating a separated sepia tone. Be sure the black-and-white image is in RGB color mode, not Grayscale, or you will not be able to apply color (the tool makes this adjustment for you). You may want to do your own conversion to black-and-white before using the tool by using any of the methods discussed in earlier chapters; the tool converts color images to grayscale using luminosity by default.

Two other tools are included to allow you to easily create custom setups for using two or more spot colors. These tools are Toning Setup and New Toning Layer, both found in the Power_Separations category of Effects. The Toning Setup tool walks you through the basic process of setting up any RGB image for toning, and the New Toning Layer tool allows you to add colors one at a time.

One of the great advantages of using Gradient Map adjustment layers is that, unlike Curve presets, these are editable and come with a gradient preview built in. Be sure to try to blend inks by setting the color tabs so that the gradients appear to be smooth and so that the influence of one ink will pick up where the next leaves off. While the gradient bar provides a solution for individual inks, it is a pretty safe bet that if each ink gradient is smooth, the result will be when they are combined.

It may be difficult to visualize what the mix of inks will look like. Hidden Power provides a means of previewing your setup as a gradient, using a gradient bar preview.

On the CD, there is a sample gradient bar (Duotone_Preview_Bar.psd). You can use this file to check how smooth your mixing is or to develop gradient maps for application in duotones. To test your duotone gradient maps, just open the preview image and drag the adjustment layers and colors to it from the duotone on which you are working. You will have to arrange and group the layers to match what you created. To use the sample gradient bar to develop mappings, open `Duotone_Preview_Bar.psd` and create the color fill and adjustment layers right in the preview file; when you are satisfied, drag the color and adjustment layers to the duotone you are creating. The gradient should appear relatively smooth and even in the preview image—unless you are using the duotone for some type of image correction or special effect. The bar is more useful for seeing where the adjustments may be failing than in generating effective duotones. To test the duotone and preview gradients directly in the image you are working on, you can use an additional Hidden Power tool that is included to work with images set up using the Basic Duotone Setup tool. Just double-click the Duotone Bar tool in the Power_Extras category of Effects. This will create a duotone preview bar right in your image. Use the Delete Duotone Bar tool also found in the Power_Extras category of Effects to remove the bar.

Even when applying the same duotone color scheme to different images, you can't always apply it with the same mapping adjustments. The result of toning really depends on the image. What works fine for normal and low-key images may not work as well for high-key images, which would probably suffer from the attention to shadow detail. You need to create mappings that are dependent on the overall tonality of the image on an individual image basis—otherwise, it could just be a pushbutton effect. Generally, high-key images should be set to emphasize detail in the highlight areas, and low-key images should be set to emphasize detail in the shadows. Experimenting and gaining experience with setting the gradient maps will make creating duotones easier and more intuitive.

Now that you have created your duotone effect, you will need to know how to use it optimally to achieve the results you want. We'll look at how to accomplish this in the following section.

Printing Duotones

To print your duotones, you could just flatten them and send them to the printer, but you'd have done all the extra work in creating a duotone separation for nothing. What you have in the layers by the time you are finished with the duotone procedure is a *bona fide* separation: each color component is held separately in the image. You should treat the image as if it is a separation. This means using the inks separately and applying them to the paper as separate inks.

Printing True Duotones at Home

A great experiment to try at home is to print the separated colors one at a time to see the duotone results. To do this, you will want to create a separate file for each of the colors in your duotone. Be sure you have safely stored the original, and then save the files for each component. Just leave one of the duotone color layer sets on (see Figure 10.11), flatten the image, and save the result as an RGB image with the name of the color. Repeat that step for each color in the image, and save a separate flattened image for each color in your duotone.

When you are finished saving the components as separate files, print these color files to your printer one at a time *on the same sheet* by running the sheet through the printer once for each ink. Print light colors first, and follow with darker. You should use photo-quality paper and allow sufficient drying time between printing each ink. If you use lower-quality paper, the paper will likely not handle the ink well, and the result might be murky and oversaturated.

> When saving black ink components or grays, you can sometimes get truer results by saving the component as Grayscale mode and printing with black ink only. Some printers will muddy up or even colorize RGB images that are grayscale because of attempts at separation and if there is a fluctuation in the ink output.

In using the component colors separately and putting down the colors one at a time on your paper, you will build your print similarly to the way it would be created on a printing press that rolls out colors one at a time. As long as your printer has reasonably accurate paper gripping, you'll get a pretty refined result in your duotone and superior results to just flattening the image and printing it out.

Figure 10.11

View only one color result at a time before flattening and saving.

Shadows areas of the image will probably be richer and darker when printed in this multiple-pass style because the inks will go on heavier than they would if printed in a single-pass. The printed effect of multiple passes is a greater tonal range, because the blacks will be darker—even though you are using the same number of grays in the image and same number of inks in the printer. This works somewhat like putting on multiple coats of paint.

Printing True Duotones on Press

To use your duotone separation with an imagesetter and for making film or creating printing plates, you'll want to make grayscale images from your duotone layers rather than color. These grayscale images should represent the density of the ink rather than the color.

To convert your separation in this case, leave one duotone component and its adjustments visible in the layers, shut off any coloring for the component, flatten the image, and save it as a grayscale with the name of the color. Do this for each component in the duotone. You'll note that the "light" layer components become dark when you do this (see Figure 10.12), and that's what is supposed to happen. What you are seeing is how the application of the color ink will look in grayscale—as density of the ink rather than ink color.

As long as you tell your printing service which file is which, they can create film for printing or impose the image without a lot of trouble. There is one other way to put these files together to avoid problems when submitting them: by turning them into EPS DCS files. We'll take a closer look at that technique in the "Using CMYK Components" section later in this chapter.

Figure 10.12

Shutting off the color and black layers (a) and then flattening gives you a grayscale depiction of the Spot 1 color plate. The darker component (b) is the Spot 1 plate and the lighter (c) is the black.

a

b

c

USING DUOTONES FOR TONAL CORRECTIONS

Duotone adjustments can be used to make subtle changes and corrections in difficult black-and-white conversions. Although the images will not retain the richness of duotoning or the effect of multiple inks, creating duotone effects to correct grayscale images can help strengthen subtle detail, and some of this may be retained in the grayscale result. Consider the duotone adjustments to be an important part of your grayscale correction arsenal.

For example, if you have an image with subtle highlight detail (such as a wedding picture in which dress detail has become somewhat washed out or faded because of harsh flash lighting), you can create a duotone to change the image emphasis in different tones. Just open the image in black-and-white and then create a duotone. For the wedding picture example, you'd pick a black ink and a light-gray ink for your colors. Use the light gray to emphasize the highlight area of the image. This can work in images where tones seem to flatten too much, as in Figure 10.13.

Figure 10.13

This image had flat medium tones (left), but applying a duotone helped make an adjustment that better defined the contrast and lightened the result (right).

Separating CMYK Color

One image mode that Photoshop Elements supposedly does not handle at all is CMYK color. CMYK stands for cyan, magenta, yellow, and black—the four colors that are the traditional standard for ink printing. Even though Elements doesn't have a CMYK image mode, there are ways to extract CMYK components, just as there are ways to extract RGB components, or luminosity and color. CMYK is just a little more complicated.

The procedure for separating CMYK color is probably not something you will need to use every day. You will use this only in situations where CMYK is a must (requested by a service), or when you want control over the separations to your home inkjet printer.

Even with the ability to create a CMYK image, many home printers would take an image you created in CMYK and print it without directly using the CMYK data. These printers would look at the CMYK file, interpret it as RGB, and then use that information to print by using its CMYK inks. In effect, what happens is that you don't really get from the printer output the CMYK that you put in.

To fully understand what's going on during the CMYK separation, you need to have a decent understanding of just about everything that we've discussed up to this point in the book. Because CMYK separation can be a complicated topic, we'll first look at the process of how to separate, and then we'll discuss additional theory. This topic could fill a book on its own, so we'll just give you enough to get started with here. You can learn more from experimentation and discussions on the Hidden Power website and in the Hidden Power newsletter (find information about the newsletter on the website: www.hiddenelements.com).

With the following techniques, you can create your own separations. You can not only use them in four-color print jobs, but you can force your printer to make a CMYK print to your specifications.

Making the Basic CMY Separation

CMYK separations start with converting color information to CMY—without the K. The representation of the black ink is added to adjust for inadequacies in the process. The easy part of this separation is filtering out the CMY. Although it isn't as straightforward and easy as making an RGB separation, the process for separating is similar.

If you remember the RGB separation, we used simple filters to draw out the red, green, and blue color components. In making the CMY separations, we will do something similar. However, it isn't as direct as filtering for cyan, magenta, and yellow, because we have to work within the limitations of the RGB additive color scheme. That means being a little more clever with filtration to get your result.

Cyan is the inverse of red. Try this out: open a new image, fill it with red (RGB: 255, 0, 0), and invert the image. The image will turn cyan. Cyan is also a combination of blue (RGB: 0, 0, 255) and green (RGB: 0, 255, 0). Test this out by creating a new image with a black background. First, create a new layer and set it to screen, and then fill it with green. Next, duplicate that layer, and use Hue/Saturation to adjust the Hue +120 degrees to blue. You will see cyan on the screen. Magenta is the opposite of green (RGB: 0, 255, 0), or a combination of red (RGB: 255, 0, 0) and blue (RGB: 0, 0, 255). Yellow is the opposite of blue (RGB: 0, 0, 255), or a combination of red (RGB: 255, 0, 0) and green (RGB: 0, 255, 0).

Screening an image for blue and green will reveal cyan, screening for red and blue will reveal magenta, and screening for red and green will reveal yellow. If you look at a color wheel, the relationship between these colors may become more evident. The target CMY color falls between the two RGB components. In other words, the cross product of mixing equal amounts of blue and green light is the RGB equivalent of cyan. Combining red and blue light creates magenta. You can see how this relationship works by opening the RGB.psd file on the CD, clicking the circles with the Move tool, and changing their positions. As one circle moves over another, the result of that color combination becomes apparent on-screen.

What we will be doing with the CMY separation is using the knowledge of these combinations to apply the same type of color filtering we applied when extracting RGB. Completing the separation will give you basic CMY image information, using nothing but pure RGB components. This separation information works to represent your image on-screen—and in a perfect world. When we're finished with the CMY separation, we'll look at why it doesn't work in real-world printing and what we have to do to offset that shortcoming.

We'll work through the CMY separation in three parts:

Preparation Set up the colors for separation by duplicating the original image. Once the image is duplicated, you are ready to start making the real separations based on existing color.

CMY separation Screen each layer by the RGB color components to reveal the CMY color separation and simultaneously create the preview for the color. This state is temporary, because to make this a really useful separation, you'll have to convert each channel to grayscale—just as you did with the RGB components.

Conversion of colors to tone Adjust each color to display tone. There is no way to represent the intensity of component color other than by using its tone. The leap here is that you have to remove the color that it seems you have already separated and then re-create it to get a usable result.

> Please keep in mind that color separation to CMY/CMYK should be done only *after* you have corrected your images. Check your image before setting out on the steps for conversion!

Preparation

All you will be doing here is creating some source layers to use in helping to make the separation:

1. Open Kush-beggi.psd (found in the Chapter 10 folder on the companion CD). The image should be flattened already when you open it.

2. Create a Hue/Saturation Adjustment layer that adjusts Hue +120 (as we did for the RGB separation in Chapter 4). Name the layer **Hue/Saturation Template**.

3. Create a new blank layer and fill it with red (RGB: 255, 0, 0), name it **Color Red**, and set the mode to Screen.

4. Duplicate the Color Red layer, then duplicate the Hue/Saturation Template (it will be named **Hue/Saturation Template Copy**), and move the copy of the template to the top of the layer stack.

5. Merge the Hue/Saturation Template Copy and Color Red copy layers. The resulting layer will be green, so name it **Color Green**.

6. Duplicate the Color Green layer, then duplicate the Hue/Saturation Template, and move the template copy to the top of the layer stack.

7. Merge the Hue/Saturation Template Copy and Color Green copy layers. The resulting layer will be blue, so name it **Color Blue**.

8. Create a new layer, fill the layer with white, and name it **Composite**. This will separate the components you will create from the setup layers and background. If you create the layer immediately after renaming Color Blue, the new layer will be at the top of the layer stack, where it should be.

9. Duplicate the Background layer, name the new layer **Cyan**, and change the mode of the layer to Multiply. Move the layer to the top of the layer stack (Command+Shift+] / Ctrl+Shift+]).

10. Duplicate the Cyan layer, and name the new layer **Magenta**.

11. Duplicate the Magenta layer, and name the new layer **Yellow**.

The image will look awful at this point, but that doesn't matter. These are only the initial steps in the separation to develop the components, and the image is not supposed to represent the final result. You'll be taking quite a few more steps to complete the separation. The layers should look as they do in Figure 10.14. Steps 1 through 7 can be completed by double-clicking (i) CMY Setup in the Power_Separations category of the Hidden Power tools in Effects.

Figure 10.14

With this layer setup, you are ready to separate the CMY colors.

CMY Separation

Just like separating the RGB components, we'll use the color layers to filter out CMY color from the image:

12. Duplicate the Color Red layer, and move it above the Yellow layer. Name the layer **Red Screen**, and make it a clipped layer with the Yellow layer by pressing Command+G / Ctrl+G.

13. Duplicate the Color Green layer. Name it **Green Screen**, and move it above the Red Screen layer created in step 12. Make it a clipped layer with the Yellow layer by pressing Command+G / Ctrl+G. The red and green combine to filter out the yellow component from the image.

14. Duplicate the Color Red layer, and move it above the Magenta layer. Rename the layer **Red Screen**, and make it a clipped layer with the Magenta layer by pressing Command+G / Ctrl+G .

15. Duplicate the Color Blue layer. Name the layer **Blue Screen**, and move it above the Red Screen layer created in the last step. Make it a clipped layer with the Magenta layer by pressing Command+G / Ctrl+G. The red and blue combine to filter out the magenta component from the image.

16. Duplicate the Color Blue layer, and move it above the Cyan layer. Rename the layer **Blue Screen**, and make it a clipped layer with the Cyan layer by pressing Command+G / Ctrl+G.

17. Duplicate the Color Green layer, change the layer name to **Green Screen**, and move it above the Blue Screen layer created in the previous step. Make it a clipped layer with the Cyan layer by pressing Command+G / Ctrl+G. The green and blue combine to filter out the cyan component from the image.

If you have completed these steps without a hitch, you'll be looking at the same image you started with. The layers will look like Figure 10.15. If you turn off the visibility for any two of the three CMY component layers, you'll see the separation named in the remaining layer. Hidden Power tools will take care of steps 12–17 if you double-click the (ii) CMY Separation Hidden Power tool in the Power_Separation category of Effects.

Converting Color to Tone

Although you have done the basics of separation at this stage of the process, it is still a color representation rather than a real separation of component color. You really have to have grayscale representations of a color as tone for it to be useful as a separation. In this segment we'll convert the color to tone.

18. Activate the Cyan layer by clicking it in the Layers palette, and merge the clipping group by pressing Command+E / Ctrl+E. This merges the three layers into a single layer named Cyan. It is a color representation of the cyan component for the image.

19. Activate the Magenta layer by clicking it in the Layers palette, and merge the clipping group by pressing Command+E / Ctrl+E. This merges the three layers into a single layer named Magenta. It is a color representation of the magenta component for the image.

20. Activate the Yellow layer by clicking it in the Layers palette, and merge the clipping group by pressing Command+E / Ctrl+E. This merges the three layers into a single layer named Yellow. It is a color representation of the yellow component for the image.

Figure 10.15

The basic RGB-CMY separation setup in layers

21. With the Yellow layer still active, open Hue/Saturation by pressing Command+U / Ctrl+U. Change the Edit selection from Master to Yellows, and move the Lightness slider all the way to the left (see Figure 10.16). Then click OK to close the Hue/Saturation dialog box. This removes the color from the Yellow layer and enhances the tonality to make tonal representation of the density of the yellow component.

Figure 10.16

The Hue/Saturation settings for changing the yellow component to a grayscale yellow plate

22. Shut off the view for the Yellow layer, and activate the Magenta layer by clicking it in the Layers palette.

23. Open Hue/Saturation by pressing Command+U / Ctrl+U. Change the Edit selection from Master to Magentas, and move the Lightness slider all the way to the left. Then click OK to close the Hue/Saturation dialog box. This removes the color from the Magenta layer and enhances the tonality to make a tonal representation of the density of the magenta component.

24. Shut off the view for the Magenta layer, and activate the Cyan layer by clicking it in the Layers palette.

25. Open Hue/Saturation by pressing Command+U / Ctrl+U. Change the Edit selection from Master to Cyan, and move the Lightness slider all the way to the left. Then click OK to close the Hue/Saturation dialog box. This removes the color from the Cyan layer and enhances the tonality to make a tonal representation of the cyan component.

Figure 10.17

A complete CMY color separation should look like this with all the layers.

The result of these steps has the desired effect of creating the color components as tone, but it also removes the color so that there is no preview. You can add back the preview by repeating steps 12–17 exactly. You'll end up with layers that look like Figure 10.17.

Hidden Power tools will perform steps 18–25 if you double-click the (iii) CMY Component Tone tool in the Power_Separations category of Effects.

Though you have the separate CMY components, this is only part of the CMYK separation. The next part is adding black (K). Black is added to the CMYK separation to make up for the fact that in the real world, process inks (and ink media) are not 100 percent efficient in reproducing color. Combinations of printed CMY inks can't absorb all the light that strikes them, so black is added to boost potential light absorption. We'll look at one way to define the black component in the next section.

Handling Black Separation

CMYK separation from RGB requires separation into CMY and then generation of elements and masks to implement the addition of a black (K) component. Black implementation can vary depending on preferences and can be finessed to achieve different results with different printers, inks, and papers. We'll look at one style, and that should give you the information you need to make variations that you find pleasing. You have the basic CMY components, and you will use the information from these to determine saturation and luminosity. You'll use the saturation and luminosity to determine where the black ink will be most effective. Like the duotone use of inks, black will be most effective in the darkest portions of the image and usually where there is less saturation (that is, grays).

We'll be continuing the separation into CMYK by using the CMY separation and preview you have created from the Kush-beggi.psd image in the previous sections. You'll have to know how to create saturation and luminosity masks to create the black component. The following steps give you the basics for completing the black separation:

1. Make the saturation mask.

2. Make the luminosity mask.

3. Combine the masks to make the black component.

4. Apply the black component.

5. Remove color under the black to reduce ink use.

We'll step through each part in the following sections. If you need to repeat the CMY separation, you can use the three separate Hidden Power tools to set up the separation (i), separate the CMY (ii), and create the components (iii), or just use the (i–iii) CMY Component Separation tool to step through all three parts in one click.

Making the Saturation Mask

Making a mask based on saturation is similar to color-masking techniques used earlier (in Chapter 6). Masking saturation will enable you to target gray (and nearly gray) areas of the image. You will then be able to substitute black in those areas of the image to enhance dynamic range. This will also help make sure ink does not oversaturate or shift color.

1. Duplicate the Background layer to a new image by activating it and choosing Duplicate Layer from the Layers palette pop-up menu. When the Duplicate Layer dialog appears, choose New as the Destination Document in the Duplicate Layer dialog box. This opens the duplicate layer in a new image.

2. Split the Luminosity and Color components in the image by using the Luminosity and Color tool in the Power_Separations category of Effects.

3. Turn off the visibility for the Luminosity layer, and move it to the top of the layer stack.

4. Duplicate the Composite layer.

5. Merge the Composite Copy and Color layers. This commits the color layer information.

6. Set the result to Difference mode. This shows a comparison between the image color saturation and the unsaturated areas. Lighter areas are more saturated; black areas are unsaturated.

7. Merge the layer result from steps 5 and 6 with the Composite layer. This commits the saturation comparison.

8. Open Hue/Saturation and move the Saturation slider all the way to the left to set the Saturation to –100 percent. Click OK. This removes any color left in the saturation mask.

9. Open Levels and move the white Input slider to 128. This adjustment can vary depending on the image and what you want to accomplish, as well as how you want to control the separation. Making a stronger change (moving the slider farther to the left) will confine black generation to areas with less color saturation.

After completing these steps, you will have a saturation mask, and it should look something like Figure 10.18. It represents a mapping of color in the image from the most saturated (lightest) area to the least saturated (darkest) area. Rename this layer **Saturation**.

Making the Luminosity Mask

A luminosity mask will help you target the darkest areas of your image, where the black can best influence the color range. This will enable you to make the most of black's effective range while reducing ink saturation.

10. Add a new layer above the Saturation layer. Name the new layer **Black** and fill it with 50 percent gray (R = 128, G = 128, B = 128).

11. Activate the Luminosity layer and turn on the visibility.

12. Make a levels correction by opening Levels (press Command+L / Ctrl+L) and moving the white Input slider to 128. This changes the mask so only 50 percent grays or darker appear as gray. This is your luminosity mask, and it should look like Figure 10.19. Making less of a correction will cause your black component to influence more of the image.

Figure 10.18

The saturation mask appears lighter in areas where the color is most pure (has the least gray).

Figure 10.19

The dark portion represents the darkest half of the image (50 percent–100 percent black).

13. Merge the Luminosity layer with the Black. This will commit the changes to the Luminosity layer. The resulting layer should be named **Black**.

14. Activate the Saturation layer, change its mode to Lighten, and move it above the Black layer in the layer stack. This helps reduce the black influence in dark but highly saturated areas of the image.

15. Merge the Saturation layer with the Black layer. The result will be your black component.

Applying the Black in the Separation

Once the black component separation is complete, you have to move the black component back to the original image with the CMY separation and then apply the black to adjust the other color components. Where black is used to influence the image, you reduce the influence of other colors—again, to avoid oversaturating the areas.

16. Duplicate the Black layer completed in "Making the Luminosity Mask" back to the original CMY separated image (use the Duplicate Layer function by activating the Black layer and then selecting the original image as the target). The layer name should remain Black.

17. Move the Black layer to the top of the layer stack in the original image. Change its mode to Multiply.

The steps of the black separation covered in the preceding two sections ("Making the Saturation Mask," "Making the Luminosity Mask") and in this section ("Applying the Black in the Separation") can be taken care of by using the (iv) CMYK Black Hidden Power tool located in the Power_Separations category of Effects. That tool will make the saturation mask and the luminosity mask and move the separation to the original image. The result will usually look a little dark. The next step is the adjustment to the other color components: removing color under the black to balance the addition of the black component.

Removing Color under Black

To keep ink use lower, to get better results on a press and in your printer, and to counteract the effect of adding the black component, you will want to reduce the amount of color in the CMY components where the black ink was added. This reduction can keep the ink from oversaturating, streaking, and drying poorly in print, as well as balance the look of the image. This procedure continues from the point where you added the Black layer back to the CMY-separated image in the previous section.

18. Duplicate the Black layer and invert it (Filters → Adjustments → Invert). You can name the layer **Black Adjustment Yellow**.

19. Open Levels and change the white Output slider to somewhere between 128 and 191 levels. This change will determine how much you want to diminish the yellow component in consideration of the black you are adding. The levels will look like Figure 10.20.

Using 128 for the white levels Input slider position will remove 50 percent of the color under the black ink, and using 191 will remove 25 percent of the color. At 25 percent removal, your maximum ink outlay in blacks will be 325 percent (C75 + M75 + Y75 + K100), which is a little higher than what is usually suggested for presswork. At 50 percent removal, the maximum ink outlay is 250 percent (C50 + M50 + Y50 + K100). We are just making a flat change here, because this can get really intricate. For example, you may choose to use the Gradient Map function for creating the adjustment, and you could adjust those mappings separately for each ink.

20. Move the Black Adjustment Yellow layer just above the Yellow layer in the layer stack, and change the mode to Screen. This reduces the gray values in the Yellow layer by the intensity/density of the black component.

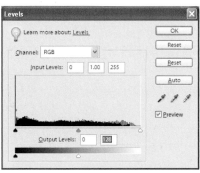

Figure 10.20
The less the change in the white slider (the greater the number), the less color will get removed from the yellow component, and the greater the final ink outlay at the printer.

21. Create the black adjustment for the magenta component. To do this, duplicate the Black layer, change the name of the layer to **Black Adjustment Magenta**, change the mode to Screen, make a Levels adjustment (see steps 18 and 19, and move the layer just above the Magenta layer in the layer stack. This reduces the gray values in the Magenta layer by the intensity/density of the black component.

22. Create the black adjustment for the cyan component. To do this, duplicate the Black layer, change the name of the layer to **Black Adjustment Cyan**, change the mode to Screen, make a Levels adjustment (see steps 18 and 19, and move the layer just above the Cyan layer in the layer stack. This reduces the gray values in the Cyan layer by the intensity/density of the black component.

Figure 10.21
Your completed CMYK separation should look like this in the Layers palette.

That's it. What you have now is a complete separation that shows the cyan, magenta, yellow, and black with color removed under the black to reduce the density of inks so there won't be overinking on press. You can merge the adjustment layers with the components by activating each adjustment layer in turn and merging it with the component by pressing Command+E / Ctrl+E. Components should retain their names, and color should continue to be grouped as clipping layers. The results appear in Figure 10.21. The steps in "Removing Color under Black" can be taken care of by double-clicking the (v) CMYK Apply Black tool in the Power_Separations category of Effects.

You can complete the entire process from setup through applying color removal by using the (i–v) CMYK Process effect in the Hidden Elements tools (under the Power_ Separations category). You will be required to make adjustments to levels to complete the processing. You may see the potential here for manually adjusting the performance of your images, in that there are many other variations you can consider. For example, cyan (traditionally a weaker, less efficient ink) is left stronger than yellow and magenta during under-color removal. An option for using the Gradient Map function is included as part of the CMYK Map Process tool included with the Hidden Power tool set. Use either the gradient mappings or the levels for adjustments during the removal; you do not need both. You will need to make separate reduction layers for each of the colors if you want the removal to be different for each component color. All of this will require a little testing to get the best output. There is an infinite number of variations.

With the separation in place, you can make changes to the image in CMYK, just as you would adjust an RGB image. In other words, if you feel that there is too much or too little of any color, you can reduce this imbalance by inserting an adjustment layer just above the component layer. The changes will be previewed directly in the image as you make them, so you can see the result on-screen.

Once you determine settings that work, you can reuse that method over and over again to create your custom separations. For example, if you note that your prints are all a little magenta heavy, you can add an adjustment to the Magenta layer as part of your process to reduce the magenta influence. At the same time, you are not subject to automatic conversions.

Using Hidden Power's manual separation of CMYK components, you have the advantage of making corrections to your CMYK content that you simply can't control otherwise in Elements—or in standard Photoshop CMYK conversions. The real glory of the process is learning how CMYK works, whether or not you implement the tools for print work. However, as with your custom duotones, you will be able to use your separations for printing, as you'll see in the next section.

Using CMYK Components

Once you have a viable CMYK separation, you'll want to be able to use it. To print the image, you can follow the same procedure you used for printing duotones. That is, you can flatten the layers individually to get C, Y, M, and K components in color and then run the sheet through your printer four times, once for each color. Your other option is to save the component layers as separate files and provide these to be used to output film. While these are viable options, the best option may be to build a real CMYK file with them.

The only problem with making a CMYK file is there is no direct way to save the file as CMYK, since Photoshop Elements won't handle CMYK channels. However, using the

Hidden Power of a DCS file template, it is possible to save your custom separations for use in a PostScript environment and create a viable CMYK file from Elements—even though there is no CMYK mode.

Creating CMYK Files in Elements

The method of creating your CMYK file may be a little bit of a horse-and-buggy approach in our modern digital-image world, but it is the only method that Photoshop Elements seems to allow, and it does let you at least complete the process and apply your CMYK separations.

What we'll do is hijack the components of a DCS EPS file. You will take your CMYK layers, split out the individual components, and then create the components of a DCS file. You'll have to know a little about DCS files and what to do with the template, but that part is relatively easy—and we'll look at how to do it all in this section.

What Is a DCS File?

DCS files (Desktop Color Separation) can come in several types, but the one we'll be concerned with here is a five-part file. It is a file that handles the components of a color image as separate files. The file has a preview (a low-resolution image that you can use for placement in layout programs that handle PostScript information) and separate grayscale files for each of the components (in the case of a CMYK file, separate files for cyan, magenta, yellow, and black). The low-resolution placement file is essentially a resource fork that points to the other files. When a PostScript device encounters the file, it will reference the high-resolution information in the separately saved component files when it goes to print.

As long as you name the files that are being referenced and save them uniformly as the proper type and format, you can fool a PostScript device into thinking that the content in a set of files will be what it needs to print—and there, a DCS template file can reference your cleverly substituted component separations.

Creating the DCS File

All you will be doing to create the file is splitting out the component parts from your CMYK separation and saving them as parts of a DCS template. You'll need to have the proper filenames and follow a rather rigid procedure, but in the end you can have a viable CMYK file.

1. Create a new folder to hold your DCS separation. Name the folder to describe the image so that you know which separation the folder contains. If necessary, you can create a text file in the folder to describe the file contents.

2. In the Chapter 10 folder on the companion CD, locate the DCS folder and the CMYK folder inside that. Open the CMYK folder and copy only the CMYK_DCS_Template.eps file

into the folder you created in step 1. The other files in the folder are placeholders to show you how the component files will need to be named.

3. Open an image that is already color-separated into CMYK components using the Hidden Power process, or open any RGB image and create the separation by double-clicking CMYK Process in Hidden Power tools in the Power_Separations category in Effects.

4. Use the (vi) CMYK Component Split tool in the Hidden Power tool set to separate out the components from the file opened in step 3. When the components are separated, you can close the original color version of the image.

5. Activate the Cyan image (it will be named according to the layer name it had in the original file).

6. Choose Save As from the File menu. When the Save As dialog opens, locate the folder created in step 1, and choose Photoshop EPS from the Format drop-down list, as shown in Figure 10.22. The template EPS file should appear named in the window. Click the template filename so it populates the File Name field; then delete the `.eps` from the name and add the component extension letter. For the cyan component, that would be `.C` (the whole name would be `CMYK_DCS_Template.C`). Click Save.

7. When the EPS Options screen appears, set the Preview to None, the Encoding to Binary, and uncheck the Image Interpolation check box before clicking OK, as shown in Figure 10.23.

Figure 10.22

Be sure to set your Save As dialog as depicted here. If the parameters are changed, the DCS file may fail when implemented.

8. Activate the Magenta image file and repeat steps 6 and 7, naming the file with an .M extension for magenta, rather than .C.

9. Activate the Yellow image file and repeat steps 6 and 7, naming the file with a .Y extension for Yellow, rather than .C.

10. Activate the Black image file and repeat steps 6 and 7, naming the file with a .K extension for Black, rather than .C.

When you have completed these steps, you will have saved the CMYK components of your image so that they can be placed in layout programs, such as QuarkXPress or Adobe InDesign, and you will be able to open the file as a CMYK file in other programs, such as Photoshop. These programs will recognize the DCS file and will reference the high-resolution components when it is time to print. You can go in at this point and rename the placement file (and the placement file *only!*). That is the file with the .eps extension. *Do not* rename the component files (.C, .Y, .M, or .K). Renaming components will cause the image to fail. The placement file is what you would place in your layout program or open with Photoshop. Elements will not recognize the DCS file.

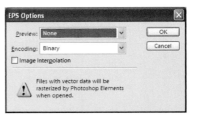

Figure 10.23

Be sure to set your EPS Options dialog as depicted here. If the parameters are changed, the DCS file may fail when implemented.

The placement file will look like Figure 10.24 as a preview. The preview is meant to help with placement of the image. Be aware that the preview will not resize automatically to the new size of your components; it shows a set 1000-pixel square for a 300 ppi image, no matter what you do in resizing the component files.

Be sure not to save more than one image (the five parts are one image) to a folder, or you will save over other image information. Using separate folders for each image will keep your files from overwriting one another. If you have a lot of DCS files to work with, place the separate folders for each image in a main folder, such as My CMYK Images. Multipart images are a little more difficult to maintain and track, but approaching them with consistency will yield consistent results.

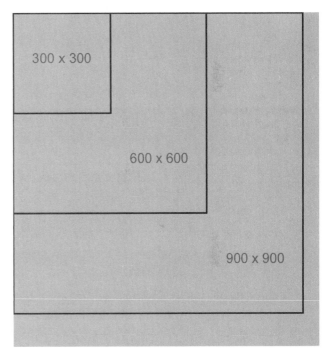

Figure 10.24

The boundaries on the preview in the placement file are meant to help you place the image in a layout program.

Templates are also provided on the CD in the DCS folder for duotone, tritone, and quadtone images so that you can use your duotone, tritone, and quadtone images as DCS EPS files. These files use a generic name for the additional colors (that is, Spot Color 1, Spot Color 2, and Spot Color 3). The generic colors can cause some mismatching when processing components, but it is possible to find solutions for output. Alert your printing technician to the generic names in the spot color files before processing. Name the files according to the extensions shown in the template folder.

If you have digested even most of what has happened in this chapter, you are pretty much a color guru at this point—well beyond the scope of what most Photoshop users know. There is almost nothing you can't do with a color image coming out of Photoshop Elements. Now we can move on to specialized concerns for printing.

Chapter 11

Options for Printing

You shouldn't just buy a printer and a ream of paper and assume you have every weapon you will ever need for your printing arsenal. First, you have to know what to expect from your printer's capabilities and the type of paper you buy. Knowing about the process can help you make better decisions that lead to better results.

While there are ways to get better results at home, at times you might need to print an image with a different process to get the best output. There is a reason why some printers cost thousands of dollars while standard home inkjet printers are much less expensive. Some of your best options for printing are just not practical for home use, but that doesn't mean you can't use them.

In this chapter, we'll look at getting better color results in print.

Understanding Printers and Printer Resolution

Making Prints at Home

Printing to the Edge

Using Other Printing Options

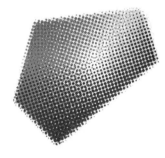

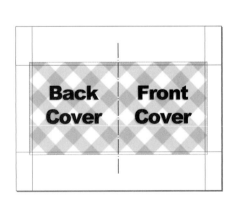

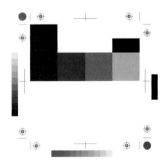

Understanding Printers and Printer Resolution

There are really only a few practical options when buying a printer for your home. Though not the only options, generally you are limited to a photo-quality inkjet printer—which is inexpensive and not a bad choice at all—or a laser printer. The latter is often quite a bit more expensive and doesn't necessarily deliver superior results. Different printer types handle the same image information in somewhat different ways. Understanding how each works can give clues as to how to prepare an image for printed output.

Both inkjet and laser printers put tiny dots (of ink or toner) on paper that represent the absolute resolution of the printer—the smallest spot of ink that the printer can make. These dots are fixed for each printer. The shape and intensity of each of the printer dots cannot be altered: each dot is either 100 percent on or off. The dots per inch (dpi) rating of a printer represents the number of these tiny dots of ink that the printer can make in one linear inch on a page. It is essentially measured the same way whether the printer is a laser or an inkjet. The dpi of a printer can be considered its maximum resolution—the finest building block of the printer's ability to represent an image. The maximum resolution of a printer is the *lower* of any two numbers reported as the resolution by the manufacturer. A 1200 × 600 dpi rating, for example, is really 600 dpi with a half step for the rows (the half step allows the dots to overprint). The dpi rating for a printer never changes—though there are other options you can use to control the output and how those dots are used.

The different dot patterns used by laser and inkjet printers account for the difference in their printed result. The dots on a laser printer are used in patterns that form larger dots in halftone screens; dots on an inkjet printer are more or less random. They form an array or tonal density (as used in stochastic printing) rather than organized halftone dots. By definition, *halftone screening* uses dot shapes (diamonds, circles, and so forth) of different sizes in rows to create tone and color in halftone screens (the arrangement of halftone dots and angles); *stochastic printing* uses randomized printer dots (not shaped dots in halftone rows) to create arrays of tone and color. A stochastic printer can print with a lower resolution (dpi) than a laser printer and appear to create finer results because of the randomized behavior of the dots.

If you can understand halftone screening, it isn't a big leap to understand stochastic printing. We'll look at halftone printing in detail first. Once you know some printing theory, it will help you understand how your images are represented in print, and you'll better understand how to achieve the best results. Different image content (vectors and pixels) controls printer information in different ways. Controlling that content on the printed page starts with understanding print theory.

Halftone Printing

Halftones are printed images that are composed of halftone screens. Halftone screens are composed of two types of ink dots: printer dots (also known as printer elements and dpi) and halftone dots (known as screening frequency and lpi, or lines per inch). *Printer dots* are the smallest unit of ink the printer can print; they are the *dot* in *dots per inch* noted in the printer specifications. *Halftone dots* are shaped dots made up from a grouping of the smaller printer dots, which create the halftone dot shape. The halftone dots are defined in rows that make up the *line* in *lines per inch (lpi)*. The set of rows of halftone dots define the halftone screen. See Figure 11.1.

Based on settings that you choose for printing (specifically the lpi), a set number of printer dots is assigned to each halftone dot. The printer dots within the set for each halftone dot are turned on or off in patterns on a PostScript printer to represent the shape of the halftone dots. Because halftone dots are made up of smaller, set-size printer dots, halftone dots, unlike printer dots, can vary in size from one dot to the next. The darker the tone, the larger the halftone dot, and the more printer dots are turned on inside the halftone dot grid. For example, if a halftone dot has 256 printer dots in it (a 16 × 16 printer dot grid as pictured in Figure 11.1), 60 percent gray will use 60 percent of the black printer dots in the halftone grid, or 154 out of the 256 printer dots. If a halftone dot were supposed to represent a 50 percent gray, 50 percent of the dots would be turned on (128 printer dots). If a halftone dot were to represent black, all the printer dots for the halftone dot would be on; if it were to represent white, none of the halftone dots would be on.

During the process of describing the image to the printer, Elements and your computer convert the shape, color, and tone of the image into rows of halftone dots based on the lpi and screening angles selected in the printing options (if nothing is selected by the person doing the printing, the printer will use a default). These dots are arranged in screens similar to the appearance of a window screen, where each square in the screen represents one halftone dot that can have a different tone than its neighbors. In turn, screens are defined for each ink color and sent to the printer. The printer is told which printer dots to print and which to keep off in order to create the halftone pattern and represent the image. The printer collects the information and then applies these rows of printer dots to paper to create a representation of the image.

The goal of applying the ink in screens is to provide a way for the inks to mix, minimize the visibility of the individual dots, and maximize ink coverage on the page so that images appear as close as possible to continuous tones to the naked eye.

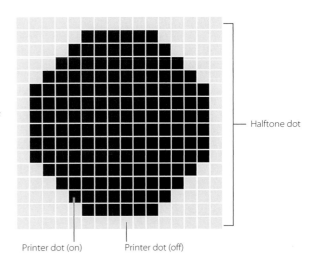

Halftone dot

Printer dot (on) Printer dot (off)

Figure 11.1

This shows a complete printer dot grid for a 16 × 16 halftone dot. The black printer dots are on; the gray printer dots are off. This halftone dot uses 60 percent of the printer dots in the grid, so it represents a 60 percent tone.

Halftone Dot Size

You can specify the size of the dot by choosing a *line screen* in the printer settings when going to print (using a PostScript or PostScript-compatible printer). The line screen setting tells the printer the number of halftone dot rows that will be put down per inch of print. The orientation of the halftone dots can be controlled by the screening angle that you choose. The *screening angle* tells the printer at what angle to offset the rows of halftone dots. Different angles are used so the dots of ink don't all land on one another and to avoid obvious patterning of the halftone dots. Knowing what the trade-offs are in selecting line screens and screening angles can help you optimize the use of the printer resolution to get the best printed result.

The lower the frequency of the lpi, the more printer dots that are used to print a halftone dot, and the larger the halftone dot will be. There is a trade-off in this relationship. Lower lpi means a greater the number of printer dots used in any halftone dot, so the halftone dot can represent more tones. A greater number of printer dots in a halftone dot leads to a greater number of possible variations that a halftone dot can represent, but it also ensures that each halftone dot will be larger and therefore more visible when printed. The opposite is also true: if you use fewer printer dots in a halftone dot (increase the lpi), it will have fewer potential variations but smaller, less visible, halftone dots. The larger the halftone dots, the easier they are to see and the more likely the halftone dots are to cause visible dot patterning (*moiré* patterns). The trick of halftone printing is to balance the relationship: keep halftone dots large enough so that the printer can represent all the image tones (by being composed of enough printer dots) but not so large that the halftone dots are easy to see.

The solution is found in the printer resolution. Just as with image resolution, if you have more information in the halftone dots than you can use, you waste it. There is no need to make a halftone dot with more information than you can extract from the image source. So, the optimal way to use the printer resolution is by selecting the right lpi for the printer.

Selecting the Right lpi

Halftone screens can be optimized for printing images that you have created depending on the maximum resolution of the printer you are using. Say your printer has a resolution of 600 dpi. This means it can print a maximum of 600 printer dots of information in a linear inch. At the same time, imaging programs, such as Photoshop Elements, deliver 8 bits/channel of information per ink color to the printer, meaning there will be 256 tones for any one color in any pixel. To be maximally efficient, any halftone dot would have to be able to represent 256 possible variations to present the information correctly (or at least potentially).

A 16 × 16 element halftone dot can have 256 variations (16 × 16 = 256) and can represent 256 shades of tone. This would be an optimal situation, where the halftone dot would be able to reliably render the information in each of the image pixels. A 20 × 20 element halftone dot, on the other hand, could represent 400 shades of gray. This may sound good, but there are two reasons it isn't: the halftone dot would be 25 percent larger, and an 8-bit source image would still provide only 256 potential variations. If you decided to use a 20 × 20 halftone dot, you would be printing halftone dots that can potentially represent a lot more information (156 percent more) than you have in your image. It is a waste of resources. A 10 × 10 element halftone dot will be smaller and less easy to discern, but it can have only 100 variations (10 × 10 = 100) and will likely be less able to show the full potential of pixels in your image.

Table 11.1 shows the size of various halftone dots and the number of shades of gray they can represent.

So, if the printer has a 600 dpi resolution and you want to run a halftone dot with 256 potential tones, then your lpi will have to be set to 38 (600 / 16 = 37.5). This setting will faithfully render the information in the image. Regrettably, a halftone dot that can represent all 256 possibilities is not always the best bet with a lower-resolution printer. The 38 lpi setting needed to have halftone dots that can reproduce 256 variations is a low line-screen frequency, producing a rather large halftone dot. If you step down to a lesser-size halftone dot with fewer elements—say a 10 × 10—you can have smaller halftone dots and a higher lpi frequency, and the printed result might end up looking better. A 10 × 10 halftone dot on a 600 dpi printer would enable you to run a 60 lpi screen (600 / 10 = 60). By trading down the number of tones each dot can represent, you shrink the size of the halftone dots.

A smaller number of elements per halftone dot means that fewer potential colors/tones can be accurately represented by a single halftone dot; it also means that there will potentially be a less smooth transition between tones. When you step down from a 16 × 16 element halftone dot to a 10 × 10, you go from 256 levels of tone representation down to 100 possible variations and a greater difference between the depiction of each level of tone. If you further decrease the number of elements in a halftone dot, the potential number of tones that can be reproduced by the halftone dot continues to decrease. Each time you lower the number of tones you can create, you increase the potential for color and tonal banding, which is a visible difference between levels of color or tone in the image. You have to decide which trade-off gives you the most pleasant result: bigger dots with more tone or smaller dots with more opportunity for banding.

ELEMENTS IN HALFTONE	SHADES OF GRAY
20 × 20	400
16 × 16	256
10 × 10	100
7 × 7	49
5 × 5	25
3 × 3	9

Table 11.1

Conversions of Halftone Dimensions to Gray Levels

The Advantage of Higher-Resolution Printers

The only way to get the full number of gray levels and small halftone dots is to have higher printer resolution (higher printer dpi; smaller printer dots). Printers with greater dpi (resolution) can show a greater number of tones than a lower-resolution printer, while using the same size halftone dot. This is why printer dpi makes a difference in the image result.

An imagesetter or professional press with 2540+ dpi will deliver better results than you could get with even good home laser printers because of the discrepancy between the printer resolutions. With at least 2540 printer dots at your disposal, you can use linescreen values of up to 150 (158, really) on professional devices and still get 256 levels of tone for each ink color. Compare this result to using 38 lpi to get 256 levels of gray on a 600 dpi printer, as discussed above, and you see that the press equipment can deliver dots that are about ¼ the size.

Breaking Pixels into Screens and Screen Angles

With the halftone rows defined by the line screen you have selected (based on the actual resolution of your PostScript printer), all that is left to do is convert the image to dots that fit neatly in rows. If everything is set up correctly, colors are separated into the CMYK components and converted to halftone dots according to default settings. If there is only one color (usually black), screening is fairly simple. The screen is converted to rows of dots at a specific angle. Often this angle is 45 degrees for black (rather than leaving the rows horizontal) in an attempt to better fool the eye into seeing tone rather than rows of dots (but screens can be adjusted however you choose).

Color halftones are a bit more complicated in their screen angles. The angles of screening for each color are offset with different angles by default, so the result doesn't cause the inks to run in parallel or cause other patterning. Default settings for the screen angles might be something like C 108 degrees, M 162 degrees, Y 90 degrees, and K 45 degrees. The colors in an area of the image are broken down into their CMYK components and then individually rendered into dot screens at the different angle settings. These screens are then printed over one another to create color and tone. See Figure 11.2.

All screening angles can be controlled with printer settings to attempt to get different effects. For the most part, you will want to leave the defaults and have the process make these decisions for you.

Vectors and Postscript Printing

A most interesting fact about halftone dots and printer dots is that they can be controlled by the presence of vectors. Clipping paths, clipping layers, and image elements defined by vectors, as described in Chapter 9, can be used to control and reshape halftone dots in a way that pixels cannot. Vectors can essentially cut through predefined notions of halftone dot shapes and redefine how printer dots are assigned. Vector shapes and type can appear to retain much sharper edges than in halftone screening. Figure 11.3 shows how a shape printed with four colors (CMYK) would print when using straight halftones and when using vectors to define the edge.

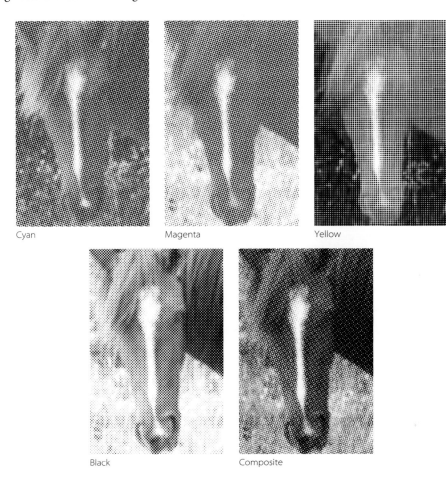

Cyan Magenta Yellow

Black Composite

Figure 11.2

Halftone dots for each ink are defined in separate arrays, or screens. When these are combined in printing as cyan, magenta, yellow, and black ink, the result renders image color and tone.

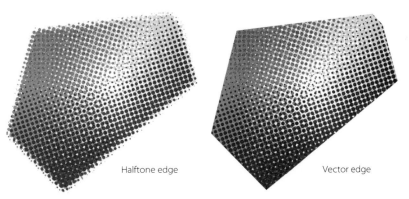

Halftone edge Vector edge

Figure 11.3

The non-vector halftone edge is softer and far less defined than the vector-edged shape, though both may look almost identical as digital images.

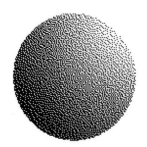

Figure 11.4
A halftone represen-
tation of an area
(left) can be com-
pared with finer
printer elements in
stochastic printing
(right) when printers
are capable of the
same resolution.

To use the advantage provided by vectors in printing your images, you will need to be printing to a PostScript printer, and you will have to have saved images in a format that allows vector information. TIFF, PDF, and EPS file types are your only options for saving printable images with vector content when using Photoshop Elements. If images are saved with the vector information and printed to inkjet or other non-PostScript printers, the results may not be as expected.

If the idea of breaking down image components into dots is clear enough at this point, understanding what goes on in an inkjet printer and how that process differs should be fairly easy to comprehend. We'll look at inkjet printing in the next section.

Stochastic Printing

If you can fathom all that is going on in printing a halftone in the previous section, stochastic (inkjet) printing is comparably simple. Instead of being trapped into halftone dot shapes, stochastic printing randomizes the use of printer dots so the printing seems smoother and there is little possibility of creating moiré patterning and other potential halftone-dot-related trouble. This is also why lower-resolution stochastic printing can seem finer than much higher-resolution halftone printing.

Figure 11.4 shows a rough approximation of how halftone and stochastic printing of the same area may compare.

While you won't have to deal with lpi settings and the trouble that halftone dots can bring, you forgo some of the refined edge sharpness you can get with PostScript printing that uses vectors. Vectors and pixels are treated essentially the same way in non-PostScript environments. Your images printed with an inkjet printer will look decidedly more like a photograph than anything you print on a laser printer. Both printing types have their advantages, both use printer dots in different ways, and neither is truly continuous tone.

Making Prints at Home

After you've made corrections to an image, you might look at it on the screen and it will look just fine. But when you print it, the color might not seem as vivid as you remember from the screen. This kind of outcome isn't unusual, as the process of printing can sap some of the strength from the color. It is a result of the necessary conversion from RGB (the light you see on-screen) to CMYK (the ink you see on paper).

Image files created by a camera are recorded in RGB color. This is a fine way to record visible color and the best way to display color that will be projected as light—that is, just about any color that can readily be reproduced on your camera LCD, your TV, or your computer monitor, by using a digital projector, or in creating digital film (film recording). All of these RGB processes play together fairly nicely.

Most printers you will use, whether inkjet, laser, dye-sublimation, or otherwise, use a CMYK process. That can mean plain ol' cyan, magenta, yellow, and black ink or a hybrid that uses additional inks (like CcMmYyK, which uses lighter tones of cyan, magenta, and yellow to create more fluid ink coverage). CMYK and RGB are not very friendly with each other—CMYK can often make RGB look bad—or much worse than it has to look—especially if there are profiling problems. Specifically, vivid red, green, and blue areas of an image can suffer in the conversion to CMYK because there are areas of RGB color that the CMYK process just can't imitate. Getting better results in print starts with that awareness. Adjusting an image specifically for CMYK results—working with an image that you've converted to CMYK or previewing the image as CMYK—can make a difference. We'll look at both of these options in this section.

What goes wrong between your image on-screen and the result in print can be hard to track down. Problems can start with your monitor not being calibrated and can range to it being improperly profiled, to having problems with color management in the image, to needing adjustment to your separations, to having trouble with your printer, and even to printing on the wrong medium. We've covered most of these areas to some extent but the last one. Before we get deeper into printing, we need to determine who is controlling your output.

Who Controls Your Output?

You can make a conversion to CMYK by using techniques from this book, but you can't always be sure that a separation setup is used for printing—unless you test your output. The reason for this is that many inkjet printers (printer drivers) make their own separations. Instead of taking what you put together as a CMYK image, they might convert the information from CMYK and then back to CMYK again. It's a problem similar to what can happen behind the scenes with renegade image profiles.

> Recall that in Chapter 2 it was suggested that profiles are almost unnecessary and using them or not depends on how you work and the processes that you use. It will often be better to avoid embedding profiles in images. You can't expect miracles from a profile, and you can't expect a digital process to know what looks right. Only you can do that.

You might guess that this double conversion—CMYK to RGB (or LAB) and back to CMYK—is not desirable if you've already gone out of your way to make a CMYK separation. Printers and drivers don't do this to be naughty; they are trying to help you get the best results. The printer will not realize that you are a sophisticated user and have created your own separation with a purpose in mind.

The first thing you need to do is find out what your printer and printer driver are doing so you'll know better how to handle your images—at least with that printer. You'll need to run a quick test to see how your printer is handling color. All you have to do is run a rich black (a black that combines black ink with cyan, magenta, and/or yellow ink rather than just using black) to the printer. Once you evaluate the results, you'll have to look at your possible options. Unfortunately, you can't print a CMYK image directly from Photoshop Elements. So that everyone can perform this test, I've provided another route using Adobe's Acrobat Reader (which is available on the companion CD).

Running the Test

Use the following steps to test your CMYK output.

1. Open CMYK.pdf from the CD by using Acrobat Reader.

> This test will not work if you open the image by using Photoshop Elements, because Elements will have to convert the file to RGB. You need to print the image as CMYK, and you can do that from Acrobat Reader.

2. Print using your usual printer and the print settings you usually use.

3. Evaluate the results in a well-lit room.

To evaluate the output, you have to know what you are looking for and what this test print is supposed to be testing. The file is set up with a rich black bar (more than just black ink) across the top. The "black" bar should actually be five colors—if your printer and driver are printing it as intended. The first three boxes are a rich black with cyan, a rich black with magenta, and a rich black with yellow, respectively. The top half of the last box will be black ink only, and the bottom half will be a rich black using 100 percent of all four inks. The next three bars in the image will be cyan, magenta, and yellow at 100 percent, 75 percent, 50 percent, and 25 percent. The separation of how that looks in color plates when separated right from the file I provided is shown in Figure 11.5.

Examining the output in the light should make apparent any differences between what you should have gotten and what you did get. If the black looks like a solid bar that is all the same rather than several different blacks, your printer (or the driver) is taking liberties with your CMYK separation. Therefore, you may not

Figure 11.5

The color in your print should use cyan (a), magenta (b), yellow (c), and black (d) in exactly the patterns shown, or your printer or driver is getting in the way of your results.

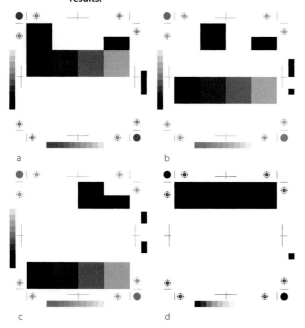

a

b

c

d

be able to use the printer as a reliable proofing device to see what you will get when using another printing device or service—unless you can find a solution.

If you want to get the CMYK out that you created, you will want to get the test image to print by using the original color in the image. It isn't so much that you want to be a control freak and never have image information change; you just don't want it to change without you knowing about it so that you can make proper adjustments and not waste your time.

There is more than one solution to the problem, but you have to be able to live with the result. Your solution could be as extreme as replacing your printer, but other options don't require making a decisive change in your current home setup. Your options include the following:

- Changing the output settings for printing
- Replacing your driver or using another method to get the right output
- Using a printing service when preseparated output is critical
- Working in RGB and accepting whatever the printer and driver give you in the conversion to CMYK
- Using a combination of the previous options

Changing Your Output Settings for Printing

Several settings that control how the printer will handle color can be hidden somewhere on the various tabs of your printer driver settings (and sometimes in the program you are using to do the output). These settings include the more conspicuous Convert CMYK Before Printing type to the type that vaguely mentions something about color management (or profiles). There may be other options more cleverly disguised. There also may be no options at all. Unfortunately, there are few standards.

If you look through all of your printer dialog box options when you are ready to print and there are no color options, then you will have to look at another potential solution. Don't give up until you get out the printer manual or online documentation of the driver interface and see what settings the driver has and what the settings affect. The documentation can point you in the direction of any settings that you might need to experiment with when the settings are not obvious.

There is no profile in the CMYK.pdf, and the result of your printing should be that the color is not manipulated by the color settings of your printer. However, some printers/ drivers may either insist that you have a profile or assume a generic profile, and this can result in a conversion. Again, that will show up as a change in the black bar, and/or as influence on the pure CMYK color bars. Alternatively, you may choose to use a work-around and/or replace your driver.

Replacing Your Driver

Most printer companies have a website for their products where you can download upgrades to system software and sometimes hardware as well (firmware). Obtaining new printer software from the website for your specific printer model can help give you functionality that was added after the printer was manufactured—or that enough people complained about to warrant an enhancement. When visiting such a website, don't pass up the option to complain, if necessary.

There may be third-party drivers that can do what you need. These will usually come at an additional expense. Sometimes you can use other drivers, but this can require a lot of trial and error and is probably impractical for the most part.

One exception where you can find a free third-party driver is on the Adobe website. Adobe makes drivers that are pretty much universal in helping create PDF files, and these can be downloaded for free. There is also functionality on the site that will help you convert files to PDF. Creating PDFs to print from is often a good solution for varied applications (it was used to create the test file). Using PDFs, you can often get the near equivalent of PostScript output from a non-PostScript printer (for example, clipping paths won't be ignored). All you do is use the driver option to Print To File. This will make a PRN (printer) or PS (PostScript) file, depending on your settings and the driver used. This file can then be turned into a PDF, and you can use that to print. PDF files are also often small (depending on compression settings) and service friendly; they can be lossless, and they can embed fonts.

Although it is not specifically changing your printer driver, exploring other options for programs to print from can be another solution. For example, layout programs often have capabilities that can help you get the output you want. For example, if you have QuarkXPress, Adobe PageMaker, or Adobe InDesign, printing from these programs can sometimes add options for output, or you can convert files to other formats such as EPS (Encapsulated PostScript).

Another clever workaround is to print your CMYK process images one color at a time by using multiple passes on the printer—as was outlined for making duotone prints in Chapter 10. While this may improve the result, it will probably not work perfectly if your driver is ignoring your separations. In other words, this only masks the problem rather than fixing it. If you can't control the settings, you still are not really controlling the result.

Using a Printing Service for Output

There are two ways to look at a printing service: 1) an expensive place that can be intimidating and inconvenient and smells like chemicals or 2) a resource for equipment you don't want or can't afford to keep at home. Services enable you to use sophisticated printers that you would probably never buy. Different services may have different equipment, and getting to know what is available—both locally in your area and through the Internet—may give you some good options for other means of output. Options can include color laser, LED (light-emitting diode), film recorders, offset printing, print-on-demand, and other processes (both high- and low-tech). For the most part, you'll know if you need a special service. We'll look at several of these options in more detail later, in the section "Using Other Printing Options."

Working in RGB

You may notice that the CMYK test gives you different results than you should get if the printer is using the information you send, but another question you need to answer is whether the results are good enough. In many cases they might be, and if they are, it saves the problem of having to make and correct CMYK separations. There is nothing wrong with sending an RGB image to your printer to be separated to CMYK *if* the results are satisfactory. At other critical times (when you are making a specific separation, as I did to create the CMYK test), you may need to explore more thoroughly how you can influence CMYK output.

CREATING PDF FILES

Adobe Acrobat (Professional, Standard, and Elements) and Adobe Acrobat Distiller will enable you to create PDF files from PRN (print) and PS (PostScript) files. These programs are usually licensed by purchase, but they may be included with other software packages or new computer purchases.

As another option, Adobe will allow you to use their online tools at their site to create a limited number of PDF files over a trial period. You can find the PDF creator here: `https://createpdf.adobe.com/` (look for the Try it for Free! link). Other free and inexpensive resources are available as well, such as these:

- Ghostscript
  `http://www.ghostscript.com`
- Pdf995
  `http://www.pdf995.com`
- PS2PDF
  `http://www.ps2pdf.com/convert/convert.htm`
- Docudesk (deskPDF)
  `http://www.docudesk.com`

Information here is likely to change; please feel free to post questions to the Hidden Power forum or search the Web for *Create a PDF online*.

Using a Combination of Solutions

What the last few sections were obviously leading to is that not every image will warrant or require the same process to get the result you need. You might use all of the discussed solutions in a single day, depending on what you need to accomplish. Being aware of the options is half the battle; the other half is realizing that using the right one at the right time saves work, time, frustration, and possibly money as well. Be sensible about your choices; be honest in your image evaluations; and be ready to change the processes you use most of the time in order to get the right result in the end. The right result will vary, sometimes from image to image.

Selecting and Testing Printer Paper

When eating soup, most sophisticated soup eaters use soupspoons. In a pinch, a teaspoon or tablespoon could do; if you are the chef, a ladle may be used for tasting. However, there is usually a reason why items we use every day have taken on slightly different shapes to perform their jobs. The same is true of printer paper. In this section, we'll discuss how to select and then test printer paper to ensure the best results.

Selecting Paper

Most people would tend not to run tissue paper through their printer in hopes of getting a good print. The same goes for toilet paper, paper towels, wax paper, litmus paper, tracing paper, shelving paper, aluminum foil, bubble wrap, plastic wrap, and so forth. What many people never consider is that different papers that look essentially the same have different qualities—and some of these qualities aren't a lot different from some of the sillier suggestions that you would quickly dismiss. Plain ol' typing paper may be too absorbent, acting more like a paper towel in absorbing the ink. It might have a texture or coating (such as an easy-to-erase surface) that impedes ink absorption. It might not be white. It may not necessarily be made for accepting ink from a color inkjet printer. Different inks in different printers can be … different. Because they can be different, paper that works well in one printer (such as a printer with an ink that dries quickly) may work less well on a different printer (such as a printer with ink that is slower to set).

> Although differences in paper can create different results when using a laser printer, it is usually much less of an issue because absorption is not part of the equation.

Manufacturers did not put expensive photo-quality paper on the market just because they thought they could sucker in unsophisticated buyers to pay 10 to 20 times more for paper they really didn't need. Photo-quality paper was made specifically to do the job of making the best-quality images from your inkjet printer. It is worth the extra money to use it when printing your best-quality, final images.

You don't have to use special photo-quality paper for every print, but you may need to change printer settings to adjust for the paper type. When using plain paper, it should be white. If not, the whites and lighter colors in your image will be influenced by the paper color (usually decreasing the dynamic range of the image). You will find that some brands of paper (even brands of the fancier photo-quality paper) will work better with your printer. Sometimes this will have little or nothing to do with price.

Testing Papers

If you are going to use a plain paper to proof images before printing on better photo-quality papers, or if you will be using different quality papers, be sure to "waste" a few sheets testing your output. Read the manufacturer's suggestions for the settings to choose for photo-quality and plain paper, and make prints of the same image on each. Make a few prints with somewhat different settings; for example, if there are settings for different grades of photo-quality paper, you might try more than one (especially if the paper you are using is not noted specifically by the manufacturer). Try several prints with the plain paper as well. As you make the prints, note the settings used for each by writing those settings directly on each print you make.

Compare the results of the photo-quality prints to the image on-screen first. Choose the result that most closely resembles what you see on-screen. (It may not be the best print!) Next, compare the print that looks the most like what is on-screen with the prints on plain paper side by side. Make note of the settings that produced the best matches, and use those settings when you print to those paper types. Retest whenever you switch papers. If you like the quality of the prints you get with a certain brand of paper, you should stick with it unless there is a good reason to change—and "because another brand costs slightly less on sale" is not a good reason. Using the same paper simplifies your process and ensures optimal results without having to retest. Testing is time consuming and really unproductive.

Testing your paper and noting the settings that produce the best results can assure you that what you see on-screen will most closely resemble what you will finally get in print. Once you make this test, it should be unnecessary to make plain-paper proofs for every image you print. With this test made, you have essentially completed the easier process of color management that I suggested at the beginning of the book: getting prints to match the screen. If you do not change the monitor settings or the paper you use, you can be assured every time of getting similar matching to what you see on-screen.

Printing with a Profile

A second use for color management and profiling arises when you print your files. Working-space color management is handled by your selection of a preference for Color Settings (see "Color Preferences" in Chapter 2). What that selection does not handle is the output profiling. Output profiling attempts to adjust for your printer and, we hope, the paper used as well. The output profile can be used whether you have your preferences for the working space set to limited color management, full color management, or none.

Printing with your printer profile can be accomplished through Elements via the Print Preview dialog box. Just choose Print from the File menu to open the dialog. Select the Show More Options check box at the bottom left of the dialog. Under Color Management, the screen displays the current Source Space (the profile embedded with your image per your color-management settings), Print Space, and Intent. Print Space is where you can select your profile. Profiles should be printer or printer/paper profiles that you have saved to the same place as your monitor profile (generally the Colorsync/Profiles folder on Mac or the System32/Spool/Drivers/Color folder on Windows).

Intent is set to Relative Colorimetric by default; other settings include Perceptual, Saturation, and Absolute Colorimetric. These options are described in Table 11.2.

Profiles that you will usually want to use for this will be either printer profiles provided by your printer manufacturer (sometimes supplied with the unit, sometimes available from the company website) or printer/paper profiles most likely provided by paper manufacturers (in some cases, the printer and paper manufacturers may be the same). You can also have custom profiles made or try third-party profiles (often the latter are created for specific combinations and purpose). Don't assign any old printer profile just because you have the opportunity to assign one.

CMYK Previews

It is not possible to preview CMYK printing in Photoshop Elements, so they say, because there is no CMYK to work with in the first place. If one can't create CMYK, there is, of course, no way to preview it—and no reason to. There is also no Preview option. Why should that stop you?

	INTENT	EFFECT
Table 11.2 **Intent Settings** **for Print Preview**	Perceptual	Attempts to maintain a view based on how we perceive color; actual color may change.
	Saturation	Attempts to render saturated color in the new space, potentially at the expense of color accuracy.
	Relative Colorimetric	Attempts to preserve as much of the original color as possible, while adjusting color outside the target space to the closest possible match.
	Absolute Colorimetric	Does not attempt to preserve or adjust color that is out of gamut for the target color space.

It is exactly because there is no CMYK that it is pretty easy to preview CMYK. That may sound contradictory. But what a preview has to do is take your CMYK information and convert it to RGB again. Because Elements won't open a CMYK image as CMYK, the preview is really automated (read: forced). As fate would have it, it is exactly the conversion from CMYK to RGB that will show you what you should be getting in print and will let you know—without printing—approximately what results you will see when you do print.

As demonstrated in Chapter 10, you can build a CMYK image by making a custom separation and saving to a DCS EPS template. To complete the process of previewing your CMYK images on-screen, all you have to do is split out the CMYK components from your custom separation and merge them. You can do this manually by copying each component out of the file, creating the EPS, and then going back to open that file so it converts to RGB. Hidden Power tools provide an easier way without having to save the image first. All that is required is that you can complete a CMYK separation and get a reasonable preview using output to plain and/or photo-quality paper. If you have accomplished this, you can preview your result before even sending the image to print by proofing on-screen. This can save paper, ink, and cost.

The preview that you will create is just a preview file and nothing more. You should never save the preview. Just look at it, see if there is something you want to adjust, and then throw it out. You can experiment with creating a Gradient Map set that makes the preview look accurate, and you can then apply that to any image you are previewing. This will take some trial and error (or testing), but once you have achieved an accurate preview adjustment, you can use it over and over to preview the result of your separations.

1. Open any image and create a CMYK separation by using Hidden Power tools functionality. Double-clicking (i–v) CMYK Process in the Power_Separations category of Effects will lead you through the separation.

2. Double-click (vi) CMYK Component Split in the Power_Separations category of Effects in the Hidden Power tools. This will separate the C, M, Y, and K components from the separation you created in step 1, leaving the original components in the layers of the first image.

3. Double-click Preview CMYK in the Power_Separations category of Effects in the Hidden Power tools. This will attempt to combine the separated components created by the split. Because Elements is an RGB program, it will stop you from viewing the image as CMYK and prompt you for a conversion to RGB (choose to convert by clicking the Convert Mode button). This CMYK to RGB conversion is exactly what you need to preview the CMYK result on-screen.

After you have completed this simple process, the image on-screen should represent the CMYK you will probably get by printing the original CMYK separation (if your printer respects your separation). I say "probably" because there can be some variation specific to the printer, the inks, and the paper, as well as your setup for color management. The solution to getting a more accurate preview is to make some adjustments to the preview image on-screen. To adjust the preview, do the following:

1. Open an image and create a CMYK separation by using the (i–v) CMYK Process Hidden Power tool in the Power_Separations category of Effects.

2. Use the (vi) CMYK component Split tool to separate out the C, M, Y, and K components to separate files.

3. Create the EPS DCS file from the component files using the CMYK Template and procedure from the "Creating CMYK Files in Elements" section in Chapter 10. Do not close the component files.

4. Create an on-screen preview for the CMYK image using the Preview CMYK Hidden Power tool in the Power_Separations category of Effects.

5. Open and print the EPS file you created in step 3 by using a layout program. Any process that you have tested using the CMYK.pdf file and the instructions in "Who Controls Your Output?" will work.

6. Compare the print to the screen, and make changes to the preview image on-screen by using adjustment layers (such as gradient maps, levels, and so forth). Your goal is to make the screen match the print as closely as possible. This may take some time. Look back to Chapters 5 and 6 for color- and tone-correction techniques.

7. Create a preview template file to store the adjustments you made. Name the adjustment layers according to their purpose and/or placement. It may be a good idea to save a screen shot of the Layers palette in the template so you can duplicate the results.

8. Use the correction layers to correct the preview of other images. All you have to do is drag the correction layers from the sample to the new preview or vice versa.

You can make your adjustments by using separations to fine-tune the preview. RGBL, explored in Chapter 4, may be a good choice. Once the corrections are stored, you can use them on any image you have separated into CMYK to get a better preview of the output on-screen *before* you actually print. Over time, you may need to adjust the correction template that you have created to make it fit better to a broader range of situations.

Creating Custom Picture Packages

Picture packages are an easy way to fit images onto a printed sheet when you go to create image prints. Packages can lay out one image in different sizes and combinations to fill a printing sheet or allow you to print more than one image. Photoshop Elements provides a bunch of presets, and you might find one that meets your needs. A good thing to know is that you aren't stuck with the presets Adobe assigned.

You can access Picture Package from the Editor by choosing Print from the File menu and then clicking the Print Multiple Photos button or by choosing File → Print Multiple Photos. Once the Print Photos dialog is in view, choose Picture Package from the Select Type Of Print drop-down menu. Mac users should see the "Using Picture Package On Mac" sidebar.

Say you want to print seven images on an 8.5 × 11 sheet—three images that are about 4 × 5 and four smaller wallet shots at about 2 × 2.5. Adobe doesn't provide this layout, so you would have to create it yourself. To create the Picture Package using the measurements from the example, all you have to do is the following simple steps:

1. Open a text-editing program such as Notepad or WordPad.

2. Type the following into the text editor exactly as you see it here. Use a single space where you see spaces, not tabs or double-spacing. You can also open the SevenShots .txt file off the Hidden Power CD to compare or use instead.

    ```
    I 8 10
    Letter (7) shots
    0 0 3.875 4.875
    0 5 3.875 4.875
    4 0 3.875 4.875
    4 5 1.875 2.375
    4 7.5 1.875 2.375
    6 5 1.875 2.375
    6 7.5 1.875 2.375
    ```

3. Save the file as a plain-text file into the Layouts folder in the Elements program directory. By default, the path to the folder is

    PC: C:\Program Files\Adobe\Photoshop Elements 4.0\shared_assets\layouts
    Mac: Applications: Adobe Photoshop Elements 4.0: Presets: Layouts

4. Choose the images you want to print in the picture package. If you are in the Editor, you can do this by simply opening the images you want to print. If you are in the Organizer, locate the images and Command+click / Ctrl+click those you want to print.

5. Open the Picture Package printing option as described earlier. From the Editor choose Print Multiple Files from the File menu, or choose Print from the File menu in the Organizer. Once the Print Photos dialog is in view, choose Picture Package from the Select Type Of Print drop-down menu.

6. Choose the printer to which you intend to send the picture package from the Select Printer drop-down list.

7. Choose Letter (7) Shots from the Select A Layout drop-down list.

8. Drag and drop the images from the thumbnail bar (at the left of the dialog) into the areas of the preview (the main panel) where you want the images to appear. Elements will automatically resize and orient these images to fit the areas that are mapped by the layout. Images will be rotated automatically to take best advantage of the layout size. See Figure 11.6.

You can reuse the layout after it is created to print other files, a folder of files, or images in the Organizer. If you are not automating printing of a folder or image group, you can change individual images in the layout by just dragging any of the available thumbnail images into any of the areas defined in the layout (see Figure 11.7). You can then save and/or print the packages when the image(s) have been completed.

If you want to create your own layouts, you can type them up like you did in step 2— you'll just have to know what those things mean that you typed in the text file. All you did was set up a data file that Elements looks at to know how to lay out the page. The first character in the first row defines the units for the layout. Here we used I for inches, but you can also use P for pixels (72 to the inch), and C for centimeters. This initial measurement type is used for all of the measurements in the file.

The number following the measurement type defines the width of the page; the next number defines the height. I don't know about you, but my paper is usually 8.5 × 11 inches. Regretfully, the picture package "logic" only recognizes layouts that are set in 8 × 10 when you select letter-size paper as the target (or 576 × 720 pixels). If you use A4 paper, you will want to use 19 × 27.7 centimeters.

Figure 11.6

The new package layout defined in this exercise will have images in an array, as pictured here.

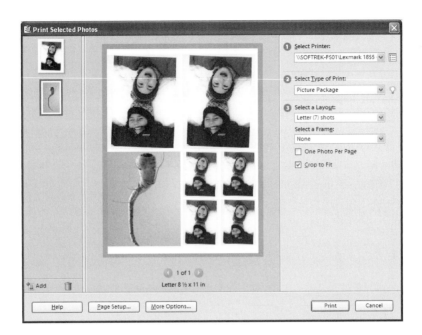

Figure 11.7

On PC, select the image you want to replace by clicking on it in the thumbnails and dragging it into place. Here, a photo of a parsnip replaces a shot of the children in the lower left of the package.

The Crop To Fit check box is a little unpredictable. While it will do more to fit your prints into the page, it really ignores the image content and can create some really bad cropping. You will likely want to keep it unchecked.

The second line of the file is the name of the layout as it will appear on the drop-down list. The name you use for the file doesn't matter in the least, so long as it is a plain-text file and you save it to the right folder. While there seems to be no limitation on the length of the description, the display is limited to 27 characters (though rolling over the listing will display the full name). It is good to name the layouts something obvious so that they are easy to locate in the list.

All the lines that follow define the location of picture areas. You will create one new line for each picture box that you want on your picture package page. The first number is the distance from the left of the page, and the second number is the distance from the top of the page. The third number is the width of the picture box, and the fourth number is the height of the picture box.

These packages can be useful if you want to print a lot of images quickly and have a favorite setup. If you are only doing a one-time setup, it is probably easier and less time-consuming to do packages manually. To make a manual setup, just create a new document that is the size of your paper, drag in the images you want to print, and then arrange them. One advantage of manual packages is that you can save them and reprint whenever you want.

Boxes will overlap if you aren't careful with the sizing—so be careful with the sizing. Don't look for these picture packages to do a lot of paper conservation: you won't have the opportunity to print close to the edge of your paper. We'll look at printing to the edge in the next section.

USING PICTURE PACKAGE ON MAC

Mac users may be a little itchy reading this methodology because it won't all seem right—especially that last step. Truth is, while the procedure above will work using the manual method on Mac, the interface is different on Mac and PC, and the Mac has some advantages. For one thing, there is a Picture Package item right on the File menu. Once the Picture Package dialog opens, there is an Edit Layout button right on the bottom right of the screen. Clicking that will open the Picture Package Edit Layout screen, and from there you can create a new layout and save it without ever leaving Elements. Once in the Picture Package Edit Layout screen, do the following:

1. Enter the name you would like the layout to appear under in the drop-down list in the Name field.

2. Select the desired Page Size from the drop-down list, or enter it manually in the Width and Height fields, and select the desired unit of measure in the Units drop-down list.

3. Click the Delete All button to clear the image boxes (called Zones). It is just easier to start fresh by deleting them all.

4. Click the Add Zone button, and change the size and position of the box that appears either using click and drag and the handles on the bounding box, or using the Size and Position fields.

5. Add as many zones as you need either by repeating step 4 or by duplicating the existing box. To duplicate the zone press Option and click on the zone, then choose Duplicate from the pop-up menu when it appears.

6. When your zones are all in place, click the Save button to save your layout and return to the Picture Package screen. You will need to select a name for the file you are saving.

Also, updating the files on Mac layouts in the Picture Package screen is done by clicking directly on the zone where you want to change the image. The Select An Image File dialog will open and you can choose an image from anywhere on your system to replace the current image in that zone.

Printing to the Edge

Another layout problem that may confound a user is making images print to the edge of the paper. On most printers, there is an edge area of the sheets you are printing that the printer will not print on—commonly called a grip edge in printing. It is often a quarter to a half-inch broad and may vary from edge to edge depending on how paper was designed to go through the printer. In most cases, you really don't want to print right to the edge of the paper if the printer was not designed for edge-to-edge printing—and maybe you don't even want to do it then. If the ink misses the page, you could end up getting ink on the printer, rollers, or something else, and the edges of the print could be smudged by handling.

There are two solutions to the problem of printing to the edge, which are really the same thing: buy perforated paper that you print on and then tear away in the shape of the print, or just do it the old-fashioned way: print on a larger sheet than you need and then crop the paper.

For example, say you are creating a CD booklet and you want to make your image on the front and back go right to the edge of the booklet. You wouldn't start with paper that was exactly the right size and then use your printer to print the image exactly to the edge; you'd start with a larger sheet, print the cover, and then cut down the paper. Figure 11.8 shows a sample layout.

The image prints a bit beyond the crop edge— say, by an eighth of an inch (which is a printing standard). This provides a margin of error for the cropping. If the cut doesn't fall precisely on the crop mark, the image will still come all the way to the edge of the cropped area. Extending the image beyond the boundaries of the area you want it to occupy and then cropping the edges of the image is called *bleeding* in printing terms. One-eighth of an inch is a standard margin of error.

Figure 11.8
All areas outside the crop hash are cut off and discarded.

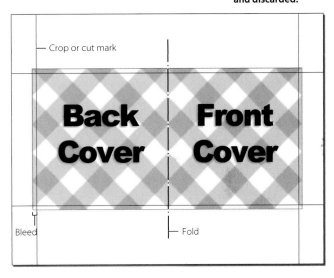

Using Other Printing Options

There are several other printing options for your images, and in this section we will focus on higher-end possibilities that are impractical for use in the home. You can turn your images into negatives or slides for use in photo printing or projection, and you can use other printing processes such as offset printing and LED that surpass home printers in quality and are designed for quantity. You will have many more options than those mentioned here, but in dealing with digital images and photography, these will be common and useful. Check with your local services and on the Internet for more ideas.

Film Recorders

A *film recorder* is a means of generating film exposure from a digital image. Film recorders can be used to create slides and negatives, which can then be used for slide presentations and print exposures.

Within the film recorder, a CRT (cathode ray tube) is employed to project a thin beam of light through a filter and onto film to expose it. Film is then processed and developed by using conventional photo processing, resulting in an image on traditional analog film.

Film recorders come in varying resolution and quality based both on the number of lines of resolution possible and the quality (and size) of the CRT. Cost for processing can vary based on the quality of the film recorder and the available resolution. Usually, it is not cheap, but when you need slides or film and have an image with enough resolution, the quality can be unsurpassed. Resolution of your images may have to be 650–1000 ppi at the final size.

In general, 35 mm film is used with 2000- and 4000-line recorders; 8000-line recorders can be used with 35 mm film, but this resolution begins to surpass the limitation of the film grain. Larger film stocks (2.25 inch) usually require 8000-line recorders, and film stocks 4 × 5 inches and larger usually require 16,000-line recorders.

A list of exactly what resolution to use would be meaningless, because the quality of these various devices may require different source resolution. You'll have to contact services both to see if they have film recorders available and what they require for output.

Offset Printing

Offset printing is usually standard CMYK printing on printing presses, though it can also be duotone printing or other processes such as six-color hexachrome printing. Printing on a press may come in handy for producing greeting cards, business cards, books (and covers), CD inserts, calendars, posters, and the like—printed materials that you will want to produce in quantities of thousands. While shorter runs may be available, this type of printing is almost exclusively effective in volume. The result is top quality in both black-and-white and color printing. Presses can be of varying quality. The better-quality presses will run upward of 133 lpi and 2540 dpi. All will use PostScript and halftone approaches.

Newer digital solutions for printing include devices such as Hewlett Packard's Indigo Digital Presses, which use up to seven inks to achieve high-quality, all-digital prints. These machines were designed for short-run production of color materials that might be impractical to run on a traditional press. They offer high print quality and reasonably low cost for runs under about 500 pieces.

Light-Emitting Diode (LED) Printing

Light-emitting diode (LED) printers generate photographic results from RGB digital files. Somewhat like film recorders, these printers enable your files to be printed without the conversion to CMYK because the process used is light-based. Exposure is created on photographic paper up to poster size, directly from digital files. Exposures are then processed as you would photographic paper, often right in the same machine.

While LED prints may be somewhat more expensive than traditional photo prints, the gap isn't very wide. The advantage is that you can use this process selectively with images that you have had the opportunity to correct and improve digitally and still get photographic results. Unlike using a film recorder, which would take two steps (record to film, then print) to get results, LED printing takes the digital file directly to print in a single step. Because it cuts out having to pay for film and photo developing, it can end up being much less expensive to process than using the film-recorder route.

Again, quality can vary with this output type depending on the machine (and the operators), but the color results will often be far superior to home printing. Files often require only about 250 ppi at final size. Check with your service to be sure, and ask to see samples of prints to check the quality of resolution and papers before you buy. Of all the output options, I use this most frequently for output of my own photographs for framing and photo shows.

At the End of the Book

By this point of the book, we have walked through setting up your equipment and defining a process and tools to use, and we've opened images and processed them for the best visible results. We've also addressed concerns for output and opened the door to additional options for creating superior prints. You've loaded tools from the CD and perhaps stepped across a few boundaries with processing images in Elements that you may not have thought possible.

There are additional pages in the Appendix on technical information, that may be useful to peruse. One of the most interesting sections for Elements users at any level will be how to run actions in Elements. This can open the door to many useful effects and techniques—like the Hidden Power tools—that are otherwise extremely difficult or time-consuming to accomplish.

To help you continue your experience and learning, I maintain the Hidden Power website, newsletter, and forums. These areas of the extended Hidden Power website are meant to nurture Elements users, and I hope they are a means of building a community and a resource. They are a resource for me to get to know my readers better and for understanding what needs to be done in further development of processing and techniques, and they are a means for you to provide feedback as to what would be most helpful for you. Please be sure to do the following things:

- Sign up for the Hidden Power newsletter (`http://hiddenelements.com/newsletter.html`) to keep abreast of tips, tricks, tool upgrades, new releases, questions and answers, errata, and troubleshooting for Hidden Power tools and techniques.

- Visit the forums to discuss your ideas with other Hidden Power readers about image editing, processing with Elements, and what new tools you'd like to see (`http://hiddenelements.com/forums.html`).

- Make suggestions and ask questions about tool use, specific techniques, and how to process your own images by responding to the newsletter or adding topics in the forum.

- Visit the website to find out about new tools, access the forums and past issues of the newsletter, and find links to actions that you can use in Elements that have been tested for use by other users.

- Let me know directly (`thebookdoc@aol.com`) about any actions you find that you successfully install and use in Elements so I can let other users know. Keep me abreast of your progress, of news and information, and of successes you have in editing your images—I may be glad to use your examples in future editions of this book.

But even at the end, as you turn the final pages, I hope that you see this as the beginning of your image processing and exploration. In other words, I hope these last words of the book open the future to your development and to learning about making your images better. I learn more about image editing every day, and I invite you to learn with me, outside the confines of the book.

Appendix

Community, Concepts, and References

This appendix provides information that doesn't fit a particular topic in the book. It is information that will come in handy when working with images. In its own way it can be considered "hidden." It is material that can be a struggle to find yet may be critical to developing your skills in image editing. Topics such as these are sometimes buried in obscure places, if they are even documented at all. They may be presented incorrectly on the Web, or they can be just plain too difficult to find when you really need them. You'll likely find that these topics will come in handy.

How to Run Actions in Photoshop Elements

The Toolbox

Resolution

File Types

Bit Depth

Blending Modes

Camera RAW Files

Advantages and Disadvantages of 16-Bit

Reader Requests

How to Run Actions in Photoshop Elements

Actions are procedures (sometimes referred to as scripts or macros) that you build in Photoshop that allow you to play back a series of events. In Photoshop, actions are built by simply recording the steps you make during corrections. All you do is turn on the Record feature and Photoshop records your steps as you make them and stores them. When you have finished recording, you can save the set of steps as an action, and you can play back the series of events on any image, just by playing the action. In this way, you can easily repeat the steps from image to image.

Actions are useful if you find a particular way to make corrections or changes to an image that are universal or if you create an effect that you would like to repeat. You can lighten your workload by recording those steps and playing them back. You can often use the same actions that you recorded for Photoshop in Photoshop Elements. In fact, many of the Hidden Power tools and techniques are recorded actions that allow you to repeat a series of steps. In other words, the Hidden Power tools ramp up the power of Elements using actions, and other actions may be available that were created for Photoshop but that may suit your needs in Elements.

A wide range of actions for Photoshop is available for free on the Web that accomplish everything from making practical corrections (such as the Hidden Power tools) to helping render interesting effects (creating a frame or changing an image to look like a drawing or watercolor). A whole store of actions is available for free download on Adobe Studio Exchange. Not all of them work in Elements as is, but many will, and the rest can be altered to work in Elements if you can edit the actions (more on that later).

All versions of Elements to date have several different ways that actions can be played. Some require knowing how to write HTML or XML and are too complex for many users to implement. However, there is a solution for running actions that works in all versions of Elements that requires no HTML or XML or programming skills. This easier solution uses the Effects palette, and it is the solution we'll look at here.

Overview

There are several steps in playing actions using this method. I go into some detail here; after you do it once or twice it will be fairly easy. The general steps are listed here. Each step will be described in more detail:

1. Locate or create an action that you want to run in Photoshop Elements.
2. Set up the preview image.
3. Install the action in Elements.
4. Delete the Effects Cache folder.
5. Restart Elements.
6. Run the action.

A sample Hello World action is provided on the CD so you can work through the steps and check to see that you can get actions to work before you start trying to add new ones. If you'd like to test out the whole experience, you can download the action from the Hidden Power website (`http://hiddenelements.com/`). This action will create a new document containing the words *Hello World*. This sample simply allows you to be sure that you can install actions correctly.

1. Get an Action

You can't play an action in Elements if you don't have one to run. While you will be able to use the sample file provided to see how this works, you'll want to use other actions at some point. You can find actions for Elements on the Web by searching for Photoshop Actions, or you can create them yourself if you have access to Photoshop (6, 7, CS, and CS2). Some great sources for Photoshop actions are `www.actionfx.com`, `www.atncentral.com`, `www.actionexchange.com`, and `www.hiddenelements.com`. At this time, only `www.hiddenelements.com` maintains actions for Elements 4. This site can expand dramatically with reader input. Action files work on both Mac and PC, without alteration. You can easily identify action files by their three-letter extension: `.atn`. A sample action file from this is shown in Figure A.1 as it would appear in thumbnail view.

Any action that you download from the Internet may be compressed (e.g., a ZIP or SIT file for PC/Mac), so you may need to first download the file to your computer and decompress it to reveal the action file. You can find free decompression utilities on the Internet, though you will likely already have some type of decompression utility on your system. See the Hidden Power website for suggested decompression utilities.

Basic Color Correct.atn
ATN File
11 KB

Figure A.1

This action file is from the Hidden Power tool set, titled Basic Color Correct.atn.

> Warning: Please be aware that actions you locate and download from the Internet may be copyrighted. This means that those creating or distributing the action claim some sort of intellectual property right to the action. Whether you paid a fee for the action or not, do not redistribute actions without consent of the copyright holder!

If you have access to Photoshop, you can use it to record and save your own actions to play in Elements. You will record and save the action using Photoshop's Action palette features. Please see Photoshop's Help menu for information about recording actions. While you can record almost anything you do in Photoshop, some behaviors will not work and may need to be recorded differently for Elements. See the "Actions That Will Not Work in Elements" and the "Troubleshooting" sections of this appendix for more information on these recording issues.

Whether you record the action yourself or download it from the Internet, you will want to begin by setting up your file structure for installation into Elements.

1. Create a new folder with a descriptive name for the category in which you want your action to appear on the Effects drop-down list. The sample folder is titled Hello World, but you can name your folder anything you want (avoiding most special characters).

2. Save the .atn file into the folder created in the previous step with the name of the file as you want it to appear in the text listing of Effects.

When you extract the sample file, the Hello World.atn file will already be in a folder called Hello World. The folder will also contain a preview file (Hello World.psd) as an example of how these files are set up. The action file contains the steps that perform the behavior; the preview file contains only a thumbnail preview of the effect and the name reference to the action file so Elements knows what action to play.

At this point, we will assume you have either located the Hello World action on the Hidden Power CD or that you have downloaded an action from the Internet. Now that you have your action, let's create a preview file.

2. Set Up the Preview File

The action preview image is the key to launching your action in Elements. This image file displays in the Effects palette and points Elements to the action you are attempting to run when you click the preview. Photoshop actions that you download from the Internet will seldom have this preview image, so most of the time you will have to create it. It is actually pretty easy to do. The sample folder will already have an action preview

(Hello World.psd) that you can look at as an example. If you want to make your own preview, just do the following:

1. Open Photoshop Elements.

2. Create a new image that is 64 × 64 pixels. Do this by choosing New from the File menu (File → New) or by pressing Ctrl+N on your keyboard. When the New dialog appears, enter the name for the action, change the dimensions to 64 × 64 pixels, and make the mode RGB Color. See Figure A.2.

3. Design your preview image as desired. It can literally be anything you want it to be so long as the image will fit on a single 64 × 64 pixel layer. You can change this image later on after you test the action. In fact, it is sometimes a good idea to use the action to build a preview by running it successfully on a sample image. After you have created the look you want, flatten the image (you may want to save the file with layers before flattening so you can make adjustments to the preview without rebuilding it).

4. After flattening the image, open the Layers palette and double-click the Background layer. This will open the New Layer dialog. Change the name of the layer to match the name of the action that you want it to run. This name has to be exactly the same as the name of the action file (including spaces) but without the .atn extension. It may be best to copy the name directly from the file.

5. Save the file as a Photoshop document in the folder where you saved the action (.atn) during the first part of the setup. When saving, be sure that the Save Layers option is checked.

You can compile previews for multiple actions in one preview file (each preview on its own layer) or compile many different preview files into a single folder. You will likely want to compile previews into one file if you have a set of actions that act as a group (again, a good example is the setup for Hidden Power tools). Keep in mind that the action files you plan to run should be in the same folder as their associated preview file. The name of the folder they are in will appear in the category listing in the Effects palette. You can also add to existing Effects categories, including those supplied by Adobe. All you need to do is add the action file (.atn) and preview image (.psd) to the category folder and then delete the cache and restart Elements. Deleting the cache is covered in "4. Delete the Cache Folder."

With the preview created and placed in a folder with the action, it is time to install the action and create the category in Elements.

Figure A.2

The New dialog with proper parameters for creating a preview file

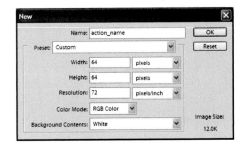

3. Install the Action Folder

After locating, downloading, and decompressing the action file and setting up the preview image, you are ready to place the action folder into Elements. You will need to place the Effects folder inside the Elements program folder; it's located on the C drive in the Photoshop Elements 4.0 program folder by default:

```
C:\ Program Files\adobe\Photoshop Elements 4.0\Previews\Effects
Applications:Adobe Photoshop Elements 4.0:Previews:Effects
```

Figure A.3 shows the location of the Effects folder.

Copy or move the entire folder that you created for your action into the Effects folder. In the case of the example action, you would want to move the Hello World folder into the Effects folder. This folder should contain only the .atn file and the preview .psd file. Once you have added the action category folder to the Effects folder containing the action file and preview file, you have effectively installed the action. You can do these steps in different order (e.g., create the category folder, then add the action and preview files), but you should vary the process only after you are sure how it works. You can also add other actions to your folder, but keep it simple until you are sure what you are doing.

All that is left to do is make Elements recognize the new files and run the action. In the next section, we look at deleting the cache to force Elements to recognize the new files.

Figure A.3

The Effects folder is located in the Photoshop Elements 4.0 program folder.

4. Delete the Cache Folder

The Effects cache file stores information about the effects that are currently installed in Elements. Regretfully, the file does not get effectively rebuilt each time Elements starts up. Although failing to rebuild will save startup time (as it was meant to do), it will not be very helpful when you have added new actions to try out, because Elements will not recognize them. What you will have to do is delete the cache folder for Effects; this will force Elements to rebuild the cache the next time you start up the program.

To delete the cache, just follow these steps (it is best to do this when the Elements program is not running):

1. Shut down Elements.

2. Locate the Elements Previews folder (see Figure A.3 for the location).

3. Right-click the Cache folder inside the Previews folder and choose Delete from the pop-up menu. (You can also drag the Cache folder to the trash if you prefer).

4. Empty the trash.

5. Restart Elements

When you restart Elements, it will look for the cache, and when it doesn't find it, Elements will rebuild the cache according to the files currently installed in the Effects folder. In effect, deleting the cache forces Elements to recognize the new files you have installed. You have to delete the cache files after every action installation in order to force Elements to rebuild the cache.

After restarting Elements, look in the Effects palette for your new action additions. If the Effects palette is not visible, open the palette by selecting Styles And Effects from the Window menu on the Elements menu bar; then choose Effects from the drop-down list at the upper left of the palette. With the Effects palette in view, allow Elements some time to rebuild the cache and previews. Depending on how many items you have in the Effects, this can take a while (two to five minutes). Be patient. When rebuilding activity seems to stop, look for your new action by viewing the category listing. The categories should list the folders you install by the folder names. Choosing your new category should list your new action. If the action appears in the list, you are ready to run it. If the action does not appear, and you have been patient with the rebuilding, see the "Troubleshooting" section for what to do next.

6. Run the Action

To run the action, be sure an image is open, and double-click the thumbnail in the Effects listing on the Styles and Effects palette. An image must be open even if the action (such as the "Hello World" sample) opens a new image during the action. The open image can be any image at all, even one you create without saving. It is best to run most actions on RGB images. When running actions, take note of specific errors that appear, if any. These error messages will help in troubleshooting any problems.

> Steps 1–6 run through a full installation of an action where you create the preview and the category. A quicker method of testing actions is described in "Actions That Will Not Work in Elements," later in this section.

Troubleshooting

It is all too familiar to me that even installations that should be easy sometimes run into problems. While it is likely that you will get through the action installation without a hitch, this section attempts to cover all manner of trouble you may have. If you cannot access the actions you believe you have installed, please follow these troubleshooting tips. The sample file was tested on *all* versions of Elements (1 to 4), so if you are unable to get the sample to work, it is not likely that it is a problem with the files (or the CD) unless you had trouble unzipping them. If you did, try another utility to unzip the files, and install the action again.

There are several places in the process where things may be going wrong, starting with the decompression. Please read through the following suggestions and take all of them into consideration before following the Last Resort. Read through the problems to see which describes your situation, and follow the suggestions there *in order*. Some of the following troubleshooting steps may seem redundant either with the installation instructions or with one another. Please humor me. These instructions were developed from years of troubleshooting experience to help you get out of installation troubles: they have to cover all the bases, and that sometimes means a little tedium. Your cooperation is appreciated.

Problem: Nothing new appears in the Effect menu after installation. If nothing appears and you have used the sample files as provided, there is a fundamental problem with the installation.

a. Reboot your machine, start Elements, open the Effects palette, and wait five minutes (to be sure the cache is rebuilt). If the actions folder you have created and installed still does not appear in the drop-down list, go to step b.

b. Be sure you are looking in the right place in Elements for the effects. The effects will be located on the Styles and Effects palette under a category named exactly like the folder in which you installed the action(s) and preview files. Open the palette by choosing Styles And Effects from the Window menu, and select Effects from the drop-down list on the upper left of the palette. Choose the category from the drop-down list immediately to the right of the list where Effects is selected. If you can locate the palette and there is still nothing listed, go to step c.

c. Be sure you are opening the correct version of Elements. Users who have multiple versions of the Elements program are sometimes prone to installing the actions into a folder that is not the one they are currently accessing with a shortcut. To be sure you are opening the right version of the program, close Elements. Locate the Effects folder where the actions folder is installed, and back out to the root of the Elements program folder. Locate the program file (.exe on PC, .app on Mac) in the program folder, and start up the program by double-clicking the program file. If this solution works, you need to delete and rebuild your shortcut for the program. If you have checked and the program you are opening is correct, go to step d.

d. Because the following step is a little more drastic, delete the Effects Cache folder again and restart Elements, even if you have done so previously. After Elements restarts, check the Previews folder to be sure the cache was rebuilt. If this does not solve the problem, go to step e.

e. Rebuild the Settings file, which may have become corrupt. To rebuild the Settings file, hold down the Ctrl+Alt+Shift keys on the keyboard when starting up Elements immediately after choosing Edit And Enhance Photos on the Welcome screen. Hold down the keys until the prompt to delete the Adobe Photoshop Elements settings file appears, and click [YES]. The deleted file will be re-created automatically. This will restore the default palette placement and tool settings and will delete your color settings. You will have to reset your preferences. If you still can't see the new categories in Effects, go to step f.

f. Close Elements. Rename the Effects folder in the Previews folder to **xEffects**. Create a new folder in the Previews folder and name it **Effects**. Copy the Hello World folder into the new Effects folder. Delete the Effects cache and restart Elements. If you see the Hello World folder in Effects after the restart, one of the effects you installed previously is corrupted. Add the Effects folders back into the new Effects folder from the xEffects folder one at a time, deleting the cache and restarting Elements after *each* effect is added. This will help you determine which folder is corrupt. If you are able to add back all the effects, delete the xEffects folder. If you do not have any change in the Effects palette after renaming the folder, go to step g.

g. Reinstall Elements. Proper reinstallation will require first uninstalling and then reinstalling the program. If you still can't get this to work, go to The Second to Last Resort.

Problem: The category appears in the Effect menu after installation, but no effects/actions appear. The Preview image files are not being recognized by Elements because of placement, configuration, or damage.

a. Be sure the action/effect is not nested in the installation folder. Folders for Effects should be inside the Effects folder with no other folders nested inside (for example, don't have the Hello World.atn file in a folder called Hello World inside the Hello World folder in Effects. Using the sample, there should be a Hello World folder directly inside the Effects folder, and the .atn and .psd files should be in that, not another buffering folder.

Correct:
```
Previews: Effects: Hello World: Hello World.psd
Previews: Effects: Hello World: Hello World.atn
```

Incorrect:
```
Previews: Effects: Hello World+: Hello World: Hello World.psd
Previews: Effects: Hello World+: Hello World: Hello World.atn
```

If there is a nested folder, move the actions and preview files out of the inner folder and delete the empty folder. After moving the files, delete the cache and restart Elements. If this does not fix the problem, go to step b.

b. The preview file was inadvertently flattened, or a Background layer still exists in the image. If the image was flattened, the references to the action files will be wiped out because Elements depends on the layer name to locate the action to run. If the Background layer exists in the image, Elements chokes on it and stops loading (likely a bug, which remains unfixed as of this writing). Rebuild the Preview file, and *be sure no other* .psd *file in the* Effects *folders has a Background layer*. If this does not fix the trouble, go to step c.

c. Open Elements, and then open the preview file (.psd) for the action you are trying to install. This should be located in the folder with the action. Make no changes to the file, but save it using Save As (File → Save As). Save over the existing file. This may correct certain errors that may have occurred in unzipping the file. Delete the cache and restart Elements. If this does not fix the trouble, go to step d.

d. Use a freshly downloaded action file and another decompression tool to decompress the files. Some decompression tools do not adequately decompress the files, and this can lead to the files not being recognized or to files being damaged. This is why the tools noted on the www.hiddenelements.com website have been recommended: they work. If even these tools are not working, there may have been a problem in downloading the file itself (for example, you are using a dial-up connection that is finicky, or the download pauses frequently). If there seemed to be significant hesitation copying or downloading the file, downloading the file again is recommended. If this does not fix the problem, go to The Second to Last Resort.

Problem: The category and thumbnail preview appears in the Effect menu after installation, but an error displays saying the request could not be completed. Action files are not being recognized by Elements because of placement, naming, configuration, or damage.

a. Be sure the action file is located in the same folder as its preview file. Using the sample, there should be a Hello World folder directly inside the Effects folder, and the .atn and .psd files should both be in that Hello World category folder. If you have to move the action into the folder with the preview file, you should be able to run the action without restarting Elements by double-clicking the preview/thumbnail in the Effects palette.

Correct:
```
Previews: Effects: Hello World: Hello World.psd
Previews: Effects: Hello World: Hello World.atn
```

Incorrect:
```
Previews: Effects: Hello World: Hello World.psd
Previews: Effects: Actions: Hello World.atn
```

b. Be sure the layer name in the preview file is an exact match to the name of the action you intend to run. Watch out for additional spaces in the name. When making such changes, change the name of the action file to match the layer name (open the preview file and copy and paste the name directly from the layer name to the file), rather than the other way around. By renaming the action file instead of the layer, you will not have to restart Elements and delete the cache to test.

c. Use another decompression tool and a freshly downloaded action file. Some decompression tools do not adequately decompress the files, and this can lead to the files not being recognized or to files being damaged. This is why the tools noted above have been recommended: they work. If even these tools are not working, there may have been a problem in downloading the file itself. Downloading the file again is recommended. If this does not fix the problem, go to The Second to Last Resort.

The Second to Last Resort If you have given the old college try to get things working, and you just can't seem to, the next-best place to look for a solution is on the Hidden Elements forums. A part of the forum is dedicated specifically to Hidden Power tools and using actions in Elements. Feel free to browse previous questions or ask brand-new ones. Find the forums using the link below. Ask the question in the forum under the version of Elements that you are using.

You can find the direct link to the forum by visiting the Hidden Power website: `www.hiddenelements.com/forums`.

The Last Resort While it is highly unlikely that you will get this far without a solution, it isn't a lost cause yet. Contact the author directly by sending an e-mail to `thebookdoc@aol`
`.com`. He will run you through these steps again, and the installation will work. You will be slightly embarrassed, and he will sound cross (his brief notes can be mistaken as such), but he is not. Please use Subject: Installation Trouble PE4 Actions. Include information about what you are trying to install, where you found it, and any information you have concerning errors (include exact wordings of those errors), along with a description of what is happening during the install.

Actions That Will Not Work in Elements

While it is likely that any effect that you are looking to achieve can be done in Elements if you can do it in Photoshop, not every action recorded for Photoshop will work in Elements as is. This may sound like a bit of a contradiction. The real problem is that you may have to tailor actions to the abilities of Elements rather than assuming Elements will do everything exactly as Photoshop will. This can be somewhat of a challenge, but it isn't an insurmountable one.

Finding Out if an Action Works

The quickest way to find out if an action works in Elements is just to install it and test it out. A good way to install is to use a Test category (a separate category folder named Test) to temporarily install actions without constantly restarting and going through creating the preview file without knowing if the action will work as is. To do the test, you can borrow an existing effect name in a predefined preview file.

Along with the Hello World effect supplied on the CD, there is also a predefined Test folder you can install that can be used to test actions. All you need to do is install the Test folder following the installation steps above used for the Hello World tool and restart Elements. It will allow you to run up to a dozen actions for test purposes. It comes with a preview file that has 12 predefined action names (see the list).

Possible Action Names

Test 1

Test 2

Test 3

Test 4

Test 5

Test 6

Test 7

Test 8

Test 9

Test 10

Test 11

Test 12

To test an action after the Test category is installed, simply copy a version of the action you want to test into the folder, and rename the action according to one of the available names. You may want to track the names of the actions you are installing and the test slots they are in to be sure you don't get confused as to what works and what doesn't. I use Notepad to do the tracking and just type the original name of the action and the test number (for example, fix_everything.atn: test 12).

You will not have to restart Elements or delete the cache folder to test actions this way after the initial installation because Elements will know which test filenames to look for per the original preview image. Even if you do not restart Elements, Elements will execute the new action when you double-click the associated thumbnail in the Effects palette. If the action runs satisfactorily, you can then create a proper preview file and install the tested action to another folder or category with a more useful and descriptive name.

Testing this way will allow you to try out many actions without restarting Elements. It is the same method I use for testing tools that I create for Hidden Power.

When Actions Fail

When an action fails in Elements, it will usually be because of a few specific things:

- The action references another action (unsupported in Elements Effects).
- The action attempts to use a function or mode that is not available in Elements.
- The action references functions incorrectly.

In order to fix these problems, you will have to edit the action. This means either acquiring a demo version of Photoshop 6 or higher (which will allow action editing and saving yet does not expire like other demos) or locating a version of Photoshop (at a school or library, for example) where you can edit actions and return them to your system to run in Elements. A third choice might be to present an action to another Photoshop user for editing (such as the author). Once you've made changes to an action so it will make use of Elements features, it will be able to create the same effect, even if it happens to do it in another way.

A key concept of successfully editing an action to work in Elements is not to throw up your hands and declare that an action doesn't work if it does not produce the expected results the first time you play it. When a step does not work in Elements, you can almost always find a good solution and workaround to produce the same (or very similar) results by editing the action and using a different approach. That is really the entire basis of how the Hidden Power tool set was created. Coming to the solution will require taking note of the errors that appear and noting the steps in the process where questionable events occur. The latter is best to do by slowing the action playback in Elements (you can do this with the Hidden Power Power_Playback tools) or by playing back the action slowly in Photoshop. In Elements, you will want to keep the Undo History in view as you play back the action; in Photoshop, you will want to view the Actions and History palettes—so long as there is room on the screen.

For example, actions that switch to LAB mode often do so to effect a color or tonal change. Instead of worrying that the LAB mode is not available in Elements, you might replicate the result by applying a change using layer properties (in this case Luminosity or Color layer modes). While it took 150 steps to replicate, I did create a tool that mimics the functionality of the Healing Brush tool for Elements 1 and 2 users, which I called the Mend tool (available on the hiddenelements.com website). This is a very good tool to study if you are looking to make other custom tools and workarounds for Elements. It explores several different workarounds that may be valuable in developing other effects.

If all else fails and you need some help, you are welcome to try The Second to Last Resort and The Last Resort described above in the "Troubleshooting" section. It is possible I may have interest in helping to develop specific tools, so long as there is time and the possibility that a broader group of users may find the actions useful (or fun).

When you have successfully adjusted actions or created actions to work with Elements, I hope you will contact me about possibly distributing them from the Hidden Power website either for free or for a fee (which you will share). Contact me directly with any prospects you might have (thebookdoc@aol.com).

The Toolbox

Table A.1 describes the toolbox tools and shortcuts for selecting them. Figure A.4 maps the tools as they appear on-screen. If you learn to use the shortcuts (from the map or the table), you don't have to waste time hunting for tools on the toolbar, and you can actually hide the toolbar to give yourself some more workspace.

To remove the toolbox from your display, choose Windows → Tools to uncheck the option for display. To cycle through tools that have the same shortcut, press Shift and the shortcut letter.

Figure A.4

An exploded view of the toolbar

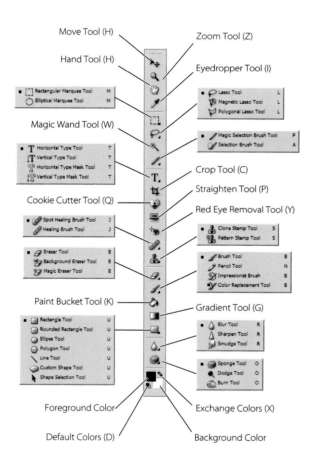

TOOL NAME	SHORTCUT	DESCRIPTION
Move	V	Moves active (and linked) image areas.
Zoom	Z	Increases (zooms in) and decreases (zooms out) the magnification of image display on-screen.
Hand	H	Enables the user to grab the canvas and scroll to navigate a magnified image when the entire image cannot be viewed at one time.
Eyedropper	I	Samples color from the image based on a single pixel or pixel area (according to selected options). Places the color in the foreground or background (when the Shift key is pressed). Often used with the Info palette.
Rectangular Marquee	M	Makes a rectangular or square selection.
Elliptical Marquee	M	Makes a circular or oval selection.
Lasso	L	Makes a freeform selection formed by dragging the cursor with the mouse.
Polygonal Lasso	L	Makes a polygon-shaped selection formed by clicking the mouse to mark the endpoints of the polygon sides.
Magnetic Lasso	L	Makes a freeform selection formed by the selection lasso snapping to the edges of contrasting tones or colors.
Magic Wand	W	Selects similar colors or tones based on a specified sample area and tolerance range.
Magic Selection Brush	F	Paints a freeform masked area based on brush size and dynamics. The unpainted area is converted to a selection when the user selects another tool.
Horizontal Type	T	Places entered text horizontally using the font selection, point size, and other dynamics selected on the Options bar.
Vertical Type	T	Places entered text vertically using the font selection, point size, and other dynamics selected on the Options bar.
Horizontal Type Mask	T	Creates a selection based on horizontally entered text, font, point size, and other dynamics selected on the Options bar.
Vertical Type Mask	T	Creates a selection based on vertically entered text, font, point size, and other dynamics selected on the Options bar.
Crop	C	Resizes canvas (can result in a larger or smaller image than current canvas). Rotation is also possible.
Cookie Cutter	Q	Crops a photo into the selected shape based on shape options (proportions, fixed size), feathering, and option to crop the image.
Straighten	P	Allows the user to create a horizontal (or horizon) line to reorient the image. Can be applied to all layers or just one. Has options for expanding the canvas, retaining size, and auto-cropping to remove background.
Red Eye Removal	Y	Replaces the color of the brushed area with the replacement color defined on the Options bar, according to a sample area (the tool samples the initial click point).

Table A.1

Photoshop Elements Tools

Continues

Continued

TOOL NAME	SHORTCUT	DESCRIPTION
Healing Brush	J	Copies sampled pixels from one part of an image to another based on brush size and dynamics (like the Clone Stamp), and then attempts to fit the correction into the target area by making "smart" comparisons between the sample and target areas.
Spot Healing Brush	J	Clones like the Healing Brush but selects the clone source automatically. Best used for correcting minor damage such as dust.
Clone Stamp	S	Copies sampled pixels from one part of an image to another based on the brush size and dynamics specified on the Options bar.
Pattern Stamp	S	Paints with a selected pattern based on the brush size and dynamics specified on the Options bar.
Eraser	E	Changes the erased area to the background color (when used on the background) or to transparent (when used on a layer).
Background Eraser	E	Changes the erased area to transparent based on the settings specified on the Options bar. Changes the background to a layer if applied to the background (using color modes that support layers).
Magic Eraser	E	Changes the erased area to transparent based on sample point and tolerance. Changes the background to a layer if applied to the background (using color modes that support layers).
Brush	B	Paints with the selected brush using the foreground color and brush dynamics (click More Options on the Options bar for dynamics).
Pencil	N	Creates a hard-edged freehand line based on the selected brush.
Impressionist Brush	B	Paints with the selected stylized brush using sampled color and brush dynamics (click More Options on the Options bar).
Color Replacement	B	Paints with the selected stylized brush using sampled color and brush dynamics (click More Options on the Options bar). Limited to Hue, Color, Saturation, or Luminosity.
Paint Bucket	K	Based on the tolerance and selections specified on the Options bar, fills an area with the foreground color or a pattern. Colors the image matte if used over the matte area while the Shift key is pressed.
Gradient	G	Fills an area with a blend of one or more colors based on the gradient, applied direction, and gradient type (Linear, Radial, Angle, Reflect, or Diamond), selected on the Options bar.
Rectangle	U	Creates a vector rectangle shape. Creates a new shape layer if a non-shape layer is currently active.

Continues

Continued

TOOL NAME	SHORTCUT	DESCRIPTION
Rounded Rectangle	U	Creates a vector rectangle shape with rounded corners. Creates a new shape layer if a non-shape layer is currently active.
Ellipse	U	Creates a vector ellipse (circle or oval) shape. Creates a new shape layer if a non-shape layer is currently active.
Polygon	U	Creates a vector polygon shape with an even number of sides, based on the number of sides specified on the Options bar. Creates a new shape layer if a non-shape layer is currently active.
Line	U	Creates a vector line with a width in pixels specified by the Weight field on the Options bar. Creates a new shape layer if a non-shape layer is currently active.
Custom Shape	U	Creates a custom vector shape by using the custom shape selected on the Options bar. Creates a new shape layer if a non-shape layer is currently active.
Shape Selection	U	Activates or moves shape layer components.
Blur	R	Softens hard edges or areas in an image to reduce detail, based on the brush size and dynamics selected on the Options bar.
Sharpen	R	Applies a sharpening calculation to the area where you drag the cursor based on the brush size and dynamics specified on the Options bar.
Smudge	R	Either smudges the existing colors in your image or smears new color through your image based on the direction you drag the cursor, the brush size, and the dynamics specified on the Options bar.
Sponge	O	Changes the color saturation or vividness of an area defined by the brush selected on the Options bar. In Grayscale mode, the Sponge tool increases or decreases contrast by moving gray levels away from or toward neutral gray.
Dodge	O	Lightens areas where you drag the cursor based on the range (Highlight, Midtones, or Shadows), brush size, and dynamics specified on the Options bar.
Burn	O	Darkens areas where you drag the cursor based on the range (Highlight, Midtones, or Shadows), brush size, and dynamics specified on the Options bar.
Switch Foreground and Background Colors	X	Exchanges the colors in the Foreground Color and Background Color boxes.
Set Foreground Color		Opens the Color Picker dialog box to allow the specification of a color to fill the Foreground Color box.
Set Background Color		Opens the Color Picker dialog box to allow the specification of a color to fill the Background Color box.
Default Foreground and Background Colors	D	Restores the Foreground Color and Background Color boxes to their default colors.

Resolution

If the initial discussion of resolution in the first chapter of the book was not enough, there is more here. Several resolution factors that occur outside of images themselves can affect your results in Photoshop Elements. These factors include input device resolution, monitor resolution, and output device resolution. Understanding resolution of peripherals is imperative to getting the best results from your digital images. That's what we look at here.

Input Resolution

Input resolution is the resolution of images coming off of the device you are using for capture. Most commonly this will be a scanner (whether you scan your own images or have them scanned for you) or a digital camera.

Scanners and Resolution

Scanner resolution is measured in dpi (dots per inch), based on the number of scanned samples that occur during scanning and how that is converted to image information. Scanners are most often rated in optical and/or interpolated resolution—the latter sometimes disguised by other terms. You should pay attention to optical resolution only. Interpolated resolutions lead to the scanner creating interpolated (assumed) information, so the results will usually not be much better than using interpolation to resize images in Elements.

All scanner types are not alike, and for best results you should use them for the purpose that they were made. You will generally not want to use a flatbed for scanning negatives— even if it has a transparency adapter or other means of scanning slides. Flatbeds start at an optical resolution of about 600×600 and can go much higher. They are generally best for making reflective scans, such as those you might make from prints. Negative scanners will start with at least 1800×1800 and are better suited to making accurate high-resolution scans from your negatives and slides. Conversely, you would not use them for reflective scanning. They are, however, usually fairly expensive. Services, such as Kodak Photo CD scanning (this is different from Kodak CD, which is a lower-end product), can provide multiresolution scans of your images inexpensively.

So long as you have the option when scanning, you should make a scan that fits your targeted need. In other words, know the purpose of your scans before you make them, and don't just blindly scan to the maximum capability of the scanner. Scan to exactly the size you need to cut down on the need for interpolation, unless you have a good reason to do otherwise. The size you need can be determined by the print resolution and the target range for image output that we looked at in Chapter 1, in the section "What Image Resolution to Use." Making your scans to the target size will require selecting options for resolution, and perhaps other settings such as scaling, in your scanner software before making the scan. These settings vary from scanner to scanner, so be sure to familiarize yourself with the settings by reading the manual and exploring the scanner's software.

Digital Cameras and Resolution

Digital camera resolution is weighted in pixel dimension, total pixels (megapixels), or both. While that is useful as a comparison between cameras, it doesn't tell you how big the resulting images will be or how the resolution is arrived at. Different types of cameras may have different types of sensors (CCD, CMOS) or sensor configuration (tri-sensor, X3, Super CCD), and the camera itself may calculate results differently.

> In extreme cases, I have seen cheap cameras advertised with high pixel counts. While there may be some other science at work that major camera manufacturers have not heard of (unlikely), these offers may be clever advertising ploys where cheap cameras are manufactured with small sensors and the stored images are digitally resized larger during processing inside the camera—without regard to quality. Be wary of an inexpensive, no-name camera wielding a high pixel count.

Table A.2 offers a brief overview using common camera technology and maximum output size (in inches).

When using your digital camera, pay attention to the resolution rather than the number of images you can get onto your memory card. Some people make the mistake of sacrificing image resolution to get more pictures on their card. It's better to buy more cards and keep the resolution and detail in your images. Unlike using a scanner, your capture of a scene with a digital camera may be your only opportunity to make the capture; unless there is a specific reason to use a lower resolution, leave the camera set to the maximum pixel dimension or highest resolution. Consider shooting in RAW if there is a RAW option to gain more bit depth and processing flexibility.

CAMERA RESOLUTION	TOTAL PIXELS	MAX. FINAL SIZE FOR WEB/ MONITOR (96 DPI)	MAX. FINAL SIZE FOR PHOTO-QUALITY (200 DPI)	MAX. NEGATIVE/ CHROME OUTPUT (650 DPI)
640 × 480	307,200	6.7 × 5	3.2 × 2.4	1 × 0.75
1024 × 768	786,432	10.7 × 8	5 × 3.75	1.5 × 1.1
1280 × 960	1,228,800	13.3 × 10	6 × 4.75	1.8 × 1.5
1600 × 1200	1,920,000	16.7 × 12.5	8 × 6	2.5 × 1.8
2048 × 1536	3,145,728	21.3 × 16	10 × 7.5	3.1 × 2.3
2400 × 1800	4,320,000	25 × 18.75	12 × 9	3.7 × 2.8
2500 × 2000	5,000,000	26 × 20.8	12.5 × 10	3.9 × 3.1
3072 × 2048	6,291,456	32 × 21.3	15.4 × 10.3	4.7 × 3.1
4536 × 3024	13,716,864	47.3 × 31.5	22.7 × 15.1	7 × 4.7

Table A.2

Common Camera Resolutions

The chart for camera resolutions does not tell the whole story. While the charting here suggests maximum sizes, there is some potential difference in camera technologies that will weigh into quality. For example, multiple-sensor configurations (Kodak Pro camera models) and X3 technology (Sigma SD9 and SD10) may yield sharper images from smaller pixel counts because they capture RGB components at every pixel, rather than using standard mosaic captures and interpolation (if you would like to discuss this further, let's do it on the Hidden Power forums: `www.hiddenelements.com/forums`).

Monitor Resolution and Settings

Monitor resolution affects how images appear on-screen. I have seen people think nothing of setting monitor resolution to the highest setting suggested by the manufacturer and assume that it is correct, preferred—or that it doesn't matter. If you set your monitor resolution too high (greater than the monitor was built to handle), you can lose detail rather than improve it, and images can appear too small (they will print larger than you see them on-screen). If you set the resolution too low, objects on screen will appear larger than they should, and you won't take advantage of the viewing landscape on your monitor.

The maximum monitor resolution setting is dictated by the monitor's viewing size and dot pitch. *Viewing size* is simply the monitor area; *dot pitch* is, essentially, the resolution—the number of image dots that can be represented. The greater the viewing size or the lower the dot pitch, the more information the monitor can show. A larger monitor will tend to have a higher dot pitch than a smaller one. Monitors with lower dot pitch will tend to look sharper.

There are more complicated means of selecting a monitor display resolution, but choosing the "right" resolution means choosing the resolution that makes the image appear correctly sized on-screen. This choice also pretty much eliminates the possibility that your monitor won't have the capacity and resolution to properly render your images. Any monitor with a dot pitch of less than .28 (about .22 horizontally) should be able to handle the range that I suggest while offering a sharp image. This does not mean that having a higher-resolution monitor is a waste; finer dot pitch almost always translates into finer image display (I prefer .25 dot pitch or lower). Using a higher resolution can also have the advantage of making palettes and menus smaller, leaving more space on the screen for you to work. However, you will want to make that decision rather than make an assumption.

Table A.3 is a guideline to help you create an accurately sized image on-screen and will give you a target to shoot for. It may not be exact, because there are variables in displays, but it should take you closer than just guessing at a size or choosing the maximum suggested resolution willy-nilly (or based on what you think might look good when you have the monitor control panel open). The point is that when you choose View → Print Size, your image will be close to displaying on-screen at the size you intend to use it.

Monitor screen size is measured from corner to corner diagonally rather than as height or width. If you are unsure of your monitor size, a quick measure of the diagonal surface area of the screen from corner to corner will tell you approximately what the view size is for your monitor (it is often slightly smaller than that). Choose an available display resolution in the monitor control panel that falls within the range shown in the table (between 72 and 96 ppi) to get the most accurate sizing.

If you prefer to have a very accurate view of print size on-screen, you can choose your resolution roughly and make adjustments in the horizontal and vertical projection of the monitor to make the display dimensions nearly exact. To do this, you can match a display ruler (show rulers on an open image displaying at 100 percent) to a household one by using horizontal and vertical screen controls. Be sure to resize in both directions for the most accurate display.

DIAGONAL VIEW SIZE	72 PPI RESOLUTION	96 PPI RESOLUTION
23″	1600 × 1200	1920 × 1200
21″	1280 × 1024	1600 × 1200
19″	1152 × 870	1280 × 1024
17″	1024 × 768	1152 × 870
15″	870 × 640	1024 × 768
13″	800 × 600	870 × 640

Table A.3

Common Monitor Sizes and Resolutions

Number of Colors

You may be able to change your color settings to anything between monochrome and 32-bit color in your control panel, and as with resolution, it might be tempting to always pick the maximum. These settings may be presented as bits or number of colors (depending on the operating system and the utility or control panel you are using for the setting). The more bits or colors, the more true-to-life color can be; at the same time, the more taxing the color processing can be, so this may result in fewer options for refresh rates (see the following section for more information on refresh rates). Optimally, you will want to choose to display the most bits you can, but if you have a less-powerful video card and a large monitor, or if your refresh rate options are limited, it may be best to choose fewer bits or colors as a trade-off. Your images generally store 24-bit information (3 × 8 bits) in Photoshop Elements, so displaying at 32-bit is not necessarily better for viewing image color.

Refresh Rate

Refresh rate is the frequency at which an image on the screen is updated or refreshed. The rate is measured in Hertz (Hz). The higher the frequency (the more Hz), the faster the screen refreshes. The faster it refreshes, the less likely you are to detect flicker, and the more likely that your view of changes and movement on the screen (such as the cursor) will seem smooth. Quick refresh rates can also reduce eyestrain. This can be important if, like some of us who edit images, you spend a lot of time staring at your monitor.

Use only suggested refresh rates for your monitor and video card or you can run the risk of damaging your equipment. Refresh rates should be as fast as you can make them within the manufacturer's suggested range without cutting into other display properties that reduce performance in other ways (see the previous section, "Number of Colors").

Output Resolution

Table A.4 shows some real-world examples of output resolution and workable ppi ranges. Calculations for the table were based on the formulas shown in the Calculation Used column; square brackets in the calculations indicate the range of values used to determine the lowest and highest resolution acceptable in that media. This table can be handy for choosing a rough estimate of file size, and you can use the equations for calculating more specific results. The table also assumes you will be printing the image at 100 percent of the image size; resizing the image in layout or another program will affect the calculations. Check with your printing service for their recommendations before blindly assigning these estimates. Say you have a pixel-based image at 5 × 7 inches and it has 300 ppi. That will print well to a variety of outputs at the original size (although there may be too little or too much resolution for some options). If you want to resize the image or apply it at a different size by changing the dimension, the ppi, or both, there are many possible results. Table A.5 looks at these possibilities (all based on an original image that is 5 × 7 at 300 ppi).

Table A.4

Approximate Resolutions for Various Media

DESIRED CHANGE	INTERPOLATION METHOD	APPLIED IMAGE SIZE (INCHES)	EFFECTIVE IMAGE PPI	RESULT	COMMENT
Increase file dimension with same ppi	Bicubic	8 × 10	300	Increasing the number of pixels causes image information to be added or faked.	The result will probably not be much better than applying the original image without interpolation. It will likely be a bit soft. Image content may affect the results. Bicubic interpolation works best with blended tones (photographs).
Increase file dimension with same ppi	Nearest Neighbor	8 × 10	300	Increasing the number of pixels causes image information to be added or faked.	The result will be almost exactly like applying the original image without interpolation. It will likely be a bit soft, and may be blockier than Bicubic interpolated results. Image content may affect the results. Nearest Neighbor interpolation works best with solid color and lines (screenshots).

Continued

DESIRED CHANGE	INTERPOLATION METHOD	APPLIED IMAGE SIZE (INCHES)	EFFECTIVE IMAGE PPI	RESULT	COMMENT
Increase file dimension with lower ppi	Bicubic	8 × 10	72	Disproportional changes in ppi and dimension (in this case, decreasing the ppi dramatically while increasing the dimension) cause image information to be changed (in this case, lost).	Even though the size of the file increases in this case, the result is less information in the file because of the lower ppi. While this 8 × 10 may display fine on-screen and on the Web, the result in print will most likely be soft and undesirable.
Increase file dimension without interpolation	None	8 × 10	210	Proportional changes in ppi and dimension result in the same image information being distributed over a new area. There is no change in file information (or file size).	This will provide a very similar result to applying the image at increased ppi. The resolution could probably be better targeted to the desired output.
Increase (double) the ppi	Bicubic	5 × 7	600	Increasing the number of pixels causes image information to be added or faked.	This file will have too much resolution for just about any type of output. It can slow processing and increase file sizes unnecessarily, without improving output quality.
No change	None	5 × 7	300	Applied at file dimensions.	This is the targeted application of this pixel-based image.
Decrease ppi	Bicubic	5 × 7	72	Decreasing ppi and keeping the dimensions the same removes information from the image.	While this can be fine for the Web, this file will have too little resolution for most types of printed output. It may look fine on-screen, but that shouldn't be the determining factor.
Decrease file dimension without interpolation	None	3.5 × 5	429	Proportional changes in ppi and dimension result in the same image information being distributed over a new area. There is no change in file information (or file size).	By decreasing the file dimension without interpolating, this file will have too much resolution for just about any type of output. It can slow processing and increase file sizes unnecessarily.
Decrease file dimension with lower ppi	Bicubic	3.5 × 5	72	Decreasing file dimension and ppi at the same time removes information from the image.	This image takes a double whammy in decreasing both dimension and ppi. While it will be suited to screen display (and may not look too different on-screen than the display of the two options that follow), results in print will probably not be satisfactory.

Continues

Continued

DESIRED CHANGE	INTERPOLATION METHOD	APPLIED IMAGE SIZE (INCHES)	EFFECTIVE IMAGE PPI	RESULT	COMMENT
Decrease file dimension with higher ppi	Nearest Neighbor	3.5 × 5	300	Disproportional changes in ppi and dimension (in this case, decreasing the dimension while retaining ppi) cause image information to be changed (in this case, discarded or lost).	Resizing an image smaller is usually less damaging to the result than attempting to add information to the image. While making images smaller shrinks the pixel base and merges and loses information, it tends to matter less than increasing image size. Nearest Neighbor interpolation, unless used with great care, is not usually your best choice in decreasing image size. Results will probably be better in most cases with Bicubic (or perhaps Bilinear) interpolation.
Decrease file dimension with higher ppi	Bicubic	3.5 × 5	300	Disproportional changes in ppi and dimension (in this case, decreasing the dimension while retaining ppi) cause image information to be changed (in this case, lost).	Generally it is fine to repurpose an image by decreasing its size. Because the result will merge and blur somewhat, sharpening is recommended. Using Bicubic resizing actually invests a little sharpening for you, so that additional sharpening may not be necessary. If possible, work with images at the intended size for best results.

File Types

When saving an image, you have to select a file type. To choose the right one, it is handy to know what the available file types are and generally what they are used for. Table A.6 gives a brief overview of file types supported when saving from Photoshop Elements. Other file types are supported as "open only," meaning that you can open the files, but you will have to save them as something else.

Compression

Compression is a means of making saved files smaller. It occurs when saving files as part of the file type, or it can be applied after saving by using a file compression utility.

Some file compression encoding is known as *lossy* in that it loses original image information during processing. In some instances, it's okay to sacrifice some image quality for file size. For example, JPEG is a lossy format used on the Web to speed image transfer.

FILE TYPE	SAVE AS COLOR MODES	PURPOSE/USE
Photoshop document (PSD)	All	Native Photoshop Elements format. Store working/in-progress Photoshop images.
Bitmap (BMP)	All	Traditionally a Windows-based file format. PC screenshot format. Lossless compression.
CompuServe Graphics Interchange Format (GIF)	All	Web graphics. Uses an indexed-color palette (256 colors max) to achieve compression—colors are converted during save if not already indexed. Conversion to GIF from images with more than 256 colors will cause image information loss.
Encapsulated PostScript (EPS)	All	Mostly used in PostScript printing to retain vector, pixel, and separation information. Does not support alphas. Can use JPEG compression.
Joint Photographic Experts Group (JPEG)	Grayscale, RGB	Often used for full-color web graphics, and digital camera image storage. Uses variable, lossy compression in storage, which can damage images over repeated saves. Better color retention than GIF.
PC Exchange (PCX)	All	Another bitmap format like PCT and BMP. Uses lossless compression.
Portable Document Format (PDF)	All	Designed by Adobe Systems to allow viewing of PostScript-encoded documents (using Acrobat products such as Reader). Uses compression including lossless ZIP encoding and lossy JPEG. Compression can be controlled separately for color, grayscale, and monochrome (bitmap) images. Highly portable between platforms and used broadly in print applications.
Photoshop 2.0	All	Native Photoshop format with backward compatibility to earlier versions.
PICT file (PCT)	All	The Mac equivalent of Windows BMP.
PICT resource (RSR)	All	Files used in resource forks (such as icon graphics).
Pixar Computer Image (PXR)	Grayscale, RGB	Specially designed for Pixar Image workstations, for editing rendered graphics to return to a Pixar format.
Portable Network Graphics (PNG)	All	Developed as a royalty-free replacement for GIF. Supports transparency and animation (but not via Elements). Supports both lossless and lossy compression (but not via Elements).

Continues

Continued

FILE TYPE	SAVE AS COLOR MODES	PURPOSE/USE
Photoshop RAW (RAW)	Grayscale, Indexed Color, RGB	Undefined or raw image data. No compression. Can be used for custom deciphering or encoding of file formats that are otherwise unsupported by Photoshop. Similar to but not the same as Camera RAW.
Scitex Continuous Tone (SCT)	Grayscale, RGB	Developed by Scitex for proprietary image-processing systems. Used with high-end scanning devices. No compression.
Targa (TGA)	Grayscale, Indexed Color, RGB	Most common in the video industry; also used by high-end paint and ray-tracing programs because of expanded bit depth. For specific application in video output. No compression via Elements.
Tagged Image File Format (TIFF)	All	A broadly used, general-purpose file type for printed output. Supports most native Photoshop Elements file features. Supports lossless compression.
Wireless BMP	BMP	For application on wireless networks.

Some of the image information is compromised during the save process to make the files smaller and allow them to be transferred more quickly over the Web. However, in most cases you should stick to lossless compression to retain the quality of your images, especially if high quality is a concern. Beware of lossy compression that gets reapplied each time you save. JPEG compression, for example, is reapplied each time you open and then save the file, so image quality will steadily degrade over time if you use JPEG format as an archival format and repeatedly open and save an image.

> JPEG is a compression type as well as a file format; JPEG compression can be used with other file types. For example, a DCS file can have component parts stored with JPEG compression.

Compression that is applied as part of the file format (JPEG, LZW, GIF, and so on) is different from file compression. Some compression schemes rely on color reduction, decimation, pattern recognition, or other schemes to reduce file size by reorganizing or reinterpreting image file information. In other words, image-type compressions may act on image information directly to achieve compression. File compression is done with utilities (ZIP, SIT, SEA, MIME, and so on) after the file is saved. Utility compression is always lossless because it acts on the file information independently of it being an image.

Bit Depth

Bits and bit depth have been known to cause confusion, and understanding them may be important to freeing those ghosts from the closets in your mind. A big deal is made of 16-bit image editing, or how many bits a scanner or camera can capture. If you don't have the foggiest idea what bits are, that can lead right to the bus stop of confusion. If you know, you can make intelligent decisions about how important specifications really are to your image editing.

Bits represent how exactly color can be measured. They are the little encoded 1s and 0s used in computer language to describe an image. Each pixel color in your image is described by bits. The more bits, the greater the potential accuracy of the color in each pixel.

Bits themselves are just tiny chunks of information—sometimes described by the term *binary*. All that term means is that each bit used in your files can have one of two values: either on (1) or off (0). If an image is 1-bit, each pixel in the image can be on or off: black or white. The more bits per pixel, the more complex the relationship gets, and the more color variations can be represented.

If your image is 2-bit, each bit has two potential values, and these values can be paired in any of these four combinations—00, 01, 10, or 11—to define the pixel. Each additional bit per pixel adds a multiple of two combinations, one additional set of combinations for each additional bit. Just to show how quickly this can add up, if a third bit were added to your 2-bit image, this would result in the following set of possibilities for each pixel: 000, 001, 010, 011, 100, 101, 110, 111—a total of eight possible combinations. So each time another bit is added, there are twice as many possible combinations—one additional full set of possibilities for each of the two possible values of the bit.

To determine the total number of bit combinations, all you have to do is multiply by two for each bit. Eight bits per channel would be $2 \times 2 \times 2 \times 2 \times 2 \times 2 \times 2 \times 2$ (or 2^8), totaling 256 combinations. However, this can get a little murky. Following that logic you would think that a 24-bit image would be 2^{24}, representing 16 million colors. That is correct. But when describing an RGB image, 24-bit images can be described as 8 bits per channel. That is, each of the three channels is allotted 8 bits. These three groups of 8 bits describe the 256 tonal possibilities for each channel: red, green, and blue. Each of the colors has 256 possibilities that can be combined in any fashion. Whether you multiply 2^{24} or $256 \times 256 \times 256$, you get the same number of bit combinations: 16,777,216. That is how many colors each pixel can represent in 24-bit color.

Bit terminology can be confusing because *bit depth* can be referred to as bits per channel or total bits. If used with care, this shouldn't pose a problem, but it can be confounding when you discover a 16-bit image actually has more image information than a 24-bit color scan. Be sure you are comparing either total bits per pixel or bits per channel when looking at specifications or comparing images. Comparing bits per channel to total bits is like comparing grayscale and color images—different representations of the same thing, but they are not equivalent.

If you add bits, you add potential colors: if you have an image with 30 bits, there would be 10 bits per channel, 1024 bit combinations per pixel per color, or 1,073,741,824 potential combinations. That is 64 times as many color combinations as 24-bit, with only a few more bits per pixel.

In other words, increased pixel depth exponentially increases the color possibilities, which is why increased color depth is considered potentially so valuable in color work. The negative effect of increased bit depth (for example, to 16 bits per channel from 8 bits) is dramatically increased image size and need for enhanced processing power. There is also some question as to the value of increased bit depth. In fact, it seems almost useless for anything but initial corrections for two reasons:

- If you have 16 million colors, it is not likely that having even more will have much effect on the way you see an image.

- Output in most cases can't reproduce more than 24-bit color.

Increased bit depth can improve the capture of detail in poorly exposed images and may be desirable for archiving (and future use). However, even 8-bit potential is more than most people actually need. (For more about 16-bit images, see the "16-Bit Images" sidebar in Chapter 2.)

Blending Modes

Blending modes are a means of calculating a result between source and target information in your image. Blending modes can be applied with brushes or layers. A blending mode controls how the content (a layer or brush) is applied, based on the image content. When a mode is used with a painting tool, Photoshop Elements uses the brush content as the source (foreground color) as if the color were being applied in a layer, using the selected brush dynamics. Brush applications change the content of the layer you are painting on to achieve the result; layer modes cause a visual (rather than actual) change based on calculated interaction with all image information below the layer.

Modes can create effects by using calculations based on select color components. For example, the result might be a calculation involving red, green, and blue components (tone and color together) or a calculation based on luminosity, color, or other components. Table A.7 describes the blending modes available in Elements. Keep in mind that layer opacity will influence these calculations.

> Adobe is pretty stingy with the exact calculations involved in blending modes. The descriptions in their "Help" sections are actually obfuscated by the language used to describe them. To simplify: the more obscure and difficult to calculate, the less useful the mode tends to be in normal use.

BLEND MODE	QUICK KEY	EFFECT
Normal	Shift+Option+N / Shift+Alt+N	Plain overlay of content. The result takes on the color/tone of the pixels in the upper layer (so long as the Opacity is 100%).
Dissolve	Shift+Option+I / Shift+Alt+I	The result takes on the color/tone of the pixels in the upper layer, but the result is dithered (randomized) according to the opacity of the application. The greater the opacity, the more the selection is weighted to the upper layer. 100% opacity will produce a 0% Dissolve effect; 50% opacity indicates 50% of the result has the applied color.
Darken	Shift+Option+K / Shift+Alt+K	Chooses the darker color value set for each pixel in comparing the two layers. Uses either the applied color or the original (not a combination). No portion of the image gets lighter.
Multiply	Shift+Option+M / Shift+Alt+M	Darkens the result by darkening the lower layer based on the darkness of the upper layer. Any tone darker than white in the Multiply layer darkens the appearance of content below. No portion of the image can get lighter.
Color Burn	Shift+Option+B / Shift+Alt+B	Burns in (darkens) the color of the underlying layer with the upper layer, darkening the result. No portion of the image gets lighter. The greater the difference between the applied pixel colors and the content below, the greater the percentage of change.
Linear Burn	Shift+Option+A / Shift+Alt+A	Similar to Multiply but more extreme. No portion of the image can get lighter.
Lighten	Shift+Option+G / Shift+Alt+G	Chooses the lighter color value set for each pixel in comparing the two layers. Uses either the applied color or the original. No portion of the image gets darker.
Screen	Shift+Option+S / Shift+Alt+S	Brightens the result by lightening the lower layer based on the lightness of the upper layer. Any color lighter than black lightens the result. No portion of the image can get darker.
Color Dodge	Shift+Option+D / Shift+Alt+D	Dodges (lightens) the color of the underlying layer with the upper layer, lightening the result. No portion of the image gets darker. The greater the difference between pixel colors, the greater the change.
Linear Dodge	Shift+Option+W / Shift+Alt+W	Similar to Screen but the result is more extreme. No portion of the image can get darker.
Overlay	Shift+Option+O / Shift+Alt+O	Multiplies (darkens) the light colors (51%–100% brightness) and screens (lightens) the dark ones (0%–49% brightness). Colors at the center of the light and dark range are affected more than those at the extremes.
Soft Light	Shift+Option+F / Shift+Alt+F	Multiplies (darkens) the dark colors (0%–49% brightness) and screens (lightens) the light ones (51%–100% brightness) depending on the applied color. If the applied color is light, the pixel lightens; if dark, it darkens. Soft, or 50% application of the upper layer.

Continues

Table A.7

Photoshop Elements Blending Modes

Continued

BLEND MODE	QUICK KEY	EFFECT
Hard Light	Shift+Option+H / Shift+Alt+H	Multiplies (darkens) the dark colors (0%–49% brightness) and screens (lightens) the light ones (51%–100% brightness). 100% application of the upper layer.
Vivid Light	Shift+Option+V / Shift+Alt+V	Similar to Color Burn when the applied color is darker than 50% gray; similar to Color Dodge when the applied color is lighter than 50% gray.
Linear Light	Shift+Option+J / Shift+Alt+J	Similar to Linear Burn when the applied color is darker than 50% gray; similar to Linear Dodge when the applied color is lighter than 50% gray.
Pin Light	Shift+Option+Z / Shift+Alt+Z	Similar to Multiply when the applied color is darker than 50% gray; similar to Screen when the applied color is lighter than 50% gray.
Difference	Shift+Option+E / Shift+Alt+E	Reacts to the difference between pixel values. A large difference yields a bright result; a small difference yields a dark result (no difference yields black).
Exclusion	Shift+Option+X / Shift+Alt+X	Uses the darkness of the original layer to mask the Difference effect (described previously). If the original value is dark, there is little change as the result; if the original color is black, there is no change. The lighter the original color, the more intense the potential Difference effect.
Hue	Shift+Option+U / Shift+Alt+U	Changes the Hue of the original to the applied while leaving the Saturation and Luminosity unchanged.
Saturation	Shift+Option+T / Shift+Alt+T	Changes the Saturation of the original to the applied while leaving the Hue and Luminosity unchanged.
Color	Shift+Option+C / Shift+Alt+C	Changes the Hue and Saturation of the original to the applied while leaving the Luminosity unchanged.
Luminosity	Shift+Option+Y / Shift+Alt+Y	Changes the Luminosity of the original to the applied while leaving the Saturation and Hue unchanged.

Camera RAW Files

Camera RAW files are an option for image capture in newer or more *pro-sumer*–level digital cameras. RAW is not an acronym; it simply stands for *raw*, as in raw image data. It is the content of the digital capture as grabbed by the camera's image sensor without processing and conversion in the camera (such as conversion to JPEG or 8-bit to save file space). It is an option that has gained popularity as camera storage media have increased capacity to allow storage of larger images and the ability to process these RAW captures externally from the camera has been supported by Adobe and camera manufacturers.

RAW files have been around for a long time. In fact, you could open and save to a type of RAW file (Photoshop RAW) in Photoshop Elements 1. When you open one of these RAW files, you get a dialog that allows you to put in parameters to decipher the image data (see Figure A.5). The RAW (or Photoshop Raw) file format was meant to provide the user a means of opening and saving nonstandard image files—possibly created before there were digital image standards or developed with nonstandard processing (for example, in scientific imaging). If you only had the file and did not know how to open it up and what parameters to use, you would have a very difficult time opening the image because you'd have to guess at what was stored in the file and how that translated into the Photoshop RAW parameters—if it did at all.

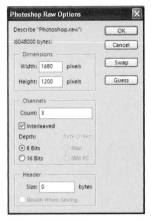

Figure A.5

The Photoshop RAW options allow the user to decipher image structure by choosing bit dimension, channel count and bit depth, and header length information.

RAW files that you get off your camera are really just another type of RAW file, though they are handled in a much different (and friendlier) way by Elements 4, using the Camera RAW plug-in. The RAW camera files are the raw data captured by your digital camera that have been assembled into proprietary image formats. When you try to open one, the plug-in recognizes the file type and steps in to handle the files acting as an intermediary in pre-processing.

You might think that Camera RAW files are the same as any image your camera spits out, but that isn't exactly true. Before you download images from your camera as more familiar JPEG or TIFF images, they start out as raw data; they are encoded, processed, and turned into one of the more familiar digital file formats so that they can be used with popular image editing programs. RAW files will be raw data, and all will be called RAW files, but all RAW files will not all be constructed the same way. If fact, the file types that come off different cameras as RAW have unique file extensions, depending on the manufacturer, so they can be identified. The Camera RAW plug-in in Elements has the ability to recognize many of these RAW file types, and it will automatically decipher the files and present them in the Camera RAW dialog, which you can then use to do some initial adjustment to the raw data from the image.

Adobe's new DNG (Digital Negative) file format is an attempt by Adobe to standardize (or create an open standard for) RAW camera images. Their hope is that this file type would be used widely as a standard by manufacturers to remove the possibility of increasing the already large number of proprietary RAW file types. Adobe offers a DNG converter for free that works with many file types. You can download it here: www.adobe.com/products/dng/.

The processing that occurs in the Camera RAW plug-in includes interpreting and merging captured information that would otherwise be handled by the camera. Since the camera doesn't have the ability to make artistic judgments per image, the advantage of shooting in Camera RAW is essentially that it allows you to control how the raw data gets combined. It is usually a finessing of image data rather than a manhandling.

Making adjustments in the dialog is an opportunity to get the most out of information captured by the camera, plain and simple. If your camera shoots in 12-bit and produces an 8-bit JPEG that is stored on your camera's media, many calculations happen along the way to compile the image from the RAW data and shrink the file size. This can be stated another way: the process of storing the file compromised the original capture data with a loss in potential for the ultimate image quality. This loss may not be huge, and in some shots you may not notice it at all (in comparing RAW and JPEG). The images where you will not see a big difference are those that are properly exposed. However, the latitude that you have in working on an image and coming up with what you need from the RAW data (and later in 16-bit) is worth the extra processing time for those who are serious about their images. If you already know about exposure, aperture, and composition and have some experience in digital image processing, you might shoot RAW images to give yourself more to work with in achieving the goals of your images in post-processing—and perhaps to give yourself better data to store as the source of your image captures in your archives for future use.

In other words, just as a user might appreciate the speed of automated processing when using auto-levels or auto-contrast, setting your camera to store JPEG images might be a godsend because the process is completed for you. However, if you don't shoot only statues outside on an overcast day at noon or so, then you may have more creative vision as to what makes an interesting image. If you shoot scenes with a lot of potential for manipulating shadow detail or highlights (low-key or high-key images), you would certainly like the advantage you have in manipulating the images from your RAW originals. If you shoot a rock concert, for example, the latitude you gain in manipulating the highlights, shadows, and light color would certainly favor storing RAW files. You would more likely be able to make drastic manipulations to the RAW, high-bit image without causing or enhancing damage that could be introduced by overworking the image in 8-bit or by enhancing the JPEG compression damage.

You can look at the RAW format as the ultimate archive version of an image, because there is no compression, artifact, or other adjustment made by the camera before delivering the image—all you have is the raw capture data. This can enable you to make adjustments and compensation to the capture, rather than the standard conversion enforced by on-camera processing.

Working with RAW Images from Your Camera

Even though you can open a RAW file in Photoshop Elements, getting the camera to store RAW files is another matter. Not all cameras will allow you to save files in RAW formats. To process the RAW data, your camera will have to offer a RAW save option, and you will have to change the camera settings to store the data in the camera's RAW format. See your owner's manual for these instructions.

To handle your camera's RAW images, you will most likely be able to use either proprietary software provided with the camera or Photoshop Elements 3 or higher. Elements 1 and 2 do not handle RAW files that come from your camera without the Camera Raw plug-in. The Camera Raw plug-in is standard in Elements 3, and it enables you to open many types of camera RAW files from the native data. The plug-in will open automatically when you attempt to open a recognized RAW image file (see Figure A.6).

When you open the image by using Elements, you will be presented with the dialog box and can make adjustments that you prefer by using the on-screen preview as a visual guide. Settings that you choose can be saved and used in actions and batch processes so that you can process your RAW images in bulk. More interesting, you can store and archive the camera's RAW files and at a later date process them differently if a different interface or process becomes available.

Figure A.6

When you open an image saved in a RAW file format, this dialog appears, allowing you the opportunity to convert the image data.

The Camera Raw dialog includes sliders that help you adjust color Temperature, Tint, Exposure, Shadows, Brightness, Contrast, Saturation, Sharpness, Luminance Smoothing, and Color Noise Reduction. Other settings that affect the output are bit depth selection (you can choose 8- or 16-bit) and rotation. Controls that affect only what you see on-screen include preview size (as a percentage of pixels viewed) and clipping previews (Highlight and Shadows). You can do all this while looking at a preview and a color histogram that provide clues as to the best mixture of these elements in the image. Some of the adjustments may be better deployed during correction stages, so don't feel obligated to use every slider, and don't attempt to make the image look perfect in the preview. In some cases you will not even want to make an adjustment at this stage.

Adjustments that you do make in the Camera RAW dialog will often be to retain the best image information possible. This means you will want to balance the histogram while getting a preview that looks good. Balancing the histogram in this case means expanding the dynamic range of the white area of the graph, while maintaining the balance of colors and keeping the individual color components from clipping (not shifting one of the three component colors too far into the highlights or shadows so that you lose captured detail). Each of the controls will help balance image qualities differently—but usually intuitively (see Table A.8).

Table A.8	CONTROL	USE/DESCRIPTION
Camera RAW Controls	Settings	Enables the user to select preset, custom, or previous settings used with the plug-in. Selected Image uses the settings from the previous conversion; Camera Default uses default settings that you created for the camera or from the image as shot (if no default is stored); Previous Conversion uses the last settings used to process images from this camera. To store a default, adjust the sliders as desired and choose Set Camera Default from the pop-up menu to the right of the Settings.
	White Balance	Adjusts Temperature and Tint based on selection from the drop-down list. Drop-down list selections include As Shot (from image data), Auto (automatically balanced), Daylight (normal daylight, 5500 degrees Kelvin), Cloudy (cool, overcast lighting 6500 degrees Kelvin), Shade (cool light full shade, 7500 degrees Kelvin), Tungsten (balanced light, 2850 degrees Kelvin), Florescent (greenish light, 3800 degrees Kelvin), Flash (balanced light, 5500 degrees Kelvin), Custom (manual slider settings). White Balance can be sampled from the image using the Eyedropper tool from the upper left of the palette; just click on what should be a gray area of the image.
	Temperature	Enables correction for the ambient color temperature (White Balance). The plug-in will counter the correction by warming or cooling the image color. Moving the slider to the right increases the ambient color temperature and warms as a result (compensates for images taken on an overcast day). Moving the slider to the left decreases the ambient color temperature and cools the image as a result (compensates for warm images such as those taken with unbalanced incandescent light).
	Tint	Allows the user to balance the magenta/green tint of the image and counterbalance the changes made by using the Temperature slider. Moving the slider to the right increases the influence of magenta; moving the slider to the left increases the influence of green.
	Exposure	Exposure simply lightens or darkens an image by increasing (right) or decreasing (left) exposure. Checking the Auto box will automatically select a balanced exposure based on other existing settings.

Continues

Continued

CONTROL	USE/DESCRIPTION
Shadows	Enhances the influence of shadows in the image. Moving the slider to the right darkens the image; moving it to the left lightens the image. Checking the Auto box will automatically select a shadow presence based on other existing settings.
Brightness	Enhances the influence of highlights in the image. Moving the slider to the right lightens the image; moving it to the left darkens the image. Checking the Auto box will automatically select a highlight intensity based on other existing settings.
Contrast	Enhances image contrast. Moving the slider to the right increases global image contrast; moving the slider left decreases image contrast. Checking the Auto box will automatically select a contrast based on other existing settings.
Saturation	Much like the Saturation slider on the Hue/Saturation dialog, this is used for adjusting color saturation in the image globally. Moving the slider to the right increases saturation; moving the slider to the left decreases saturation.
Sharpness	Enhances local contrast in the image much like the Unsharp Mask filter set to a short radius. Moving the slider to the right increases the local contrast, sharpening the image; moving the slider to the left decreases the intensity of the sharpening.
Luminance Smoothing	Helps to attenuate tonal noise somewhat like blurring. Moving the slider to the right increases the softening; moving the slider to the left reduces the intensity of the blur.
Color Noise Reduction	Mediates color noise. Moving the slider to the right increases mediation; moving the slider to the left decreases mediation.
Bit Depth	Enables the user to open the image at standard 8-bit depth or use the RAW file bit depth to render a 16-bit image. If you select 16-bit, RAW camera images with less than 16-bit (e.g., 12-bit) will be converted to 16-bit so no image information is lost. Select the desired result from the drop-down list.
Rotation	Rotates the image for the preview and opened image. Clicking the rotate button at the left rotates the image 90 degrees counterclockwise; clicking the rotate button at the right rotates the image 90 degrees clockwise.
Auto	These check boxes appear above adjustment sliders for Exposure, Shadows, Brightness, and Contrast. When they are checked, the corresponding slider will adjust automatically whenever you change any of the other settings.

CURRENTLY SUPPORTED CAMERAS

As of this writing, the Camera RAW plug-in supports many camera types. Adobe may enhance the list of supported cameras over time as new cameras come onto the market and upgrades to the plug-in are made available. Check Adobe's site for updates and information:

`www.adobe.com/products/photoshop/cameraraw.html`

Advantages and Disadvantages of 16-Bit

Once your images are processed and you are ready to go to print, you will be printing to an 8-bit color device (I don't know of any printers that claim to handle 16-bit images). This is a current technological impasse, which may be changed in the future, because 16-bit images haven't been around all that long in common practice. However, whether printing to 8-bit with 16-bit information is a "loss" at this point is questionable. Technically, you will be changing from trillions of colors to millions, but the difference might be beyond human perception.

The real thing that you are trying to do with 16-bit files is not to print them; it is to get the best-darned image information you can off your camera. One of the maxims for ending with the best result is starting with the best image—not one that you will use digital image editing to enhance later merely for fixing mistakes. That means trying to capture what you imagine you see in the viewfinder and in your imagination by using the equipment you have. If you are a creative shooter, your images (and correction possibilities) could benefit from using 16-bit files, but it is not critical, and not everyone needs them for image editing. Using 16-bit format offers the opportunity to fine-tune images coming from the camera. For many who are critical of their work, this can provide advantages.

The biggest drawback to using 16-bit format is that the files tend to be much larger than those stored as JPEG. This means that you will either need to get more storage for image capture (more media cards, or cards that have greater capacity) or be prepared to fill up your media many times faster. In short, it can cost you more space when shooting, more processing time when correcting, and more archival space when storing. However, the potential gain in quality and possibilities when processing may be worth the drawback.

Whether the ability to work with 16-bit files is a benefit depends on your camera, its processing, and your workflow. If your camera does not capture images with increased bit depth, the advantage gained by working in 16-bit may be a wash. An honest evaluation of images you open from RAW against those processed by the camera should give you a good idea of whether it is worth the additional space—and the cost of additional storage. In most cases, it is likely that it will be, to whatever small extent, at least for manipulation.

Reader Requests

If you think of anything you'd like to see in a chart or table that would simplify what you do, please make a request on the website or newsletter for the book, or send the request to me by e-mail. If you need something, it can probably prove useful to a lot of people. I'll make requested information available as I can (possibly as part of the Hidden Power tools). Your input is invaluable! I can't guarantee I'll get to everything, but I may have a quick answer to help you out.

E-mail: thebookdoc@aol.com
Website: www.hiddenelements.com

Index